ALL TOO HUMAN

ALL TOO HUMAN

A POLITICAL EDUCATION

GEORGE STEPHANOPOULOS

LITTLE, BROWN AND COMPANY BOSTON NEW YORK LONDON

First Edition

Library of Congress Cataloging-in-Publication Data

Stephanopoulos, George
    All too human : a political education / by George Stephanopoulos. — 1st ed.
      p.   cm.
    ISBN 0-316-92919-0
    1. Stephanopoulos, George   2. Presidents — United States — Staff — Biography.   3. United States — Politics and government — 1993–   4. Clinton, Bill, 1946–   I. Title.
E840.8.S675   1999
973.929'092 — dc21
[B]   99-13817

10 9 8 7 6 5 4 3 2 1

MV-NY

Printed in the United States of America

TO MY PARENTS

CONTENTS

ALL TOO HUMAN

PROLOGUE

ays after the Monica Lewinsky story broke in January 1998, I had a dream about President Clinton: I had returned to the White House after a year away, and I was sitting in my usual chair just next to the president's desk in the Oval Office, prepping him for an interview with CBS News. *Seems like old times*, I thought, *it's good to be back.* But moments before the interview was scheduled to start, we got word of some vague but terrible tragedy. The whole country would soon know about it, and the president would need to respond. I pulled out my notepad and struggled to scratch out appropriate words of consolation and hope. Nothing came, but it didn't matter. Clinton did what he always seemed to do so well at times like this, saying exactly the right thing, in exactly the right way. *He's still got it — best politician I've ever seen.* Then I walked across the Oval, opened a door, and found myself in a pocket-sized room — windowless and bare, except for nude pinups of Monica pasted on its walls.

I was struggling in my dream with the Clinton I loved and the Clinton I feared, the president I served and the man I didn't want to see. As I write these words, a popular president presiding over an America prosperous and at peace has been impeached. Clinton's lawyers are skillfully defending him in a Senate trial against the charge that he committed perjury and obstructed justice to conceal his sexual affair with a twenty-two-year-old intern. The battle is all but over, and I'm still mystified by the Clinton paradox: How could a president so intelligent, so compassionate, so public-spirited, and so conscious of his place in history act in such a stupid, selfish, and self-destructive manner?

I don't know how to answer that question, and I never thought I'd have to try. When I first considered writing about my time with President Clinton, I envisioned a political memoir shaped like a human comedy — a story of good, talented but fallible people acting on Vaclav Havel's hope that politics "can be not only the art of the possible, especially if 'the possible' includes the art of speculation, calculation, intrigue, secret deals, and pragmatic maneuvering, but that it can also be the art of the impossible, namely, the art of improving ourselves and the world." I wanted to write a candid story that neither shied away from showing the "art of the possible" nor surrendered to the cynical notion that there is nothing more to know about politics. I hoped to explain how an ambitious and idealistic president of uncertain personal character grew in office — how he outsmarted his enemies, out-hustled his adversaries, and overcame his failings and those of his team to help our country and achieve what no Democrat had done since Roosevelt — two full terms in office and a successful presidency. I believed it would be a story with a happy ending.

But the plot took a turn.

The events of the last year have changed the shape of the story I set out to write. It can no longer have a truly happy ending. I have done my best to recount accurately my thoughts and feelings and the events as I perceived them at the time, but I couldn't avoid the filter of the president's affair with Monica and its aftermath. Throughout 1998 and early 1999, I lived in two separate Clinton worlds: the past I had experienced from the inside, and the present I was observing from the outside. As the stories unfolded, one on my word processor and the other on the news, I came to see the connections more clearly, and was tempted at times to think of the Clinton story as a tragedy. That doesn't seem quite right either. For all his talent, Clinton lacks the grandeur of a tragic hero.

His presidency, however, does have the momentum of classic drama. The roller-coaster ride from Clinton's improbable election in 1992 to his impeachment in 1998 is a narrative stocked with dozens of characters, hundreds of decisions, and a thousand coincidences — all driving toward a conclusion that feels somehow, sadly, inevitable.

This book tells my part of the Clinton drama. It covers two presidential campaigns and four years in the White House. From the day I met him in September 1991 to the day I left the White House in December 1996, he was the dominant figure in my life. Our relationship was intense, intimate at times, but not a personal friendship. The Clinton I know is the Clinton I show in this book: the politician and president at work, a complicated man responding to the pressures and pleasures of public life in ways I found both awesome and appalling.

As I wrote and rewrote, I came to see how Clinton's shamelessness is a key to his political success, how his capacity for denial is tied to the optimism that is his greatest political strength. He exploits the weaknesses of himself and those around him masterfully, but he taps his and their talents as well. I have not lost my conviction that President Clinton has done a great deal to advance our country, and that he has acted out of profound patriotism and concern for others. For every reckless and expedient act, there are others of leadership and vision. I don't know how President Clinton will react to the portrait presented here, but I have tried to provide a fair representation of his many-faceted personality.

I have also tried to show the modern White House at work. For most of my tenure, I held a relatively amorphous job that was an amalgam of political troubleshooter, public-relations adviser, policy expert, and crisis manager. Having vaguely defined responsibilities was often frustrating, but it allowed me to participate in a wide range of White House decisions: from preparing a budget to writing presidential jokes, from helping to choose a Supreme Court nominee to smothering another "bimbo eruption," from passing legislation to preparing for press conferences, from organizing a peace ceremony to advising on military action. So much of the excitement of being a White House aide comes from having the chance to be a witness to history, and to feel like you're making it. I hope my account will be a useful tool for presidential historians.

In the end, however, this is neither a biography of Clinton nor a comprehensive history of his first term. It's a more personal narrative, the story of what happened to me in the White House — what I saw and did, how I felt and reacted to the pressures and pleasures of public life. Theodore White once wrote that "closeness to power heightens the dignity of all men." I now know that's not always true. I know how often I let my own ambition, insecurity, and immaturity get the best of me, and I have tried to be honest about that as well. But I also know that even having the chance to make the mistakes I made was a tremendous privilege. Because for all the compromises and disappointments, for all the days when my job felt like an exquisite jail sentence, working in the White House was the greatest adventure of my life.

— Morningside Heights
January 31, 1999

1   BACKGROUND CHECK

On the Saturday before Christmas 1992, I was feeling lucky. A few weeks earlier, with my help, Bill Clinton had been elected president — and soon I'd be working for him in the White House. But first I had to visit the Rose Law Firm. If you've read John Grisham, you've got a pretty good idea what Rose Law was like — Little Rock's version of "The Firm." Not that anyone's ever been murdered there (as far as I know), but its pedigree, power, and aura of buttoned-down mystery had made it a force in Arkansas for more than a century. It was also Hillary Rodham Clinton's firm.

All that made me a little nervous as I walked through the empty streets of Little Rock. I knew my background check was just a formality and believed I had nothing to hide. Still, I couldn't help worrying as I crossed the parking lot and, as instructed, let myself in the back door.

Waiting for me in the conference room was Webster L. Hubbell, a Little Rock legend — football star, former mayor, former judge, law partner of Hillary, golf partner of Bill. We had met only once before, and I thought of him as part of a pair. Webb and Vince. Hubbell and Foster. Vince Foster was Hillary's other close partner, and closer friend. Upright, quiet, and rail thin, Vince reminded me of Gregory Peck as Atticus Finch in *To Kill a Mockingbird*. Webb looked more like the linebacker he once was. A massive man with a beefy grip and thick lips that made you forget there was a brain behind all that brawn.

I had often heard their names invoked by the Clintons, as in, "I spoke to Webb, and he thinks . . ." Or "Vince isn't sure about that. . . ." It was a way to end the argument. Webb and Vince meant influence, integrity, and judgment. We lived in parallel but separate worlds. They were Little Rock; I was Washington. They were lawyers; I was an operative. They were friends; I was staff.

"This shouldn't be too difficult," Hubbell assured me as we shook hands across the table. First, he asked the basics: where I went to school and whom I had worked for. Then more serious stuff: Had I ever been arrested? Any money problems — potential conflicts or large debts? Unlike, say, Bob Rubin (the Wall Street investment banker and incoming head of the National Economic Council), who probably needed half a law firm to vet his portfolio, I had no stocks or bonds. My only investments were a mortgaged condo in the Adams Morgan section of Washington and a small 401K from my work on Capitol Hill. The financial review took about a minute.

"Drugs?"

"About what you'd expect," I replied. "A little marijuana in high school and college, but I haven't touched it in years. Nothing else."

Then came a couple of oblique questions about my "social life," designed to give me an opportunity — if it were true — to admit to being gay or the secret father of a small child. We both knew where Webb was going. He was circling in on the one big question. I had been summoned here so that this man, who symbolized probity and proximity to the next president, could lean over the table, look me in the eye, and say, "Now George, I want you to think hard about this. Is there anything at all, anywhere in your past, that could ever come back to embarrass the president?" From now on, everything I said or did would reflect on Clinton and affect our mission, even if it happened long ago. The president's welfare had to be my first concern; everything else came second. In return, I would get to be part of something bigger than I ever imagined.

"Well," I began, "you should know I'm the subject of a criminal investigation by the FBI." Republican complaints had forced a probe to see if I had conspired with Iran-Contra independent counsel Lawrence Walsh to damage the Bush campaign. I hadn't, but maybe it would lead to something else — like the time I tried to prove that Dan Quayle was a drug dealer.

In the fall of 1988, when the Dukakis campaign was going down the tubes, I was part of a "rapid response" team doing a remarkably ineffectual job of rebutting Republican attacks. But late in the race, a federal prisoner named Brett Kimberlin (aka the Speedway Bomber) was telling reporters he once sold drugs to Dan Quayle, and that Quayle might have sold some himself. A rumor reached me that years earlier, a grand jury examining the evidence had covered it up under pressure from prosecutors close to Quayle's family. If I could find the disgruntled grand jurors and convince them to talk, we'd win — and I'd be a hero.

So I bought a plane ticket to Indianapolis and holed up in the airport Holiday Inn with photocopied courthouse records. After a day of cold-calling people who had no idea what I was talking about, I knew I was on a fool's errand. My sleuthing wasn't illegal, just criminally incompetent and a little slimy. I suppose we would have used the information if it were true, but how naive and desperate could I have been to believe that I would uncover a last-minute bombshell that every news organization in America had missed? That was embarrassing — maybe not to President-elect Clinton, but certainly to me.

After racking my brain looking for trouble, I even told Webb about the night before I left for college, when I went out egging cars with my high school buddies one last time. Not much to report or worry about. Nothing in my background would keep me out of the White House.

I was born the second child of a solid Greek family in Fall River, Massachusetts, and baptized George after my grandfather, a missionary priest who left the Peloponnesian village of Neohorio in 1938 for Montana to minister to Greek immigrants scattered across America's west. His job was to make sure the members of the flock kept their faith as they sought their fortunes, to remind them of who they were and where they came from. More than a place of worship, the immigrant church was a piece of home. A year after his arrival, just before the war, my grandfather was joined by his family. The oldest was a five-year-old boy they called Lamby, Bobby, who would also grow up to be a priest — and my father.

A boy when he sailed from Patras in 1912, my mother's father worked on the railroads from Ellis Island to Salt Lake City before settling in Rochester, Minnesota, where he opened a shoe repair shop. Only after he made his start did he return to his village, Kalithea, to bring the teen bride chosen for him back to America. When he died in 1974, his business was the oldest in town, and his fellow merchants marched down Main Street in his memory. But he was most proud of the fact that all five of his children, including my mom, Nikolitsa, had attended college.

My parents met at a church youth convention in Minneapolis, where my mom was studying public relations at the University of Minnesota. Dad was on a field trip from seminary, and there was probably no better place to meet a woman willing to become a *presbytera*, literally "priest's wife" — a word that captures the idea that everybody in the family of a priest has a responsibility to the family of the church. The presbytera is a kind of first lady. She has an official role as hostess and helpmate but can't let people get the idea she's assuming authority that isn't hers. The daughters, like my sisters, Stacy and Marguarite, sing in the choir and teach Sunday school. The sons, like my brother, Andrew, and me, become altar boys.

I was only four when I first served. Going to the office with my dad meant going to church. He would slap a little Mennen on my cheeks after he shaved, and we would head to the place only men could go — the altar, an inner sanctum separated from the rest of the congregation by a screen of icons. Often it was just the two of us back there. I would watch him whisper prayers as he vested himself in satin robes. Then I would hold out my own robe for him to bless, and the service would begin.

My first job was carrying a candle, making sure to hold it straight without staring at the flame. Once a year an altar boy forgot, hypnotizing himself and fainting to the floor. Responsibilities increased with age and size: Bigger boys took lanterns, and the biggest carried the cross. My favorite job was tending the censer. After placing a pebble of incense on the charcoal in its gold bowl, I got to walk backward, waving the perfumed smoke in my father's path as he carried the bread and wine around the altar.

I soon became a reader as well. When I was six, the bishop came to my father's new parish in Rye, New York, and placed his stole on my head before clipping a bit of my hair to symbolize my servitude to the church. *"Axios,"* the bishop proclaimed. "He is worthy." *Axios* echoed back from the pews — a word weighted with expectation, a word I would hear again if I were ordained. On Sundays after that I would read the Epistle or recite the creed, remembering to speak "loud and slow" — the instructions my dad silently mouthed to me before I faced the congregation. At nine, I appeared on my biggest stage yet. Archbishop Iakovos opened our church convention with a liturgy at Lincoln Center, and I was chosen to stand by his side and hold his staff. Monday's *New York Daily News* ran a picture of the bearded prelate in a tall gold crown next to a small boy with bangs and hands clasped in front of him. For a day, I was a star.

But most of my work was backstage. Maybe one reason I've never been queasy about the grubby work of politics, the mechanics of running campaigns and making laws, is that I spent so many of my early days behind the altar screen, where mystery is rooted in the mundane, where faith and duty are one, where my father's prayers were my cues. *Agios o Theos.* . . . Get the candles. *Wisdom, let us attend.* . . . Lanterns and cross for the Gospel. *No one who is bound by carnal desires is worthy to approach.* . . . Light up the censer and line up the other boys. *The doors, the doors . . .* Read the creed. *Our Father . . .* Heat the water for Holy Communion. *O Lord, who blesses those who bless thee . . .* Cut the bread.

Behind the screen, I learned to stay composed in the presence of power and was swayed by the illusion of indispensability. After all, the miracle of transubstantiation couldn't happen that Sunday if I forgot to boil water on the hot plate in the room off the altar. Altar boys are as much like young operatives as little monks. We serve the priest so he can save everyone else, doing the little things that need to be done. Sometimes I got lost in the details, lost sight of the spiritual essence of the service we were producing, but I hoped that doing the right things in the right place at the right time would help do some good and save some souls, including my own, even when I was just doing my job.

All this was also preparation for what I would eventually do — but not in the way I imagined. I assumed I would be a priest before I knew what it meant. That's what my father did, and my grandfather, and my godfather, and my uncle, and all their friends. When I recall summer barbecues, I see them lounging in plastic-webbed lawn chairs, highballs in hand, wearing the hot-weather uniform — short-sleeved black dress shirts with detachable cleric's collars that flopped to the side when the top button was unfastened. By night's end, even our backyard became a kind of church. Smoldering briquettes and burnt-orange cigar butts served up the social equivalent of candlelight and earthy incense as my dad and his buddies sipped Greek brandy and sang Byzantine hymns.

As soon as I could talk, I knew how to answer the question of what I would be. At home, I would preside at play liturgies with a towel draped over my shoulders, or sneak through piles of books in my dad's office to suck on the sweet metallic stem of his pipe while tapping out a pretend sermon on his typewriter. When my father was finishing his doctorate in theology, I added a twist, telling dinner guests I would be "a priest *and* a theologian," relishing the weight of the big word as it rolled off my seven-year-old tongue. Everyone smiled at my use of a word I didn't really understand, while I basked in the attention that was my reward for carrying on a family tradition.

But sometimes an expectation nurtured through childhood can come undone in a single moment. In 1974, when I was thirteen, my final eighth-grade assignment was a paper on a potential career. As expected, I wrote on being a priest and brought home my A. But that autumn, after we moved from New York to Cleveland, I started high school, and it hit me. I was sitting in homeroom one morning shortly before eight, thinking about nothing in particular, when the idea that I wasn't *meant* to be a priest, that I wouldn't bear the family legacy into the next generation, revealed itself with an intensity others must feel when called *to* the priesthood. I hadn't lost my faith, just my vocation, but I knew the decision was final. I was growing up and growing away from the only future I had allowed myself to imagine. Now if only I could tell my father, and my grandfather. When asked about my future, I started to slip around the questions until they stopped. I didn't know yet what I wanted — just what I didn't want, and that whatever career I chose had to be worthy.

I also felt a need to answer to my extended family. Greeks came to America from dozens of islands and hundreds of villages, but here they formed a single clan, united by heritage, language, and a need to achieve. Those of us in the second generation understood that honoring the sacrifices of our parents and grandparents — the laborers, cobblers, waiters, and cooks — meant getting a good education and putting it to good use — as doctors, lawyers, professors, and politicians. Assimilation for Greeks didn't mean blending in; it required standing out. If a Greek like Ike Pappas was on television, all of us watched; if another like Nick Gage wrote a book, all of us read it; when Congressman John Brademas missed his chance to be Speaker of the House, we all felt his loss; when Vice President Agnew resigned, we all felt ashamed — a disgrace lessened only by the grumbled observation that he got what he deserved for changing his name and leaving his church. The rules were so clear they didn't need to be said: Make your name, and don't change it. Make us proud, and don't forget where you came from. Drilled into me were two awkwardly compatible ambitions: public service and professional success. Priests serve; immigrants succeed. I would try to do both.

But first I wanted to blend in. Here's where I'm my mother's son. As a boy, I would spend hours upstairs, lying on the floor with my feet pressed against the radiator, leafing through yearbooks to find pictures of my mom — a pretty girl with dark hair and a wide smile whose American friends called her Gloria instead of her Greek name. Her picture was everywhere: Gloria at the newspaper, Gloria in the glee club, Gloria behind the wheel of an old jalopy filled with friends.

In high school, that's the life I wanted. I still served in the altar and studied enough to get good grades. But I wanted to be one of the guys. So I snuck onto the golf course next door, went to the track, and played poker on Friday nights with the money I earned on Saturdays as a caddie, dishwasher, and busboy. I noticed girls, but they didn't notice me.

Politics didn't interest me. Instead, I poured myself into sports. I was a chubby kid, pretty well coordinated, decent at soccer and softball, but no natural athlete. I was barely five feet tall, so instead of basketball, I tried out for wrestling. The first practice was murder. Afterward, I could barely drag myself to the car out front, where my mom was waiting for me. I got in and announced I was quitting. Then came a surprise. Usually my mom let me do what I wanted so long as I stayed out of trouble. This time she just said, "No. Stick it out."

I'm still grateful. Not that I became a champion, far from it. I lost my first match 19–2 and never caught up. I guess I never developed the killer instinct. Before a bout I would look up at the clock from the side of the mat and remind myself that win or lose, the ordeal would soon be over. You could pretty much sum up my high school wrestling career with an item from our local paper my sophomore year: "The agony of defeat is etched in the face of Orange High School's George Stephanopoulos," read the caption beneath a picture of me getting pinned.

Wrestling, in short, was more about what the sport did to me than what I did to my opponents. Cutting weight was an extreme exercise in self-control. I woke up extra early to run a mile or two before school; did sit-ups and push-ups while watching TV at night. I dieted on oranges and ran through the school hallways wrapped in plastic to sweat out that last pound. Even water had to be rationed in the hours before weigh-ins. To this day, when I put my mouth to a fountain I unconsciously count the sips. On Labor Day freshman year, I weighed 120 pounds. By November, I was wrestling at 98. My body showed me what it could take, which helped my mind turn around and instruct my body to take a little more. Though I wasn't a champion, what lingered for me was an addiction to exercise and a belief in the power of discipline.

But for all my desire to be one of the guys, I still wanted to excel — and it wouldn't be as an athlete. Columbia University spoke to my ambition in a different way. It was in New York City. It offered a distinctive core curriculum based on the great books, music, and art of Western civilization, and no one from my high school had gone there in decades.

I thrived at Columbia, and junior year I had my first taste of Washington life, as a summer intern for our congresswoman, a Democrat named Mary Rose Oakar. The big legislative debate that summer was about Reagan's budget. I helped write speeches explaining how it would hurt Oakar's constituents in the working-class ethnic enclaves of Cleveland. Before that experience, I had considered volunteering for George Bush in 1979 and voted for John Anderson in 1980. But working against Reagan's budget made me a Democrat. I didn't think supply-side economics would work, and I didn't believe it was fair. Perhaps it wouldn't have happened had I had a different summer job, but unlike the millions of Democrats whom Reagan inspired to vote Republican, I was a Republican he pushed the other way.

By 1982, my senior year, I still didn't know what I would do with my life. Law school seemed like the natural choice: finishing school for ambitious liberal arts majors who didn't know exactly what they wanted to do. It would also meet the Greek standard for achievement. The only problem with law school was that when it was over I would be in real danger of becoming a lawyer.

I almost leaped in a completely different direction. As a volunteer Big Brother whose major was international politics, I was drawn to the Peace Corps and applied one day on an impulse. Around eight the next morning, I got a call from the on-campus recruiter: "George, you're in. We've got a spot, but you have to say yes right now." I did, and went back to sleep. An hour later, I made a pot of coffee and wondered what I had done. Teaching English in Tunisia seemed like good work, but it didn't speak to the part of me that wanted to play on a bigger stage, in a world where a single act could affect the lives of millions. It didn't satisfy my drive for secular success. After my second cup, I called back and said no.

I wanted to do good *and* do well. Returning to Washington offered the promise of both. At Columbia's work-study office, I saw an announcement for internships at the Carnegie Endowment for International Peace, and won a job where I wrote book reviews and helped draft speeches about nuclear arms control, the subject of my senior thesis. The only problem was that the stipend ran out after six months. Unless I found something else, I had promised my parents that I would spend the next six months as a paralegal in Cleveland before starting law school in the fall.

I couldn't have planned what came next. Everyone needs a break or two to get ahead. Mine came the night Norman Mayer was shot.

Norman Mayer was an older man with a deep tan who wandered the streets of Washington in a nylon windbreaker, sunglasses, and a golf cap, looking like the caddie master at a country club gone to seed. He too was working on disarmament, but in his own peculiar way. If he caught your eye on the street, he would hand over a pamphlet that promised ten thousand dollars to anyone who could actually prove that nuclear weapons prevent nuclear war — a pretty lucid point for a deranged person. Occasionally, Mayer walked into our offices off Dupont Circle to lobby for his proposal. Since I was the lowest person on the totem pole, he was my responsibility. I'd offer him a sandwich, and we'd chat uncomfortably until I could find a reason to excuse myself and usher him out the door. Not exactly what I had in mind when I imagined Washington power lunches, but Norman seemed harmless enough. Until December 8, 1982.

When I returned from lunch, my boss was waiting for me with a weak smile. "Your friend is holding the Washington Monument hostage," he said. "You'd better call the police."

Dressed in a homemade space suit, Norman Mayer had driven a van he said was loaded with dynamite up to the monument and threatened to blow it up unless he could broadcast his plan to prevent nuclear war. Washington was paralyzed, and the world was watching on live television. After I called the police, reporters started calling me.

So began my first foray into a media feeding frenzy — one of those times when everyone in the country responsible for bringing "the news" to the rest of us focuses for a moment on a single event. TV bookers who fill the airwaves with talking heads work the phones to find anyone with even the most tangential connection to the event. That day, that someone was me: I was the guy who knew the guy who was holding Washington hostage. *Nightline* sent a limo. I actually said, "Well, Ted . . ." on national TV, before telling what little I knew about Norman. My parents made a video, and calls came in from friends all over the country. To top it all off, a newly elected congressman from Cleveland named Ed Feighan was watching — one day after I had applied for an entry-level position in his office.

Feighan called the next day: "If you can get yourself on *Nightline*, maybe you can do some good for me." The job title was legislative assistant, which meant I would draft letters, memos, and speeches on whatever the congressman was working on. The salary was more than double my intern's stipend — $14,500 a year.

I was thrilled with my new job but spooked by how I got it. Norman Mayer had been bluffing. There was no dynamite in his truck. But the police couldn't know that, so they shot him down near midnight when he tried to drive off the Mall. *It's not my fault Norman got shot. I didn't drive the van or pull the trigger. Why couldn't he just surrender after making his point? Besides, I would have gotten the job anyway. I'm qualified, I'm from Cleveland, I'll work hard. Still . . .* No, it wasn't my fault Norman got shot, but I couldn't escape the fact that his fate was my good fortune.

Around this time, one of my new friends, Eric Alterman, introduced me to his mentor, the legendary journalist I. F. Stone. Nearing eighty, Stone had spent the last fifty years covering Washington on his own in his own way, always exposing hypocrisy, always challenging power, never getting too close to it. Eric arranged for us to meet at the bagel bakery on Connecticut Avenue. I can still see Stone at a small table, picking at his late afternoon lunch of a toasted bagel, raisins, and a cup of tea. With his wispy curls and clear eyes, he looked like Yoda come to life in a fraying flannel suit.

"You've covered Washington so long," I asked, "weren't you ever tempted to go into politics yourself?"

"Once," he answered. Sixty-five years earlier, when Izzy was in high school, the political "boss" of his class had offered him a place on the editorial board of the school paper — his dream job — in return for campaign help. But whatever temptation Izzy felt was quickly overwhelmed by a wave of nausea and a vow never to approach active politics again.

I respected that sentiment, envied it, felt slightly shamed by it, but didn't share it. My new work seemed too thrilling to renounce, and I was a natural at the game of politics: at knowing who knew what I needed to know, at absorbing the rhythms of legislative life by walking the halls, at preparing committee hearing questions for my boss that might get picked up by the press, at learning to anticipate his political needs and to use his position to advance my issues too, at succumbing to the lure of the closed room and the subtle power rush that comes from hearing words I wrote come out of someone else's mouth.

A democracy needs people like Izzy on the outside to keep it honest, but it also needs people on the inside to make it work — people who will play the game for the sake of getting good things done. But you have to be careful. Your first deal is like your first scotch. It burns, might make you feel nauseous. If you're like Izzy, once is enough. If you're like me, you get to like it. Then to need it.

In October 1983, two days after a terrorist attack on American marines in Beirut, President Reagan ordered an invasion of Grenada. To me it seemed like a transparent diversion: Invade a tiny country in the Caribbean in order to keep people's minds off a terrible tragedy in the Middle East. I rushed into work that morning to write a speech for Feighan lambasting the president. "The whole country will see through this," I assured him, "and you should be leading the charge."

Feighan questioned the invasion from the floor of the House — and he never let me forget it. Few other members of Congress joined him, and the public loved the pictures of those rescued medical students kissing American soil. I had made a tactical error in allowing my personal views to cloud my political judgment. Even if I believed I was right on the merits, I was wrong about the politics. I should have known enough to warn my boss that the invasion would be popular even as I advised him to speak out against it.

Would that have convinced him? Maybe not; maybe it was my passionate certainty that opposing the invasion was a political winner that made my case. Whatever the truth, I learned that day to separate what I thought was right from what I thought would work, a skill that would serve me well — at a price. Judging how the world will judge what you do — how a position will "play" — is an essential political skill. If you can't predict what will work, you can't survive in office. If you don't keep your job, you can't achieve what you think is right. The danger is when you stop caring about the difference between being right and being employed, or fail to notice that you don't know what the difference is anymore.

That month I also applied for a Rhodes Scholarship, a second try after being rejected as a college senior. Studying at Oxford would give me the opportunity to spend more time thinking about what was right rather than what would work, and would reassure my parents about my future. Only half joking, my father asked, "When are you going to stop playing around in Washington and get a real job?" So I made a deal with him. If I got turned down again, I really *would* go to law school.

The selection committee saved me from that, and the scholarship offered the professional security of law school without the drudgery. The Rhodes is a passport to the Establishment. While it may not assure success, it guarantees opportunities to interview for great jobs. And the romantic vision of Oxford life passed down from scholars perched in the corridors of power is that while you're there, you get to read what you want, absorb the wisdom of brilliant tutors, argue into the night, and travel around the world. All this without a career penalty; it's an idyll off the fast track.

Unburdened for a time by the need to prove myself by getting good grades or impressing the boss, I had the chance at Oxford to learn and explore on my own. That fall a famine broke out in the Sudan. I went to volunteer in the camps and see the famine for myself — to understand why it happens, what it does to people, and write about it if I could. Helping feed a few kids or keep the camps clean was worthwhile work, and the articles I intended to write might heighten awareness. But the return ticket zipped in my knapsack reminded me that I was no Albert Schweitzer. This trip was as much about adventure as altruism, and I knew it.

While I was in Sudan, the general who'd ruled for a generation with CIA backing was overthrown. On the day of the coup, I found myself in the middle of a silent riot. Mobs were milling about, but the only sound you heard was the squeak of sneakers on pavement. Then the radio announced that the general was gone, and the crowds started to race through the streets with joyful screams.

The rest of the day I wandered through Khartoum wondering if this was what a real revolution was like. The air was charged with happiness and hope, energized by the belief that everything would be better now that the bad guy was out and the new guys could govern. But I was struck by the sight of a dazed old woman who was observing the celebration from her cardboard home by the side of the road. *What does she think of all this? Will her life be any better tomorrow than it is today? Or is some human misery beyond the reach of any revolution? Is it possible things will get worse?*

Years later, that image sticks with me — not as a counsel of despair or an excuse for cynicism, but as a reminder to be humble about the promise of politics and the potential of government. Because I believe in original sin, because I know that I'm capable of craving a cold beer in a village of starving kids, because I understand that selfishness vies for space in our hearts with compassion, I believe we need government — a government that forces us to care for the common good even when we don't feel like it, a government that helps channel our better instincts and check our bad ones. But I also believe in containing government and tempering the claims we make for it. I don't think government is good, just necessary. I'm a liberal who accepts limits.

My second year at Oxford was an attempt to reinforce my intellectual instincts with systematic study of Christian ethics. Back to basics. I wanted to build a better foundation for my political views, to ground my personal beliefs and partisan experience in philosophy and theology — another way of reconciling the life I was leading with the life I had imagined as a boy. I knew a lot about the "how" and "what" of politics. Now I wanted to think more about the "why." So I read Augustine and Aquinas, Martin Luther and Reinhold Niebuhr, analyzing the fundamental questions of politics — war and peace, life and liberty — from the perspective of what was right rather than what would work. This would offer me a guide to which questions to ask and a reminder of where I was going wrong when I got too caught up in the game.

And I still loved the game. After my Rhodes I went back to Washington, where Congressman Feighan made me his chief of staff. The next year I signed on with the Dukakis-for-President campaign. This was a no-brainer: a Greek American liberal from Massachusetts was running for president. How could I *not* work for him? After volunteering in the primaries, I moved to Boston for what I thought would be a short, happy hiatus before returning to Washington with a new president.

When I arrived, we had a seventeen-point lead. Then came the summer assault. The Bush campaign, led by Lee Atwater, opened up a disciplined, ruthless, and sustained series of attacks on Governor Dukakis's record and character. Flags, furloughs, the Pledge of Allegiance. Willie Horton became a household name, and President Reagan even joked that Dukakis was an "invalid." This "joke" was a calculated effort to ignite the false rumor spread around Washington by Republican operatives that Dukakis had been treated for depression — and, politically, it worked. Though the allegation was false, Dukakis was forced to call a press conference with his doctor to deny it. By August's Republican convention, our lead was gone, our candidate was a caricature, and our campaign was effectively over.

A few months after the election, I left politics to become the assistant to Father Tim Healy, the new president of the New York Public Library. Father Healy, a brilliant Jesuit with the bearing of Jackie Gleason, wanted to rebuild the branch libraries that had meant so much to him when he was a kid growing up in the Bronx. I wanted to learn how to manage a major institution and to be part of that educational effort — and, with the Republicans still controlling Washington, Manhattan seemed like a good place to be.

But just after I found an apartment, Newt Gingrich's campaign to topple Speaker Jim Wright succeeded, and the shake-up in the Democratic congressional leadership that ensued ended with Tom Foley as Speaker, Richard Gephardt as majority leader — and my getting a call from Kirk O'Donnell. A veteran of former Speaker Tip O'Neill's operation, Kirk had been my boss in the Dukakis campaign and was now a Washington lawyer scouting talent on the side for Dick Gephardt.

Kirk called my office overlooking the library lions on Fifth Avenue and got right to the point: "I know you just started with Father Healy, George, but would you consider coming back to Washington to be Dick Gephardt's floor man?"

Consider? Are you kidding? Kirk was offering me a starting job in the Democratic Party's major league — the House leadership. The majority leader was one step away from the Speaker, who was two steps away from the president. As executive floor assistant to Gephardt, I would be his shadow, his surrogate, his eyes and ears. In my old job with Feighan, our successes had been satisfying but small, like successfully petitioning for the release of a political prisoner or sneaking an amendment onto the foreign-aid bill to create microloans for third-world farmers. With Gephardt, I would get the chance to help set a national agenda for the Democratic Party, to figure out how to blunt Bush initiatives and force Bush vetoes. With Feighan, I couldn't get my phone call returned by the majority leader's floor man. With Gephardt, I would be that guy. Although I had never met the man, I knew Gephardt was a good Democrat, and there was a bonus: In 1992, he was planning to run again for president. So much for getting out of politics.

My new job was as exciting as I expected, even though I couldn't explain exactly what it was. Someone once compared it to being an air traffic controller at a busy airport on a foggy night; and as I stood near the Speaker's chair on late nights at the end of session and tried to explain to frustrated legislators why they had to stay for the last vote even though they had nonrefundable tickets for Florida with their families, I knew exactly what he meant. But most of the time, being the floor guy was a more substantive mix of policy and politics. It boiled down to two central tasks: knowing what was going on and getting things done.

I spent my days in perpetual motion, walking the marble halls from meeting to meeting, member to member, getting information and giving it out. Members would grab me by the tricep if they had a message for the leadership or wanted to know what was going on. Reporters slipped around the columns in search of news. Everything you needed to know had to be in your head, in your pocket, or no more than a phone call away.

But it wasn't enough to know the rules, or the fine points of policy. In the House, the personal is political and the political is personal. To know the House you have to know the members — their home districts, their pet projects, their big contributors. You have to know what votes they'll throw away and which lines they'll never cross. You have to listen for the message in a throwaway line and laugh at the joke you've heard a thousand times. A personal feud might persist for decades, or an alliance could shift in a moment. The most fascinating part of the job was following those patterns, figuring out who held the key votes or which amendment would lock in a majority, watching the coalitions form, crack apart, and come together again.

I felt justified in my work, and that we were making a difference. The budget fight of 1990 was the best. We Democrats saw ourselves as fighting to reverse the Reagan-era priorities by pushing for tax increases for the wealthy and protecting programs for the working class, and we forced Bush to eat his words on "Read my lips," sweet revenge for what he'd done to Dukakis two years earlier. We spent weeks at Andrews Air Force Base, wrestling with the numbers and the Republicans. Late at night, Ways and Means chairman Dan Rostenkowski broke out a bottle of gin and told stories of all the presidents he'd known up close. By day we'd make charts out of the Republican proposals, showing how they would benefit the wealthy and burden ordinary workers. Then we'd feed them to the press to build public support for our side.

Our efforts strengthened the budget and weakened Bush politically, but as when I first came to Washington, ten summers earlier, a Republican president was still running the show and setting the agenda. All we Democrats could do was play defense, defining ourselves more by what we could prevent than by anything we hoped to create. We could block a capital gains tax cut, but not enact a tax credit for the working poor. We could stop cuts in Head Start or Medicare, but not expand student loans or pass national health care. We could piece together a bare majority to pass a gun control bill, but never get enough votes to override the inevitable veto. We could make a lot of noise about a Supreme Court appointment — maybe even block the president's top choice — but conservative judges would control the federal courts for another generation. We could win moral victories on Capitol Hill, but we couldn't make history.

It didn't look as if we'd have the chance soon, either. By the summer of 1991, America had won the Gulf War and President Bush was being rewarded with 90 percent approval ratings. Another election was on the horizon, but no one I knew believed Bush could be beat.

Gephardt was still looking at the 1992 presidential race, commissioning polls, testing the waters in Iowa and New Hampshire. Although my job was legislative work, he took me aside in the early summer to ask me what I thought. Should he seek the Democratic nomination in 1992?

"Absolutely," I told him. "You're well known, and you've run before. You can beat anyone else in the race." (Only Senator Tom Harkin of Iowa and former Senator Paul Tsongas of Massachusetts had announced.) "Even though Bush is popular," I continued, "someone has to take on this fight. It will be good for the party and the country."

Nice little speech. Sincere too — as far as it went. But I was also motivated by something I couldn't say: *I hope you'll run, if only for my sake. I've always wanted to be at the heart of a campaign, right by the candidate's side. You could win the nomination, and if you do, who knows? Bush stumbles, and I'm working for a president of the United States.*

But Gephardt had voted for Bush's unpopular tax increase and against his popular war, and he was coming from a Congress that had raised its own pay and been bogged down in a check-cashing scandal. It seemed as if the only voters not angry at Congress in 1991 were the ones too alienated from politics to care at all. In an outsider's year, the majority leader was Mr. Inside. Knowing that, he wisely decided to stay where he was.

But I didn't want to stay. Restrained idealism and raw ambition — the pistons of my character — were powering up again, pushing me to find someone new.

2 BECOMING A TRUE BELIEVER

New York governor Mario Cuomo seemed like a potential soul mate. Fresh to professional politics when I first read his published campaign diary, I thought it was the best possible story — the chronicle of a successful candidate who thought like a moral philosopher.

Watching his 1984 Democratic convention keynote was even better. Here was a politician who could use words like *love* and *compassion* without seeming like a wimp, who talked about the "mosaic of America" and called on the country to replace Reagan's "social Darwinism" with "the idea of family." Cuomo was saying everything I believed, in a way that made people want to fight. Pacing the floor of my place on Capitol Hill, I screamed at my TV and hoped the convention would get carried away and nominate him from the floor. Mario immediately became the great liberal hope — our Ronald Reagan. If only he would run. But by the summer of 1991, Cuomo still wasn't running — at least not yet.

Bob Kerrey was glamorous. A Medal of Honor–winning senator from mainstream America, he was irony personified, balancing a dark side with whimsy and intellectual conviction in a way that would play well at the Georgetown, Manhattan, and Hollywood cocktail parties where campaign funds were raised and fashionable opinions congealed into conventional wisdom.

Kerrey would also make the Republicans squirm. They couldn't do to him what they did to Dukakis, pillory him as a soft-on-defense, hate-America-first Democrat. A war hero is a patriot by definition, so Kerrey could pull off feats few other Democrats would dare, like when he had transformed the fight against a constitutional amendment banning flag burning into a winning political battle. Kerrey had the charisma of a Kennedy without the baggage — and he didn't share Cuomo's ambivalence. The day I heard he was running, I let his staff know I was interested in signing up.

Paul Tsongas, a Greek American, was my intended. Joining his campaign would have felt like accepting an arranged marriage. He had been a good senator, and I had once sent him a fan letter after reading his book about his struggle with cancer. But Tsongas had no charisma, and his economic plan read more like a corporate report than a populist manifesto. He was for cutting capital gain taxes and cutting Medicare spending, precisely the policies I'd been working against. And after 1988, there was no way the Democrats would nominate another cerebral Greek from Massachusetts.

Which put me in a bind. But for the fact that he was Greek, I wouldn't have even considered working for Tsongas. Because he was Greek, I had to explain to my extended family why I wouldn't. In my community, ethnicity still trumps ideology. Although Greek Americans generally vote Republican, they support Democrats who are Greek. They would line up behind Tsongas just as they had for Dukakis — and expect me to do the same.

Bill Clinton wasn't my type. He was a Southern conservative; I was a Northern liberal. He was a governor; I was a creature of Congress. I hadn't met him, and I had heard him speak only once: at the 1988 Democratic convention, where his droning nomination of Dukakis drew sustained applause only for the words "In conclusion . . ."

But friends of mine who knew him well insisted I would like him. Mark Gearan, the Dukakis spokesman who was then heading the Democratic Governors' Association, said Clinton was more liberal and less boring than I thought. My Gephardt colleague David Dreyer said Clinton's philosophy of personal responsibility would appeal to me, and he introduced me to John Holum, George McGovern's former issues director, who was collecting résumés for Clinton. If they all liked this guy, he must have been better than I thought. And any Democrat beat four more years of Bush. Maybe Clinton's more conservative side would make him more appealing. Maybe it was time for the party to sacrifice ideological purity for electoral potential.

Not all of my friends thought it was wise for me to join a campaign. Kirk O'Donnell took me to breakfast in the House dining room to talk me out of it. We were surrounded by the world I knew. The white-coated waiters had saved my regular table. Members came by to ask for a favor or pass a message to the leader. I was a big shot, or at least felt like one.

"Be smart," Kirk said. "You've got one of the top jobs in Congress. Why throw it away? Stick with Dick. If you really want to work in the campaign, wait until after the convention."

This was a kind voice of reason and prudence, but I was restless and willing to gamble. Although waiting to work for the nominee was a safe bet, the sooner I signed up with a candidate, the closer I'd be to the center of the action. And for someone like me, with more ambition than actual campaign experience, it was an ideal time to be looking for work. Like the top tier of potential candidates who had already announced that they wouldn't challenge Bush — Gephardt, and Senators Bill Bradley, Jay Rockefeller, and Al Gore — most top staffers were sitting this one out. They had upended their lives for two losing campaigns in a row, and they weren't going down that road again for an effort that appeared hopeless. The best jobs were still open.

I met Kerrey and Clinton on the same day in September 1991. It was a sunny Friday morning, and I walked to the Senate side of the Hill from my office in the Capitol aware that whatever happened that day could start a chain of events that would change my life.

Kerrey was announcing the next Monday. My "interview" was an invitation to join the prep for his post-announcement press conference — a "murder board" in which staffers played reporter and peppered the boss with all the tough questions he could expect to hear. I joined Kerrey's core team on the sofa across from his desk. The senator waved an offhand hello, and we began, with me trying to ask questions that were challenging enough to be useful but not so harsh as to seem hostile. After all, I didn't even know the guy. But I liked what I saw.

Later in the meeting, Kerrey started reading aloud a draft of his announcement speech, which closed with a quote from Dietrich Bonhoeffer, the German theologian who was executed for plotting to assassinate Hitler. *Nice: Bonhoeffer — the noble martyr willing to dirty his hands and sacrifice his life for a righteous cause.* The me that had studied Bonhoeffer's *Ethics* and admired his moral heroism was captivated. Then my internal political twin kicked in, reminding me that quoting a German minister on the subject of sacrifice might not be the ideal way to open a campaign for the hearts and minds of middle-class Americans who already felt squeezed. It would appear obscure at best, condescending at worst.

There was also something vaguely unsettling about the atmosphere in Kerrey's office. Staffers always defer to senators, but as Kerrey spoke to us from behind his enormous desk, I noticed a slow nodding of heads that suggested that the words Kerrey spoke were deeper than your average political talk — that the senator's terse replies were political koans. A cool but unmistakably messianic zeal hummed just below the surface of the Kerrey campaign.

I wasn't immune to it, and had I joined his team, I probably would have succumbed to it. But after the meeting, when I met with Kerrey's campaign manager to discuss the logistics of a possible job, she was distracted and slightly dismissive, unsure how I'd fit into their top-heavy hierarchy. As the interview crept on, I felt more like the son of a big contributor seeking an internship than a political pro applying for a top job. When I said I would appreciate a quick decision because I needed to give Gephardt notice, she looked at me and said: "You have to understand something. This is about a cause, not a career."

I was beginning to figure that out.

The Clinton meeting was at the town-house office of Stan Greenberg, a former Yale professor turned pollster who had signed on with Clinton. I didn't know what to expect but had plenty of time to wonder, because Clinton was late. When he walked into the room with Stan and Mark Gearan, I got the full treatment.

Bulky and butter-cheeked, Clinton looked like an overgrown boy in his light summer suit. But he had the gait of a man used to being obeyed, admired, courted, and loved. Slow but not stately, almost lazy but loaded with self-confidence. Gearan introduced me with a light setup: "You know George's work. He wrote jokes for Dukakis."

"Not really," I demurred. "They just needed a short Greek with no sense of humor to test-market the lines."

Clinton held my eye with a smile while he shook my hand. His was soft, and the grip was surprisingly light for a politician. "Sounds to me like you have a sense of humor," he said. "What else do you do?"

Mark and Stan left us alone, and Clinton started to putter around the office, picking up books, poll questionnaires, photos, anything that caught his eye. Before we really began talking, the phone rang. Democratic Party benefactor Pamela Harriman was calling, and she wanted to know Clinton's position on campaign contributions from political action committees (PACs). While he listened, Clinton perused a polling report, licking his finger as he leafed through the pages, looking up at me every moment or so as if to apologize for the interruption. When the call was over, he asked for my advice. Tsongas was refusing PAC money; should he do the same?

"PAC money isn't morally worse than other contributions," I said. "But attacking PACs is an easy sound bite right now, so unless you can raise a ton, it's probably not worth ceding the high ground. Besides, Harkin's sucking up all of the labor money anyway. You're not giving up as much as you'd gain with the editorial boards. I'd take the pledge."

"That sounds about right," Clinton said. For the next half hour, I joined him on the first of countless stream-of-consciousness tours across the political landscape of his mind. He seemed to know something about everything — from the party rules for picking superdelegates to turnout in black precincts on Super Tuesday, from how the credit crunch was bankrupting small businesses in New Hampshire to how microenterprise loans could help farmers in the Mississippi Delta — and he swooped from issue to issue without losing his thread, punctuating his soliloquy with questions for me. By the time he closed with the prediction that the nomination would be decided on the day of the Illinois primary, I was blown away.

Before he left for lunch, he asked me about the 1990 budget deal, one of my areas of expertise. What was good about it? Where was it weak? Could Harkin and Kerrey be hurt by their votes? He wasn't testing me, just looking for advice, and it seemed as if he was taking it in, filing it away for future use. We were working together from the moment we met. He walked out with a wave and a promise to call. When I asked if I could hear soon because of Gephardt, he turned in the doorway and said, "Of course."

That evening I felt pulled in different directions. The idea of Kerrey was still appealing, and I thought he had the better chance to win. But compared to Clinton, the man I had encountered was distant and unfocused. He didn't seem to know what he would do as president, and his team didn't seem as enthusiastic about having me on board.

Clinton was more impressive up close, smart and ready. Yes, he was more conservative than I. He supported the death penalty; I was against it. He had supported Bush's Gulf War; I was for extending sanctions. He supported the Nicaraguan contras in the 1980s; I thought this policy was both illegal and wrong. But all of the potential nominees supported the death penalty, and most executions were carried out under state law. As for our foreign-policy differences, what was past was past: By late 1991, Bush had won the Gulf War, Nicaragua had held a free election, and the cold war was over.

More important, Clinton and I were in sync on the issues I cared most about. His belief that the role of government was to open opportunities to people who "work hard and play by the rules" appealed to my Greek work ethic. So did his devotion to education — from Head Start to student loans to worker retraining — and he had made progress in Arkansas. He wanted to raise taxes on the rich and cut them for the working poor. He wanted national health care and a domestic Peace Corps. Unlike most Southerners, he didn't kowtow to the National Rifle Association. On race, he was willing to fight for what was right in a state where they once had to call in federal troops to end segregation in the schools. He'd never let the Republicans get away with Willie Horton.

But I was moved by more than what he stood for or how much he knew. It was how I felt around him: uniquely known and needed, as if my contribution might make all the difference. Clinton spoke to the me yearning to be singled out for a special job — the boy who had wrapped his fingers around the archbishop's staff and waved the censer in the path of his dad.

The day before Clinton announced, I was formally offered a job: deputy campaign manager for communications, a loosely defined slot in which I'd be responsible for figuring out how policy issues would play in the media and the political world. Although my duties were not defined with precision, I didn't press for clarification. I wanted the freedom to freelance, and I was too excited and grateful to raise the other awkward questions my friends were urging me to ask before signing on.

My girlfriend, Joan, was especially wary. She thought Clinton was way too conservative and Little Rock was too far away. We had first met on the Dukakis campaign. Both of us knew that campaigns have the same effect on relationships as the first year of law school or a new doctor's internship. Sometimes the trial strengthens the relationship; more often it breaks the couple apart. But that wasn't the only thing bugging her. There was something about Clinton. The stories. Everyone we knew seemed to know someone who knew someone who had a tale to tell about Clinton and women.

That night, we celebrated at my neighborhood Greek restaurant with our friends Richard Mintz and Helene Greenfeld. By the time the baklava arrived, we got to the subject lurking beneath the surface of our little party. They all lowered their voices and questioned me in the same protective tones you reserve for a good friend you suspect is marrying the wrong girl. "What about his past? Are you sure you know what you're getting into?" We kicked around the idea of my raising the issue with Clinton, but I couldn't imagine doing that. I was too young and too junior to be interrogating my future boss about his personal life. His marriage was his business — and Hillary's. Besides, if adultery were a disqualifying offense, half the politicians in Washington would be out of work.

I had no problem defending Clinton against interrogations into his past. What I cared about was the present — and the immediate future. Was he fooling around *now?* Was there any danger that he would pull a Gary Hart and sabotage his own campaign? Impossible, I thought. After Gary Hart's 1988 meltdown on the *Monkey Business,* everyone knew that was against the rules. Getting caught in the act could end a campaign in a heartbeat. I was certain that Clinton was too smart and too ambitious to be so self-destructive.

I was also reassured by what Clinton had already said publicly. Shortly before he announced, Clinton had attended a Washington ritual known as the Sperling breakfast. About twenty reporters invited by Godfrey Sperling, the longtime *Christian Science Monitor* columnist, gathered a couple of times a month over eggs and coffee to give a politician or policy maker the chance to talk about an issue at length without the confrontational tone or live cameras of a press conference. Aware that the womanizing rumors were the most worrisome cloud over his potential campaign, Clinton tried to inoculate himself against future questions by bringing Hillary to the breakfast. Toward the end of the hour, he acknowledged that his marriage had "not been perfect or free of difficulties," but assured the room that he and Hillary had worked it out and expected to be together forever. The message was clear: His past wasn't prologue.

Nothing more had appeared in the press, but the rumors didn't stop — and not everyone wanted them to. Congressman Dave McCurdy, a conservative Oklahoma Democrat, was conducting a whispering campaign against Clinton on the floor of the House. McCurdy wanted to jump in the race, so he was presenting himself to centrist fund-raisers and activists as the clean-cut alternative to Clinton — a Clinton with "character." It didn't work. After the tawdry excesses of 1988, political elites were groping for a shared understanding of how much privacy a public figure deserved and what was fair game in the heat of a campaign. It seemed like a zone of privacy was being staked out.

So despite the well-intentioned warnings of my friends, I wrapped

things up at work, sublet my apartment, and packed my bags for
Little Rock. Then, one more hiccup. The Friday before I left, the
Northeast corridor was buzzing with a new rumor: Cuomo was getting in. At a fund-raising breakfast in Manhattan, he had cracked
open the door to a candidacy. The news hit me like a kick in the
stomach. *Why now? Where were you a month ago?* But the discomfort
faded faster than I expected. Something *had* changed for me.

The messianic streak in Kerrey's camp had left me cold. But I
was yielding to a similar temptation with Clinton. I barely knew
him — one meeting, a couple of phone calls. But the feeling I had
when we first met was taking root, putting him and his cause at the
center of my life. Maybe I couldn't help it. Maybe I had to romanti-
cize the mission in order to survive the impossible hours, the inevitable compromises, and the intense personal pressures that I
knew would come with any campaign. Maybe I had to turn it into a
crusade. How it happened is still a mystery to me, but I was on the
road to becoming a true believer, developing an apostle's love for
Clinton and the adventure we were about to share.

Bruce Lindsey met me at the Little Rock airport. Clinton's old
friend and aide-de-camp, he was smaller than he sounded on the
phone, with short hair and a handsome, dark face hidden by thick
black glasses. He wore a standard-issue blue blazer, gray pants,
and white shirt, and his voice was friendly but flat. His whole demeanor seemed designed for the job he held: Clinton's shadow.
Wherever Clinton went, Bruce followed — hanging backstage,
collecting names, keeping secrets, shuffling cards for a game of
hearts.

We drove straight to the governor's mansion, where Clinton
swung open the aluminum screen door by the kitchen to welcome
me in and show me around. The heavy autumn haze had left him
with a swollen head and a red nose. "I have a hard time thinking when allergy season hits; always sleepy," he explained. But
that didn't stop him from picking up our conversation right where
we had left off in Washington. "I feel good about it, but we're
behind. . . . Got a lot to do. . . . Trips to New Hampshire and
Chicago. . . . Need to set up a network to get me ideas from my
friends. . . . Decide what to do about the Florida straw poll."

He kept on talking as I followed him to the bedroom, where he started to change out of his jeans for a downtown lunch, then stopped to hand me an article from a pile on one of the night tables. There were two of them — one for him, one for her — both loaded down with novels, magazines, issue papers, and spiritual books. I hadn't yet met Hillary, but seeing the night tables made me picture the two of them propped up late at night, passing their reading back and forth, arguing, laughing, educating each other, sharing a passion for ideas.

Then she appeared in the bedroom door. Hillary was prettier than the pictures I'd seen, with a dimpled smile that didn't match her high-powered reputation and a tailored suit that did. Walking over in his briefs, Clinton smacked a sloppy kiss on her cheek and introduced us. "I've heard so much about you," she said, her Midwestern accent slowed just a touch by her years in the South.

Nice start. Warm. But it was one thing to be working with the boss while he changed; with his wife there, I just wanted to excuse myself. Hillary insisted I stay and stepped right into the conversation, asking questions, analyzing the upcoming primaries, and reminding me of all the work we had to do. My awkwardness was flushed away by an adrenaline-enhanced sense of arrival. This was exactly what I wanted to be doing: building a presidential campaign — and exactly where I wanted to be: in its inner sanctum.

Clinton left for lunch, and I made my first visit to the Clinton for President headquarters, a converted paint store in downtown Little Rock. *This is it? Where's the buzz? The staff? Why aren't the phones ringing off the hook?* It felt like the headquarters of an incumbent state senator with no opponent. On my left were the volunteer receptionists, a pair of gracious but elderly ladies putting in a few hours a week. On my right was the bare table that would serve as my desk. Nancy Hernreich, the governor's executive assistant, sat in the back. She was the whole scheduling operation, accompanied only by the black binder that went everywhere she went. No one else in the office seemed to be doing anything. Now I felt like Dustin Hoffman in the closing scene of *The Graduate* — the pullaway where he's sitting in the back of the bus, Katharine Ross finally by his side and that weak smile on his face that says, "*I have no idea what I've done or where I'm going, but I guess I have to make the best of it now."*

For the first couple of weeks, I stayed in the office, working the press by phone, helping Nancy with the schedule, recruiting friends to come down, following through on the fifty ideas a day Clinton called in from the statehouse: Hillary's friend in Chicago had a tax plan he wanted me to review; a smart New Hampshire supporter had some good ideas on bank reform; could I make a call to Dade County and check on the straw poll?

After first bunking with some "Friends of Bill," I moved into an apartment behind the governor's mansion with Richard Mintz, whom I had persuaded to take the plunge with me and work on Hillary's team. Our home was part of a complex of converted crack houses in a neighborhood made attractive only by its proximity to Clinton. One night, Richard came home to find a pair of burglars in the process of stealing our television. Apparently on a work break, they were sprawled on the couch eating take-out chicken when Richard arrived. They politely picked up the bones and left; we moved a few days later.

I didn't much care about the apartment because I expected my real home to be on the road with Clinton. Our first trip together was to a Democratic Party dinner in Chicago, where both Clinton and Kerrey would be speaking. Because this was the first event of the campaign to feature both candidates, a few members of the national press would be there. For me, this dinner had additional meaning: the road not taken. *What if Kerrey turns out to be better than Clinton? What if I made the wrong choice?*

Bruce Lindsey and I accompanied Clinton on a commercial flight, and we all flew coach. Clinton carried a huge saddle-leather satchel stuffed with papers and books. As he worked his way through the bag, he reached across the aisle to pass me memos for follow-up before turning to his crossword puzzle and taking a nap. Sitting a row behind him, I noticed that some of the other passengers kept glancing at him in a way that seemed to be saying, *"This guy looks like someone I should know."* When I caught one of their glances, I smiled back with knowing pride and a look I imagined to say, *"If you don't know him now, you will. Just wait."*

We took the El into town — not just to save time at rush hour, but also so that Kevin O'Keefe, a local pol and high school friend of Hillary's, could call the *Tribune*'s political gossip columnist with a little nugget about the governor of Arkansas who was running for president. Riding the El was a nice tip of the hat to the city's working-class spirit, and all the little messages add up. We also made local news by announcing that David Wilhelm, a veteran of Mayor Daley's operation, would now be Clinton's campaign manager. He would give us an edge if, as Clinton expected, the March 17 Illinois primary really turned out to be the decisive contest.

The trick to speaking at party fund-raisers is to treat them like dinner theater. People are there to have fun and feel good. No heavy lifting. The postmeal speech has to be easy and light, with just enough inspiration to make people feel that being there is a kind of civic duty.

Clinton began his speech by working his way down the dais with a special word or inside joke for every politician there. *Nice stroke. People remember being remembered.* Then he made a couple of quips about how much Arkansas had given Chicago, including Scottie Pippen of the Bulls, and launched into his stump speech — a condensed version of his announcement speech on how we needed a president who would fight for the middle class and fix our problems here at home. When he tested a line we had worked on about how America needs a president who cares as much about the "Middle West as the Middle East," the crowd rewarded him with laughter and applause. I made a note to remind him to use the line again — as if he needed reminding.

Kerrey arrived moments before the dinner and didn't work the crowd, just stood off to the side cracking jokes with his traveling aide. When he spoke about Vietnam, it was still moving, but there was an edge of bitterness beneath his words that he couldn't hide. And he made no real attempt to tailor his message to this particular crowd on this particular night. Over the course of a campaign, despite all of the artifice, the public usually picks up a reasonably true picture of a candidate, for better or worse. The Chicago crowd saw an engaged and optimistic Bill Clinton, a man who loved his work. He wooed his audience, forged a connection, and paid them the compliment of delivering a speech that didn't seem canned. Kerrey didn't work hard enough to win the room, giving people the impression that he expected them to support him because of who he was rather than what he would do for them.

After the speeches, Kerrey left right away. Clinton stayed for another reception with the local VIPs and greeted each one with a personal word while I stood off his left shoulder and collected their business cards for our field and fund-raising efforts. Pumped up by the people and the speech, Clinton fished for compliments as we hustled through the back hallways to our suite: "How'd I do? . . . You think it was OK? . . . Find out what Joe thinks." Joe was Joe Klein, a short, bearded writer for *New York* magazine who had his eye on Clinton. I found him outside by the curb waiting for a cab, and we schmoozed for a few minutes. He was as high on the speech as I was, confirming that Clinton had cleaned Kerrey's clock. Good news to report.

Our campaign grew fast through the fall. We traded up headquarters, and Wilhelm built up our field organization, working back from Illinois to Florida, where the first symbolic votes would be cast at a straw poll in December. His buddy Rahm Emanuel came down from Chicago to run the money. All I knew about Emanuel at first was that he had once mailed a dead fish to a rival political consultant. But when the former ballet dancer arrived in Little Rock and leaped onto a table to scream his staff into shape, I knew the money side would be OK.

I divided my time between setting up shop in Little Rock and accompanying Clinton on the road. Bruce took care of the "body"; I concentrated on press and policy, briefing Clinton before interviews on likely questions and the reporter's angle, checking in with our consultants back in Washington, reading newspapers, magazines, and policy journals for news hooks and new facts to freshen the stump speech. When Clinton spoke, I took notes — partly so I could help explain his thinking and point out his best lines to the press, partly to help remind Clinton which riffs were especially effective. I was there to hear what worked and to help whittle away what didn't. On the plane, I tried to absorb the thoughts he revealed in snatches of conversation between catnaps and countless hands of hearts. Each hand was a tutorial: Either he was reaching across the table to teach me how to pass the cards, or leaning back into his headrest with a meditation on, say, the right way to confront David Duke: "You can't question his being born-again. . . . We Southerners believe in deathbed conversions. . . . Just say we can't go back to the days when his kind of thinking held us all back."

On a late Friday night in November, Clinton expounded on that theme before his largest campaign audience yet — at the Church of God in Christ convention, in Memphis. Clinton was flying in from New Hampshire, but I had spent the week in headquarters and was missing the road. With Memphis only a couple of hours away, David Wilhelm and I decided to take a drive.

Entering the convention, I was struck by the sensation of never having been in a room like this before. David and I were about the only white faces in a crowd of men in immaculate suits and women in elaborate hats. Stray organ chords drifted over the murmurs of the congregation. The arena was alive with expectation, fellowship, spirituality, and a sense of fun — somewhere between a Sunday service and a rock concert.

But if I was at sea, Clinton was at home. He knew this place and its people, had prayed with them in tiny churches on the back roads of Arkansas. Here, too, he had made it his business to know who they were and what they cared about. If Chicago had been politics as theater, this was politics as liturgy.

He entered the hall, a lone white man surrounded by a cluster of black clergymen, looking like a heavyweight with his cornermen before being called into the ring. He was staring straight ahead, almost in a trance, oblivious to the crowd. I would soon learn the meaning of that look: Clinton was composing his speech.

As he moved toward the stage, I sat on a concrete step in the aisle, ready to be carried away. This was my guy, and I wanted him to succeed — especially here, in front of an African American audience, where he could preach his message of drawing black and white workers together in common cause. Just like Bobby Kennedy had tried to do before an assassin's bullet struck him down. Then came court-ordered busing, urban decay, the Democrats' drift toward identity politics, and a generation of Republican candidates from Nixon to Bush whose winning formula was crime, quotas, and welfare queens. By 1991, RFK's "black and blue" coalition was a distant memory.

Maybe Clinton could put it back together. That was his dream, and mine. I wanted him to be the Bobby Kennedy I first heard of in second grade, when our whole school was ushered into the auditorium to pray for the great man who'd been shot the night before and was fighting for life on an operating table. The Bobby Kennedy I read about when I first moved to Washington. Jack Newfield's elegy to RFK's 1968 campaign introduced me to a world of young men like Jeff Greenfield and Peter Edelman and Adam Walinsky, who had hooked up with a Kennedy to help change the world — brash, tough-minded idealists who wanted to stop the war in Vietnam and start a war on poverty at home, from Bed-Stuy to Appalachia to the Indian reservations in the mountain west. Young guys who helped make history.

If Clinton could be Kennedy, maybe I could be one of them — and maybe tonight would be part of that process. Maybe this speech would pass into the realm of political myth, like John Kennedy's 1960 speech on church and state that put him over the top in West Virginia, or his younger brother's sermon against violence, delivered impromptu in Indiana the night Martin Luther King was shot. Or maybe, more likely, this would be just another Friday night in a campaign that would never be remembered at all. But campaigns are fueled by fantasy too.

Clinton delivered that night. After a hug for Bishop Ford, he started out slow, easing into the speech as if he were groping for words. Picking up speed, he praised the church, "founded by a man of God from my state," and reflected on his own Baptist faith, making connections, drawing them in. With a lilt in his voice, he told this mostly black, mostly Southern crowd that he had flown here through the night from a very different place — New Hampshire, "almost all white, very Republican." But for the first time in their lives, Clinton said, people in New Hampshire had something in common with "people like you who have known hard times."

"Amen," called the crowd.

"America is hurting everywhere tonight," Clinton continued.

"Our streets are mean." More amens, more speed. Clinton picked up the pace, moving from a prayer for Magic Johnson to a condemnation for David Duke before settling on the heart of his message — the "new covenant, a solemn agreement which we must not break." Government must provide opportunity; people must take responsibility. "If you can go to work, you ought to go to work."

"Yes, sir. . . . Tell it now."

Clinton was talking straight, and the crowd was responding. If anyone dared to attack Clinton for playing the race card on welfare reform, I had the perfect counterpunch: *You don't know what you're talking about. When Clinton told twenty thousand African Americans in Memphis that people on welfare must work, he got the biggest applause of the campaign.*

But he didn't stop there. Clinton quoted Abe Lincoln, praised the "power of oneness," and promised to take this same message of personal responsibility not only to this black audience in Memphis, but all over the country, from the "high-tech enclaves of Silicon Valley to the high-powered barons of Wall Street." He was challenging, preaching, reminding all of us that "we're all in this together."

Right as Clinton closed, I jumped up to catch him backstage before the next task of the evening — an interview with Dan Balz of the *Washington Post*. I had been talking to Balz nearly every day and had urged him to be there that night to see Clinton at his best.

During the formative weeks of a campaign, long before the Iowa caucuses or the New Hampshire primary, the candidates fight for scraps and angle for the slightest bit of coverage, especially in national newspapers like the *Post*. If Balz, the top political reporter at the country's top political paper, wrote about the Memphis speech, people would pay attention. Even what didn't make it into the paper might make a difference. At the beginning of a campaign, key reporters create a kind of bush telegraph, sending messages from one outpost to another. Balz would trade information with a source, who would tell his boss, who would chat with a big donor at a cocktail party. The buzz would begin.

My job was to help it along. In the holding room, I pulled Clinton aside to brief him on what Dan was working on and to suggest some points that would play into Balz's story line on the black vote. I felt a little bit like I was introducing two of my friends who didn't know each other, hoping they would get along. We needed this meeting to go well; people had to know how moving Clinton was that night. Before I left to get Balz, I urged Clinton to talk about Bobby Kennedy's example in the interview. He absorbed my mood and fed it back with his memories of 1968.

But I returned with Balz to a terrible sight. Clinton was shaking hands and having his picture taken with Gus Savage, an Illinois congressman infamous for his anti-Semitic views who had been reprimanded by his colleagues for hitting on a Peace Corps volunteer during an overseas junket. What made the moment even worse was that there was nothing I could do about it. If I tried to stop the photo, it would only call attention to the problem. It was awful: Balz was watching me watch the photo op, while I was watching Dan watch me. He could sense my discomfort, I just knew it, and he started to tease me, pretending — at least I hoped he was pretending — that Clinton posing with Savage was the real story in Memphis. *He's kidding, right? That's all we need: an article on Clinton the hypocrite. Talks about "bringing people together" on stage, curries favor with a sexist and racist congressman backstage.*

Dan *was* kidding. The interview went well, and the evening couldn't have gone better. I saw the inspiring side of Clinton and felt I'd done my part. Before driving home, David and I stopped for eggs, grits, and country ham at an all-night diner near the arena. There was nowhere else I wanted to be just then, as the convention delegates streamed in well after midnight for food and talk. Wilhelm and I were jazzed up by the crowd and the speech and our candidate and the excitement that comes with being at the top of a new campaign for the first time, when it's early enough to know you have little to lose and everything to gain. Early enough to believe that anything is possible.

I wanted to wander from table to table to eavesdrop on imagined conversations. *"Who was that fellow Clinton? I liked what he had to say."* But I knew from experience at church conventions that the delegates would be too busy catching up on family, friends, and church politics to pay much attention to a young politician they might never hear of again. So I just ate my ham and hoped for a good article in the *Post*.

Before New Hampshire, there are stretches in the campaign when nothing happens for weeks, and occasional days when it seems as if everything happens at once. Monday, November 18, was one of those days. The previous Friday, all the candidates had been in New Hampshire to roast Dick Swett, a Democrat running for Congress. Clinton and Kerrey were swapping jokes behind the dais before the official ribbing began, and Kerrey told Clinton a dumb and dirty joke about Jerry Brown and lesbians. Clinton laughed.

Three days later, as we flew to Washington, Richard Mintz called the plane from Little Rock to warn us that C-Span had a videotape of Kerrey telling the joke. Chris Matthews of the *San Francisco Examiner* also had the story and was staking us out in Washington to get Clinton's response.

Not good. Slow news day. Two leading candidates in the race. Sex, feminism, and political correctness all rolled into one. Matthews has a scoop, and we're stuck right in the middle of it. By this time we were using a Learjet, and when I leaned across the lap table to tell Clinton what was going on and ask him to tell me the joke, he smiled over his reading glasses and said he couldn't remember exactly how it went. If he was bluffing, it was probably for the best. The fewer details coming from our side, the better.

Our mission was tricky: How did we extricate Clinton from this embarrassing incident without exonerating Kerrey? This story was both an opportunity and a threat. A threat because any sentence containing the words *Clinton* and *sex* would always be bad news. Opportunity because Kerrey was our main rival, and getting caught telling an offensive sexist joke would cut against his soulful image. It was time to apply a corollary to Napoleon's rule: "Never get in the way of your enemy when he's heading for a cliff. But give him a push if you can get away with it."

Of course, we couldn't pretend that Clinton had been offended by a joke he had obviously enjoyed. Explaining that he was laughing just to be nice was disingenuous, and it would call too much attention to the fact that Clinton had laughed at the joke rather than focusing fire on our rival who told it. So we would try to keep Clinton out of the story. Our official response was this statement from me:

"What Governor Clinton has said is that he and Bob Kerrey are good friends. . . ." The opening phrase sends a double message: Not only is the story old news, but it's not even important enough for Clinton to make his own statement. "Good friends" is a signal to Kerrey's people that we won't go out of our way to hurt him, which is not to say that we will go out of our way to help him.

"Senator Kerrey clearly thought it was a private conversation, and Governor Clinton is going to respect that. . . ." This is Senator Kerrey's problem; Clinton is merely a forgiving observer. Our guy just *listened* to the joke, as opposed to the poor sap who told it. But we do "respect" Senator Kerrey's right to lose sight of the fact that he's in the middle of a presidential campaign, where everyone knows there's no such thing as a private conversation.

"There were a lot of bad jokes flying around that auditorium . . . some more tasteless than others." We're not saying Clinton's never told a bad joke; you press guys probably have one on tape. But yes, if you insist, Kerrey's joke was worse. It was — and this is the key word, the most vivid word in the statement, the one that turns the knife — "tasteless."

I was pretty happy with the language. Even better news for us was the fact that Kerrey was in San Francisco just as this was breaking. That alone guaranteed a second-day story, and Kerrey prolonged his agony by going on a binge of self-recrimination. Telling this joke, he said, had caused him to confront "an unpleasant side" of himself. It was time, he continued, "for me to evaluate my own behavior."

There is such a thing as apologizing too much. Kerrey's response kept the story going and made him look weak. At a stage in the campaign when even the most trivial incident is dissected by the punditocracy to distinguish between the candidates, Kerrey was sending the message that he wasn't yet ready for prime time. While his blunder wasn't the talk of the nation, it was the subject of no less than four stories, plus a column in the *Washington Post*.

The joke drowned out any coverage we might have gotten on

Clinton's congressional testimony advocating D.C. statehood. But the real point of our visit to Washington was a private meeting later that night with Jesse Jackson. Jackson had just announced that he wouldn't run for the Democratic nomination, so the black vote was up for grabs, and Clinton's relationship with Jesse could make the crucial difference.

A few of us accompanied Clinton to a dinner meeting on Jackson's turf — the private room on the second floor of a restaurant in his Northeast Washington neighborhood. It felt like the meeting of two gang leaders, each with a small entourage, sitting down to see if there was an alliance to be formed or a battle to be fought. This was the first time I had seen Clinton and Jackson together, and I was struck by their size, their huge hands and oversize heads.

Clinton and Jackson needed each other. Clinton wanted Jackson's endorsement and the votes that went with it, but without appearing to ask. As the titular leader of African American Democrats, and a man who'd won more primary votes in the past than anyone now in the race, Jackson expected to be courted — and to play the role of kingmaker. Jackson probably also calculated that Clinton was the only other candidate in the race who could cut into the campaign of the only African American in the race, Virginia governor Doug Wilder. Wilder and Jackson were more rivals than friends. If Wilder did well in the primaries, it might threaten Jackson's preeminent position in the black community.

Dealing with Jackson was a delicate task, which we had muffed in the Dukakis campaign. The only strategy that would work in 1992 was tough love. Clinton had to treat Jackson with the respect Jackson had earned and craved, but he couldn't kowtow to him or enter a no-win public negotiation for his endorsement that would only add to Jackson's power and cost us some white votes. Clinton's leverage was increased by his independent relationship with a new generation of black leaders, such as Congressmen Bill Jefferson, John Lewis, Mike Espy, and Bobby Rush.

Clinton struck the right balance that night. Over baked chicken and sweet potato pie, he talked policy and politics: statehood, civil rights, justice, and jobs — both in the country and within the campaign. Jackson didn't say much at first, just took it all in. Then he weighed in with expectations expressed as opinions. I was impressed not so much by what they were saying as by how they said it, circling each other with their words, half showing off, half holding back. This was not the time for promises or threats, although both were palpably in the room, like a pair of bodyguards at the door.

So this is it. This is how the big guys talk to each other. I'd been behind my share of closed doors on Capitol Hill, but this was different — more self-conscious, almost cinematic, as if everyone was aware of playing a part in a drama that was being written as they spoke. This was the classic smoke-filled room, minus the smoke. I watched and listened and tried to look cool, too dumbstruck to say a sensible word and half convinced that somebody would look up any minute and say, "Hey, what are *you* doing here?"

Clinton and Jackson could have talked all night, but we had to leave for the last meeting of the day — a late-night rendezvous with James Carville and Paul Begala at the Grand Hotel on M Street.

Theodore H. White's *The Making of the President, 1960* described the major political advisers of the day as a few dozen Washington lawyers, "who in their dark-paneled chambers nurse an amateur's love for politics and dabble in it whenever their practice permits." By 1991, that description had the dated feel of a sepia-toned photograph, harking back to an era when political consultants, like tennis players in long pants, were not paid for their work. There were still amateurs who loved the game in 1991, but campaigns were now run by professionals.

The professionals with the hot hands that fall were Carville and Begala. Earlier that month they had guided former JFK aide Harris Wofford to an upset landslide victory in his Pennsylvania Senate race against Bush attorney general Richard Thornburgh. Every Democrat in the country hoped the race was a harbinger for 1992, and most of the candidates wanted to hire the men who had helped make it happen.

Paul Begala and I were friends from our days together on Gephardt's staff. I spent most of my day on the House floor, but whenever I got back to the office, there he was, at the desk across from me, having more fun in front of a word processor than I thought was humanly possible. Watching him write a speech was like watching Ray Charles play the piano. He would rock back and forth and talk to the screen, groaning one minute, laughing the next. The speeches he produced had perfect populist pitch: pithy, funny, aimed straight at the lazy Susans of middle-class kitchen tables. With his lizardlike looks and colorful patois, Carville was the better-known partner, but James wouldn't have been James without Paul.

James had his own gift — a sixth sense about politics, a down-home genius that can't be taught. He was the first person I heard say that President Bush could be beat. It was in May 1991, at Paul's thirtieth birthday party. We met by the bar, where James was pouring himself a bourbon. He filled my glass too, while assuring me that Bush was going to lose if we had the right candidate. I remembered the prediction because I wanted it to be right but was sure it was wrong.

We went to the bar, where Clinton ordered decaf and the rest of us had a drink. Within minutes Carville and Clinton were competing. Who knew more about politics, who was the real Southerner, who had the most sophisticated take on Super Tuesday's primary chessboard. Everyone agreed that the black vote could make the difference for Clinton — and that New Hampshire was a crapshoot. After Carville and Begala left, Clinton turned to me in the elevator and said, "Those guys are smart." Which meant, of course, "They agree with me." They signed up with us a couple of weeks later, and the *Post* reported that we treated it "as the December equivalent of winning the New Hampshire primary."

True — and that wasn't the only good news coming our way at the end of 1991. Clinton was catching on, even with liberals who had been suspicious of him. At the early cattle calls, he'd tell the crowds, "I'm a Democrat by instinct, heritage, and conviction. My granddaddy thought he was going to Roosevelt when he died." The party regulars would stomp and yell, oblivious to the unspoken yet unmistakable "but" at the end of the sentence. Clinton was establishing his bona fides, rallying skeptics with words he knew they wanted to hear. But the fact that he had to do so out loud was an implicit warning: *"I come from your world, but if you don't change with me and cut me some slack, we'll never get anything done, because we'll never win."*

Most liberals knew this, understood that Clinton wasn't really one of us. But it felt good to get lost in the partisan reverie, to be carried back to a time when photos of FDR graced Democratic mantels like the icons of a patron saint, a time when the Kennedy brothers epitomized the best and the brightest, a time long before McGovern, Carter, Mondale, and Dukakis were caricatured into a sadly comic Mount Rushmore, symbols of a party out of touch and doomed to defeat. It felt good, again, to think about winning.

Only one other Democrat could still stir the party faithful in the same way, and he was the cloud over our heads as 1991 drew to a close. No matter what we said or did, the campaign wouldn't feel entirely real until the eternally ambivalent front-runner finally declared his true intentions. Nobody knew what Cuomo was going to do. He was teasing the press, the party establishment, his potential opponents — and the longer he took to make up his labyrinthine mind, the more frustrated we got. He had frozen the race.

Reporters were dying for Cuomo to jump in. It seemed as if every time the governor of New York scratched his nose he received more fawning coverage than we could get with a series of substantive speeches. What could be better than an enigmatic and eloquent intellectual who quoted Saint Francis of Assisi and didn't dirty his hands by actually entering the race? Few figures are more appealing than the reluctant statesman untroubled by ambition but willing to accept the burden of office for the good of all. "Cuomo Sapiens," the *Post* called him. "The Thinking Man's Non-Candidate."

Although I had shared those feelings, I was ready to engage. Clinton resisted most of our efforts to draw clear lines with Cuomo, but we got an opening when Cuomo took the first shot. Joe Klein was stirring the pot. In a *New York* magazine interview with Cuomo, he got the governor to criticize Clinton's plans on welfare and national service. Schmoozing on the phone with E. J. Dionne of the *Post*, I saw we had the opportunity we'd been waiting for. Maybe if we lobbed the grenade back to Cuomo, E. J. would have enough material to write a story and frame the debate.

I scratched out a statement and drove my battered Honda to the mansion to show it to Clinton. In his makeshift basement office, Clinton edited the statement and stood over me while I dialed the phone, wishing, I knew, that he could pick up the phone and talk to E. J. himself but knowing it wouldn't be smart: Candidates don't debate noncandidates. But by attacking Clinton's signature issues, Cuomo was helping define him — as the un-Cuomo, the new Democrat who wasn't afraid to challenge party orthodoxy. An attack from Cuomo was also a sign that we mattered. Maybe he was hearing footsteps.

Dionne wrote a small story that included a quote from me defending Clinton's ideas and challenging Cuomo to "let the debate begin." Any ambivalence I felt about taking on one of my political idols was balanced by my frustration at the way Cuomo was toying with the race, by my convincing myself that Cuomo was criticizing a caricature of the Clinton proposals rather than the ideas themselves, and by Dionne's observation that the Clinton campaign "fired back immediately." E. J. was sending a signal to the political world, telling it, I imagined, *If you hit Clinton, he hits back. His campaign won't repeat the mistakes of the past.* But I couldn't help wondering what Cuomo thought when he read my words, or what I would have thought and said had I been working for him instead.

Cuomo was telling people that he couldn't decide about the race until he finished work on his budget in Albany. Thankfully for us, an external deadline forced his hand: the final filing date for the New Hampshire primary was December 20.

The twentieth was a Friday, and that entire week felt like one long election day, waiting for results you could no longer pretend to control. Work was impossible; all we cared about was information about Cuomo's intentions. We scrutinized every statement, rumor, and hint for possible clues. Cuomo chartered a plane for a flight to Manchester — *must be getting in.* But Republicans in his state senate were holding firm in budget talks — *maybe he can't get in.* We seemed to have the most to lose if Cuomo entered the race, which is why we were desperately trying to convince ourselves that we wanted him in, that his entry, which was probably inevitable, would actually work to our advantage. "The only way to be a heavyweight is to beat a heavyweight" was our new mantra.

Clinton was on his way to Tennessee that Friday, where a throat specialist would make the first try at treating his persistent hoarseness. Anticipating the worst — or the best, depending on your point of view — we had prepared a statement for Clinton welcoming Cuomo into the race. As the filing deadline approached, CNN went live with cameras in Albany and New Hampshire. They even had a camera trained on the idling plane. Then Bernie Shaw broke in with a bulletin. Cuomo was out. The first big break of the campaign.

Clinton was just about to exit when I reached his plane. "Don't get off," I said. "Listen to this." Cuomo approached the microphones to make it official, and I simulcasted his statement to Clinton over the phone. Clinton seemed unfazed by the news, but I knew he was making the calculations in his head, and I guessed he was pleased. One of the reasons he had been so reluctant to hit Cuomo early was to avoid prodding him into the race in a fit of personal pique. Without pausing to comment, Clinton dictated a gracious statement for me to release to the press.

Meanwhile, Rahm Emanuel was playing the tough guy. "Damn." His fists pounding his thighs. "It would have been so great if he came in. We'd rip his head off." But he didn't linger. Cuomo's decision would free up a lot of New York money, so he had to hit the phones.

David Wilhelm then came into my office, and for a moment we just looked at each other across the desk. Like me, he was more liberal than centrist, more old than new Democrat.

"You didn't want him in, did you?"

"What, are you kidding?"

"Me neither."

Not a single vote had been cast, but the complicated, almost alchemic process that creates conventional wisdom had made Clinton the front-runner. A similar process was solidifying my spot in Clinton's inner circle. The daily phone calls, endless meetings, late-night games of hearts on the plane, and early-morning reviews of the headlines were deepening the bond. Clinton seemed to have confidence in me, and he coached me on what I needed to know — even taking me into the bathroom once to deliver an important message on how to deal with a particular woman friend of his.

The night before, I had shared a car with Susan Thomases, a brassy New York lawyer and Democratic campaign veteran who was also one of Hillary's best friends. Exhausted from an all-night speech meeting and a full day of events, I didn't make a good impression. Bad move: She apparently told Hillary, who told Clinton that I was rude. When we got to the airport that morning, he gave me some advice over the urinals: "George, you know that Hillary and I have a lot of good women friends our age. You have to pay attention to them, ask them what they think so they don't resent you. You're smart, but you're a boy. You have to go out of your way to be nice to them."

By the end of the year I was doing better in that department. Every Tuesday, before her weekly "ladies lunch" in Little Rock, Clinton's mother, Virginia Kelley, would stop by my office to chat before leaving me with a powerful hug as thanks for "taking care of my Bill." Hillary knew she could count on me to get things done and let me know how much she appreciated it by inviting me to the family Christmas party along with a dozen or so longtime friends of the Clintons. We played parlor games and sang carols — an old-fashioned American-style Christmas in the South. The ethnic in me found the whole scene exotic but warm. I was becoming part of the family.

3   HEARING HOOFBEATS

After a few days off with Joan at a funky Ozark resort called Eureka Springs, I caught up with Clinton on New Year's Day in Charleston, South Carolina. He and Hillary wanted a quiet family night after their annual visit to Renaissance Weekend — a gathering of credentialed baby boomers who flew to Hilton Head every New Year's for earnest talk and energetic networking. Once they were settled in their suite with Chelsea and her choice of movie rentals, I went out for a walk. The warm salted breeze and the gaslights guarding the turn-of-the century town houses by the bay connected me to another time. But I was thinking about the year ahead.

Things were looking good. Not only were we succeeding, but our rivals were stumbling. Cuomo was out, and Wilder would soon follow. Nobody took Tsongas seriously yet, and Harkin signaled that *he* wasn't a serious threat by taking a two-week vacation in the Caribbean. Jerry Brown was still a joke, and Kerrey had been hampered by a staff coup, weak fund-raising, and the revelation that he didn't provide health insurance to employees at the fitness centers he owned — a devastating charge given that the senator was trying to make universal health care the signature issue of his campaign.

Our team was starting to gel. Dee Dee Myers came in from

California to be press secretary, and Bruce Reed moved down from D.C. to run the issues shop. I was back on the road — this time for good. I couldn't have been happier with where we were or how I fit in. If our luck held, we'd get the nomination. If it held a little longer . . .

The next day's main event was in an antebellum mansion with a staircase out of *Gone with the Wind*. As night fell, about a hundred supporters crowded up the stairs to watch Clinton go to work. These were his people — progressive Southern Democrats. And this was his place — a room big enough to perform in but small enough to forge personal connections. Mellowed by his brief holiday and building hopes for the new year, Clinton spoke in a soft drawl stretched out just a touch for his neighbors' ears. The crowd was rapt with parochial pride and the hope that this night might be a memory in the making — the year we began with the next president.

Clinton didn't simply speak to the group; he conducted it. When he recounted the daily struggles of single women working their way off welfare, they nodded in empathy. When he left rhetorical questions hanging over the foyer, they responded with murmurs and muffled shouts. When he condensed his life's ambition into a single closing sentence — "I desperately want to be your president, but you have to be Americans again" — the applause wrapped around him like a communal hug.

Joe Klein and I took it all in from the back of the room with tears in our eyes — moved by the emotional moment, expectation, and apprehension. Reporters are paid to be dispassionate, but Joe was either smitten with Clinton or doing a smooth job of spinning me. We talked openly and often now, either on the phone or when he hooked up with us on the road. As the paying guests sat down to dinner, we retreated to the basement. The campaign was going so well that we slipped into what Joe called a "dark-off," whispering fears of future misfortune like a couple of black-robed crones spitting in the wind to ward off the evil eye. *We're peaking too early. It can't stay this good. Too tempting a target. What goes up must come down.*

"I come from Russian Jews," Joe said. "Whenever things are good, we start to hear hoofbeats — the Cossacks."

"Yeah, I know just what you mean."

"Don't try to out-dark me on this one, George. It's in my genes."

"Mine too," I replied. "The Turks."

The hoofbeats we heard that night weren't Cossacks heading for a Russian *shtetl* or Ottoman Turks bearing down on a Peloponnesian *chorio*. They were the ghosts of Clinton's past, summoned to life by his campaign's success. From Hot Springs and Little Rock, Fayetteville and Oxford, they were gathering together and galloping north — to New Hampshire.

New Hampshire's not only the first presidential primary; it's also the most intimate. You meet people where they live and work and play, and talk to them over cake donuts and Greek pizza, over Friday night boilermakers in the dimly lit Manchester men's clubs, and in bowling alleys on Saturday afternoons where families roll games of duckpins. Only in New Hampshire do presidential hopefuls still go door-to-door. Salt stains crept up my loafers as I followed Clinton through the snow.

A master at what James Madison called the "little arts of popularity," Clinton was made for this kind of hand-to-hand campaign. No one could match him at a house party. He'd greet each guest individually while I checked in with headquarters from the kitchen phone. Then I'd settle on the second-floor landing with a Styrofoam cup of strong coffee and watch him do his stuff in the living room below.

Clinton would lay out his economic plan, and they'd fire back questions. Flinty and frugal, New Hampshirites wanted to know exactly how he was going to pay for his programs. But that year they also needed help. New Hampshire was mired in recession. Clinton's new ideas on health care, jobs, and student loans sounded sensible, and he answered every question — in detail. No one could stump him, and people walked away impressed. Here was a politician who cared enough to really know the pressures families faced, and with definite ideas on what could be done to ease them.

I summed up that sensibility in a quote I gave Joe Klein for his January profile of Clinton in *New York* magazine. "Specificity is a character issue this year," I said. Like all good spin, it was a hope dressed up as an observation. We wanted Clinton to be seen as the thoughtful candidate — the man with a plan who knew what to do — and we needed that to be the character test of 1992. A good spinner is like a good lawyer: You highlight the facts that help your client's case and downplay the ones that don't. When the facts are unfavorable, you argue relevance. That's what I was trying to do: blunt the questions about Clinton's private behavior by pointing to his public virtues and saying that was what voters cared about most. It was, but "specificity" obviously wasn't the only character issue in 1992.

Which brings us back to Clinton and women. That front had been mostly quiet through the fall, except for "sweet, sweet Connie." Immortalized in the Grand Funk Railroad classic "We're an American Band," Connie Hamzy was a Little Rock groupie who was infamous on the rock circuit for her lusty backstage adventures. But in November 1991, she claimed that her favors had also been bestowed upon a certain Arkansas governor.

My assistant, Steve "Scoop" Cohen, heard about it on a local talk-radio station. They were promoting an upcoming issue of *Penthouse*, in which photos of Connie would be accompanied by her claim that Clinton had propositioned her eight years earlier in a hotel lobby. Hamzy's charge felt like a mortal threat to our embryonic campaign, so we scrambled into action.

I contacted Clinton on his way to a Texas fund-raiser, but he didn't seem too concerned. Sure, he'd met Hamzy, he recalled, but not the way she said. As he quickly recounted the story over the phone, I imagined his eyes getting wider and detected a little laugh in his voice. They had run into each other in the lobby of the North Little Rock Hilton. The governor was leaving a speech with a few associates when Hamzy, who had been sunbathing by the hotel pool, ran up to him, flipped down her bikini top, and asked, "What do you think of these?" Clinton seemed to take great pleasure in picturing the scene again.

Hillary was less amused. "We have to destroy her story," she said from her seat next to him on the plane. I was with her. Hamzy's story didn't sound funny to me either. It was flimsy, but it could still do some damage if we didn't snuff it out fast. Thankfully, the facts seemed to be on our side. This wasn't just a "he said, she said" case.

Working with Clinton's gubernatorial staff, I was able to round up sworn affidavits from three people who'd accompanied Clinton, witnessed the encounter, and corroborated his account.

The story broke before dawn on CNN *Headline News*. Barely into my first cup of coffee, I called CNN central in Atlanta. It took a little while to find someone with responsibility, but when I finally reached a night editor, I started screaming: "You can't run something like this without proof. You have to check a charge before you run with it."

Stopping CNN was key. If they ran the story all day, however briefly, other news organizations could cite them to justify running their own stories. Our denials would be folded into the accounts, but the damage would be done. All of the trashy images — *Penthouse*, rock and roll groupie, bikini — would be out there, and they might stick. If a bad joke merited four stories in the *Post*, who knew what this would get?

When other reporters started calling, I refused to comment on the record. A denial, just like a mention on CNN, could become a pretext to run the story. So I denied it off the record and offered to fax the affidavits rebutting the charge on the same basis. The strategy was to convince legitimate news organizations that Hamzy's charge wasn't credible enough to be aired. It worked. CNN dropped the story after a single mention, and none of the other networks picked it up.

We'd survived our first bimbo eruption. The Hamzy episode was a test — of Clinton's character, our campaign's competence, and the media's resistance to tabloid trash. We all passed. Clinton was telling the truth, we defended him aggressively on the facts, and the media ignored the story despite the juicy details. Too bad it was only a drill.

My reward that night was an appreciative phone call from Hillary and the governor, who thanked me between spoonfuls of mango ice cream from the Menger hotel in San Antonio. This wasn't exactly the job satisfaction I imagined getting from a presidential campaign, but the exhilaration at being shot at and missed was tangible, and I told myself that the situation might have spun out of control if I hadn't been there. This first dustup also planted seeds of indignation and resentment in my psyche against Clinton's accusers and their potential accomplices in the press. I was mirroring the Clintons' mood, absorbing their anger and fear and turning it into my motivation. We weren't about to let "them" steal the campaign. I didn't know where the next charge would come from, but I was ready to fight.

Over the next month, my combativeness was calmed by rising poll numbers and the absence of dropping shoes. But that artificial sense of security disappeared on January 16 — our first "garbage day." The *Star* tabloid was faxing around a story alleging that Clinton had had affairs with five Arkansas women, including Gennifer Flowers, a former lounge singer, and Elizabeth Ward, a former Miss America. The allegations had first been raised in Clinton's 1990 gubernatorial race, when a state employee named Larry Nichols filed a libel suit against Clinton. But the women denied them, the story evaporated, and Clinton won reelection.

After we landed in Boston that afternoon, I read the just-received *Star* story to Clinton. Although he said it was false, his manner was less breezy than with Hamzy, more agitated and insistent. But any doubts I had were assuaged when Clinton went on to explain that Nichols and his right-wing allies were out for revenge because Clinton had fired Nichols for using official state phone lines to raise money for the Nicaraguan contras, and when he added that all five women had filed sworn affidavits in 1990 denying the charges. That was all the ammunition I needed: The facts still seemed to be on our side, and Clinton's accuser had a motive. This was a smear campaign.

The narrative we developed that day was a variation of the Hamzy defense. We wanted to avoid an on-the-record denial if possible, not only because it could create a story but also because if Clinton denied some allegations, his silence about others could be construed as confirmation. Since Clinton had admitted to "problems" in his marriage, we knew there had to be at least one woman out there whose charges he couldn't deny. More likely, many more. So we tried to avoid the trap by attacking the tabloid messenger. Paul cooked up some lines about other *Star* scoops like the discovery of "alien babies," and I came up with a no-comment denial: "I'm not going to comment on that tabloid trash."

When we arrived at the fund-raiser, a reporter from Fox TV was waiting in the lobby. To me that constituted proof of a conspiracy. The *Star* and Fox were both owned by ultraconservative Rupert Murdoch. *It's a setup. Clinton* is *a victim. It couldn't be any more clear.* Now my initial doubts, which I had partially pushed aside earlier on the plane, were swept away by righteous anger. I seethed as Clinton answered the Fox reporter and blew up when CeCe Connelly of the Associated Press asked Clinton if the *Star* story was true.

"You can't do that," I barked at CeCe. "You're trying to create a story with our response." Fox TV we could handle, but the prospect of a credible news organization like the AP broadcasting this garbage around the globe was trouble — and it drove me crazy. I went straight to a phone to call John King, the AP's chief political reporter in Washington. "You can't put this crap on the wire," I said. "Just because it's published in a tabloid doesn't make it news. Before you run with the charges you have a responsibility to check them out yourself." While I was talking to King, I noticed that Clinton had pulled away with Bruce Lindsey for a hushed conversation on another pay phone across the lobby.

The AP held off, but Friday's *New York Post* ran a full account of the *Star* story under the headline WILD BILL. Another Murdoch paper, more evidence of the right-wing conspiracy at work. The mainstream press still resisted, but it was certainly following the story. Our candidate was the front-runner now, and he was throwing off the scent of scandal. When our van pulled up to the mock-Tudor Sheraton Tara Hotel in Nashua the next day for a health care forum, we were greeted by a pack of reporters, cameras, cords, and boom mikes bigger than anything we'd seen yet in New Hampshire. Our first "clusterfuck."

Seeing all those reporters waiting in the snow was both scary and a little thrilling. They weren't there to hear what Clinton had to say on health care, but the fact that so many showed up was proof that we were in the big leagues. "Keep smiling," I reminded Clinton as we prepared to climb out of the van. "We can't let them think they're getting to us." Images of Senator Edmund Muskie passed through my head. While defending his wife against a Republican dirty trick, the 1972 Democratic front-runner against Nixon had wiped a tear — or was it just a snowflake? — from his eye. It was the beginning of the end of his campaign.

Clinton was in no danger of repeating Muskie's mistake. As we walked toward the lobby, a mass of reporters surged toward us. Wearing a smile and sticking with our strategy, Clinton calmly explained that the *Star* story was both old and untrue. Whatever he was feeling inside, whatever uneasiness I witnessed behind closed doors, Clinton stowed it away before facing the cameras.

Inside the hotel, two different campaigns were going on simultaneously, separated only by a wall. At the candidates' forum, Clinton held forth on health care. I was out in the lobby with most of the reporters, trying to suppress the scandal that threatened to consume our campaign. Under the gaze of the suits of armor posted by the registration desk, I tried to pick off the journalists one by one to explain why the *Star* story was not only irrelevant but wrong — and part of a plot.

My main job now was damage control, the front lines of spin. Not only was I an ersatz defense counsel, I was also learning to deconstruct the text of tabloid stories like a literary sleuth, searching for unsupported statements, hearsay, logical inconsistencies, and, most valuable to us but most difficult to find, charges that could actually be disproved rather than merely disputed. A single demonstrably wrong accusation could call an entire story into question, allowing us to focus attention on the accusers rather than the accused.

Beating back the first *Star* story was relatively easy — the sworn affidavits did the real work. Besides, I believed Clinton, and believed even more in what he was trying to do. But I was conflicted in another way. Crisis management was starting to consume my time and define my character. My better side cared about the substance of the campaign, but the competitive warrior in me was more engaged by the street fighting. The pull to be part of the battle felt more urgent than shaping the policies we were trying to advance. I wanted to be in the lobby, not the forum. In the heat of the moment, this impulse was easy to justify. I told myself that if this allegation, or the next one, or the one after that metastasized into a full-blown scandal, the campaign would die — and nobody would ever hear or remember or benefit from anything we proposed on health care or education or the economy. I would also be out of a job.

What began as a strange, even sordid, way to spend my time soon felt natural. Wake me up in the middle of the night, I could have told you the lies in the Nichols story before I even opened my eyes. I began to think that doing the dirty work was not only necessary but noble, a landmark on the road to greater good. I began to fool myself, because fighting scandals can be fun; the action is addictive.

But any fun I was having faded fast a week later, when Gennifer Flowers flipped. Another Thursday, another *Star* story, another garbage day. But this one was more serious. A key witness for the defense was now part of the prosecution — and she said she had tapes. Early that morning, from a pay phone at National Airport's private terminal, I made my daily predawn call to Carville.

"You gotta get to the airport," I said. "We need you to come to New Hampshire with us."

"What's goin' on?"

"Some woman in Arkansas is claiming she slept with . . ."

"Ah shit, George. Is that all?"

"No, it's bad. You gotta come."

James resisted, but he wasn't going to miss this. There hadn't been much for him to do when everything was going so well in December; now we needed his gut. I felt better just having him around. The Cajun in him spoke to the Greek in me. As with Klein, we fed each other's dark side, and I loved just listening to him talk.

We landed in Manchester in an icy rainstorm and drove straight to the Holiday Inn. Inside was a gaggle of reporters, smaller than the mob scene of the week before but more select — "big feet" like Al Hunt of the *Wall Street Journal*, Jules Witcover of the *Baltimore Sun*, Curtis Wilkie of the *Boston Globe*, and James Wooten of ABC News. Seeing them, I was painfully aware that we were poised on the brink of a Big Moment. These reporters were some of the original "boys on the bus." They'd seen it all up here in Manchester, from McCarthy's peace movement to Muskie's meltdown, from Carter's surprise to Hart's surge, from Romney's "brainwashed" gaffe to Reagan's stolen microphone to Bush's tractor pull to victory over Dole. The New Hampshire primary had been the springboard for a few lucky candidates — and the graveyard for so many more who once seemed promising. We'd either survive now and go on to fight other battles, or the big feet would file our eulogies on deadline, and we'd become just another anecdote in the long lore of New Hampshire.

As the reporters talked among themselves, I imagined their conversation: *"Should we ask him? . . . Don't we have to? . . . Hate to, though. . . . Remember Paul."* In 1987, Paul Taylor of the *Post* had broken a barrier by asking Gary Hart flat-out if he'd ever committed adultery. After that uncomfortable moment in a crowded room, many reporters and their papers vowed to resist sex stories. But reporting the news is as competitive as running for office, and while established reporters weren't eager to break a story that violated a candidate's privacy, they didn't want to get scooped either. How a candidate handled controversies like this, they also reasoned, was relevant to how he would confront the pressures of the presidency.

We tried to hustle Clinton up to our suite, where Bruce, James, the governor, and I all read the article at once, trading the pages back and forth. "They Made Love All Over Her Apartment," read one headline. I winced, but from our perspective, a wilder story was actually better. The more sensational the charges, the less likely they'd be taken seriously.

Clinton read the piece with a running commentary that picked up speed as he skimmed the paragraphs. Every time he spotted a detail he knew was wrong, he seized on it, even squeaking out a laugh when he found charges he knew we could disprove — like the time Gennifer said they rendezvoused in Dallas. His reaction was rooted in some nervous relief. Whatever had happened between him and Gennifer — and I still didn't know — he could prove that elements of her story were untrue.

I was happy to make a list of the details that were false, but I didn't press Clinton to say which ones were true. Not knowing made it a bit easier to deal with the press; "I don't know" is often the best defense against a reporter on deadline. But my reluctance to question Clinton further went deeper than that. Reading the second *Star* story, I couldn't help but assume that *something* had happened with Gennifer. When Clinton wasn't listening, James and I speculated on exactly what that something might have been: a blow job in a car ten years ago? A one-night stand or two? But I couldn't bear the thought that an old dalliance dredged up by a tabloid would curtail the professional experience of my life, or the promise I saw in Clinton. I wanted to believe that it was all malicious fiction, to see Clinton as he saw himself — the target of unscrupulous enemies who would try to destroy him personally because they opposed his policies. And I needed Clinton to see me as his defender, not his interrogator, which made me, of course, an enabler.

OK, say he's lying about some stupid one-night stand; it's still not fair for him to have his whole past picked apart. He's already said he didn't have a perfect marriage; what more do they want? And what does it matter — what does that have to do with being president? The tabloids are targeting him to make money; the right-wingers are attacking because they're afraid he'll win and afraid of what he'll do. We can't let them get away with it or they'll never stop.

By the time we returned to the lobby, I was in a lather. We didn't have the silver bullet of Gennifer's sworn denial anymore, but her story *was* full of holes, and she *did* have a motive to lie — the *Star* was paying her to tell this tale. The year before she had threatened to sue a radio station for mentioning her name in connection with the Larry Nichols allegations. Bruce had called down to Little Rock to get a copy of her previous denial and her lawyer's threat, then gave them to reporters to bolster our contention that her change of heart was a case of "cash for trash."

Above all, we couldn't appear to let the story throw us off track. The heart of our strategy was to pursue the peoples' business no matter what obstacles our opponents put in our path.

First, though, Clinton had to talk to Hillary. She was in the middle of an Atlanta fund-raiser, but he finally reached her from a pay phone off the men's room at the Manchester airport. After a brief conversation, Clinton emerged looking more calm than he had appeared in the suite. That bucked me up too. During those stressful days it was easy to forget that Clinton's problems might go beyond politics. What did all of this mean for his marriage? Or for Chelsea? I wondered what Hillary had said to him, but he didn't volunteer any details. All I knew was that if she felt better, he felt better — and if he felt better, I felt better.

An ice storm grounded our scheduled flight to a brush factory in Claremont, so we piled into vans for the three-hour drive. As we inched along the icy road, Clinton sat up front, seemingly absorbed in a book called *Lincoln on Leadership*, a gift from Mario Cuomo. But I'm sure he was keeping an ear tuned to my backseat conversations on the cell phone. I was beating back the story with any reporter who asked, checking in with Carville in Manchester and Wilhelm in Little Rock to see how the scandal looked from there, and talking to Ted Koppel about a possible Clinton appearance on *Nightline*. Koppel and other network representatives were trying to lure Clinton on the air to address the *Star* charges, but we didn't want to take that big a risk unless we absolutely had to. When two of the three network news broadcasts that evening made no mention of Gennifer Flowers, we rejected all of the interview requests and returned to Little Rock.

Our reprieve was short-lived. The next day's papers were filled with stories, and Gennifer scheduled a press conference for Monday. We had seventy-two hours. Clinton retreated to the mansion while the rest of us held one conference call after another to decide what to do. *60 Minutes* offered us airtime right after the Super Bowl — the biggest audience of the year. If we accepted, the first thing most Americans would know about Bill Clinton was that he had some association with a lounge singer. But our situation was so serious that the only hope was the media equivalent of experimental chemotherapy. *60 Minutes* was strong enough to cure us — if it didn't kill us first. The interview was scheduled to be taped on Sunday morning.

Across Arkansas, Ricky Ray Rector was awaiting a decision on his fate, but he didn't know it. Convicted of murdering a police officer, Rector had lobotomized himself with a bullet to his brain. Unless

Clinton intervened, Rector would be executed that night by lethal injection.

I spent the evening with Clinton, waiting for the execution, a moment out of time. We stood around the mansion's kitchen island, absently shuffling paperwork that had piled up while the governor was in New Hampshire. But our attention was on the adjoining butler's pantry, where a phone receiver lay overturned on a small table — the open line to the execution chamber. Just in case. A new fact. A last-minute stay from the Supreme Court.

But that only happens in the movies. The sole drama that night was whether the prison doctors would find a vein in Rector's arm. They called periodically with progress reports, interrupting our discussion on how Clinton had come to support the death penalty after opposing it early in his career. He described how meeting with the families of murder victims had pushed him over, and he told me how he had talked it through with his pastor and mentor W. O. Vaught, who had explained that capital punishment was not a violation of Christian teaching because the original translation of the Ten Commandments prohibited "murder," not all killing.

But the stories we tell ourselves rarely match what others see. To Clinton's critics, the switch was pure expedience, especially in Rector's case. What better way to change the subject from personal scandal, what better way to signal that you're not a stereotypical Democrat, than to execute a man, a black man — a man so uncomprehending that he set aside the pie from his final meal for "later"?

But that night, I saw something else — honest engagement with a difficult dilemma. I told Clinton that I opposed the death penalty because I believe the state should take life only in the active defense of life. We argued over whether it was a deterrent. But I couldn't quarrel with how Clinton reached his decision. Rector's verdict had already been reviewed by a judge, a jury, and two separate hearings of the state's Clemency Review Board. In four terms as governor, Clinton had never overruled the board. Had Clinton broken precedent and spared Rector, I would have been proud, but the devil on my shoulder would have whispered that we were handing the Republicans a huge issue.

Thoughts of Gennifer faded as we talked and Clinton governed. In a horrible and ironic way, Clinton's kitchen seemed like a sanctuary from the storm of scandal we'd left behind in New Hampshire. Cold comfort for Ricky Ray Rector. But Clinton's stoicism comforted me. Wielding ultimate power made him sad, the appropriate sensibility, I thought, for a statesman sanctioning death.

60 Minutes would be taped Sunday at the Ritz-Carlton hotel in Boston. After a spirited Saturday-night rally in Manchester, we gathered at the hotel. Executive producer Don Hewitt and correspondent Steve Kroft showed us the room with the fireplace where the interview would take place. The Clintons didn't say much, just took it all in with clinical eyes.

Up in our suite, our team was on edge. All of the regulars were there: Carville, Lindsey, Paul Begala, Dee Dee Myers, Stan Greenberg, and our media consultants, Mandy Grunwald and Frank Greer. Susan Thomases also flew in, along with Tommy Caplan, Clinton's college roommate and erudite campaign companion.

Cracks were starting to develop in our normally cohesive group. Who would lead the prep? Whose advice would be heard and followed? Who really knew what they were doing and had the Clintons' best interest at heart — the friends or the staff? Mandy was supplanting Frank on the strength of her star turn on *Nightline* a few nights earlier. I was insinuating myself as gatekeeper and prep coordinator. James paced around the edge of the room and waited for the power that would flow his way. Handling crises like this was the reason he was hired. Susan watched us all, including Clinton, with a wary eye. Her client was Hillary.

Ordering room service broke some of the tension. Hillary reminisced about how this was her ultimate childhood luxury, and we talked about what we were going to order as if it were the most interesting topic in the world. Hillary even let her campaign-bloated husband have a cheeseburger, but she kept an eye on his intake of fries. All of this was just a way of avoiding the question at hand: What were the Clintons going to say — and how were they going to say it?

Clinton insisted that the Flowers story was untrue, so any admission of a sexual affair with Gennifer was off the table. But we discussed whether he should make a general admission of adultery — explicitly, unequivocally, using that word instead of a euphemism like "problems in our marriage." Initially, some of us, including me, thought that he should. Better to be straight, I argued; you earn extra credit for candor. I also believed that a concession like that would, at some level, make Clinton's denial of Gennifer's story more credible. But I backed off fast. Both Clinton and Hillary were adamant about not using the A word, arguing that it was too grating, too harsh, too in-your-face to the viewers at home. And with Gennifer's press conference the next day, any explicit admission of adultery — no matter how it was couched — *would* appear to confirm her story, and call the past denials into question.

Once the two threshold questions were pushed aside with our empty plates, Mandy and James took control of the meeting and focused us on our goals: to appear candid about past marriage troubles, to define character as a constant struggle for personal improvement, and to confront the country with the question of whether the presidential campaign should be about one candidate's past or the whole country's future. I synthesized the strategy in hand-lettered notes that I gave to Clinton when Hillary adjourned the meeting around one A.M.:

- YOU'RE FORTUNATE, RATHER THAN AGGRIEVED. YOU REALIZE IT'S A PRIVILEGE THAT THE SON OF A POOR, SINGLE MOTHER FROM ARKANSAS CAN RUN FOR PRESIDENT.
- YOU'RE SAD ABOUT GENNIFER, NOT ANGRY. YOU DON'T KNOW WHY SHE CHANGED HER STORY, BUT YOU'RE NOT GOING TO BE DIVERTED.
- USE YOUR FAMILY AS A METAPHOR FOR CHARACTER. YOU'VE HAD PROBLEMS IN YOUR MARRIAGE, YOU'VE FACED THEM, YOU'VE WORKED THROUGH THEM, AND YOU'RE COMING OUT STRONGER THAN EVER.

After the Clintons left, the rest of us went up to Stan's room for a drink. No one could sleep anyway. With the gallows humor and guilty pleasure that accompany being in the middle of the action without really being in the middle of the fire, we talked about the day ahead and whether we'd even be together a week from now. For us, no matter how tomorrow turned out, it would be a war story, the day we bet a whole campaign on a single interview.

But what about the Clintons? Alone in their room now, what are they discussing? Is this what they bargained for? Was there a deal between them? These questions swirled through my head and seeped into our conversation. I admired their ability to sacrifice privacy and pride for the chance to do some good — but wondered if I should be appalled. *Is it about power's potential, or just power? When is the price too high?* Mostly, though, I just felt sorry for them. I had a hard time talking to my parents about my girlfriend. Tomorrow the whole country would be discussing their marriage.

Around eight the next morning, I went to Carville's room and found him screwing his fists in his eyes to wipe away nervous tears. Mandy was there too, working out her anxiety with cigarettes and talk. We all knew that last night's prep wasn't crisp, that we had wasted too much time on side conversations and unnerved the principals with too much conflicting advice. Clinton is a small-*d* democrat; he takes counsel as it comes. A good quality, but not when you're in a crisis and the clock is ticking. We knew these last few hours had to be different, more focused and disciplined.

I walked across the hall to get the Clintons to agree. Hillary opened the door with a wan look, and as I slipped into the room she rested her hand on my shoulder for an extra second. Clinton's face looked like a soft, pale stone.

"How do you want to handle this morning?" I asked them. "Another big meeting, or would you prefer to do this with just a couple of us?" A loaded question, but I was leading them where I thought we needed to go and giving back what I thought I read in their expressions. They didn't want to hurt their friends or pick and choose among their advisers. But Hillary also knew that another bull session would just heighten the tension. Instead, the two of them crossed the hall to James's room, where we spent a few quiet minutes reviewing the strategy. But there wasn't really much to say. They were on their own.

The rest of the team was down the hall. They were irritated at my going behind their backs, but I told myself I was doing what the Clintons wanted and needed — a conviction strengthened by my desire to inhabit the smallest ring of the inner circle. Any jealousy I created was exacerbated when I followed the Clintons into the interview. The negotiated ground rules allowed one staffer in the room, and James and Mandy agreed it should be me. They trusted me not to freelance if Clinton had a last-second question or qualm, and he had become accustomed to having me around in moments like this. Whatever I felt inside, I could be relied on to stay calm and anticipate his needs. From my seat behind the camera, I would also serve as a human TelePrompTer, a visual reminder of our collective advice. Clinton would see me and remember the talking points I'd handed him.

Twice during the interview, Don Hewitt called a break and emerged from the control room. He told the Clintons how he'd made John Kennedy president by producing the debates in 1960 and said he could do the same for them. Like a director coaxing his leading couple, he crouched down in front of the couch and whispered, "Just say yes or no. Yes or no, and we'll move on to other things." I shook my head in slow motion. We had to stick to our strategy, not Hewitt's.

Kroft kept pushing, but Clinton denied Gennifer's story and refused to directly acknowledge adultery. He admitted to causing "pain" in his marriage and added that most Americans would "get it." And most viewers did. People heard that Clinton hadn't always been faithful, but they also saw a talented and idealistic couple who were committed to their marriage and the country's future. The performance was infused with the message of the Sperling breakfast from months before: What's past is past; it's time to move on. On the plane to Little Rock that night, we all thought the interview had gone about as well as we could have hoped. We had given it our best shot, and everything was out in the open now.

The next afternoon, three hundred and fifty reporters showed up at Gennifer's press conference, and CNN was broadcasting live. I pleaded with them to check out Gennifer's story before putting her on the air, but they ignored me — in retaliation, I was then convinced, for our decision to pull the Clintons from *CNN Newsmaker Saturday* and put them on *60 Minutes*. A bunch of us gathered around the television in my office to watch.

It didn't start out so badly. Gennifer's red suit and dark-rooted hair sent exactly the right message. A question about Clinton and condoms from Stuttering John of the Howard Stern show helped make the event seem like more of a circus than a serious political scandal. Gennifer even said she'd been approached by Republicans to tell her story. *There's an opening. Maybe we can turn this into an "anatomy of a smear" story instead of a morality play about Clinton's character.*

Then came the tapes — scratchy but apparently authentic recordings of Clinton and Gennifer talking in intimate tones about their personal relationship and the presidential race. Hearing Clinton's unmistakably husky voice felt like picking up the phone to catch your girlfriend whispering with another man. My whole torso tightened as I was hit by a wave of nausea, doubt, embarrassment, and anger. Mostly anger.

He lied. Even if he didn't, what's he doing talking to her in the middle of the campaign? That must have been her Clinton and Lindsey called from that pay phone in Boston. How could he have been so stupid? So arrogant? Did he want to get caught? How come he let me hang out there? Never said a word that whole ride to Claremont while I swore to reporters her story was false — just sat there, pretending to read Lincoln.

As the senior staffer in the room, I kept my anger inside to avoid demoralizing the interns and volunteers. This was a new challenge: I was used to keeping calm to convince my bosses they could count on me. Now I had to be strong for the kids who looked up to me. I tried to identify hopeful signs. *The conversation did sound stilted; her questions were leading — maybe the tapes were doctored? It's a setup.* Later investigations by CNN and KCBS would show that the tapes were "selectively edited," but there was no getting around the fact that by talking to her on the phone, Clinton had put everything we worked for at risk.

When Gennifer finished, Rahm Emanuel, David Wilhelm, and I retreated to a private office. We didn't know what was true anymore or what was going to happen. All we could trust right now was each other. There comes a time in every campaign when even a candidate you admire becomes your worst enemy. As if by design, each of us in turn expressed our disgust while the other two bucked him up. Tag team venting.

It worked, and as the night passed, we were back to fighting for Clinton even more fiercely. A dynamic had already started that would repeat itself many times in the years ahead — one explained well by Reinhold Niebuhr: "Frantic orthodoxy," he wrote, "is never rooted in faith but in doubt. It is when we are not sure that we are doubly sure." I now had doubts about Clinton, had seen his flaws up close, which caused me to focus even more intently on his strengths and believe even more fervently in his ideas. I didn't want to throw away what he could achieve as president and what I could achieve by his side, and I didn't want our enemies to win. They'd stop at nothing to defeat him, so nothing would stop me from defending him. Now I was a true true believer.

Hillary rallied all of us that night with a conference call from Minneapolis, foreshadowing another pattern that would be repeated again on a larger stage. If she was standing by her man, then so were we. A Boston TV poll showed that Clinton was still leading in New Hampshire, and a national survey on *Nightline* found that 80 percent of the country thought Clinton should stay in the race.

We had survived to fight another day.

Colonel Gene Holmes was the Gennifer Flowers of the draft. In 1969, he was the ROTC commander at the University of Arkansas. After a year at Oxford, Clinton returned to Fayetteville, enrolled in law school, and sought to fulfill his obligation for military service by joining the ROTC unit commanded by Holmes. Later that summer, Clinton changed his mind and returned to Oxford, but avoided military service by drawing a high number in the lottery that determined who would be drafted. This is what I knew about Clinton and the draft when I signed up. What I didn't know was what had not been reported: that Clinton's version picked up the story *after* he had received an induction notice from his local draft board. In 1969, Clinton gamed the selective service system — and got lucky.

The full story of Clinton and the draft is an anxiety-ridden tale of manipulation and mendacity similar to thousands of others from the 1960s. But as an aspiring Arkansas politician in the 1970s, Clinton didn't want to be defined by his unflattering draft history. So instead of telling the whole story, he pointed anyone who asked about the draft to Colonel Holmes, who as late as October 1991 assured reporters that he had dealt with Clinton "just like I would have treated any other kid."

Holmes's quote seemed like all I needed to know when I signed up. The fact that Clinton hadn't served in Vietnam was likely to come up in the campaign; but like adultery and marijuana, military service was a topic on which the political establishment was setting new standards. Adultery was survivable if it was a discrete event in the past. Smoking pot was acceptable if you stopped in college and professed not to like it very much. Failing to serve in the military was not disqualifying as long as you didn't "pull strings." You didn't have to be a war hero, but you couldn't be seen as a draft dodger.

Of course Kerrey's campaign would get a boost from his background. There was nothing we could do about that. We couldn't win the Vietnam issue; we just had to avoid losing — and change the subject. That was our strategy in early December 1991, when Dan Balz began working on a joint profile of Clinton and Bob Kerrey. "Bookends from the Vietnam generation," Balz called them, referring to the unavoidable contrast between the war hero and the civilian.

Balz's interview with Clinton was a few minutes squeezed into a ride to National Airport — a dumb scheduling move on our part given the sensitivity of the subject. I rode up front while Clinton and Balz talked in the back. Just as we reached the airport, Clinton told Balz that the fact that he wasn't drafted in the summer of 1969 was a "fluke."

Uh-oh. Where did that come from? When discussing a topic you want to go away, boring is better; Clinton knew that. *Fluke* was too provocative a word, almost a taunt. I didn't know all the details of Clinton's draft history, but I doubted it fit the word *fluke*. Balz was skeptical too. "At a minimum," he wrote, Clinton "was lucky to have survived more than a year classified 1-A." Balz was letting his readers know that Clinton's explanation wasn't persuasive, and sending his colleagues in the press a signal to dig deeper.

The better we did, the more scrutiny Clinton's draft history would get. Two days after Christmas, over mansion fare of pimento cheese–spread sandwiches on white bread with corn chips on the side, about twenty of us sat in the Clintons' basement to review the year ahead. When we got to potential problems, I brought up the draft. "We need some tighter answers," I said, recalling the car ride with Balz. "It's going to come back."

You would have thought I had called Clinton a draft dodger. Hillary spoke first, and she was incensed. "Bill's not going to apologize for being against the Vietnam War!" Ignited by her intensity, Clinton launched into a red-faced tirade against the war and said he'd rather lose the race than say it was right.

That wasn't my point, of course. But in trying to look tough and smart in front of my colleagues, I had painted the Clintons into a corner. They didn't have to blow up, but I had made a rookie's mistake: Pros don't raise sensitive subjects in big meetings. Later, Wilhelm, Carville, and I approached Clinton when he was alone. "We're not saying you have to apologize," I said. "But we need the same information our opponents have." Clinton nodded, and we hired a research firm to review his draft history, but it was already too late.

Flash forward six weeks to Wednesday, February 5. We were still in the lead despite the Gennifer story, but Clinton had come down with a bad flu. So we canceled our schedule for the day and put him to bed in a New Hampshire motel. As he rested in the next room, I returned a phone call from Jeff Birnbaum of the *Wall Street Journal*. The Post-it note read "Clinton and the draft."

The moment Jeff answered the phone, I knew we were in trouble. He wasn't interested in having a conversation or in getting a feel for how our side assessed the campaign and our opponents. He had specific questions about when Clinton joined the ROTC and whether he enrolled in law school in the summer of 1969, and he didn't want to have a debate with me on whether that information was relevant to voters in the winter of 1992. He didn't want me to change the subject or stall for time. You could almost hear Joe Friday coaching him off-line: *Just the facts, George. I'm not in the market for spin today.*

Jeff's manner was a tip-off, what professional poker players call a "tell." Reporters often clam up when they think they have a big fish on the line. Their counterspin techniques may include holding off calling until just before deadline to deny you the chance to learn more about their angle or question the credibility of their sources. Sometimes they worry that if you know what they're up to, you'll try to blunt the edge of their story by providing them with new information that muddies their lead. Or that you'll release the same information they're after to the competition, which deprives them of their scoop while making you appear candid.

I don't blame Jeff for being circumspect. Had any of those legitimate spin options been available to me, I would have used them in a minute. But I didn't have much to tell him. When I went into Clinton's room, he was flat on his back and too groggy to get worked up. Even so, he was fairly convincing about having nothing to hide — in part because I wanted to be convinced, in part because he had convinced himself over time that his relatively benign memory of traumatic events a generation ago was exactly how it happened, in part because the research we had commissioned hadn't turned up anything troublesome beyond what had already been in the papers. "I have no idea what he could be getting at," Clinton wheezed through his congestion. "Tell him to call Gene Holmes."

Which was exactly what Birnbaum had done. But Holmes, like Gennifer Flowers, had changed his story. Now he was saying that he felt Clinton's promise to join the ROTC was merely a pretext to avoid the draft, suggesting that Clinton had manipulated both him and the system. When I read Birnbaum's article early the next morning, I tried hard to offset my natural pessimism. *Holmes is old. Maybe he's confused; maybe it's a misquote; maybe Birnbaum trapped him, twisted what Holmes was trying to say. Why's he turning now? Who got to him?*

It was still dark when I walked across the freezing parking lot to the health club next to our hotel. I was working up a sweat on the StairMaster, and working hard to convince myself that the *Journal* article wasn't so bad, when Larry Barrett from *Time* came over to say hello. Barrett is a gruff guy, and no reporter is especially friendly at 6:20 A.M. after spending the night in a second-rate motel during a New Hampshire winter. "Good morning," he said, shaking his head. "Looks like you've got some day ahead of you." There went any illusions I had mustered. If Larry Barrett was getting avuncular on me, we were definitely in trouble.

How should we spin this? Clinton explicitly denied manipulating the system and seemed genuinely puzzled by Holmes's account. None of us knew about Clinton's induction notice — and if he remembered, he wasn't telling. We would certainly point out that Colonel Holmes had changed his version of events. But where Gennifer had changed her story for money, what was driving Holmes? We couldn't attack a veteran who, for all I knew, was also a war hero. So all we could do was try to poke factual holes in Birnbaum's story. But except for failing to mention the fact that Holmes had changed his account, Birnbaum's article was more solid than we knew or could admit.

My age was also a handicap. Later that day, Paul Begala and I faced another media mob at the Sheraton Tara. Any ambivalence reporters may have felt about prying into a candidate's sex life was supplanted on the draft story by a righteous intensity deepened by personal experience. For male reporters around Clinton's age, the draft was a defining moment; how you dealt with it spoke volumes about who you were. Some had served honorably, while others were self-proclaimed experts at evading the selective service or connoisseurs of cover stories told to local draft boards. They knew in their bones that Clinton's good fortune was not a "fluke."

But those of us born in 1961 came of age in a different America. My class of eighteen-year-olds was the first to register for the peacetime draft. Vietnam was over, and no other war was on the horizon. To a suburban kid with a latent political consciousness, signing up was such a casual procedure that I did it at the post office with a few friends on the way to play golf. The emotional investment of the reporters I encountered was foreign to me, and I could see they weren't putting much stock in anything I had to say. For good reason: Not only did I not really know the facts, I didn't understand their meaning.

Frustration was building on both sides. After fifteen minutes of getting screamed at in the lobby, I finally gave up. "*You* guys don't understand," I blurted out. "I can't help you on this one. All I cared about in 1969 were the Mets."

The draft did all the damage Gennifer didn't do. As Clinton would later joke, we dropped "like a turd in a well," falling to third place in three days. But on the Sunday night we found out, he wasn't in a humorous mood. Pacing around his family room in jeans while Hillary sat at a card table in her sweats, Clinton went on a tirade. "It's that damn middle-class tax cut. It's killing us," he thundered in a fit of self-delusion. *Grow up. If it weren't for that tax cut, we'd be dead last. That's what people like about you. It's everything else they're sick of.*

But I stayed silent, and Hillary stayed focused. She knew the self-pity would pass if we had a plan. We spent the rest of the night drafting new commercials and a "fight like hell" strategy for the last ten days. The next morning, we flew back to Manchester, light-headed from lack of sleep but liberated by the prospect of having little more to lose. It was February 10, my thirty-first birthday, and Mark Halperin of ABC News had a present for me.

When we landed in Manchester, he was waiting on the tarmac. Mark had been with our campaign nearly as long as I had, and we were as close to friends as possible given our adversarial roles. The look on his face as he walked my way was all the commentary I needed on what he held in his hands. "Nobody else has this," he said, giving me a couple of pages. "Read it right away. We're going to need a response."

Even before the document touched my hands, my eyes took in three details: the Oxford University seal at the top of the first page, the phrase "Dear Colonel Holmes," and a line I still can't read without getting slightly sick to my stomach: "I want to thank you, not just for saving me from the draft . . ."

My knees went wobbly; lack of sleep and scandal fatigue were taking their toll. *That's it. We're done.* I told Mark we'd get back to him, although I had no idea what we would say. But my overdeveloped damage control instincts kicked in immediately. *The letter's a fake*, I decided as I took it over to Clinton. *The Republicans are at it again. They're doing to us what they did to Muskie.*

That had to be it. The alternative was too grim.

Inside the terminal, Paul, James, Bruce, Clinton, and I squeezed into a small men's room. Hillary marched in right behind us. For a minute or two we silently passed the pages back and forth. Hillary spoke first. "Bill, this is *you!* I can hear you saying this."

So much for the dirty-trick defense. So much for my fantasy of making the Republicans pay for every nasty act from Watergate to Willie Horton. Hillary not only authenticated the letter, she seemed moved by it — misted by a nostalgic memory of the Bill Clinton she fell in love with across the stacks at the Yale Law Library.

You guys can relive Woodstock some other time. Again, the generation gap. "This must have been what they were all going through in 1969," Paul told me later, "while you and I were asking if we could stay up late to watch *Mod Squad.*" The two of us were convinced that the press would use the letter to prove that Clinton dodged the draft. James had a different take. "This letter is our friend," he said. "If you read the whole letter, you end up thinking, 'I wouldn't mind having a president who could write a letter like that when he was twenty-one.'"

We both turned out to be right. But at that moment I was certain we were holding the political equivalent of a death warrant. Although it was a thoughtful letter that expressed both respect for the military and principled opposition to the Vietnam War, Clinton didn't post it until after he had received a high number in the draft lottery. At a minimum, it suggested that Clinton was stringing Holmes along and holding on to his coveted ROTC slot until after he was certain he wouldn't be drafted. I also couldn't believe that we hadn't known about the letter, and just wanted the whole ordeal to be over. *How long will people give us the benefit of the doubt? How much of this stuff can they take? How much more can I take?*

Our next stop was the Stonyfield Farms yogurt factory in Londonderry, where Jim Wooten would do the interview we had promised Halperin. As Clinton toured the factory floor, I stayed in the back room, where I lay on the floor feeling sorry for myself. Staring up at the ceiling, I felt as if I were back on the high school wrestling mat, just before a match against someone who would probably kick my butt. *At least it will be over soon. We'll be knocked out of the race in eight days, and here's where it all began to end. On the cold stone floor of a yogurt factory, waiting for the final interview. Happy birthday.*

Begala was as bleak as I was. We tried to prep Clinton, but there was really nothing we could say. Only he knew what had happened and why. Wooten taped a short interview before turning off the camera and asking for five minutes alone with Clinton. Paul, Halperin, and I watched them talk through a window in the hall, trying to read their lips for any sign of how it was going. Expecting the worst, I was certain that Wooten was just doing his best to soften the blow of a killer story. Neither of them said a word after they shook hands, and we parted company with Wooten. But thirty minutes later, Halperin beeped me. The story was off. We had a stay of execution.

But not for long. The next day, *Nightline* also had the letter. I was in a van with Paul and James when my pager vibrated with a call from Ted Koppel. We pulled off the road at a nearby hotel to find a pay phone. No luck, so in what seemed like an essential extravagance, we rented a room. The clerk raised an eyebrow but must have decided that what three consenting adults did in the privacy of a paid-up room was none of his business. We passed him a credit card and made the call.

I asked Koppel how he had received the letter. "It's my impression it came from the Pentagon," he replied. *The Pentagon? Then maybe the Republicans do have something to do with this. Isn't it illegal to rifle through someone's draft records? Do we have enough evidence to actually make the charge? Or is Koppel trying to trick us into coming on?* Within fifteen minutes we were back on the road and pumped up again by the prospect that Clinton really was the victim of a dirty trick.

We made the Pentagon charge, but it didn't pan out. And Clinton went on *Nightline*. Answering the questions was our only hope. Koppel first asked Clinton if he wanted to read the letter on the air, but we weren't that dumb. A clip of Clinton reading one damaging line out of context would be replayed endlessly. Instead, Koppel read the letter and gave Clinton the whole show to explain himself. Clinton was masterful — calm about the past, impassioned about the future, with just the right degree of indignation about the kind of issues that ought to matter in electing a president. In the final minute of the show he squeezed in a sterling sound bite: "Ted, the only times you've invited me on this show are to discuss a woman I never slept with and a draft I never dodged."

Even had I known for certain then that Clinton's closing statement wasn't really true, I would have had a hard time admitting it to myself. I was in battle mode, and nearly anything we did, I believed, was justified by what was being done to us. Tabloid reporters were prowling the streets of Little Rock, offering cash for stories about Clinton. Almost all the rumors swirling around our increasingly gothic campaign — that Clinton sanctioned drug running from Arkansas's Mena Airport, that Clinton was a cocaine fiend, that Hillary was a secret lesbian — were both malicious and untrue. And on the Friday before the vote, one more person emerged from the more recent past with a story that could sink us.

I first heard about it while Clinton was appearing at a senior citizens' center in Nashua. All through the afternoon he listened to the testimony of people struggling to get by. When a tiny, frail woman named Mary Annie Davis confessed tearfully that she had to choose each month between buying food or medicine, he knelt down, took her hand, and comforted her with a hug. Even the hardest-bitten reporters in the room were wiping tears from their eyes.

I missed it. As we walked in, a reporter for the *Nashua Telegraph* pulled me out of the entourage and confronted me on the sidewalk. "We have to talk," she said. "I have a witness to a recent conversation that Governor Clinton had with you and Bruce Lindsey about getting Gennifer Flowers a job in state government. He says you were planning to pay her off."

"I have no idea what you're talking about," I said, "but you can't run a story like that without giving us a chance to respond." We agreed that at six that evening, Bruce and I would go to the *Telegraph* and meet with the editors — our only hope of killing the story.

James was hanging with some reporters on the edge of Clinton's event. Pulling him into the laundry room, I paced around in my parka while he sat on a washing machine and tried to calm me down. Now I saw a different side of what Clinton was going through; someone was telling stories about me too, and sullying *my* reputation. Over time, I developed calluses against the personal attacks that come with high-stakes politics — that's the price that accompanies the privilege. Then I was distraught. I knew I wasn't guilty, but if the charge was published at the height of the New Hampshire primary, a lot of my peers would see it and believe it despite my denial. We'd tank in New Hampshire, and the last thing anyone would hear about me was that I tried to get a government job for the governor's girlfriend.

A part of me was almost hoping we'd get knocked out. Then, at least, I wouldn't have to face another reporter asking me another question about another story I couldn't control. The hoofbeats weren't just in my head anymore; they were everywhere. The whole experience was dirty, draining, and depressing. So much for recreating Bobby Kennedy's crusade. We looked more like Gary Hart's campaign every day.

Bruce and I arrived at the *Telegraph*, where the editorial board was behind closed doors. Then a man emerged from the conference room with a young girl, and it all came together in an instant. The man had been our driver on a Saturday in early January, a lifetime ago. All afternoon he talked about a charity he'd started to send household goods to Russia. Perfectly good cause, but the driver's chatter had a manic quality. We made a vague commitment to appear at his booth at an upcoming fair but forgot about it in the tumult that followed.

This must be payback for the broken promise. When Bruce and I denied the charge and explained the situation to the editorial board, they killed the story. I'd like to think it was our persuasive power that carried the day. More likely they realized the allegation was too thin. It might not have made a difference even if it were published, but then I was sure it was the tipping point — the final piece of information that would make everyone conclude all at once that Clinton was more trouble than he was worth.

I wish this episode had ended there, but it didn't. While the driver had a final word with the editorial board, his daughter — who couldn't have been older than eight or nine — waited for him in the lobby. Flushed with our tiny victory and frayed from a month of crises, I approached the driver's daughter on our way out: "Your father," I said, looking at her as if she were to blame for all our troubles, "is a really bad man." I felt ashamed the second the words escaped my mouth, but it was too late. The girl just stared back at the brutal zealot I'd become, and I couldn't argue with her, or change the subject, or even spin myself.

The final weekend was a blur. I was sure all was lost, but Clinton demonstrated the power of pure will. He was determined to touch and talk to every voter in New Hampshire. We staffers left the suite in shifts to accompany him, but we were superfluous. This was all about Clinton — his pride, ambition, and anger, his need to be loved and his drive to do good. Watching him made me wonder if you had to be a little crazy to become president. What did it do to you to want something so badly?

What I didn't realize at the time was how the focus on Clinton's problems was paradoxically helping him, turning the New Hampshire primary into a referendum on what politics should be about. Clinton was channeling public disgust and transforming it into a reason to vote for him. The best way to strike a blow against the obsession with scandal was to vote for the candidate most plagued by scandal. Never mind that Clinton brought many of the problems on himself; he also offered a way out — and he was a kick to watch. No matter how hard you hit him, he popped up smiling.

On election day, I was so dark that I couldn't pull myself out of bed. The bond Clinton was forming with the voters of New Hampshire wasn't showing up in our polling, which predicted we would fade to third or worse. Clinton kept his promise to keep pushing for votes "till the last dog dies," but there was nothing the rest of us could do. James and I considered killing time by going to see *Bill and Ted's Bogus Journey* at the Cineplex across the street, but we didn't want to be far from a phone when the first exit polls came in.

A bunch of us retreated from our makeshift headquarters and gathered on the twin beds in Carville's room. James was pacing around like a medieval penitent, lightly lashing himself over each shoulder with a small piece of rope. Stan and Mandy ducked in and out with news from their network contacts. On the road with Clinton, Dee Dee called in for updates, and our New Hampshire communications director, Bob Boorstin, joined us to help draft that night's speech. When the exit polls started to come in, we ordered cheeseburgers from room service and started banging out a victory memo on Bob's laptop.

Of course, coming in second to Tsongas wasn't technically a victory, but it sure felt like one after all we'd been through. Even Clinton, the eternal optimist, seemed surprised by the news. I spent the late afternoon with him as he sat through a series of satellite interviews to news outlets in the states we would visit next. Between questions, I fed him updates. Although he had been suspicious of exit polls ever since they falsely predicted his reelection as governor in 1980, he silently signaled his growing excitement by slowly pumping his fist just below camera range. "I'll feel like Lazarus if these poll numbers hold up," he told me as we headed to the elevator, where he pounded his open palms on the closing metal doors.

Our near-victory suppressed my new doubts about Clinton. Success has a way of doing that. My initial infatuation was maturing into a more complicated bond. Clinton wasn't a hero, just a man, with flaws as profound as his gifts. But he was by far the best politician I'd ever met. He had more ideas than anyone in the race, his heart was in the right place, and he refused to quit. Together, we still might do some good, and he was still my ticket to the top.

Late that night, we staffers took a victory lap around the bar of the Sheraton Tara, accepting congratulatory cocktails from reporters just steps from the lobby where we'd been mauled on Gennifer and the draft. Across the bar, I spotted Pat Buchanan, holding court with a bare-toothed grin. Beer-and-shot populist in union halls by day, sipping an incongruous chardonnay with his Beltway friends at midnight, he'd shocked President Bush that day by winning 37 percent of the Republican vote. With Bush that weak, working in the White House wasn't just a fantasy anymore.

But we had to keep the hoofbeats at bay.

4 HIGHER UP, DEEPER IN

The Secret Service agents made it real. The morning after the New Hampshire primary, when I cracked open my door to collect the newspapers, there they were, guarding the governor's suite down the hall. Molded ear pieces, microphones hidden in their sleeves, magnums strapped to their backs — concrete reminders that Clinton might be a target of more than the tabloids. All through the fall I had a recurring fantasy about wrestling a gunman to the ground to save Clinton. From now on I would share that imagined responsibility with the United States Government.

We flew south with our new security detail, a bigger jet, and a surge of confidence to soothe our New Hampshire hangovers. In a single day, we'd gone from doomed back to unbeatable. Lazarus, just like Clinton said. Kerrey and Harkin hadn't met expectations; both would soon drop out. Cuomo's write-in campaign fizzled; he'd never get in. That left Paul Tsongas as our prime opponent, which was fine with all of us except the one who counted most. On the flight out of Manchester, Clinton called Paul Begala and me to the front of the plane in a fury and waved an *Atlanta Journal* in our faces. The fact that editorial pages were bashing Clinton's middle-class tax cut and praising Tsongas's call for fiscal pain drove him crazy. Our more populist approach would win us the primaries, but Clinton felt as if he was slumming and hated getting called on it.

The nomination was ours to lose — but we did our best to make it a race as the spring unraveled a skein of oddly joyless victories. We were winning ugly; every week we'd snuff out an incipient scandal, grind out a majority, and watch Clinton grow more unpopular. No candidate had ever compiled such high negative ratings while winning the nomination. Primary exit polls consistently showed that Ross Perot — the weird little man who was a ventriloquist's dummy for voter anger — was outpolling Clinton. Establishment Democrats wondered aloud whether a Bradley, a Bentsen, or a Gephardt could jump in and save the party from its damaged front-runner.

When we formally clinched the nomination with a win in California on June 2, the *New York Times* ran a front-page story on the prospect that delegates to the Democratic convention would throw Clinton over for someone new. A "brokered" convention — the dream of political junkies and our worst nightmare.

We bottomed out that night. Clinton was a wreck — exhausted, overweight, angry, and in danger of doing permanent damage to the asset no politician can do without: his voice. Our campaign was broke in every way. We hadn't been paid in months, and our team was split into squabbling camps: the consultants in Washington, the headquarters in Little Rock, and Clinton on the plane. Polls forecasting the November election put us in third place, behind Bush and Perot.

Which set the stage for our comeback. By late spring, the still-stalled economy was making the country increasingly impatient with President Bush, but Clinton was not a credible alternative. To the general public, he was a slick Southern yuppie educated at silver-spoon schools like Yale and Oxford who had dodged the draft, cheated on his wife, and lied about smoking pot. But a crash research effort (dubbed the Manhattan Project) led by Stan Greenberg discovered that a simple story line could change minds. If you told voters that Bill Clinton was the middle-class son of a single mother who had worked his way to the Arkansas governorship and made progress in his poor state by focusing on job creation and education, it put the questions about his character in a new context and gave people permission to pay attention to Clinton's ideas. We didn't have enough cash to advertise these facts, so we booked the governor on every television interview show that would have him — from *Today* to *Charlie Rose* to *Arsenio Hall* — where Clinton would have the chance to talk at some length about his background and his plans. He demonstrated independence from Jesse Jackson over Sister Souljah but unified the party with a new economic plan that promised to both cut the deficit and increase government investments in jobs, education, and health care. In the single best decision of the campaign, Clinton broke with tradition and picked another young Southerner as his running mate. By the time the Democratic convention opened in New York, we were in first place — this time for good.

It was only my second convention. Four years before in Atlanta, struggling to establish myself in the Dukakis campaign, I had spent the entire week in a basement as a volunteer, booking press interviews for the senior staff. They would bustle through the windowless room, each with an intern as shadow, on their way to the upper floors — where the real work was done. The highlight of my week came when I borrowed a floor pass and burrowed through a small claque off the convention floor to shake the hand of my political hero. "Your diary was an inspiration," I told him, just before the crowd carried him away.

Here in New York, Mario Cuomo was looking for me. But when he dialed my room on the fourteenth floor of the Hotel Intercontinental, I was in the presidential suite helping Clinton revise his acceptance speech. My friend Eric thought it was a joke when he answered the phone, so he hung up. When Cuomo called again, Eric figured he'd better find me.

So much had happened in a year. Bill Clinton was now the Democrats' best hope, Cuomo was nominating him, and I was Clinton's guy — a man to see if you had a message to send or a problem to be fixed. Cuomo's call to me was both a sign of my growing power and a source of even more. When I excused myself to return the call, I made sure Clinton knew where I was going and why.

Cuomo wanted to give me a sneak preview of his speech. The

relationship between Clinton and Cuomo had been tense, especially after the Gennifer tapes, in which Clinton was heard calling Cuomo a thug. Cuomo picked me out because I wasn't from Arkansas or the conservative wing of the party. His former economic adviser Gene Sperling, a friend of mine from the Dukakis campaign whom I'd recruited to run our campaign's economics shop in Little Rock, had also told him that I was his biggest fan in Clinton's camp. During the vice presidential selection process, I had written Clinton a memo advocating that he choose Cuomo as his running mate.

So even though I was trying to act cool, I was thrilled. Hunched over the edge of my bed, my ear pressed tight to the receiver, I heard Cuomo in full performance mode. The reluctance he showed when Democratic Party chair Ron Brown had to cajole him into nominating Clinton was not in evidence now. Cuomo was proud of his speech, and the more he recited, the more he seemed to convince himself that Clinton really was our "new captain for a new century." His Flushing-inflected bass flowed over the phone in a pumped-up rush, punctuated by jokes about Captain Queeg and questions that answered themselves. "You like that? You *like* that!"

Later that night, I watched the actual speech in the governor's suite. Watching the Clintons watch Cuomo with their arms wrapped around each other's shoulders and Chelsea on the floor between them was a small revelation. It was all starting to sink in. The two of them slowly shook their heads from side to side, as if to say what they saw just couldn't be true. But it was, and they were already planning ahead. Clinton mused that Cuomo would make a perfect chief justice; Hillary nodded.

As Cuomo accepted his cheers, I went straight to the floor. There are times in politics when you experience the pretense of a private moment in public. Cuomo stood at the base of the towering podium that moments before had been his national perch. He was flushed, encircled by an entourage, and throwing off an aura that felt like a force field. As I approached, the crowd around him parted to let me in. "The governor asked me to give you his personal thanks," I said in a shout that had the intimacy of a whisper. Then I reinforced my message with a point that also underscored my place in Clinton's constellation: "I was up there watching it with him. Governor, he was crying."

The people around us watched Cuomo and me talk in a way that made me feel as if we were actors in a silent movie. In a way, we were, with Cuomo in the role of elder statesman and me playing new kid on the block. Not only had my months with Clinton brought me political power, I was also becoming a political celebrity.

It starts out slowly. You're quoted on behalf of your boss, and the circle of people who follow politics the way most follow professional sports takes note of the unusual name. You do a call-in on C-Span and get photographed next to the candidate on a tarmac in New Hampshire. A few more people take notice, especially Greeks, who love seeing a big name like Stephanopoulos on the small screen. Political reporters do profiles of the new candidate's team. Then the campaign takes off, leading to a series of firsts: first *Today* show, first *Face the Nation*, first press conference of your own. When you're on the rise, political celebrity creates a self-fulfilling prophecy: The more you're known, the more you're approached for information and political favors, which increases your influence, which makes you even better known and more powerful.

I enjoyed the attention, encouraged it, loved it — even when I was embarrassed by it and wished I didn't need it. But the convention also brought some deeper satisfaction. Shortly before Clinton's acceptance speech, I left our holding room and stood on the floor of the arena at the base of the podium. In front of me, the standing-room-only crowd was singing, screaming, and swaying, with signs held high, creating a swirl of color and sound that cut all the way to the rafters. Until that week I had never been on the floor of Madison Square Garden. The closest I had come was front row for the circus, or the imaginary ringside seat supplied by the transistor radio stuffed under my pillow the night Ali and Frazier met for the fight of the century.

Now I stood in the center of the floor, hypnotized by the motion and emotion, feeling tiny and ten feet tall at the same time. I normally don't like crowds; they scare me. But that night, the crowd filled me with pride and awe, with a sense of ownership — and possibility. I wasn't always proud of the way I had handled myself during the campaign. I had learned to calculate, scheme, and maneuver — to say things I didn't fully believe and do things I might later regret while telling myself that, maybe, it would do some good. That night, I had no doubts. I had faith in my candidate, his crowd, and myself. I believed that our compromises and our trials were our contribution to the common good — and that anything was possible if only we could do what had seemed improbable back in that Little Rock paint store. If only we could win.

Back in the holding room, Clinton pulled his face out of the inhaler long enough to tease me. "George, you didn't think I could do it, did you?"

"No, sir," I replied, "but I'm awfully glad you did."

The next morning, Clinton and Gore rode a fleet of buses across I-80 toward New Jersey, Pennsylvania, Ohio, and Illinois — the "battleground" states. I stayed behind to enjoy a lazy day in Manhattan before flying to Little Rock with James.

Not being on the bus made me wonder if I was missing something — the excitement of the crowds and connection with the country. But two months before, on a flight to Minneapolis, Clinton had pulled me aside on the plane and reassigned me to Little Rock headquarters. Our campaign was balkanized and adrift, and our whole team of consultants threatened to quit if things didn't change.

James outlined the demands — a complete overhaul of our headquarters and operating philosophy. The Republicans were pros. They had won three presidential campaigns in a row, and they were ruthless. We had to be battle ready just to be in the game — to break down the bureaucracy and replace campaigning by conference call with a single strategic center for attacks and counterattacks. Hillary got it immediately. "What you're describing is a war room," she said, giving us both a name and an attitude.

The purpose of the War Room wasn't just to respond to Republican attacks. It was to respond to them *fast*, even before they were broadcast or published, when the lead of the story was still rolling around in the reporter's mind. Our target was the public's filter for information; our goal was to ensure that no unanswered attack reached real people. James summed up our approach on a T-shirt saying, "Speed Kills . . . Bush." The fact that we had a War Room would be as important as anything we did there. Its purpose was to make us appear relentless, to intimidate, to make anyone who was paying attention think of us as aggressive, different, and a little unpredictable — pretty tough for Democrats.

James would be the general, but he needed a second in command. Paul was the logical choice, but his wife was due to deliver their first baby that summer, so he couldn't move to Little Rock. That left me. Clinton knew I was reluctant to leave his side, to relinquish the power that accompanies proximity. Out of sight, I feared, out of mind. I had seen it happen. So he made a point of making my transfer seem like my choice, of telling me how much he trusted me and how much *he* needed me to do this job. Aware that my reaction would be noticed, I pushed myself to appear eager. Instead of completing this last trip with Clinton, I dropped off in Minneapolis and took the next flight back to Little Rock.

Working in the War Room gave me the chance to prove myself away from Clinton's shadow. Back in Little Rock, we traded up headquarters again — to a four-story gray stone building that had recently housed the *Arkansas Democrat-Gazette*. Our fourth-floor War Room was the paper's old newsroom. Carville's command post was a fold-out conference table flanked by a couch, where we held our twice-daily meetings. Scattered around the room were outposts for every campaign department: research, press, issues, field, and all the rest. Four TV sets suspended from the ceiling provided us with instant access to CNN, network news, and other necessities like *Seinfeld*, sports, and Showtime.

While I was constantly in and out of the War Room, I spent most of my time in the old managing editor's office down the hall, making phone calls, holding meetings, talking to the road, and reviewing a constant flow of speeches, statements, and press releases.

We had a team of writers led by Bob Boorstin, but I was ultimately responsible for accuracy and tone, and the counterattacks to Bush charges were released over my name.

The War Room never closed. Day and night, teams of young volunteers worked in shifts, tracking every Bush move on their computers. On the roof, a satellite dish pulled in broadcasts, including the occasional intercept of a still-unaired Republican commercial on its way to a local affiliate. Much of this technology was relatively new. At the Dukakis headquarters in Boston, the AP wire had reached us via a clickety-clack teletype machine. Now our kids were downloading stories onto their laptops.

We also subscribed to the *New York Times* on-line news service. At first, the *Times* inadvertently included an internal midday preview of the stories scheduled for the next day's front page. This was inside information, and it reminded me of the scheme in *The Sting* where Paul Newman booked bets on horse races after receiving the actual results on a hijacked wire. Knowing what the *Times* was working on, we could adjust an attack, prepare our defense, or springboard off a story to advance our agenda. When Bruce Lindsey made the mistake of mentioning our new research tool to a *Times* reporter on the plane, our windfall came to an abrupt end.

But for all of our high-tech toys, the most useful item in the War Room was a low-tech template — a hand-lettered white board that James stuck on a pillar in the middle of the room. It said:

> *Change vs. More of the Same*
> *The economy, stupid*
> *Don't forget health care*

I thought of it as a campaign haiku — an entire election manifesto condensed to nineteen syllables. James drilled it into our heads, and every speech, every event, every attack, and every response had to reflect one of these three commandments: New unemployment numbers are released? Put out a statement — it's the economy, stupid. Bush repeats the ludicrous charge that as a student Clinton was a KGB tool in Moscow? Closer call, but see line 1 and go with it: The president is at it again, giving us more of the same old negative politics. A new controversy over the National Endowment for the Arts? Tempting, but let it go. We can protect the NEA later, from the White House, but talking about it won't help us get there. In our world, the only mortal sin was to be "off message."

I was the first senior staffer to arrive in the morning, getting in around 6:15, unless I had an even earlier appearance on one of the morning shows (Little Rock is in central time). When I was on the road with Clinton, he knew he could count on me to have read the papers, reviewed our overnight polling, checked in with headquarters, and checked out our opposition and the rest of the world before I walked into his room. As he cooled down from his morning jog while munching his morning bagels and bananas, I wanted to be able to tell him things he didn't already know. To make myself indispensable.

In my War Room office, I'd plow through a pile of Xeroxed clips while our overnight researcher filled me in on any new developments since the papers were printed. Around 6:45, James would call from his room at the Capitol Hotel. I was his third call of the morning. First came Mary Matalin, his future wife, who was a senior staffer on the Bush campaign. He then checked in with Stan Greenberg to review our overnight polling before calling me. Getting those numbers from James was as essential to me as a second cup of coffee; I couldn't function without them. After that, we would waste a couple of minutes speculating on the state of the Bush campaign — a rigorous analysis based entirely on James's take on the tone of Mary's voice that morning. "She's really ragging on me today," James might say, "so their numbers must be as bad as we think." Or, "I'm scared. Mary's being a little too nice. You think they have something on us?"

James wanted to win this election even more than I did. He was forty-seven; just a few years earlier, he was broke and unemployed. Now he had the opportunity of a lifetime. A lot of talented strategists get the chance to run presidential campaigns. Only the lucky ones have it happen at a time most suited to their talents, and the sense of frustrated ambition fueling the country's desire for change in 1992 was something James understood in his bones. He was smart enough to know that the stars would never line up like this for him again. This was his one big chance, and he ran our War Room with a combination of intuitive genius, intensity, and eccentricity — as if Machiavelli, a marine drill sergeant, and an extra from the movie *Deliverance* had been morphed into a single Cajun creature.

After the morning meeting, James and I would retreat to my office with a handful of other staffers for a conference call with our counterparts on the road. Clinton would then get on the line to make sure that we weren't making strategy without him. He knew how easily a candidate could get out of the loop of his own campaign. We would brief him on the polls, our new commercials, and what Bush was doing, then get braced for the morning outburst about his grueling schedule, or our flaccid speeches ("Words, words, words — all you write is words — they don't mean anything"), or the fact that Chelsea had seen a blistering Bush attack on Arkansas television without a response from our side. Mostly he was just letting off steam and letting us know he was watching our every move. If the yelling got real bad, I would disconnect the speaker-phone by picking up the receiver. No reason for the rest of the campaign to hear the candidate melt down — and even getting yelled at can be a power play. While he talked, I'd pretend to slap myself on the face.

I spent the rest of the morning gathering intelligence, swapping information, and trying to shape the news, concentrating on our beat reporters, the journalists on President Bush's plane, and my old contacts on Capitol Hill. After lunch at my desk, I'd check in with the producers at the national networks. In the afternoon, we'd meet with the other consultants to review the research, draft ads, look over the long-term schedule, and bullshit about the race. Sometimes I'd grab a quick nap on Carville's couch. Then we'd enter the chute toward news time.

If either side had drawn blood during the day, I'd spend the late afternoon chatting up the networks and trying to get our licks in, beeping the Bush reporters one last time, and checking in with our team on the road. In the end, a political campaign boils down to talk, talk, and more talk. What are they saying? What are we saying? What are they saying about what we're saying in response to your question? And on, and on, and on. The official War Room day ended with our evening meeting following the top of the network news. James went for a run, and I stayed around another hour to make sure the next day was set before heading off for my evening bout with the StairMaster.

Around 9:30, we'd have a late dinner, usually at Doe's. A spartan steak house with Formica tables and linoleum floors, Doe's was where the reporters wanted to eat when they came to town, which made our back-room table the campaign equivalent of the cool corner at the high school cafeteria. We always invited journalists to eat with us, partly because it was our job, partly because it was fun, and partly because they paid for dinner. Nothing made Paul and Dee Dee madder than to call the War Room and be told that James and I were at Doe's. We worked long hours, but their day was even longer. While we devoured rare rib eyes washed down with Heinekens, they were calling from a holding room in some anonymous hotel, waiting for Clinton to leave a fund-raiser so they could return to the plane to fly half the night on a moldy sandwich for the privilege of getting up three hours later to start another day. I sometimes envied their place at the center of the action, but not when I was at Doe's.

My day ended around eleven. I'd fall asleep on a full stomach within minutes of getting home. About six hours later, I'd beat the alarm by a minute and get up to do it all again.

The War Room's best moment was the Republican convention in Houston. Working with a SWAT team who had sneaked into the Astrodome, we countered every Republican attack and managed to write and release an annotated response to Bush's acceptance speech even before the president reached the podium. Our tactical triumph was picked up by the press and made us feel like winners. But nothing we did helped us more than what the Republicans did to themselves. By turning their convention over to Pat Buchanan, Pat Robertson, and the rest of their right-wing base, they turned off the rest of the country — and gave me a chance to be Hillary's public defender.

When the campaign started, it didn't look as if Hillary would need to be defended. She was an unqualified political asset — her husband's chief adviser and candidate in her own parallel campaign.

Clinton would cite her work on education and children as a reason to vote for him and refer to her in every speech: "My wife, Hillary, gave me a book that says, 'The definition of insanity is doing the same thing over and over again and expecting a different result.'" We circulated "Buy One / Get One Free" buttons, and progressive primary audiences, especially women, loved the modern-marriage pitch. The fact that Clinton was with such a strong, smart, and successful woman made people like him even more.

I liked most of what I saw in private too. They really were complete partners, businesslike in meetings, often childlike with each other. Hillary adored him despite herself, giving him a Nancy Reaganesque gaze when he tightened his tie and talked nonstop about his upcoming speech, or later, when he loosened it with his arm around her and laughed about the evening's events. She could soothe him too. One night, after a particularly useless debate prep during which Clinton was hoarse and cranky, I went up to their suite with the next day's schedule to find her on the couch with him, legs laid over his lap, feeding him lemon slices dipped in honey. In playful moments, Clinton called for her in baby talk: *"Hee-a-ree, Hee-a-ree."*

Of course, they fought too, and it wasn't fun to watch. She lit into him when she thought he wasn't being tough enough on himself or the people around him, particularly the "boys" like Paul or me, or the more encompassing "kids on the plane," a term that included Dee Dee. One morning during the New York primary all I saw as I walked in their door was her standing over him at the dining-room table, finger in his face, as he shoveled cereal into his mouth, his head bent close to the bowl. I backed up without turning around and quietly shut the door.

The Hillary backlash began with *60 Minutes*. Tammy Wynette took offense at Hillary's derisive-sounding reference to "Stand by Your Man" and publicly demanded an apology. Most viewers were happy with Hillary's defense of her husband; it made them think his affairs were the Clintons' private business. But the undercurrent we couldn't eradicate was the notion that their partnership was less a marriage fired by love than an arrangement based on ambition. Hillary's prominent public role also made her a more legitimate political target. If voters were being promised two presidents for the price of one, the press and our opponents figured that we ought to expect twice the scrutiny. They examined Hillary's private law practice and whether she did business with the state while Clinton was governor. The *New York Times* started to ask about one of the Clintons' joint investments, a resort development project called Whitewater.

Hillary's litigator instincts made her hunker down. Whitewater and Rose Law Firm questions were directed to her friend and fellow lawyer Susan Thomases. A pattern began of revealing as little as possible as slowly as possible, which was stupid, because the underlying information — about Hillary's investments and legal practice — was embarrassing but not scandalous. The early stories were too convoluted to do any real political harm, but the Hillary controversy reached a fever pitch during the Illinois primary.

In a Sunday-night debate, Jerry Brown charged that Hillary was profiting from Rose Law Firm business with the state of Arkansas. Anticipating the attack at the predebate prep, we had urged Clinton to hit back hard. Anger in defense of his wife would play well; it was a form of chivalry — and the least he could do after Hillary had stood up for him during Gennifer and the draft. Standing on a chair at the dining-room table, I got carried away: "The minute you hear the word *Hillary*, rip his head off. Don't let him finish the sentence." Clinton didn't. The counterpunch was perfect, leaving Brown looking petty and confused on the facts.

But Sunday night's planned confrontation gave rise to an unscripted moment Monday morning. At the Busy Bee coffee shop in Chicago, Clinton was bantering with reporters when they asked to speak to Hillary.

"Sure," he said, catching her off guard. Andrea Mitchell of NBC News asked Hillary whether it was ethical for the governor's wife to be a partner in a law firm doing business with the state. The question struck a nerve. Hillary prided herself on her integrity and resented the fact that it was being challenged, especially since she had refused her share of Rose Law's profits from Arkansas state business. "I suppose I could have stayed home and baked cookies and had teas," she replied. "But what I decided to do was to fulfill my profession, which I entered before my husband was in public life."

From her mouth to the nation's ears. There are few things more unnerving to a staffer than the buzz created when a press corps that's heard the same speech six days in a row captures a spontaneous gaffe that's guaranteed to lead the news. Hillary's sound bite sent them scurrying for the phones. We knew immediately we had a problem. "Tea and cookies" was so rich and resonant a phrase that it could be the subject of a graduate seminar on semiotics. It also seemed to reveal what many voters most feared about Hillary, that deep down she wasn't really a "traditional" woman. Most of the reporters shared her progressive side and kind of liked her sarcastic sense of humor. So did I, but the Republicans would have a field day if Hillary didn't clean this up before the close of the news cycle. We had to make her take it back.

Right. That'll happen. Too bad Mandy's not around. Hillary might be more open to the advice if it came from Grunwald rather than a couple of guys like Paul and me who didn't intuitively understand the struggles women faced. Paul took the lead and convinced Hillary to appear before the cameras again. She did, explaining that she had the greatest respect for women who chose to stay home with their children and that one goal of her husband's campaign was to make sure more women had more choices. But the damage was done. "Tea and cookies" was all over the evening news — and it stuck.

A month later we were reviewing campaign research with Clinton at a Holiday Inn in Charleston, West Virginia. Part of the presentation was the videotape of a "dial group," where a roomful of voters are hooked up to handheld meters and asked to respond to news reports, TV spots, and tapes of speeches to gauge what works and what doesn't. The results are superimposed on the screen in real time, so you have an instant analysis of voter response.

When a shot of Hillary speaking was played, the line on the screen dropped like a downhill ski run.

"Oh, man," said Clinton, demonstrating both husbandly concern and his capacity for denial, "they don't like her hair."

Nobody said a word, but James — who was sitting next to me on the couch across from Clinton — started grinding his fist into my thigh. That pressure and the laughter building up inside me made me double over until James mumbled something and burst out of the room. I was right behind him. We collapsed in hysterics the second we hit the corridor. From then on, whenever I wanted to make James laugh, all I had to say was "They don't like her hair." To him, it was the single most memorable line of the campaign. To me, it was just a sweet moment.

But the Republicans remembered "tea and cookies." Frustrated by their inability to close the gap before their convention opened, they tried to make Hillary a major issue. Party chairman Rich Bond opened the attack. In a gross distortion of views that Hillary had expressed in a 1973 journal article on the rights of abused children, Bond charged that if Clinton became president, he would be advised by "that champion of the family Hillary Clinton, who believes kids should be able to sue their parents rather than helping with the chores as they are asked to do. She has likened marriage and the family to slavery."

Big mistake. "Tea and cookies" hurt Hillary because her words seemed to reveal a secret, somewhat scary, side of her. Bond's broadside helped her by transforming her from a radical feminist with a secret agenda into a political victim of the Republican right. The attack was a willful misreading of Hillary's text, and we saw it as an opportunity to defend her and return the fire. Hillary was controversial, but people liked the fact that she was a children's advocate, and hated political attacks that were perceived as personal. What could be more personal than attacking a candidate's wife? We accused them of trying to turn Hillary into Willie Horton.

Nightline scheduled a whole show on the issue, and after studying Hillary's writings, I volunteered to argue our side. Having Hillary defend herself was too big a risk; it would send the message that the charge was substantive rather than a nasty symptom of political desperation. It would also subtly reinforce the Republican subtext — that Hillary couldn't wait to advance her extreme agenda on the national stage. Hillary knew this, and I was relieved that she agreed to have me be her surrogate. To prepare me for the show, we reversed roles: She was the staffer and I the principal. On a phone from the road, she pelted me with the toughest attacks she could make on herself and asked what a nice boy like me was doing defending a radical feminist like her. Although she doesn't show it much in public, self-deprecating humor comes a bit more easily to her than it does to her husband. She also likes a good political rumble.

From my perspective, the show couldn't have gone better. The Bush campaign didn't even send an official representative; instead I got to debate Phyllis Schlafly. If anyone was going to attack Hillary, who better than a far-right old-timer with a beehive hairdo? Of course, I could also imagine the other side thinking they could do worse than opposing a liberal punk with a mop top. The pictures were probably a wash. What turned the debate was Ted Koppel's using his anchorman's authority to subtly suggest that the attacks on Hillary were misleading. All I had to do was fall in behind and remind viewers that the Republicans were up to their old tricks.

After the show, Hillary called with thanks for "defending my honor." Good thing too. Her best friend, Susan Thomases, was constantly looking to replace me with a "serious, gray-haired" talking head, like their friend Arkansas attorney Jim Blair, or Don Fowler, who would later run the Democratic National Committee. She and Hillary were suspicious of how much I enjoyed the spotlight and rightly worried that I simply looked too young to be serious. My response to this was passive aggression: agree in principle, ignore it in practice. I appreciated the argument but also resented it. Didn't the fact that I had effectively defended the Clintons in difficult situations for most of the last year count for something? Of course it did, but my vanity and arrogance were also creeping in. Both would later come back to haunt me. But that night, and for the rest of the campaign, Hillary's blessing brought me all of the job security I needed.

When Hillary was angry, you didn't always know it right away — a calculated chill would descend over time. Clinton's anger was a more impersonal physical force, like a tornado. The tantrum would form in an instant and exhaust itself in a violent rush. Whoever happened to be in the way would have to deal with it; more often than not, that person was me. I guess Clinton figured that I could fix whatever problem was causing his frustration, and he must have sensed that I didn't take his temper personally. The trick was to have a kind of thin skin — to understand that Clinton didn't really yell *at* you; he yelled *through* you, as the rage passed through him. My job was to absorb the anger and address its cause.

One function of our daily morning phone calls was to give Clinton a chance to take out his frustrations on us so that they wouldn't come out in public. We also tried to provoke him in prep sessions before press conferences and debates, which created a kind of perverse pleasure. You got to put your boss on the spot while telling yourself that it was for his own good: "Governor Clinton, electing a president is ultimately a matter of trust, and polls show that the American people just don't trust you. What's your response?" Silence. His eyes would become slits, and his lips would disappear. "So what do you want me to say," he would finally reply in a voice muted by contempt. You could almost hear the next word: "smartass."

Clinton's anger was often well placed. Once, in rural Georgia late in 1992, we needed a good picture to highlight a Medicare event, which meant that a hundred senior citizens had to sit for hours under a baking sun. Clinton was steaming. He got on the phone and screamed at us for "grinding these peoples' faces in the dirt. You're treating them like props." He was right.

But we all have limits to how much we can take, and mine came on a late night in early October. I was asleep in Little Rock when my beeper went off at about one A.M. with a message to call Clinton in Milwaukee. My telephone was broken, or maybe I hadn't paid the bill, so I called him back on my cell phone. Clinton was upset about a foreign-policy speech he was scheduled to give in the morning, and Bruce handed him the phone in midrant. He wanted to cancel.

I tried my usual technique: listen for a spell, concede a point or two, then remind him of the underlying facts — that we had invited ethnic leaders from all over the country to the event, that we needed one more foreign-policy speech before the debates to establish his credentials as commander in chief, that the press was primed and the speech was solid. Nothing worked; he was overtired and anxious. Then the battery died on my cell phone, which left me with a real dilemma. At 1:30 in the morning, should I get dressed, get in my car, and drive a mile or two to find a working pay phone for the privilege of being yelled at again about a situation we couldn't change?

The answer to that would be no.

Three months earlier, when I was less secure in my new role, I would have done it. Three months later, when Clinton was president, not calling back would never cross my mind. But now, I took a stand and went to bed. *Go yell at somebody else. Try California, where people are still awake.*

It's true that no man can be a hero to his valet. But every day Clinton also showed how extraordinary he was. Like when he spent his downtime stroking the hand of a little girl, bald and yellow with cancer, and looked into her eyes until she believed she'd grow up to be a movie star. Or when you would prep him for a late-night car-ride-to-the-airport interview after sixteen hours of nonstop campaigning. His eyes would float, the lids fluttering with fatigue, but once the reporter ducked into the backseat, Clinton would repeat the briefing word for word and add six points we missed. We called him Secretariat, the ultimate political Thoroughbred. Most of the time I was just happy to be his stablemate, the little goat by his side who usually knew what to say and had a knack for keeping him calm.

By the fall, the rest of the country was starting to believe that Clinton was one of a kind too. As his bus rolled across the Midwest and down through the South, he promised hope and personified change, which was exactly what people were looking for after eight years of Reagan and four more of Bush. In late September, Stan Greenberg conducted a national poll that tested all the charges the Bush campaign could throw at us and every rebuttal we would give. Nothing the Republicans could try would work. On paper, at least, the election was ours.

Of course, we were usually way too superstitious to say so out loud. That would be like mentioning a no-hitter in the bottom of the eighth. But on the first Sunday in October at the Washington

Hilton, we were revising a speech on the North American Free Trade Agreement that Clinton would give later that afternoon. Clinton had decided to endorse the treaty if it included provisions to protect labor rights and the environment, but getting the wording right in a way that didn't enrage our labor base was tough. The prep wasn't going well. Clinton cut it off and called me into the bedroom.

He was lying on the bed in jeans and a T-shirt, propped up on pillows, with his speech draft and reading glasses lying untouched beside him. As I walked in, he launched into his ritual complaint about how nobody on his staff could write a speech. But I could tell that his heart wasn't in it. He gestured toward a chair by the bed, and when I sat down he just stared at me. Then he said it.

"You think we're going to win, don't you?"

He rarely asked me a direct question. We always seemed to be in the middle of a conversation, speaking in sentence fragments with a familiar tone. His more deliberate approach that morning was as significant as the fact that he was reading my mind. I hadn't said it to anyone and had barely acknowledged it to myself, but even I, the prince of pessimism, was optimistic. If he was asking, I had to answer.

"Yes, sir," I said with some solemnity. "I think we will."

"I do too."

His words seemed to hang there in the space between us. Maybe he hadn't intended to issue a kind of encyclical, but he knew that I knew this wasn't a random comment either. We had known each other for just over a year, and every moment had been dedicated to transforming this man from governor of Arkansas to president of the United States. When he said he expected to win, I felt it had to be true.

Only years later did I realize that Clinton's unconvincing anger earlier that morning was somehow connected to growing awareness of his impending responsibilities — that his uneasiness was the product of hope and fear and God knows what else a man feels when it dawns on him that he might actually achieve the goal of a lifetime and become the most powerful single person on the planet. You say a lot of things in campaigns that you never really expect to be called on — you overpromise — but the closer you get to victory, the more weight every word carries. Clinton knew this, and he was starting to think more like a president than a candidate — more about how he would implement his agenda than whether he would get the chance. In the final weeks of the campaign, he salted his stump speeches with an important reminder: "We didn't get into this mess overnight; we won't get out of it overnight."

I left Clinton's room floating on the notion of victory, tethered by its prospective burdens. But as we entered the homestretch of the race, fear of success wasn't my big problem. I was much more scared of blowing our big chance. "Buyer's remorse," Clinton called it. At the last minute, the voters might return to the devil they knew rather than take a chance on the new guy. We had seen it happen in Britain that spring, when Neil Kinnock, the Labour challenger to Prime Minister John Major, lost a big lead in the last few days of the campaign.

The closer we got to election day, the more fearful we all became. With the press speculating openly about a Clinton landslide in public, we started to drive each other crazy in private. James stopped changing his underwear; I stopped sleeping. We were both convinced that Clinton's former chief of staff, Betsey Wright (who had joined the campaign to defend Clinton against attacks from his Arkansas past), had such a twisted relationship with Clinton that she was sabotaging the campaign by inadvertently giving damaging information to reporters under the guise of defending him. I was so on edge that at a dinner with some reporters, I lashed out at E. J. Dionne and stormed away from the table over a single adjective he used in an otherwise straight piece. Clinton, egged on by Hillary, obsessed about Perot: "I'm telling you — this guy's coming on, and it's all going to come from me."

Our anxiety peaked on the Thursday before election day. Bush had spent Wednesday barnstorming Ohio by train, and our overnight polls there showed a drop from seventeen points up to three points down in twenty-four hours. If the same tactic worked in Michigan, Iowa, and Wisconsin over the weekend, we could actually lose. CNN confirmed our fears by releasing a national poll that showed our overall lead had dropped to a single point, within the margin of error. Even though we suspected that CNN was cooking the results to inject a little excitement into the race, we couldn't be sure.

As we all gathered around the speakerphone in my office for a strategy call that quickly turned into a screaming match, only Stan Greenberg was calm, maintaining the manner of a physician treating a roomful of hypochondriacs. The little box was vibrating from the force of fifteen people all talking at once. This was the last chance to change our ads before election day, and everyone wanted to win his or her own way: Hillary wanted to put up ads attacking Perot; Clinton wanted to defend Arkansas, which was now being portrayed in the Bush ads as a wasteland watched over by buzzards; the rest of us were seized by a bloodlust backed up by our research into what was working. All we wanted to do was keep our foot on Bush's neck by running "Read my lips" ads right up through election day.

Clinton finally conceded. "All right," he said. "I'm not saying I agree, but you guys do what you think is right." It was a vote of confidence that failed to conceal a warning: *"But if I lose this election, it'll be all your fault."*

In my own craziness, that's how I was starting to think too. *If we lose after holding a lead like this, it will be all our fault. Democrats all over the country will hate us.* In the final days of the campaign, Carville and I spent more and more time crouched in my corner office, making dark jokes about our exile in Europe after allowing Bush the biggest comeback in presidential history. But our worries that Thursday ended when President Bush stopped his minisurge by calling Clinton and Gore "bozos" at a campaign rally in suburban Michigan. The next day, his fading hopes and our remaining fears were put to rest.

After lunch on Friday, James ran into my office with his black gloves in the air. He was jumping up and down like an underfed club fighter who had startled himself by knocking out the champ, and screaming obscenities in the singsong meter of a nursery rhyme: "He's going to have a clus-ter-fuck; he's going to have a clus-ter-fuck." "He" was President Bush. Iran-Contra independent counsel Lawrence Walsh had just indicted former Secretary of Defense Caspar Weinberger, and a note included in the indictment indicated that Bush had both known about and supported trading arms for hostages — a charge the president had repeatedly denied. The Weinberger note was the closest thing yet to a smoking gun. Bush's campaign was dead anyway, but this was the nail in the coffin.

That night I did a little jig on the grave. I was at the gym when Michael Waldman, our campaign's specialist on Iran-Contra and other Bush scandals, beeped me to let me know that Bush was on *Larry King Live*, challenging Larry to "ask me anything." I jumped into my car with a cell phone and dialed Tammy Haddad, King's executive producer. "Tammy," I started, "Larry's letting Bush off the hook. How could he not know they were trading arms for hostages?"

"Good question," she replied. "Why don't you ask him yourself?" Figuring a little confrontation would make for good television, she gave me a special number to connect directly with the show.

Good television, maybe, but was it smart politics? We had the lead, why take a chance? If I said something stupid and the election turned, then I personally — not Clinton or James or anyone else — could conceivably be responsible for the loss. It really *would* be all my fault. But we had come this far by never letting up, by being in their face every minute of every day. This was no time to change tactics.

James was all for it, but I wanted higher clearance. I couldn't reach Clinton, so I tried Gore. Had he vetoed the idea, I would have backed off. Had he been unavailable, I would have had to make a choice. "Go for it," Gore said. I dialed the number.

As I waited on hold, all the moisture in my mouth drained into my palms. Suddenly, the line opened into what sounded like a wind tunnel. I was on the air. King announced a call from Little Rock, Arkansas, and for the first time in my life I was talking to a sitting president. "Mr. President, you asked us to find out what the smoking gun was," I said, before citing the Weinberger memo as evidence that Bush had to know Iran-Contra was an arms-for-hostages deal.

"May I reply?" Bush said, sounding peeved but still in control.

He then surprised me by reciting my résumé on national television. *Where's he going with this?* He told the viewers I was a very able young man who had once worked for Congressman Richard Gephardt. *That's it, trying to tie me to the congressional Democrats, but pretty nice to call me "able" considering I'm trying to throw him out of office.* Then he finally answered my question by saying that President Reagan didn't believe it was arms for hostages and that he believed President Reagan. *Nothing new.*

Larry King: "George, want to respond?"

President Bush: "I didn't come here to debate Stephanopoulos."

Wait a minute. He's debating six-foot chickens all over the country, but he won't debate me? King tried again to get me to respond, but Bush cut him off. He filibustered by praising me again, saying I was a "patient fellow" and that "every time we'd say something, he was out there with a —"

A response. A rejoinder, a retort, anything. Just finish the sentence!

"And they did a very good job on it," the president concluded.

In that spontaneous encounter, Bush revealed his state of mind and the condition of his campaign. He seemed to be acknowledging that our team was better than his. And by speaking in the past tense, Bush seemed to be admitting that the election was over — an idea that became even more explicit a moment later, when he offered what sounded to me like a presidential seal of approval: "So I would like to take this opportunity, because I might not have a chance to see him before the election, to commend him on all that."

Bush was the first presidential candidate I thought about working for and the only one I had ever worked against. Defeating him and his agenda had been the focus of my career for the last five years, and I had heard that my campaign press releases had gotten under his skin. One of the altar boys at my dad's church was a page at the Republican convention, and he attended a speech in which Bush complained about "some guy named Stenopoulos" who was always messing up his stories. But that was nothing compared to hearing the president of the United States praise me on *Larry King Live*. I hoped my parents were watching.

Later that night, Clinton called to congratulate me. But from the tone of his voice I could tell that he was a little annoyed. And why not? Calling Larry King's producer was my job. But confronting an incumbent president was a risk, and not necessarily a prudent one. Good thing it had worked.

"The wai-ai-ting is the hardest part." Tom Petty's song was my anthem the last weekend. The last commercials were in the can and on the air, and the schedule was set. Only two news cycles to go: No new charge could hurt us now, and nothing more we could say about Bush would make any difference. People had made up their minds; they were going to take a chance on Clinton. But knowing that wasn't the same as believing it. James and I spent the final hours in my office figuring out how we could still manage to lose. All day Monday, he folded his body across the club chair in front of my desk and burned off nervous energy by ad-libbing a series of Clinton concession speeches:

"We tried hard; we came up a little short. To those who embraced our crusade, we say thank you. . . . Throughout this campaign, I have endeavored to bring my message of change to the American people. Over forty-two percent of you embraced that message, and I am grateful to each and every one of you. Hillary and I will never forget you. The way you welcomed us into your homes, your towns, and your cities. It is not that we have lost this battle. It's whether we endure in a larger war."

"Shut up," I pleaded, still half convinced Clinton would be saying these same words tomorrow night. Part of me simply couldn't believe we were going to win, just like President Bush and his team never really believed they would lose. But by late Monday afternoon, I began to relax. Lying on James's couch and bouncing a Wiffle-ball bat on my knee, I wondered what to call Clinton after we won. I had never called him Bill; it was always Governor. Tomorrow it would be — what? Mr. President-elect. Of course I'd address him as Mr. President in public, but I wondered if in private he'd still let me call him by what I thought of as his first name. Governor had a nice ring to it, kind of stately and Southern, like when you honored a senator who had served on the bench by calling him Judge.

The final War Room meeting was Monday night — a time to say thank you and good-bye, to voice our hopes for the days ahead.

More than a hundred of us were crowded together on the floor, standing on tables, spilling out into the hallway, our numbers expanded by family and fans from all over the country. My job was to introduce James, but I hoped to be inspired, to say something that would sum up our collective experience, knowing that all of us in the room would always remember this night. Now I was crossing a threshold, from a person who had read history to one who had helped shape a slice of it; from a person who had dreamed about working in the White House to one who would do it; from a person who professed that politics could change peoples' lives to one who would have the chance to prove it.

In a voice choked with fatigue, gratitude, and hope, I talked about Clinton and James, and summed up my expectations in a few sober sentences: "For the first time in a generation tomorrow, we're going to win. And that means that more people are going to have better jobs. People are going to pay a little less for health care, get better care. And more kids are going to go to better schools. So, thanks."

It wasn't soaring rhetoric, but I was a little scared, and my skeptical soul was aware of the all-too-human imperfections that prevent promises from being fulfilled. It had been a tumultuous campaign, upsetting and exciting at the same time. It had toughened me up, hardened me more than I liked, but I still believed we could make it all worthwhile with what we would do. Camus spoke to me that night in a passage I had carried in a notebook for years: "Perhaps we cannot prevent this world from being a world in which children are tortured. But we can reduce the number of tortured children. And if you don't help us, who else in the world can help us do this?"

For James, the obligations would end. His job was done, and his speech that night was a version of the ode to brotherhood and honor and battles well fought that Shakespeare's Henry V delivered to his troops on Saint Crispin's eve. James talked about love and labor as the two most precious gifts a person could give. He said his work was finished, and as tears clouded his eyes and quivered his body, he thanked the kids he'd been tormenting for months and told them he loved them.

For a moment we were silent, subdued by the private feelings of one man and the public weight of what lay before us. Then the room broke into a chant — "One more day! One more day!" — and when Clinton's voice cracked through the speakerphone in the middle of the table, the room erupted in a cheer that I could have listened to forever.

Outside, the streets were blocked by tractor trailers and satellite trucks, the Old Statehouse had been transformed into a Hollywood soundstage, and downtown was teeming with people ready to party. Later that night, our celebration was almost spoiled by a final sleazy attack: A Republican congressman called an airport press conference to accuse Clinton of sleeping with a reporter on the campaign plane. *At least all that will end tomorrow.*

After the eleven A.M. exit polls confirmed an electoral college landslide, election day was a blur of high fives and hugs. But Clinton didn't trust exit polls. Back in the mansion, he inhaled the results I fed him in hourly phone calls but refused to let himself believe them. Only when the official tally came in later that night did the anxious man revert to the hypercompetent pol. As I read off the list of states we'd won over my cell phone, Clinton became nonchalant. "I knew that. . . . Yeah, I figured we'd win there too." I tried to thank him for changing my life. Helping him win was the best thing I'd ever done. But he wanted an update on Nevada.

Our campaign relationship ended as it had begun. Two men at work, talking shop, a candidate and his staff. The formalities were for the rest of the world. They would get the waves and smiles, the gracious words, the promise to face the future with humility and hope. I got "How'd we do in Nevada?" My own personal victory speech. An ocean away, in my grandfather's village, the village where my father was born, they roasted lambs in the square for their young cousin making their name in America. Priests serve; immigrants succeed. Perhaps I'd done both.

The next day, I drove out to the mansion for my first meeting with the president-elect. I called him Mr. President, of course; nothing else seemed possible once I saw him face-to-face. But this was a family visit. Clinton and Hillary were in the den off the butler's pantry, a staircase below the bedroom where I had first been admitted to the Clintons' private world, a floor above the basement office that was now the operations center of the Little Rock White House.

When I walked through the door, Clinton called me "Master of the Universe," and the two of them wrapped me in a three-way hug. We were all washed out, but as we sipped tea and talked about the future, I could already see sparks beneath their pale skin and exhausted eyes. Their dream was just beginning, and they wanted me to "keep on doing what you did in the campaign." Exactly what that meant would be worked out later; for the moment, it was just nice to hear.

Clinton also offered me some personal advice. "George, when I was your age, I was the youngest ex-governor in America. Don't make my mistakes. You get too wrapped up in what you do." He was right. I was too intense, too tightly wound, too impatient for my own good. Later that day, my father followed his congratulations with another word of caution. "Be careful," he said, after reminding me of the myth of Icarus. "Keep your balance."

5   OPENING DAY

*S**hit. I can't cover it up.* I was staring at the mirror of the single-stall washroom by the press secretary's office on the first floor of the West Wing of the White House. In a few minutes, I would call my first official press briefing as communications director, and I had a problem. My beard. With all the craziness of the inauguration, I hadn't had the chance to buy new razor blades, and the powder I was pasting on my cheeks gave me the pallor of a corpse with a five o'clock shadow. I was about to face the world from the White House podium looking like an adolescent Richard Nixon.

My job that day was to act like one of his henchmen — to hang Zoe Baird out to dry. Our nominee for attorney general, Baird was in the middle of a firestorm because her background check had belatedly turned up both that she had failed to pay social security taxes for her household help and that the workers were illegal immigrants. As I prepared to face the White House press corps, she was getting pummeled by the Senate Judiciary Committee. She didn't know it yet, but she was toast.

I had just left a meeting in the Oval Office with the president, the first lady, Bernie Nussbaum, the White House counsel, and Howard Paster, our liaison to the Congress. Clinton and Hillary were frazzled from the festivities of the night before and a morning spent shaking hands at an inaugural open house. Clinton sat behind the broad but still bare desk he had requested from storage — JFK's desk, the one John-John crawled from in that famous photo. Hillary stood parallel to Clinton but off to the side, the hard look on her face set off by her pastel blue suit.

"So where are we with Zoe?" Clinton asked in a tone that suggested he knew the answer.

Howard told him her testimony was costing her votes, and I urged a quick, relatively clean kill. Bernie wanted the president to fight. "No, he can't do that," said Hillary, arguing that this was Zoe's problem, not his. That was Clinton's cue to complain that he hadn't known about Baird's nanny problem when transition chairman Warren Christopher recommended her and that he never would have picked her if he had. But he also wanted to give her the chance to make her case to the Senate and make the decision herself. That meant that she and I were in limbo. My orders were to support Baird without defending her, to say that she'd make a strong attorney general but to leave the president room to cut her loose.

A difficult balancing act, but I wasn't complaining. This was the big leagues. As the loudspeaker announced that my briefing would begin in one minute, I stood behind the wooden door to the press room with a stomach full of pleasant butterflies. I couldn't wait to get behind the podium and show what I could do. The sound of the door sliding open set off dozens of camera shutters. I walked to the podium, adjusted the glasses I had started wearing again in a vain attempt to look older, and took in the scene with a deep breath.

The long, low room was more compact than it looked on television. A bank of video cameras on tripods anchored the back, and every movie-theater seat in front was filled. Photographers crouched on the floor by the podium, and the aisles were stocked with an assortment of staff and other spectators. An attractive older woman standing off the side wall looked just like Lassie's mom — because she was. After retiring from television, June Lockhart had moved to Washington and become a regular in the White House press room. She just liked to watch. The rest of the world could tune in live on CNN.

What they saw that day was a White House press secretary fall flat on his face.

It opened well enough. I read a statement about the president's getting down to work. Helen Thomas, the red-haired UPI reporter who had covered every president since Kennedy, started with a softball. "Are there any more executive orders to be signed today?"

Mr. Stephanopoulos: "I don't believe there are any more today, Helen."

Then the real questioning began.

Q: "How about all of these stories on the lifting of the ban on homosexuals in the military?"

How about you guys give it a rest and report decisions we've actually made? I know, it's too good to let go: sex, a fight with the military, gays feeling betrayed, a crisis right out of the box. If you reporters weren't pumping it so much, maybe real people wouldn't think it's the only promise we're trying to keep. But we can't get Nunn and the Joint Chiefs to give us a break yet, so I have nothing to say.

Mr. Stephanopoulos: "I think the president intends to end discrimination against homosexuals in the military . . . and it would be very soon — probably within the next week, but not today."

Q: "George, would the president like Zoe Baird to offer to withdraw her nomination?"

Well, duh. Of course he would, wouldn't you? We're sucking wind on our first day with a candidate for attorney general who broke the law. But she says she told Warren Christopher about it before Clinton chose her, so it's our fault — and she doesn't want to quit without clearing her name. We're stuck.

Mr. Stephanopoulos: "No, he thinks she'll make an excellent attorney general. . . ."

Q: "If Mrs. Baird decides to withdraw her name, would the president accept it?"

In a heartbeat. I wish that's what I was announcing right now.

Mr. Stephanopoulos: "Right now, Mrs. Baird is testifying before the Senate Judiciary Committee, and President Clinton continues to believe she'll make a good attorney general. . . ."

Damn. They caught that "right now"; everyone's writing it down. They smell blood. Hope that doesn't make Zoe fight back harder.

Q: "Did Mr. Clinton understand fully before naming her as his nominee for attorney general that she had employed illegal aliens for this long period of time?"

Bingo. The $64,000 question. Wish I knew the answer. He says no. Christopher says yes. Christopher probably mentioned it, but who knows exactly what he said or how Clinton heard it? All I know is that Zoe is saying publicly that she told us, so we're screwed either way. If we didn't know, we're incompetent hacks. If we did and appointed her anyway, we're unethical elitists. Some choice: I can't blame it all on Zoe; the president's not ready to accept responsibility and move on; but if I dump it in Christopher's lap, it will hurt his credibility as secretary of state. Gotta punt.

Mr. Stephanopoulos: "Again, I don't know the exact nature of his discussions on this. . . ."

Nice try. But they were just getting warmed up. This was the heart of the matter, the old Watergate question: What did the president know and when did he know it? I didn't know and couldn't say. But I *did* know that I was dying out there — a fact confirmed by the flop sweat pouring out from under my arms and across my chest. A trickle started to stream down the side of my face, but I was afraid to wipe it away, certain the image would be flash-frozen into a metaphor of the new administration under siege. The only relief I got was halfway through the briefing, when someone asked if I was enjoying my first day with the press in the White House.

Mr. Stephanopoulos: "It's not bad. It's a little tough." (Laughter)

They're laughing at me. Jerks. I'm a joke my first day on the job.

Then we got to what was *really* bothering them: the closing of the door. We had decided to close off the corridor connecting the press room to the rest of the West Wing, which meant that reporters would no longer have walk-in privileges to the press secretary's office — my office — on the first floor. They were confined to the basement, and they were pissed.

Helen Thomas led the charge. For more than thirty years she had started her day a little before seven A.M. by planting herself outside the press secretary's office and asking him a question as he walked through the door. Now she couldn't do that anymore. With a voice that sounded then like the Wicked Witch of the West's, she went on the attack.

Q: "Are you going to continue to block us from going up the steps?"

You guys are being such babies about it that I wouldn't mind. But I'm not your problem; Hillary is. She and Susan Thomases cooked up this plan to move you to the Old Executive Office Building so we could reopen the indoor pool that used to be right below your feet before Nixon made this the press room. Barbara Bush told her we should show you guys who's boss right from the start. Easy for <u>her</u> to say; she doesn't have to deal with you anymore. Closing the door was our fallback position.

Mr. Stephanopoulos: "Well, right now we're just figuring out how to structure all of the offices upstairs. . . . I mean, there are often changes between administrations. . . ."

Q: "Not like that."

Q: "Are you going to block us from going up the steps to your office?"

Mr. Stephanopoulos: "We will review any of these kinds of plans with you before we do any—"

Q: "What does that mean?"

Mr. Stephanopoulos: "That's exactly what it means. We're reviewing everything right now."

And I hope we change our minds tomorrow. I don't want to go through this again. Clinton seems to be on my side. He asked me again this morning why we were closing the door. Um, have you talked to your wife about this, Mr. President? She says you wanted to be free to walk around without reporters looking over your shoulder.

Q: "You've done it. You just said you were going to review it with us."

Mr. Stephanopoulos: "For the time being, we're doing it before we make any permanent decisions. We'll be discussing this with you."

Q: "Well, I want to tell you that I've been here since Kennedy, and those steps have never been blocked to us, and the press secretary's office has never been off limits. Ever."

Helen was letting me know who was really in charge. I may have been working for the new president, but she was part of the institutional presidency. She could wait us out, and she intended to win.

My untenable positions on Zoe and the press office were made worse by the fact that I wasn't prepared with simple facts and a few anecdotes to fill the reporters' first-day columns. Better preparation wouldn't have stopped the bad stories, but it would have helped soften the blow: Talk about how the president and the first lady feel on their first day; throw in a little color on the president's first night in the residence and first morning in the Oval Office; bring Tony Lake, the national security adviser, into the briefing room for a backgrounder on the ongoing confrontation in Iraq. But no, I wanted to do it all by myself, and I wasn't ready. When a reporter saved me from myself by saying thank you after twenty-seven minutes of pounding, Helen shouted, "Welcome to the big leagues," and I hustled out of there with my head down like a rookie knocked from the mound in the first inning of his first game.

Only hours before, I had gone to bed feeling like a world champion after a round of inaugural balls capping off the headiest week of my life.

We had arrived in Washington on Sunday of inaugural week and gone straight to Blair House, the president's guest house. A handsome hostess with silvery blond hair and a continental accent greeted me at the door and offered me tea as if I were one of the guests they were used to — royalty, a head of state — not just one of the staff. Only a handful of us were invited to stay with the Clintons at Blair House. As the butler ushered me up to the second floor, I pocketed the gilded card that carried my name, spelled correctly, in an elegant calligrapher's script. Closing the door, I lay back on the feather bed and luxuriated in the feeling of being one of the chosen.

But for the next couple of days, I didn't spend much time in that room. Inaugural week was a manic mix of public celebrations and private chaos. The Sunday we arrived, there was Hollywood pageantry on the Mall and a parade across Memorial Bridge to ring a replica of the Liberty Bell. Later that night, we were back at Blair House for another speech revision. A small room on the third floor had been set up with a TelePrompTer and podium to simulate the scene on the West Front of the Capitol. As usual, Clinton's speech was far from done. Whoever managed to wander in — friends, family, the caterer — could have a say on the new president's first words. He'd recite a few lines from the podium, then we'd talk about them — and talk about them some more. The speech was getting longer by the hour.

The next day I paid a visit to my predecessor and former adversary, Bush press secretary Marlin Fitzwater. The campaign had been bitter, but he was friendly now, and the untroubled way he slumped in his soft chair gave him the air of a man who was ready to go. I understood for the first time how losing the White House might seem like a relief and made a mental note to think about how to prevent it when the time came for us to compete for a second term. Marlin offered advice about maintaining perspective and told me to remember that the press was less of an enemy than it seemed. But he probably knew I couldn't hear him then, that this was a lesson I had to learn for myself. So before he left for his last briefing, he simply opened the closet and let me in on a White House tradition — the bulletproof vest. Inside the pocket was a note from every press secretary to the man who succeeded him.

At Monday night's inaugural gala, the backstage scene was straight out of a Robert Altman movie, with Elizabeth Taylor wrapped in an elaborate boa, Aretha Franklin leading her courtiers like a Nubian queen, and even Michael Jackson, wearing white gloves, dark glasses, military dress, and a pet monkey on his shoulder. But the spectacle barely registered on me because I was in desperate search of Zoe Baird. Her nomination was already on life support, and I needed some answers for the press.

But that wasn't our only problem: The speech was still a mess. A military sedan with a sergeant at the wheel was assigned to me for the week, and the minute the show was over I rode back to Blair House. By that time, I cared about the length of the speech as much as the substance. Though Clinton's August convention address had been full of information voters needed to know about him, it had also run on for more than an hour, evoking memories of his interminable nomination of Dukakis in 1988. Another rambling effort would send a signal of indiscipline and self-indulgence. The Inaugural Address had to be different: crisp, concise, Kennedyesque.

Our process couldn't have been less like Kennedy's. Legend has it that JFK reviewed his Inaugural Address alone in his bath while puffing on a cigar. Our whole team slogged through another all-nighter. Adrenaline and anxiety were fueling Clinton, but the rest of us started to sag. From his folding metal chair facing the mock podium, the vice president–elect fought to keep his chin from sinking into his chest, but it was a losing battle. Every few seconds, Gore would jerk awake, then fall back asleep — as we all should have been at 4:30 in the morning on the biggest day of our lives.

At seven A.M., President Bush's friend and national security adviser, General Brent Scowcroft, arrived for his final official briefing. This was it, the transfer of power, awesome and ordinary all at once. One minute, Clinton was grumbling about getting up early and fretting about his speech. In walked Scowcroft, a slight man in a rumpled raincoat and fedora who at that moment looked more like an accountant than a general. But the contents of his briefcase made all the difference — the instructions the new president would need in case of nuclear attack. In less than an hour, another dramatic mood change. Scowcroft slipped out of Blair House and into the street with tears reddening the rims of his eyes. The man who would soon command the most powerful military force in the world emerged a few minutes later, silent and more somber than I'd ever seen him.

Then we went to church, where my father had the honor of delivering a public prayer at the ecumenical service for America's new president. Watching from the balcony in the back, I saw the president nod his head to the rhythm of my father's reading and I started to cry — tears of gratitude, joy, and pride. Over the course of those early days, I was numb from so much happening so quickly. But seeing my family and friends swirl through the events of the week made me appreciate the moment and understand how big a deal it was. I was feeling it through them, through the sparkle in my mom's eye as she talked about the parties she'd been to the night before, through the smile on my uncle's face. Cancer had cost him much of his strength and all of his hair, but he wouldn't miss this. For him, a lifelong liberal Democrat, this inauguration would be once in a lifetime.

For me, it was still a job. After church, it was back to Blair House for one more speech prep. Then Clinton and Hillary left for the White House, and my girlfriend, Joan, and I headed up to Capitol Hill, with me holding Clinton's copy of the Inaugural in my hands. That's when the transfer of power started to hit me more personally. Pennsylvania Avenue was closed, but our official car was waved through for the mile-long ride. The day was bright and bone chilling, but the sidewalks were already packed. As we drove down the avenue in a one-car parade, I looked up and saw the Capitol dome, the most heart-stopping architecture in Washington, the sight that had inspired me as a young intern. Now it was where I would start my new life, a life centered on the *other* end of Pennsylvania Avenue, in what I hoped would be the real center of power.

When we arrived at the Capitol, Joan and I waited for Clinton in the Speaker's office on the second floor. I had spent hundreds of hours in that room, standing on the periphery, staffing Gephardt, staring at the impressionist paintings, but never once sitting on the stark white couch against the wall. That was for principals, not staff. When I arrived with Clinton's speech, we were invited to sit. But as we sipped our coffee, I started to worry about what was taking so long. It was getting awfully close to noon. I called the White House, and they said the motorcade had left a little while ago. *Then where are they? Uggh, EF-100, the Speaker's downstairs office!* I told Joan she'd better head to our seats herself and tore through the Capitol clutching Clinton's manila folder, my new shoes sliding on the freshly polished floors.

Clinton just laughed when I skidded through the door to the anteroom where he was getting made up for the cameras. As I handed him his speech, we reminisced for a minute about our mutual friend, Father Tim Healy. A month before, Healy had died suddenly. But his notes for Clinton's Inaugural Address were saved on his computer, then passed on to Clinton through me, and his "forcing the spring" theme was at the heart of the final draft. I wished the president luck. All he said was "Thanks," but he looked me in the eye and took my hand between both of his. He knew this was an important moment for me, the last one we'd share before he became president.

The ceremony passed in a flash. Joan and I were sitting about ten rows back, and the seats around us were filled with the old guard and the new, senators, Supreme Court justices, generals in full dress uniform. I couldn't see much over all the women's hats, and the mile-long crowd's cheers reached us in time-delayed waves. But the ceremony transported me outside of my present harried self. For a moment I left behind logistics and little decisions, lost myself in the constitutional splendor, and daydreamed about what we had done and what we might do: Force the spring.

Joan and I spent the early afternoon walking our way back up Pennsylvania Avenue. We waded through the crowds, soaking up the carnival atmosphere yet eager to reach our destination — the walled compound where I would spend nearly every waking moment for the next four years. Until now, the White House had always been a slightly alien place for me. It was where the president worked, and for as long as I had been in Washington, the president was a Republican. Before this week, I had been behind the gates only once, during the 1990 budget negotiations, but I never got past the lobby.

Now we were ushered through the heavy oak doors to the cluster of staff offices surrounding the Oval. Except for the furniture and four TVs, the bulletproof vest was all that was left of Marlin's office, my office now, when Joan and I entered on inauguration day. Dust frames took the place of pictures on the walls. The bookshelves were bare, and empty file drawers stuck out into the room. A disemboweled computer stood on the corner of my desk; the hard drives in every terminal had been removed with the old regime. We were told later that they had to be examined to see if anyone in the White House had been involved in the illegal search of Clinton's passport files during the campaign, but then we were sure it was sabotage.

Even lingering campaign paranoia, however, couldn't wreck this moment. Walking through the office door was like crossing the threshold of a new house. The room was empty but inviting, with a fireplace and wide view of the North Lawn; all it needed was a personal touch. Joan pressed her hand lightly to the wall, as if to prove it wasn't fake, that we were really here. Then we flopped full-length onto the couch, caught each other out of the corners of our eyes, and just started laughing out loud.

A day later, I was sitting on the same couch with my feet on the coffee table, sipping a Diet Coke and wondering what went wrong. My debut was a bomb, that much I knew. What I couldn't gauge was just how bad it was, and how unprepared we all were for what lay ahead. The campaign, coupled with my own genetic code, had trained me to flatten my feelings, to stay steady through the daily, hourly, ups and downs. I just kept plowing through — to the next task, the impending crisis, the decision that just couldn't wait.

Today that decision was Zoe Baird, but it was already out of our hands. No matter what we did, she wasn't going to be attorney general. The only questions were how this had happened, and how to get out. Her selection, the ensuing controversy, and the way we responded were emblematic of our early troubles.

Smooth and supersmart, Zoe Baird had worked her way up from "red diaper" baby to chief counsel of Aetna Insurance by doing well at all the right schools and impressing mentors like Warren Christopher in early career stints at the Carter White House and top-flight law firms. She would have made an excellent White House counsel but had neither the high-level government experience nor the close personal connection with the president that had always been the traditional requirements for attorney general.

She did, however, meet the qualification we had allowed to become the bottom line. Although I can't point to a discrete moment of decision, we worked from the assumption that keeping Clinton's pledge to have an administration that "looked like America" meant appointing a woman to one of the "big four" cabinet posts: state, treasury, defense, or justice. This was a worthy goal, but by turning it into a quota, we put ourselves in a box. After twelve years out of power, the pool of Democrats with high-level government experience was limited; the pool of women Democrats was even smaller. But now that the first three positions were filled (with men), the transition team was scrambling to find the best female attorney general rather than the best attorney general period. Arguably more experienced candidates, like federal judge Patricia Wald, took themselves out of the running, and Clinton wasn't about to appoint a Republican as attorney general, so Baird rose to the top of the list on the strength of her solid credentials and her connection to Christopher.

If Baird had not had a "nanny problem," she would probably have been confirmed and performed competently as attorney general. But she didn't have the independent stature to survive a confirmation battle, and a new president could hardly be expected to take a stand on the principle of not paying your taxes. That all dictated that we should never have let Baird's nomination get as far as it did, but our systems failed us at every crucial step.

Christopher was understandably but overly protective of his protégé, and his lawyer's reasoning told him that Baird's problem was survivable because she had relied on legal advice in making the arrangements. Clinton pressured himself to make a decision that was both quick *and* historic, and he relied too much on *his* lawyer, Christopher, rather than his political gut. The rest of us on the political team just blew it. Though we were brought into the process late, we still should have raised more of a fuss. But our antennae went down after the election, and we lost our common touch. Other elites missed the story too, because they all had housekeepers, many of them illegal, almost all with unpaid tax bills. The first *New York Times* story was a brief item buried inside the paper, and Senator Orrin Hatch, the ranking Republican on the Senate Judiciary Committee, endorsed Zoe despite her admission. The normal political signals were flashing yellow, not red, and we plowed through the light.

What we failed to see was Rush Limbaugh and Newt Gingrich bearing down on us from the right. They started to hammer us as self-indulgent, overprivileged yuppies who thought it was permissible to break the law if you were wealthy and went to Yale. The attacks were effective, and unlike many of their later attacks against Clinton and our administration, not entirely unfair. Absent the grassroots firestorm right-wing talk radio ignited, we might have gotten away with the Baird nomination, but that's what it would have been — getting away with it.

So that's where we were on our first day — managing a crisis before we had functioning computers, before we understood our political opponents and the White House press corps, before we even knew how to work the phones. The president tried to dial out a couple of times, but every time he picked up the receiver, an operator picked up on the other end, which he didn't seem to like at all. We may have been snakebit, but we were also suffering from our own ineptitude and arrogance. We had won a campaign, but we didn't know yet how to govern — and we didn't know what we didn't know.

The Baird nomination ordeal lasted through the first night. Christopher was dispatched to convince her to withdraw, but she relented only after we agreed to take the hit. Her letter to the president stressed that she had fully disclosed her household situation to the transition team, and the letter we drafted for Clinton praised Baird and accepted full responsibility for the failed nomination.

Clad in sweatpants and a baseball cap, chomping on a banana smeared with peanut butter, the president came down from the residence after midnight to sign the letter. He was in a pretty good mood, considering — the product of relief from a crisis put to rest and his usual late-night second wind. He told the group of staff waiting for him in my office that he was disappointed to lose Zoe, but added that he was happy to end it with a measure of grace. After he signed the letter, I introduced him to the man who wrote it, my new deputy, David Dreyer. Leaning back into my leather chair, his feet up on the curved wooden desk, the brim of his cap pulled down to his eyes, Clinton stared at Dreyer's long beard and asked when he had started.

"Yesterday," answered David.

The president smiled. "Well," he said. "It sure didn't take you long to screw everything up."

6   BUNGEE JUMPING WITHOUT A ROPE

he president slammed the magazine on his desk with enough force to kill a family of cockroaches. But on that first Monday morning of our first full week in the White House, his target was another species of vermin — leakers. "They're killing us," he fumed. A column in *Time* carried a challenge from a "top administration official" to Senator Daniel Patrick Moynihan, chairman of the Senate Finance Committee. "He's not one of us," the unnamed blowhard swaggered. "We'll roll right over him if we have to."

Since Moynihan's committee controlled the heart of our agenda — health care, welfare, the budget — it was the president who had to roll over first. "If I find out who did this, they'll be gone, I promise you that," he told Moynihan over the phone. "Well, if you're upset, I'm not," Moynihan responded graciously, but he would remember this slight and exact his revenge many times over the next few years. And the president *was* upset. The fact that he had to waste political capital apologizing for something he didn't do drove him crazy. Standing behind his desk, hammering his index finger into his magazine, he ordered me to find the offender and fire him.

Such a search-and-destroy mission was futile, because the insult could have come from any one of a hundred people. But I was as angry as Clinton. Not only because I didn't want to be blamed for bad leaks, but also because I'd be expected to answer for them in press briefings, where other reporters would take the quotes as evidence that my podium responses were spin and the phantom's analysis was unvarnished truth. That was often the case, but not always. Sometimes a colorful anonymous quote just fits the reporter's thesis more snugly than on-the-record boilerplate; sometimes it reflects the staffer's personal wish more than the president's official position; sometimes it sounds more candid simply because it isn't the party line.

All administrations obsess about leaks. But the underlying attitude the *Time* comment betrayed was even more damaging than our paranoia about the enemy within. Through this one anonymous official, it seemed as if our administration were revealing its self-satisfied, self-destructive subconscious.

"He's not one of us. . . . We'll roll right over him if we have to."

Most of us were discreet enough not to say such stupid things, but that didn't always stop us from acting as if we believed them. We saw ourselves as smart, and tough, and good; above all, we had won, deposed an incumbent president. Now we had work to do, lots of it. Sure, it wouldn't be easy, but we'd waited a long time — the *country* had waited a long time — for our chance to change America, and we were going to do it all in one hundred days, just like FDR. Nothing was going to stand in our way.

Or so we thought.

The Moynihan insult was merely an irritant compared to our other problems that first week. We didn't have a new nominee for attorney general. We didn't have an economic plan yet, but we were already getting hit for dropping the middle-class tax cut, and Monday's *Post* reported (correctly) that we were also considering an energy tax that would amount to a middle-class tax increase. Three people were killed in a shooting at the CIA, and we had a showdown that afternoon with the Joint Chiefs of Staff over gays in the military.

"Roll right over them. You're commander in chief. Order them, just like Truman did when he demanded full integration in 1948." That's what our gay and lesbian supporters wanted us to do. David

Mixner, the president's old friend and leading gay fund-raiser, argued that Clinton should issue an executive order lifting the ban on homosexuals in the military and tell the Joint Chiefs that he expected them to implement it with enthusiasm.

I wish Mixner could have been in the Roosevelt Room on the afternoon of January 25, when all four service commanders — army, navy, air force, marines — entered in full uniform with their chairman, Colin Powell. On our first postelection visit to Washington, Clinton and Powell had met for a friendly late-afternoon talk about this and other issues in a Hay-Adams hotel suite overlooking the White House. But today was different — high noon, not high tea; a summit, not a visit.

The president stepped around the oblong oak conference table and welcomed the chiefs one by one. Then the delegations took their seats — the military on one side, the president's team on the other, Powell and Clinton facing each other across the center of the table. Multicolored military service flags stood at one end of the room; Teddy Roosevelt's Nobel Prize sat on a mantel at the other. Oil portraits of both Roosevelts looked down on the scene. I sat below them, behind Clinton, in a chair against the wall — seen but not heard.

It started out pleasantly enough. The president's navy stewards poured coffee and passed around plates of Pepperidge Farm cookies. The chiefs congratulated Clinton on his victory. But while Clinton was their host and their boss, he didn't hold the balance of power in the room. Yes, he was commander in chief, but Clinton's formal powers were bound by the fact that he was a new president, elected with only 43 percent of the vote, who had never served in the military and stood accused of dodging the draft. Presidential power, in Neustadt's classic formulation, is the "power to persuade," but the chiefs weren't there to be persuaded, and they had the congressional troops they needed to fortify their position. Their message was clear: Keeping this promise will cost you the military. Fight us, and you'll lose — and it won't be pretty.

Our initial skirmish with the military was a war that couldn't be won. One by one, the chiefs made that point to Clinton in measured but uncompromising tones. The crew-cut marine commander, Carl Mundy, was most vehement; he saw it as an issue of right versus wrong, military discipline versus moral depravity. But Colin Powell was the most effective. He leaned his thick forearms into the table, his clasped hands pointing straight at the president, and laid down a marker: The armed forces under Clinton's command were in "exquisite" shape, he said. We shouldn't do anything to put that at risk. We'd never had full civil rights in the military, and it would be impossible to maintain morale if gay and straight soldiers were integrated.

The president stood his ground, but his voice was still soft and scratchy from the inaugural all-nighters. He said he intended to keep his commitment, making the irrefutable point that gays and lesbians had served — and were serving — in the military both honorably and well. The only question, he said, is whether they should have to live a lie. "I want to work with you on this," he told the chiefs.

I was proud of his argument, but I also knew that we had no cards to play. If we didn't work out a compromise with the chiefs, they would sabotage us on the Hill. While they were obligated to obey their commander, they had the right to present their personal views to congressional committees publicly. That's all we needed: the top military brass led by Colin Powell, lined up in a row in direct confrontation with a new president who, they said, was sacrificing national security for the sake of a campaign promise to a special interest — all live on CNN.

Impassioned testimony from the highest-ranking black man in America denying the parallels between skin color and sexual orientation would trump our strongest civil rights argument for ending the ban, and legislation overturning an executive order would fly through both houses of Congress by veto-proof margins. Gays serving in the military would be denied new protection, and the president would have another embarrassing defeat his first week on the job. The rest of the country would wonder what happened to the moderate "New" Democrat they had elected to fix the economy. Nobody had told them that his opening legislative fight would be gays in the military. Nobody had told us either; in fact, it was the last thing we wanted. Like so much else in those first few months, it just seemed to spin out of control.

I had first encountered the issue when candidate Clinton spoke at Harvard on October 30, 1991. During the postspeech Q & A, a student questioned Clinton about discrimination against gays and lesbians in the military. If they want to serve their country, Clinton replied, they ought to be able to do it openly. The exchange was so unremarkable that it wasn't highlighted in press accounts of Clinton's appearance. After that, Clinton repeated his position at a couple of fund-raisers before gay groups and in a questionnaire for the Human Rights Campaign Fund, but it wasn't mentioned in the convention speech or our advertisements, and it didn't come up in the debates. Fearing that pressing the issue would make them look intolerant, the Bush campaign never brought it up, and Ross Perot came out against lifting the ban one day, then took it back the next. Gays in the military was the stealth issue of the 1992 campaign.

A week after the election, Clinton gave a Veterans Day speech to reassure skeptics that he honored the military and would strengthen our armed forces as commander in chief. He didn't mention gays in the military because it wasn't one of our immediate priorities. But a federal court had just ruled that the navy should reinstate a sailor named Keith Meinhold, who had been discharged for being gay. In light of that ruling, NBC's Andrea Mitchell asked Clinton if he would fulfill his campaign pledge to end discrimination against homosexuals in the military. "I want to," Clinton replied blandly. "How to do it, the mechanics of doing it, I want to consult with military leaders about that. There will be time to do that."

Clinton was trying to downplay the potential conflict by stressing his desire to work with the military rather than impose the change on them. His remarks could easily have been interpreted as a hedge on his pledge, but that's not how they played. The network news led with Clinton's response, and the *New York Times* ran two front-page stories, which left the impression that Clinton was throwing down a gauntlet at the military's feet. The media bias I detected most often in the White House was neither liberal nor conservative but a tendency to play up conflict and controversy. A story that included Clinton, the military, and sex was irresistible.

We scrambled to quiet the political storm. Clinton said that he wouldn't make any final decisions until he consulted with the military. I spoke with reporters on background, insisting that while we wanted to keep our promise, we weren't spoiling for a fight. But we soon found ourselves trapped between the military brass who wanted no change, gay leaders who insisted on all or nothing, delighted Republicans who couldn't wait to vote against us, and appalled Democrats who couldn't believe that gays in the military was going to be their first vote with a new president.

During the transition, Clinton's old friend John Holum, who was slated to head the Arms Control and Disarmament Agency, and Congressman Les Aspin, our nominee for secretary of defense, tried to develop a workable compromise that would buy us some time. But nothing came together until the close of the January 25 meeting in the Roosevelt Room, when Colin Powell raised an alternative that he'd been discussing with Aspin: "Stop asking and stop pursuing," he called it. Gays and lesbians still wouldn't be allowed to serve openly, but recruits would no longer be questioned about their sexual orientation, and commanders would stop investigating personnel suspected of being gay or lesbian. General Gordon Sullivan, the army chief, seconded Powell's proposal on a conciliatory note: "Permit us to participate with you in the change." What he meant was: "Permit us to allow you an honorable surrender."

Senator Sam Nunn, the chairman of the Senate Armed Services Committee, was called in to negotiate the terms, because any new policy would be subject to congressional review. Nunn had headed Clinton's Georgia campaign, but with friends like him, we didn't need enemies. As a matter of policy, he supported the military ban on homosexuals, but he was also peeved by Clinton's failure to name him secretary of state and happy to throw some pebbles in the path of his former House counterpart, Les Aspin. All through our first week, Nunn held our first bill — the Family and Medical Leave Act — hostage until he got his way on gays in the military.

The gay community was convinced Nunn was a homophobe, a view the president and I decided we agreed with after an interminable negotiating session in the cabinet room with Nunn and his fellow Democrats on the Armed Services Committee. But our discussion of the meeting didn't dwell on Nunn. There was too much to say about Senator Robert Byrd's tour de force.

A compact man with pale blue eyes, a long, straight nose, white hair tapered to a widow's peak, and tightly tailored three-piece suits, Byrd looked just like his name — an elegant, elderly popinjay. He had been a senator since before I was born, and his hobby was writing Senate history. No man loved the institution more. When ignorant House members or imperial presidents threatened Senate prerogatives, he would unsheathe his weapon of choice — the filibuster — and pace the floor for days, reciting history by rote, recalling the glory days of Clay and Webster, England and Rome.

The cabinet room was a smaller stage. Only a dozen of us, including the president and vice president, were seated around the table, but Byrd still stood to speak. The fingertips of his left hand rested lightly on the table; his right hand clutched the buttons of his jacket — a classic orator's pose. Rome was where he began.

"Suetonius writes that Tiberius, under whom Caesar served, had young male prostitutes in his service," Byrd began, before reeling off other tales of emperors, generals, and the men who served and serviced them. "We're talking about something that has been going around for centuries," he stated flatly, echoing one of the president's central arguments. *Wow, are we going to get Byrd? Can't be.* It wasn't. After a pause for emphasis, he delivered the opening blow. "But Rome fell when discipline gave way to luxury and ease." Then he traveled through time from the decline of the Roman Empire to the Christian Coalition's slippery slope. "Remove not the ancient landmarks thy fathers have set. I am opposed to your policy because it implies acceptance. It will lead to same-sex marriages and homosexuals in the Boy Scouts." These were the concrete concerns he would hear in West Virginia that weekend. The senator's closing peroration struck a note of deferential defiance: "Oh God, get me home safely," he exclaimed. "I will not help you on the procedural issue."

In a flight of rhetorical empathy, Clinton countered Roman history with the Old Testament. "When the Lord delivered the Ten

Commandments, Senator Byrd, he did not include a prohibition on homosexuality. As a matter of conscience, the very fact of homosexuality should not prevent you from serving if you must." Vice President Gore followed with a mix of hard science and homespun theology. "How could God permit people to be born in such a way that denies them the opportunity to live up to their God-given potential?" They were making similar points, but there was a subtle difference. Clinton was simply stating his position on the senator's terms; Gore was trying a little harder to change Byrd's mind, which wasn't going to happen.

Our whole first week was overwhelmed by gays in the military. We didn't reach a final agreement with Nunn until late Thursday night, when he agreed to permit a six-month review of the proposed compromise as long as the ban was maintained during the review period. Six months later, the president announced "Don't Ask, Don't Tell"— an outcome essentially identical to Powell's initial proposal and not far off from the earlier ban. The compromise satisfied no one, except Republican political strategists, who now had a killer issue for the 1994 midterm elections. The military resented the intrusion, Democrats were furious, the public was confused, and the gay community felt betrayed.

But gays in the military was a defeat, not a betrayal. Our administration can be fairly faulted for raising hopes that couldn't be fulfilled, but not for abandoning a cause that could have been won if only we'd had the courage to try. The military and the Congress had the votes to keep the ban because the country was not ready for the change. Issuing an executive order only to see it overturned in twenty-four hours would have been a setback for gay rights, and it would have looked as if Clinton were throwing the fight. The president had to balance one of many campaign promises against the rest of his agenda and his constitutional responsibilities. He tried to keep his eye on the ball and ask, "What is the best achievable policy for those people who happen to be in the military, in the closet, and are getting harassed?"

Supporters of lifting the ban have a right to be angry at how "Don't Ask, Don't Tell" has been implemented. The heightened attention sparked by the debate has led to increased harassment of gays and lesbians serving in the military, in defiance of the president's orders. Given that result, I now believe that promising to lift the ban was our big mistake. Focusing instead on Clinton's pledge to pass legislation banning discrimination against gays and lesbians in the workplace would have been far wiser strategy. That effort already had bipartisan support, but the bitter debate over the military ban probably stalled its passage for several more years. Confronting the military before legislating against discrimination in the civilian workforce was a losing proposition from the start — for both the new administration and the cause of gay rights.

By the end of the week, I was just glad this storm had passed. Early Friday, I walked into the Oval as the president reviewed his clips with the sun streaming through the curved windows behind his desk. In a reflective mood, he wondered if he should have pressed Colin Powell to be secretary of state. (After an initial approach to Powell from Vernon Jordan, a confidant of both men who was cochair of Clinton's transition, Clinton had let the matter drop.) "I think he would have taken it," he said. "But the moment's passed." We fantasized for a minute about how if Powell had been on the inside, maybe we could have smoothed over gays in the military before it erupted; and if Warren Christopher had been attorney general instead of Zoe Baird, maybe we could have avoided a national debate over "nanny problems." But the moment had passed.

What we really needed just then was a weekend off. Instead, the administration's elite headed to Camp David the next day for a weekend retreat. About forty of us — the Clintons, the Gores, the cabinet, and several consultants and staff — were going to spend a day "setting goals" and "getting to know each other."

Driving to the White House around 6:30 on Saturday morning in a grumpy mood, I felt the same dread I used to get on my way to summer camp. The prospect of organized play and forced camaraderie made me want to fake a stomachache, which, in turn, made me feel like an ingrate. *Here you are heading up to Camp David with the president of the United States and his cabinet! Appreciate it.*

I did my best. As we drove up icy, winding roads to the hilltop retreat, I psyched myself up. By the time we arrived, I almost believed that building team spirit in this manner was the best way to begin our presidency. Camp David, a rustic lodge on a wooded hill surrounded by saltbox cabins with screen doors, reminded me of a Poconos resort. The president had already arrived on *Marine One* and was tooling around with Gore in a golf cart, the only vehicle he was allowed to drive. The rest of us scavenged through the lodge for Camp David matchbooks and coffee mugs.

But when we assembled for the meeting, I was back to longing for home. The aluminum easels sealed it. A pair of them stood at the front of the room, holding giant pads of blank white paper just waiting to be filled with our objectives, goals, and feelings. Two sensible-looking middle-aged ladies with *Romper Room* smiles on their faces and jumbo Magic Markers in their hands completed the picture. They were "facilitators," brought in by the vice president to help us bond. This weekend was Gore's baby, an amalgam of management science and New Age sentiment that he'd used with his Senate staff.

But what works for a senator isn't necessarily appropriate for a president. As the day wore on, we papered the walls with our "personal" goals for the next four years. Hillary talked about the need to write a "narrative" for the country, and the facilitators divided us into "breakout" groups for "brainstorming" sessions. I fought the impulse but couldn't stop wondering: *Wait a second. Who cares about our "personal" goals? Isn't that what the campaign was for? We made promises, and now we have to try and keep them. Why aren't we back at the White House working on the economic plan and picking an attorney general? Or home getting some rest — instead of up here talking about our feelings?*

After dinner, a smaller group of the cabinet secretaries and senior staff sat around the fireplace to share intimacies with the Clintons, the Gores, and our friendly facilitators. The only thing worse than being there would have been not being there. Of the invited, only Lloyd Bentsen — the silky and distinguished secretary of the treasury — was secure enough not to show. The rest of us dutifully shared a revelation about ourselves, as if we were a bunch of preteens on a sleepover playing "What's the most embarrassing thing you've ever done?"

Clinton talked about how getting teased for being fat made him a tough kid, and recounted that when he was five or six, a wild boar bowled him over but he got right back up. Warren Christopher confessed to sipping chardonnay in smoky jazz bars late at night. I told them that as a little kid I loved watching the *Today* show and that I would supplement my small allowance by being an altar boy for pay at weddings and baptisms. It was excruciating.

Near the close of our final Sunday session, I made my obligatory communications director speech cautioning against leaks, which was the functional equivalent of handing out Ann Devroy's phone number: 334-7459. Everyone talked to Devroy. She was a staff writer for the *Post*, but that generic title underplayed her importance to the paper and her influence in official Washington.

Ann's account of the retreat was a signal to the Washington establishment that things were a little screwy at the new White House. Under the headline "A Bonding Experience at Camp David," Devroy proceeded to piece together the events of the weekend and put them in perspective — pointing out, for example, that while these types of retreats may have been common in the corporate world, they were relatively foreign to the White House. She wrote that the weekend was a sign of how "different this presidency will be" and added the tart reminder that the last time a president had brought so many staffers to Camp David for a working session was during the malaise depths of Jimmy Carter's tenure.

The scoop was vintage Devroy. A chain-smoking reporter's reporter with a gravelly Wisconsin accent, she was the undisputed queen of the White House beat. From her desk in the newsroom she'd work the phones all day long, conferring with telephone operators, top officials, and everyone in between. I didn't know her at first, and she was suspicious of me from watching my extraheavy spinning during the campaign. But James and Mary were her good friends, and they put in a word for me. Soon we were talking up to ten times a day.

Most of the calls were short and to the point. She wanted to check up on a tip and see what we were thinking. More often than not, she had a bead on what we would do even before we'd made a final decision. Her sources were solid, and her body clock was timed to the rhythms of the White House process. "Ann, we haven't made that decision yet, I swear," I would yell into the phone. "I know, I know, George," she tutored me. "But you will." She was usually right, but I came to respect her integrity even more than her insight. Ann would hype a damaging story if the reporting was solid, but unlike many of her colleagues, she'd put the same energy into burying a scurrilous one if the reporting was shaky. She was a great gossip, but she kept that out of the paper.

The cabinet retreat article revealed the presidential scholar in Devroy — the part of her that revered the White House the way Byrd revered the Senate. In August, she would escape to a phone-free cabin in Maine with her husband and daughter to sip whiskey and study the latest monographs on the presidency. The touchy-feely, baby-boomer patina of the Camp David weekend offended both her sensibilities and her conviction that the White House was a special place, steeped in tradition, that deserved reverence. By treating it like just another corporate headquarters, Ann believed, we were throwing away that aura and devaluing the office.

Our way wasn't working, but we resisted change, convinced that it was a kind of surrender. At first, we staff wouldn't always stand when the president entered a room, a throwback to the informal, insurgent style of the campaign. If people did, Clinton hurried to say, "Don't get up" while impatiently patting the air with his hands. His unaffected air may have been refreshing, but it was also a mistake. The same with the jogging shorts; only a series of bare-legged photos on the evening news convinced the president to wear a warm-up suit. Slowly, we learned that maintaining a slightly regal aura in office is as effective as the populist touch during a campaign. Americans want their president to be bigger than life. We started playing "Hail to the Chief" at all public ceremonies.

Clinton's military salute took longer to fix. Sheepish at first, he seemed to be working out his internal conflicts every time he tentatively raised his hand. The tips of his fingers would furtively touch his slightly bowed head, as if he were being caught at something he wasn't supposed to do. The snickering got so bad that National Security Adviser Tony Lake came to my office one afternoon to strategize on how to approach the president about it. The message had to be delivered in private, but who was the right messenger? Not me; I was too young, and not a veteran. The vice president was out; too much competitive tension in their relationship for something so personal. It had to be Tony; though he hadn't served in the military, he had served in Vietnam as a foreign service officer, and Clinton's salute came under the heading of national security. After their talk, it grew crisper.

Meantime, we tried to press forward with our agenda. The president signed executive orders on abortion rights and ethics. Hillary took charge of the Health Care Task Force, an appointment that demonstrated, we believed, how much the president cared about the issue. With gays in the military out of the way, the Family and Medical Leave Act sailed through the Congress by Thursday, February 4. Fighting for legislation like this was why we were supposed to be in the White House. For six years, it had been foiled by Republican presidents with veto power. Now Bill Clinton would sign it into law and make it possible for millions of people caring for sick children or other ailing family members to take time off from work without fear of losing their jobs. *See, a president can make a difference; elections do matter.* We set our first Rose Garden bill ceremony for early the next morning.

I got home that night after ten, but I still hadn't eaten. So I ordered Chinese takeout, cracked open a beer, and rifled through my paperwork. It had been a good day. Not only had we passed our first major piece of legislation, but Clinton's daily sound bite on the economy finally made the evening news. *We're back on track, and tomorrow will be our best day yet.*

Then my phone rang. It was Ricki Seidman, a veteran of the War Room and the Senate Judiciary Committee who was now shepherding federal judge Kimba Wood, our next nominee for attorney general, through the confirmation process. If Ricki was calling at this hour, the news couldn't be good: Kimba had a "Zoe problem." The facts were more complicated and slightly less incriminating this time, but the outcome would be the same. Another memorably named nominee with an illegal nanny was going down the tubes — and taking us with her. The president hadn't technically made a final decision, but it was no secret that Kimba was at the top of our list. Her reluctant withdrawal would embarrass us and block out any media coverage of the Family and Medical Leave Act.

My job on Friday was to prevent that from happening — to find some way for Kimba to postpone her withdrawal until after the evening news, and to convince the networks that legislation affecting millions of families was more newsworthy than whether one person whom most of the country had never heard of was still in the running for attorney general. But my negotiations with Kimba's husband, *Time* political columnist Michael Kramer, deteriorated into a shouting match, and when I confronted the network correspondents with my case, they just laughed. On the news-value meter, an expected legislative accomplishment was no match for a political gaffe. While I understood their argument, I was apoplectic — at Judge Wood's failure to disclose the problem fully and our failure to ferret out the information earlier, at the media's insatiable appetite for bad news and our uncanny ability to provide it.

I was also upset about losing another weekend. We couldn't catch a break — and I needed one. Joan was coming down from her judicial clerkship in Philadelphia for a "talk," something I wouldn't be able to concentrate on while cleaning up the Kimba debacle all day Saturday. Joan tried to be understanding but became understandably annoyed as the day wore on. I would dash out of Oval Office meetings and swear that we'd be done in less than an hour. Then another. And another.

By seven o'clock, we were still discussing our options, and Clinton invited a group of us up to the residence for dinner and more discussion with Hillary. Now I really had to choose: my girlfriend or my glamorous job. False choice, I decided (Clinton was teaching me well). "Sir, I don't want to impose," I told the president, "but would you mind if Joan joined us? It would be a real treat for her." False choice, maybe, but I was oblivious then to how inappropriate my request was — both professionally and personally.

"Sure, bring her on up," Clinton said. Hillary made Joan feel at home, and we spent hours going over names, even leafing through the congressional directory in search of the perfect candidate for attorney general. The president consulted others over the phone: David Boren, Bill Bradley, even Carville. By the end of the evening, he had settled on Judge Richard Arnold, an old friend on the federal bench in Arkansas. But Arnold pulled out for health reasons on Sunday, so we were back at square one.

Soon I was too — as a single man. The evening was special; the sense of privilege that accompanies dinner at the White House is somehow enhanced when you're wearing jeans in the family's private solarium on the third floor. But it was also Joan's final straw, a sure sign of where my heart was. First the campaign, then the transition, now this. My job would always come first. She dumped me a week later — exactly what I deserved.

But my job did come first, for better or worse. Besides, I didn't have time to be lonely, with work consuming twelve, fourteen, sixteen hours a day, six days a week, and several hours on Sunday. Every day was a dozen meetings, a hundred phone calls, a new crisis, another first.

A short time later, Janet Reno was appointed attorney general, but most of our time behind closed doors was spent struggling with our number one campaign promise — an economic plan to "get the country moving again." From election day on, we'd been in endless meetings about how to reconcile our incompatible campaign promises: to reduce the deficit, cut middle-class taxes, and increase investments in research, education, and training. Our economic team was split into battling camps: National Economic Council Director Bob Rubin, Treasury Secretary Lloyd Bentsen, and Budget Director Leon Panetta were the deficit hawks, with Gore on their side as the champion of a new energy tax; liberal Labor Secretary Bob Reich led the charge for new investments, assisted by Gene Sperling and me. But Gene and I saw ourselves above all as guardians of the campaign promises. Our job was to see that what we did conformed to what we said we would do. Too bad that wasn't really possible. All our campaign estimates were off: The deficit was now larger than we had projected, our investments cost more, and our proposed budget cuts saved less.

The president presided over the rolling Roosevelt Room meetings in shirtsleeves, with glasses sliding down the end of his nose. Sometimes it felt more like a college bull session than presidential policy making. Clinton let everyone have a say, played us off against one another, asked pointed questions, and took indecipherable notes. But the reminders of who we were and what we were doing were never far away. Late one night, we ordered pizzas. When they arrived, the president grabbed a slice with the rest of us and lifted the dripping cheese to his lips. But just before he took his first bite, an agent placed a hand on his shoulder and told him to put it down. The pie hadn't been screened, and the way the president frowned when the steward replaced his hot pizza with stale cookies reminded me of the old Peanuts Halloween special. While all the other kids got candy, Charlie Brown got a rock.

The economic plan we finally developed also seemed disappointing at first to a liberal like me. We had to drop the middle-class tax cut and drastically reduce the human capital investments proposed in the campaign. But we were hamstrung by the size of the deficit and the demands of the bond market. If we didn't reduce the deficit, the Federal Reserve and the market wouldn't force interest rates down; if interest rates stayed high, the economy wouldn't create jobs and growth. I didn't fully appreciate it then, but to achieve our overall goals for the economy, we had to sacrifice some specific promises. But many survived: the earned income tax credit for the working poor; our investments in education, including a national direct student loan program; and the Americorps national service proposal. Maybe we couldn't achieve everything all at once, but we were making progress.

We were still fiddling with the numbers on Monday, February 15, the day Clinton was set to give an Oval Office address designed to break the bad news on taxes before he outlined the popular agenda items in the State of the Union two days later. All day long Clinton scrawled over the text in black felt marker, ignoring the clock. I gave up on getting an advance copy to the press. At 8:48, the text was loaded into the TelePrompTer, and Clinton raced through a single practice before the networks went live at nine.

Later that evening, I had to give my own talk to the Judson Welliver Society. Named after the "literary clerk" to Calvin Coolidge who was the first White House speechwriter, the society was a group of former White House scribes from both parties who met periodically at the home of William Safire, the Nixon speechwriter and *New York Times* columnist. That night they gathered to critique the new president's speech and to ask me some off-the-record questions about the new team.

I arrived after ten, still flustered from the day's events, but we thought the speech had gone well, and the president was pleased. The verdict from the jury sequestered in Safire's basement was not so favorable; they thought the "class warfare" rhetoric was too hot and the delivery too hurried. Arrayed before me were speechwriters from every president since Eisenhower — Stephen Hess, Ted Sorensen, Jack Valenti, Pat Buchanan, Jim Fallows, David Gergen, Peggy Noonan, and several more. While I was deflated a bit by their reviews, I felt protected in that room, as if I were being inducted into an exclusive club where I wasn't just Clinton's guy anymore but part of the community of people who would always know they had written for a president.

Safire handed me a drink and asked me to say a few words about the process. As I recounted the chaotic details, the members began to stare, their jaws dropping in disbelief. Pat Buchanan finally broke the spell. "You mean, you mean," he faltered, "he didn't practice for the first time until ten minutes before *nine?*" Incredulous murmurs swept over the tables. I hung in for a few more minutes, until Bush speechwriter Tony Snow finally exclaimed, "George, you guys are bungee jumping without a rope."

He was right, of course; I just didn't know it at the time. It's hard to develop a sense of perspective from the cramped quarters of the West Wing, which is at once the most intimate and transparent corner of the government, where you're bombarded hourly with more information, advice, and attacks than you can possibly absorb, where snap decisions may shape history and thoughtful deliberations can lead to nothing, where the mundane details of daily life mingle with majesty and mystery. As the evening ended, Safire pulled me into his book-lined study and urged me not to get too lost in the details, to "take time, no matter what happens, to smell the Rose Garden." No single piece of advice was more simple, more valuable, or more difficult to follow.

I did my best. My favorite time was Saturday morning, before the president's weekly radio address. I'd get in a little later than usual, around eight. If the sun was out, I'd take my newspapers and coffee to the steps leading from the Oval Office to the Rose Garden, savoring the feeling of being the first one up in a quiet house that happened to feel like the center of the world. Once, I ventured out to lean against a tree on the South Lawn. Lost in my reading, I looked up to see three uniformed guards standing over me. The trees were wired, and alarms were ringing all over the White House grounds.

Our first real Saturday crisis came on March 20, when Boris Yeltsin announced that he was dissolving the Russian parliament and assuming emergency powers. The president summoned Tony Lake and his deputy, Sandy Berger; Secretary Christopher and Strobe Talbott came over from the State Department, and I joined them around the small television in Clinton's private study to watch Yeltsin's speech on CNN.

The president needed an official reaction. Yeltsin may have been acting outside of the new constitution, but he seemed to be doing it in the name of democratic reform. Talbott, a Russian expert and former journalist who had translated Khrushchev's memoirs, insisted that Yeltsin was the only horse the forces of reform had. His Oxford roommate, the president, agreed. But what if Yeltsin turned into a tyrant and we got tagged with a "Who lost Russia" challenge two months into the job?

To avoid ratcheting up the sense of crisis, I was sent to the briefing room to read a statement instead of having the president, Lake, or Christopher appear in person. Now I was really nervous, aware that what I said would be dissected in capitals around the world. After the statement, I answered a few questions, sticking to our agreed-upon script: "We support democracy and reform, and Yeltsin is the leader of the reform movement." That mantra gave us some wiggle room if Yeltsin abandoned reform, but not much.

On Monday morning, there was a cream-colored envelope on my desk. Inside was a single handwritten sentence: "You could not have handled a delicate situation better. Sincerely, Richard Nixon." *Wow, Nixon thought I did a good job. Wait, Nixon's the president liberals like me are supposed to hate. I'm going native. Oh, c'mon, George, lighten up; it's just a nice note. Take it for what it's worth.*

I did, and secretly hoped the former president was watching a few weeks later when we had our first summit with Boris Yeltsin. The setting was an estate overlooking Vancouver's harbor, and the photo op was Clinton and Yeltsin strolling through the forest, an echo of the "walk in the woods" between Soviet and American negotiators that had sealed the European nuclear missile accord of the 1980s. The cold war was over, and this summit was about trade, investment, setting up a stock market, fighting crime. But both sides, and the media that covered us, were still a bit nostalgic for the dark brinksmanship of summits past, when adversarial superpowers seemed to hold the fate of the earth in their hands. In Vancouver, I delivered my first briefing to several hundred members of the international press, feeling less like a political operative than a patriot — America's spokesman.

As always, though, the event was a mix of high politics and low. There was a quiet struggle over who would accompany the president to his private meeting with Yeltsin. Secretary Christopher and Tony Lake were veterans of the Carter administration, in which the rivalry between Secretary of State Cyrus Vance and National Security Adviser Zbigniew Brzezinski had deteriorated into a daily battle. They wanted to avoid repeating that experience but still jockeyed for position. Each thought that he should get the seat that signaled prominence in the new president's universe. Which meant that Strobe Talbott ended up in the room by default. Since he spoke Russian and was outranked by both Christopher and Lake, having him there meant the other two didn't lose face.

The person who was really losing his face that day was Yeltsin. He opened strong in his tête-à-tête with Clinton. "I liked him a lot, full of piss and vinegar, a real fighter," Clinton told me after the meeting, the first of several authorized clichés I would pass to reporters on background. "I do my best when I'm under the gun; so does he," Clinton continued. "This guy's not deterred by long odds, and now he's at the top of his form."

But Yeltsin's form faded as the day wore on. That afternoon, I bumped into Martin Walker, the Washington bureau chief for Britain's *Guardian* newspaper. He said that Yeltsin had had three scotches on the boat ride to Vancouver Island — on top of wine at lunch. At dinner, Yeltsin ignored his food and downed wine in single-gulp shots. Christopher slid me a note during the second course: "No food, bad sign. Boat ride was liquid." By the end of the evening Yeltsin was extending his arms across the table toward "my friend Beeel," and I finally understood what people meant when they described a drunk as "tight." Yeltsin's skin was stretched across his cheeks in a way that nearly obliterated his features. With his slicked-back white hair, he looked like a boiled potato slathered in sour cream.

Fortunately, it didn't seem to impair his performance the next morning. The summit was a success, marred only by a mistake on our part. Richard Gere, Cindy Crawford, Sharon Stone, and Richard Dreyfuss were all in Vancouver making movies. Dreyfuss had been a campaign supporter, and he invited the president over to his hotel suite for a late-night drink, which inevitably and justifiably led to clucks in the press for hobnobbing with Hollywood stars at a superpower summit.

As we slogged through April, that seemed to be the least of our problems. Obsessed by the idea that we had to keep all our promises at once, we were trying to do too much too fast. My daily schedule illustrated an administration-wide condition. Here's a note I made to myself on the events of a single day, April 14, 1993:

> What a full day, too many meetings, too little time.
>
> Came in pressed. Saw P at nine before he left for summer jobs event. He yelled at me for a few minutes, feeling he is losing control of his presidency. Feels we are making incremental, day-to-day decisions because we don't have a core vision. Fears that many of his appointees aren't committed to his goals. Also fears that his schedule and his government are not organized to achieve what he wants to achieve. Not enough time on welfare reform.
>
> We had a diverse, kaleidoscopic campaign: You can find justification for any of our actions sometime in the campaign.

Our central dilemma is that the deficit has hamstrung us. We can't achieve all that we called for.

Because we're not coming through on investments and stimulus, we feel more pressure to respond on abortion, gays, and other liberal issues. This is an unthinking kind of reaction. Our appointees are generally more liberal than our core vision.

Jesse Jackson came in to see me. Even when you're alone with him, there's still an element of performance. Complained that the president is too quiet about jobs, and that he, JJ, isn't being talked to by the administration. Also wants P to appear on his CNN show. But he was most concerned about the upcoming anniversary of the L.A. riots (April 30). Thinks L.A. is about to blow.

Tom Brokaw came in to discuss a prime-time special with Hillary and Katie Couric.

Meeting with Mack's working group on stimulus strategy. VP reported on phone calls to Republicans. Final negotiations after initial vote.

Met with Tony [Lake] on various subjects, including Bosnia.

Met with Howard [Paster] on VAT and Bosnia.

Press briefing.

Lunch with Susan Zirinski, Dan Rather's producer. Doing a segment on people's dreams about Clinton.

Meeting with Johnny Apple and Andrew Rosenthal on *NYT*'s policy on background briefings. Interrupted by roomful of Hollywood stars: Billy Crystal, Christopher Reeve, Lindsay Wagner, Sam Waterston, and others, who came to discuss environmental policy. My office was part of the tour.

Lots of phone calls.

Meeting with P on campaign finance.

Meeting with P on stimulus strategy.

Traded jokes with Susan Spencer [CBS White House correspondent]. Why don't Junior Leaguers like group sex? Too many thank-you notes. Told P.

False alarm on King verdict in L.A.; just a sick juror.

Talked Walter Kirn out of profiling me for *NYT* magazine.

Health care meeting. Ira [Magaziner] presenting elements of plan. I'm listing my day's events during meeting because I'm too brain-dead to pay attention.

Not far from an average day.

When you're brain-dead, you make mistakes. My worst came the day of the FBI raid on cult leader David Koresh's compound in Waco, Texas. On April 19, as I stood at the podium for my daily noon briefing, CNN started broadcasting pictures of the compound in flames. Informed by his headquarters, CNN White House correspondent Wolf Blitzer asked me about the fire, but I had no idea what he was talking about. Then someone handed me a note, and I left the podium to find out what was going on.

The rest of the day I was in constant contact with Associate Attorney General Webb Hubbell, who was monitoring the situation for the Justice Department. They didn't have good information on what was happening in the compound, or where David Koresh was, or whether the children were still alive. Later in the afternoon, I issued a statement saying the president was monitoring the situation and took full responsibility for its consequences, but the press was clamoring for the president in person. That's where I erred. Dee Dee Myers and Bruce Lindsey pushed to have the president do it, and he agreed at first. But I convinced him not to out of fear that if he said something that triggered Koresh to kill the kids who might still be alive, then we'd be culpable.

My motive may have been unassailable, but my judgment was dead wrong. The odds were high that everyone inside had already perished and that nothing the president said could make the situation worse. Beyond that, the first rule in a presidential crisis is to take responsibility fully and openly. Don't duck. That's the Bay of Pigs lesson that should have been burned in my bones. When Attorney General Janet Reno appeared before the cameras, she was praised and the president was criticized, but it was my fault.

My Waco error stemmed from inexperience and misplaced sentimentality. Other missteps, like the failed nomination of Lani Guinier for associate attorney general for civil rights, were the product of sloppy staff work coupled with an overactive desire to appease our liberal base with appointments because we couldn't deliver on policy. The defeat of our economic stimulus was the price we paid for legislative arrogance. Thinking we could roll right over the Republicans in the Senate, we rejected a moderate compromise offered by Senators Breaux and Boren, and lost everything. That was Republican Senate leader Bob Dole's turn to show us who was boss.

So much for opening like FDR or JFK. Our first hundred days were no honeymoon — and the president hadn't even had his hair cut yet.

It's the kind of thing you'd never plan. Clinton was finishing a long day in Los Angeles. Returning to the airport, he decided that since he was in his favorite barber's neighborhood, he might like a trim. A normal person might act on a similar whim, but if it took too long he'd miss his flight. A normal person might also request his favorite barber, but he couldn't get Christophe, hairstylist to the Hollywood stars, to pay a visit to his private plane. For a president's personal comfort, however, almost anything is possible. What he requests, the world provides, and the public tends to accept without question or resentment. Until that invisible line is crossed: Nixon's plumed guards, Nancy Reagan's new china, Clinton's $200 haircut on *Air Force One*.

The first I heard about it was when my deputy Jeff Eller called me from the plane to say that the members of press on board were grumbling about being late because of Clinton's haircut. "What haircut?" I asked. Jeff filled me in, and although we both thought it might turn into a problem, we didn't do anything, hoping it would pass into the ether of late-day events on Pacific time. What we should have done was issue a preemptive apology. Even if he didn't mean it, Clinton should have walked to the back of the plane and said, "Sorry about the delay, folks, I screwed up."

But we missed our chance. By filing time the next day, we were in crisis mode. Aided by some inaccurate leaks from the Federal Aviation Administration, the press reported that thousands of air travelers had been delayed for the sake of the president's personal convenience. Clinton and Hillary demanded a hard-line response. "They are lying," Clinton spat in the tone he usually reserved for complaints about the press. "I had the agents check, and I was told that there would be no delays."

"I know, Mr. President," I replied. "And that's exactly what I told them, but the FAA's not really backing us up on this."

The truth is that while the reporters traveling with the president were delayed, no other air traffic at LAX was affected. But that didn't stop the paralyzed-airport myth from hardening into accepted fact. The perception was more powerful than the reality, and the underlying truth — that Clinton had been self-indulgent and insensitive to the image of having a Hollywood hairstylist cut his hair on a busy airport runway, and that his staff had been too stupid to stop it from happening — was bad enough. The controversy also created new leads for the press, such as, Did the president pay for his pricey haircuts? Finances were Hillary's department, and her staff said I was supposed to tell reporters that the Clintons had a "personal services" contract with Christophe. *Oh, that'll help.* Naturally, they next wanted to see the contract, which nobody would give me — because it probably didn't exist.

The haircut might have been just another embarrassment if we hadn't simultaneously declared war on the press corps. The formal declaration was issued a little before noon on May 19, when Dee Dee announced that seven members of the White House travel office — the people whose job it was to care for the press on the road — had been fired.

At the time, I was receiving an award at the commencement exercises of Columbia University, my alma mater. Sitting on the steps of Low Library in front of thousands of graduates and their families, I felt my beeper buzzing ceaselessly beneath my gown. All hell was breaking loose back at the White House, and I had to get back. I raced through my speech and flagged a cab to the airport. As I rode, I pulled out my cell phone and started to return calls. The first was to Andrea Mitchell of NBC. "George, what are you guys doing firing the travel office?" she asked in mild disbelief, letting me know without saying so that we were making a big mistake.

"Andrea, believe me," I replied. "Don't start defending the travel office. You'll be embarrassed."

But we were the ones who ended up with egg on our faces. All I knew at the time was that we had uncovered some sloppy accounting in the travel office and that we were taking swift action. In hindsight, it's obvious that we should have quietly eased out the office director, Billy Dale, and his colleagues; summarily firing them created a story about our management style rather than Dale's accounting practices. The more the press dug, the worse the story looked: Clinton's distant cousin Catherine Cornelius was angling to replace Dale, and a company run by Clinton's friend Harry Thomason appeared to be lining up for a piece of the White House travel business. The whole episode looked like small-time Arkansas self-dealing.

I should have been paying enough attention to prevent the firing. After all, the office that made travel arrangements for the press was technically part of my department. But the issue involved two areas I did my best to avoid: administration and Arkansas. I knew that the Clintons' old Arkansas friends David Watkins and Harry Thomason were examining how the travel office was run, but my deputy Eller was handling it. After the story broke, I compounded our problems by asking the FBI public affairs officer to attend a meeting in my White House office so we could coordinate our public statements. Three White House lawyers attended the meeting, and I was only trying to make sure that what I was saying from the podium was true. But assured of my own good intentions, I was blind to how the meeting looked to the press. *How could they possibly think that we are doing what Nixon did?*

Within a few days, I resembled Nixon's infamously incredible press secretary, Ron Ziegler. In the briefing room, I did the Clintons' bidding — giving no ground, aggressively pushing back the inquiries, taking perverse pride in my daily pummelings as proof of my loyalty to Clinton and our cause. But much of what I said from the podium about the travel office matter turned out to be, as Ziegler used to say, "inoperative."

In the Oval, however, I was taking a different tack, arguing for more concessions, an apology here, more access there. That only made the Clintons believe I was going soft, pandering to the press at the president's expense. In the end, I wasn't strong enough to convince the Clintons that we were making a mistake, or skillful enough to give the press what they needed even if it wasn't what the Clintons wanted. There was plenty of blame to go around: The Clintons were intransigent, and the reporters were self-absorbed. But they could all agree on at least one point — that George was doing a poor job. And they were right.

Which meant that by Memorial Day I was in the same condition as Zoe Baird on inauguration day. All through the spring, tensions had simmered between the Clintons and the press. The haircut and travel office debacles brought them to a boil, with me as the proverbial experimental frog who didn't realize that his warm bath was becoming frog soup.

I should have seen it coming. A few weeks earlier, on a sunny afternoon in early May, Clinton's secretary, Betty Currie, had buzzed me on the intercom and said the president wanted to see me on his putting green. She didn't say what he wanted, but that's where Clinton went to calm his nerves or wrestle with a problem he couldn't figure out how to handle.

I strolled down the sloping lawn to the manicured patch behind the Oval, where Clinton was hunched over in shirtsleeves. His suit coat lay by the side of the green, several golf balls were at his feet, and he was aiming at the farthest tiny flag. Without looking up, the president asked me what I thought of David Gergen, the former Reagan aide turned pundit. "He seems like a good guy," I answered, unaware of what Clinton was getting at. "I don't know him that well, but we had dinner once at Doe's."

"Well, I was talking to him," Clinton continued, still putting. "He thinks maybe you're doing too much, and that you should think about dropping the briefing."

The president doesn't like personal or personnel conflict. But here he was being a pretty good guy. He was letting me know what he wanted in a nice way, but I was too proud to take the hint. Back in Clinton's Little Rock family room during the transition, we had agreed that I would ease out of the briefings after the first six months. Now I resisted for fear it would look like a demotion. Although I wasn't very good at it, I liked the press job. It was public, it was concrete, and the briefer could always argue for a seat at the table. I didn't have to fight for access or worry about whether the president was listening to me that day. The briefings were also a challenging game of wits, but I wasn't playful enough from the podium. I failed to learn how to deflect difficult questions with humor or to develop an ironic "wink" — the successful press secretary's ability to serve two masters, to defend the president while giving the press the impression that he's on their side too. The Clintons perceived the press as the enemy. Instead of co-opting reporters, they wanted a confrontational stance — and I took it.

After my tip-off from the president, I should have prepared a graceful exit from the press room. Instead, I slipped into the passive-aggressive stance that had worked for me in the campaign. But my lucky streak was over. White House Chief of Staff Mack McLarty was worried about his own job, and he knew that if he didn't make a high-profile change, then he would pay the price. First he contacted Bill Moyers (whom Clinton had invited to Little Rock in December to discuss the chief of staff's job), but Moyers wasn't interested. Then Mack started serious talks with Gergen.

On Thursday night, May 27, just as our economic plan passed its first hurdle in the House, Mack reached a tentative agreement with Gergen to join the White House staff. Part of the deal was that I would give up the White House briefings and move into an undefined advisory role. Right after we won the House vote, Mack pulled me aside by the grandfather clock at the entrance of the Oval Office with the news. "George," he said, "David Gergen's going to be joining us. Don't worry, we'll make it work for you." Then he hurried out the door to meet with Gergen. The president was back in his study, and all I could do was go home. My high from the House victory was now dampened by how I knew the Gergen appointment would look — as if I'd been fired.

The next morning, Mack told me he hoped to announce the appointment after the long Memorial Day weekend. Then he left for Arkansas. Hoping to minimize the appearance that Gergen was coming in to replace me, I started to think about ways we could separate any announcement of my job shift from the news of Gergen's appointment. But once a decision like this is made, the details rarely hold for more than a day. By midday Friday, CNN's Wolf Blitzer had the story. "What's this about David Gergen coming in?" he asked. With nothing to say, I had to stall. "I'll get back to you, Wolf."

Then I tried to find someone who knew what was going on, but it was futile. Mack was in Arkansas, and Clinton was traveling too. Gore told me everything would work out but said I had to talk to Mack or the president for the details. Dee Dee called from the road with Clinton, where she was picking up the same rumors. "What's going on, George?" she asked. "Are we OK?" From the little Mack had told me the night before, I knew there were no immediate plans to move anyone else, and that's what I told her. As for me, I still didn't know what my job would be, what my title would be, where my office would be, or who would take over the daily briefings. The only other news Dee Dee had was that the president had told her he would talk to me when he got home that night.

My staff drifted through the office the rest of the afternoon, looking to console me and be consoled in turn. Many of them were friends who'd worked their way up with me on Capitol Hill and the campaign. We were "the kids": once celebrated, now scapegoats. I was angry and hurt, but I knew I couldn't show it. My position was tenuous. In the conventional-wisdom culture of Washington, any disappointment I displayed would become self-fulfilling. If I acted defeated, I would be defeated. "This will be a good thing," I told my staff with more hope than conviction.

With Clinton not scheduled to call until late, I killed some time over an Indian dinner with David Dreyer. Only here did I vent my resentment. *So it's all the kids' fault. It wasn't the kids who chose Zoe, or Kimba, or Lani. It wasn't the kids who got their hair cut or fired the travel office.* No, we kids hadn't made all those decisions, but we were part of the problem — I was part of the problem — and our headstrong clash with the Washington culture was obstructing the rest of our agenda. Here's where Gergen would help; he was the ultimate establishment man. That much I understood. *But why did it have to be a Reagan guy? We were elected to reverse the Reagan revolution, not celebrate it. What's wrong with Moyers or Hodding Carter?* Choosing Gergen was adding ideological injury to personal insult.

Obviously, the president didn't think so. He liked the bipartisan glow that Gergen would add to our team. While I was crying in my curry with Dreyer, Clinton was sealing the deal with Gergen over dinner at the White House. I went back to my apartment and called my parents to let them know what was coming. "There might be some stories in the paper tomorrow that will look bad," I told them. "But I think it will turn out OK." This was the hardest conversation of the day. It's no fun to think about having your parents read about your failure on the front page of the *Times*.

I finally went to bed around midnight, with no word from Clinton. As far as I knew, the official announcement was days away, and I was heading to California for the rest of the holiday weekend. In late March, I had met the actress Jennifer Grey on a blind date brokered by our assistants. We began dating after that, and I was looking forward to my first full weekend off since starting work in the White House. But my phone rang at 1:36 A.M. It was the president.

"George, I'm sorry to wake you," he said in his most soothing voice. "I know you already talked to Mack about this Gergen thing. But I wanted to call now because we have to do this tomorrow. I know this is for the best, and I want you to believe it. I need to have you close by me."

"I need to have you close by me." Exactly the words I needed to hear. I fell asleep feeling better.

The words the rest of the world would hear were another story. The announcement was scheduled for the ridiculous hour of 7:30 on a Saturday morning. (Gergen had convinced Clinton that we had to get it done fast.) I went to my office around 6:30, booked myself on a later flight to California, and walked into Mack's already crowded office. Gergen was at the table, sipping coffee, and he got up immediately to pull me aside for a few gracious words. The vice president was sitting at a word processor in the outer office, tapping out the president's statement, with Dee Dee and new communications director Mark Gearan standing over his shoulder to watch out for my interests. Knowing that the press would dissect the statement for clues to my new status the way Kremlinologists used to study May Day photos in *Pravda*, I wanted the same title as Gergen — counselor. But Gergen resisted, so my new title was the nebulous "senior adviser for policy and strategy." Only time would tell what it would mean.

A little after 7:30, the president arrived in the Oval. Before heading to the Rose Garden, he approached me *first* and congratulated me on my new job. *What new job? Nobody's really said what I'm going to do.* Clinton's touch was perfect. Now if only I could convince the rest of the world to congratulate me. I hadn't prepared a statement of my own, but my actual words wouldn't matter much. My mission was to look like a man who was getting promoted.

Inside, I felt like a little kid who was being punished for something that wasn't all his fault. Standing next to Clinton and Gergen didn't help; they both had nearly ten inches on me. I fixed a big smile on my face and stared straight into the cameras, determined not to look like a loser. But when Clinton started to compliment me, my reflexive reaction was a modest, momentary bow of the head. The sound of a thousand cicadas ravaging through a field snapped my head back up, but the photographers had the shot that told the story: *"Brash young presidential aide, head bowed in humiliation, the agony of defeat etched on his face . . ."*

My comeback strategy could wait until Monday. Now I just wanted that weekend off. But I hadn't lost all my chutzpah. Before I headed to the airport, Mack asked me if there was anything he could do for me. "Thanks for asking," I replied. "Can we start with a raise?" He laughed, but I got the money — and a small piece of evidence that I really had been promoted. Then I got on the plane and slept. The flight attendants woke me when we landed.

Right then, Malibu was the best place for me to be. At a diner by the beach, a group of college kids who were listening to the radio came by my table to congratulate me. *Hey, maybe this is going better than I thought.* Wrong. I might have been playing OK in the town where only no publicity is bad publicity, but on the East Coast my public double was taking a beating. For every winner in a Washington power play, there must be a loser, and that weekend it was me. The *Times* story was headlined "An Offering to the Wolves." A pissy piece in the *Post* style section claimed that I broke up with Joan for Jennifer Grey and speculated that my new status would lead

Grey to throw me over for Gergen. My whole life was fair game now. Live by celebrity, die by celebrity.

But my ritual sacrifice also created a mildly surprising sense of relief. If ancient myth, modern political culture, and my professional failings had all ordained a fall — and they had — better that it happen when Clinton still claimed he needed me by his side, before I was too shot up to have any chance of recovery. Public humiliation also had its private consolations. My answering machine was packed with "hang in there" messages from all my friends. The old bull Dan Rostenkowski tracked me down on the Pacific Coast Highway to ask: "Are you OK? Because if the president didn't treat you right, he's going to have to answer to me." The only call I didn't return was from a headhunter who thought I might be interested in joining the private sector.

No, I wasn't ready for that. I believed in our work and wanted to prove that I could take a punch. Just like my boss. On the flight back Monday afternoon, I plotted out a strategy. My touchstone was a piece of advice phoned in from former Congressman Tony Coelho: "Nobody will remember what happened to you. They'll remember how you handle it." My first day back would set the tone.

Tuesday morning it seemed as if everyone in town were stopping by on a condolence call or phoning in an encouraging word. Hillary, who had thoughtfully noticed that I hadn't fought my fate with off-the-record comments to reporters, called to say, "You're a class act, Mr. Stephanopoulos." Warren Christopher walked into my office with moist eyes: "This can be a cruel town. I went through this under Carter. For a week, I was supposed to be secretary of state after Vance resigned, then I was passed over and everyone pounced." Colin Powell said exactly what I wanted to hear: "I always feel better when you're in my meetings." Washington elder Bob Strauss added exactly what I needed to hear: "You may be a young punk, but you've been around long enough to know that all this stuff doesn't make a bit of difference. Time and performance take care of these things."

Listening to the past-tense praise was a little like hearing my eulogies, which was fitting, because that afternoon I would have to perform the political equivalent of speaking at my own funeral. Gergen wasn't set to start for another week, and they hadn't decided who would do the press briefings once he came on board. So I had four more days of facing the reporters who'd become my tormentors. Tuesday noon was the start of my final run.

"Nobody will remember what happened to you. They'll remember how you handle it."

My whole staff gathered in my office to help me prepare. The substance I could manage, but style would matter more. A little California sun helped, and I had shaved extra close that morning. Even more important was my opening line: Should I act as if nothing had happened and get right to work? No, that would ring false, look like I was in denial. Everyone was going to ask about it anyway. Someone suggested Mark Twain's old saw "Reports of my death are greatly exaggerated." No, too obvious and too defensive. What I needed was something light, a little ironic, with just the right touch of self-deprecation. I had to acknowledge that the press had won and show good-humored dignity in defeat. Gene Sperling came up with the line:

"So . . . how was *your* weekend?"

My comeback had begun.

7   CLOSE ENCOUNTERS

Out of nowhere, P's half-brother turns up. P talked to mother about it. Agrees to call him before noon; nobody's home. We're trying to round up the Senate vote, NAFTA meeting, welfare reform meeting, prepare for G-7, but I spend much of the morning deciding what to do about the new half-brother. What does the P do? What do you do when you're forty-nine years old and you discover a brother you never knew you had? His mother didn't know either.

Lots of Arkansas jokes in the WH. But this is a real human problem; there's no precedent. P going to call him, invite him to the WH. Just another odd moment. No advance warning on this one. Just something to deal with.

Note to myself, June 21,1993

Just another manic Monday. The day before, a Father's Day story in the *Post* broke the news that Bill Clinton had a second half-brother he'd never met, Henry Leon Ritzenthaler of Paradise, California. Their charming rogue father, a traveling salesman named William J. Blythe II, had died in a car accident three months before the boy who would be president was born.

Back in Dogpatch. How could you not know you had a brother? That's what they'll say. Accuse us of covering up. Poor guy; can't catch a break. Every time he turns around another surprise pops out of his past. What's he going to say to his mom? What's she going to say to him? How do we ex-

plain this — and keep it from becoming another excuse to dissect Clinton's "character"?

These were my preoccupations as I followed my morning routine: up at six; drive down Connecticut Avenue to the Southwest Gate; wait while the German shepherd from the Secret Service K-9 division sniffs my Honda for hidden explosives; grab a black coffee from the basement mess and walk up the single flight to my new office.

The room was a study in small. All the furnishings were miniature — from the twelve-inch television to the CD Walkman with four-inch speakers; from the spindly table five feet across to the squat club chair planted by the back door behind my desk. That door was the best. With its peephole peering directly into the president's private dining room, it meant that I was connected and protected.

When it comes to White House offices, it's not the size that counts. Location, location, location. Proximity, like celebrity, is a source and sign of power. The closer you are to the president, the more people believe he listens to you. The more people believe he listens to you, the more information flows your way. The more information flows your way, the more the president listens to you. The more the president listens to you, the more power you have. This particular cubicle had even played a small role in history: Nixon aide Alexander Butterfield kept the Oval Office taping system in the back closet.

In our White House, Clinton's longtime aide Nancy Hernreich had it first. But after Memorial Day, I didn't just covet that office — I needed it. All the other first-floor offices were taken — by the vice president, the national security adviser, the chief of staff, the press secretary, and they weren't going anywhere. I could have secured space in the basement, or even a spacious corner suite with eighteen-foot ceilings in the Old Executive Office Building across the street, but that would be like owning a palace in Siberia. Even if it was just a matter of inches, my new office had to be closer to the Oval than my old one.

Proximity, after all, was now my professional reason for being. The public rationale for my job shift was to have me work "more closely" with the president. "One of the reasons for this move," Clinton had said in the Rose Garden, "is that I have missed very badly, and I have needed, the kind of contact and support that I received from George in the campaign." Putting me by the back entrance to the Oval would be proof that the president meant what he said, a sign that his kind words weren't just a graceful pat on the back as he pushed me out the door. Not quite Harry Hopkins being invited by FDR to live in the residence, but the next best thing — a space in the Oval Office suite.

The trick was figuring out how to get the prize without groveling. Asking the president directly was out of the question. It would look petty and weak and make Clinton think I didn't take him at his word. Mack couldn't really help because he had his own job worries and was thinking about bolstering his position by commandeering the president's dining room (where Michael Deaver had worked for Reagan). Gergen was maneuvering for turf too. So I called on the two biggest guns I knew: my old friend James Carville and Clinton's pal Vernon Jordan, who had befriended me upon my arrival at the White House. Both understood power and the perception of power, and both would try to help. I still don't know exactly how it happened, but one day in early June, Vernon called to let me know that Nancy Hernreich was moving into a cubbyhole on the other side of the Oval that would put her even closer to Clinton, and that her office would be mine. Five minutes later, Mack walked in to make it official.

Relieved of the burdens of managing a fifty-person staff and confronting a dyspeptic press corps, I was free to do the job I did pretty well, the job I had first started doing for Clinton early in the campaign.

Which was what, exactly? Sometimes I'd take on a special project, like helping shape the final compromise on gays in the military. But mostly my job was just to be there, by the president's side; to help give background to the press on the president's thinking and background to him on theirs; to know what was going on, what the president should say, and how to get things done; to help corral decisions to closure, assess the political impact of policy decisions, and contain mistakes before they became scandals. The president tended to take each discussion and each decision as it came. My job was to think about whether they formed a coherent whole, and to help ensure that others who met with the president didn't mistake his empathy for agreement. Clinton told the world that I was to focus on "day-to-day decision making, helping me to integrate all the complicated debates that confront my office." He told me that he liked having me around because I had a "good bullshit detector."

After a predictable flurry in the press, the president's new half-brother passed back into private life. But throughout the summer of 1993, President Clinton was confronted with close encounters of a more consequential kind: episodes of intimate decision in which individuals from Clinton's past held a piece of his presidency in their hands.

"IT WAS DIRECTED AGAINST YOU"

Jumbo shrimp and canapés on silver trays were being offered by the serenely silent staff who served from president to president. It was eight P.M., June 23, and summer light was still filtering into the parlor by the Lincoln Bedroom. You couldn't ask for a better setting at cocktail hour. But the waiters were wearing business-black jackets, not their formal whites, and no one ordered a gin and tonic or champagne — it was Diet Cokes and club sodas all around.

This wasn't a social evening at the White House. President Clinton was about to order air strikes in defense of the president he had defeated.

Two months earlier, Kuwaiti authorities had arrested fourteen men for planning to place a 175-pound car bomb in the path of former President Bush as he received an award in Kuwait City. Immediately after the arrest, Clinton ordered the FBI and CIA to determine if this assassination attempt was authorized by Saddam Hussein. The official report was due on June 24, but we already knew that the investigation had established a link between the bombing suspects and the Iraqi Intelligence Service.

Our job that night was to help the president decide how to retaliate. All of the top guns were there: Colin Powell, Les Aspin, Warren Christopher, Tony Lake, and Sandy Berger (deputy national security adviser), the vice president and his national security adviser, Leon Feurth. Mack McLarty, David Gergen, and I rounded out the group, but we were there largely for Clinton's political comfort and to provide counsel on presenting the decision to the public. For now the meeting was top secret. We met in the residence because, unlike the West Wing, it had a side door that the cabinet secretaries could enter without being detected by the press.

As the president ambled over from his bedroom on the other end of the second floor, we arranged ourselves around the parlor's coffee table. We didn't sit until the president sat; our early pretensions of informality were gone now, overtaken by the task at hand. This would be Commander in Chief Clinton's first military strike.

Before then, our foreign policy had been more a matter of words than deeds. During the campaign, it amounted to little more than a couple of speeches and a series of press releases. But winning the White House added retroactive weight to everything we had said before. Poor Haitians heard that the new American president had promised not to turn them away, so they built hundreds of rickety wooden boats to head for the promised land. Besieged Bosnians heard that he had vowed to bomb the Serbs, and they hunkered down with heightened expectations, waiting for the American cavalry. Promises that were briefly considered and barely noticed during a presidential campaign, we had learned, could set entire worlds in motion, proving again the poet's words: "In dreams begin responsibilities."

After the election, that lesson was hammered home every day. We had to reverse our Haitian refugee policy, cave on gays in the military, stall on Bosnia, and flip-flop on Iraq. In a pre-inaugural interview with the *Times* devoted largely to expressing support for President Bush's policy of "containing" Iraq, President-elect Clinton had refused to rule out the prospect of a more normal relationship with Saddam Hussein. "I'm a Baptist; I believe in deathbed conversions," Clinton had said in the familiar surroundings of his Little Rock living room. "If he [Saddam] wants a different relationship with the United States and with the United Nations, all he has to do is change his behavior."

Clinton wasn't trying to signal a shift in U.S. policy. In his own mind, he had already sent a tough message by publicly supporting his predecessor's approach. He was just being himself — the relaxed, reflective, and reasonable Bill Clinton who liked to shroud conflict in soft language and shape his thoughts by hearing how they sounded out loud. It had almost always worked for him in the past.

Not this time. Sitting on the couch across from Clinton, I winced when he raised the possibility that Saddam might be redeemed and hoped that it might escape attention. *Right.* Tom Friedman, the Pulitzer Prize–winning diplomatic correspondent who'd just been shifted to the White House beat, was the lead questioner. He was accustomed to covering Bush secretary of state James Baker, a man of notorious verbal discipline who wouldn't utter a provocative sentence on the record unless he was deliberately trying to send a signal. Noting Clinton's colorful language, Friedman wrote a front-page story saying that Clinton was ready for a "fresh start" with Iraq.

Hours before most people would read the paper, Iraq's foreign minister was on *Nightline* welcoming the new American initiative. Middle Eastern leaders wondered aloud whether the tough-talking presidential candidate was really a dove, and I was desperately in search of the *Times.* Too impatient to wait for a fax from New York, I phoned Friedman. "All hell's breaking loose, Tom. What did you write?" No one likes being awakened near midnight, but Friedman's crankiness was quickly calmed by the pleasant realization that my call meant that his competitors were chasing his scoop. I was still hoping we could fix the story for the final edition, but though Friedman may have misinterpreted Clinton, he didn't misquote him. Once Friedman finished reading me the article off his computer screen, all I could say was, "Yeah, that's what he said. Good night."

The next morning, Clinton knew he had to adamantly deny any normalization of relations with Iraq, but he wasn't happy about it. At a press conference announcing the appointment of the new White House staff, he responded to the inevitable question with a flash of temper: "Nobody asked me about normalization of relations," he said, before reasserting his intention to pursue Bush's policy. Now I was in real trouble. The olive branch to Saddam had been retracted, but Clinton had just declared war on the *New York Times*.

My beeper was already vibrating. It was Tom Friedman, and he was as angry as Clinton. "George, was I dreaming or did we have a conversation last night where you acknowledged that my reporting was right?" Friedman began. "I have won not one, but two Pulitzer Prizes, and I won't stand for being called a liar by the next president." But Friedman didn't have only his reputation to rely on; he also had the transcript. So did everyone else who had seen the *Times*. There was no denying that a question on normalization had been asked and answered.

A quick apology was our only out. For the foreseeable future, Tom Friedman would be one of the relatively few people filtering Clinton to the rest of the world; we couldn't afford to antagonize him and his newspaper any more than we already had. Convinced that Friedman had deliberately twisted his words to distort their meaning, Clinton refused to issue a personal apology. But he said I could do it for him — if, that is, I did it right. So my first job as White House communications director–designate was to publicly contradict the president-elect without making him look like a liar or a fool. The best I could do was a statement saying that President-elect Clinton "inadvertently forgot that he had been asked that specific question about normalization and he regrets denying that it was asked."

Five months later, as Clinton opened the Lincoln Bedroom meeting, we were all determined to send an unambiguous, unapologetic message to Saddam — but with weapons, not words. Even the new members of our team were acutely aware of the president's tendency to overexplain himself in streams of sentences. When Clinton was "on" (the first State of the Union), he was dazzling. But when he was exhausted or embarrassed ("I didn't inhale"), he courted political disaster.

"Don't oversell and don't undersell," advised Colin Powell — the only man in the room who'd actually commanded a battalion or directly counseled a president in wartime. David Gergen reminded Clinton that the Reagan administration had rushed to judgment after the shooting down of KAL 007. Warren Christopher, whose taciturn North Dakota nature appeared to restrain his loquacious Arkansas boss, offered a one-sentence conclusion: "You'll be judged on whether you hit the target."

Wise counsel. But that night, President Clinton didn't need to be coached. He wasn't ill informed, insecure, or itching for a fight. As Tony Lake reviewed the evidence and asked Aspin and Powell to outline the military options, Clinton silently jotted notes on a small pad. When he spoke, the questions revealed a man determined to make his decisions in the right way for the right reasons: "Are we sure the evidence is compelling?" "Is this a truly proportionate response?" "How can we minimize harm to innocent civilians?" The president pressed Powell on the best time to strike. A predawn raid, Clinton reasoned, would kill fewer people, but those most likely to be killed would be the least culpable, security guards and janitors. An attack later in the day would create more casualties but also increase the odds of killing the real culprits.

I sat by the president's right shoulder, taking it all in from an armless chair pulled a few inches back from the tight circle. But I couldn't catch every word because I had another job: keeping tabs on the president's budget, which was facing its first vote on the Senate floor. Every few minutes a waiter would hand me a note from a senator calling from the cloakroom for the president. I would take the call in the Queen's Bedroom and try to handle it myself, but a couple of the senators demanded to speak to the president. *Don't you know he's got better things to do right now than beg for your vote?*

Of course I didn't say everything on my mind, either on the phone or in the room. While I was impressed with the president's cautious deliberations that night — and more convinced than ever that he wouldn't prosecute a war to prove his manhood or improve his political standing — I also wondered if the worthiest option was the one we weren't allowed to discuss: assassination. *Sure Saddam is difficult to target, but why not go for it? What could be more moral than killing the man most responsible?* But while I believed assassination was justifiable, I understood it wasn't practical: Hussein slept in a different bed every night and was surrounded by Republican

Guards. Assassination is also prohibited by American law. Although I hadn't yet been hauled before my first grand jury, I knew that you shouldn't discuss what you know you can't do.

As the meeting wound down, the president polled the room. One by one, each of the principals voted for a cruise-missile strike. I was last in line, but I fully expected, and half wanted, the president to pretend I was part of the furniture. I was honored to be there and engrossed by the serious deliberations after weeks of defending half-brothers and haircuts, but I didn't want any attention called to my presence. Something about my age and my ignorance of war made me feel as if I didn't quite belong. I knew I didn't know all I needed to know. Maybe no one ever does. The president asked me what I thought. *OK, George, don't blow it. Say something memorable and mature. But don't try too hard. Keep it simple. No one ever got in trouble for something they didn't say.* "I don't think there's a choice, Mr. President."

It was unanimous. The first missile strike of the Clinton presidency was set for Saturday night.

Our secret held through Friday as we drafted the speech the president would deliver from the Oval once the missiles landed in Baghdad. On Saturday, Clinton maintained the illusion of business as usual with jogging and a round of golf. On a smaller scale, I did the same, running errands I never had time for during the week but returning to the White House as zero hour approached.

At 4:22 P.M. (EDT), cruise missiles were launched toward Baghdad from the USS *Peterson*, a destroyer, and the USS *Chancellorsville*, an AEGIS cruiser. Simultaneously, President Clinton sat in the Oval at a desk fashioned from the timbers of the British warship HMS *Resolute* (a gift to the U.S. from Queen Victoria) and began to consult with his counterparts. I sat in a maple chair by the president's phone, taking notes for the "tick-tock" accounts of the decision-making process that all the major newspapers would be writing that night.

President Hosni Mubarak of Egypt was first on the line: "Hello, Mr. President," Clinton said. "Can you hear me? Thank you for taking my call. I'd like you to see my ambassador right away. I know what time it is. We need to maintain secrecy. But I'd like your support on this. Sorry for calling you this late." I heard only Clinton's end of the conversations, but the calls were short and to the point. Yeltsin, true to form, was indisposed; his people couldn't find him. Yitzhak Rabin was already the foreign leader Clinton most admired: "He's a tough son of a bitch!" Clinton said after putting down the phone. The Kuwaitis and Saudis were enthusiastic, and Prime Minister Major offered his full support.

Ironically, the president who seemed most reluctant was the one whose life and honor Clinton was defending. Yes, as Clinton would later tell the world, the plot against Bush was "an attack against our country and an attack against all Americans." But it was also an attack against one man. I can only imagine what President Bush was thinking at 4:40 P.M. that Saturday afternoon when Clinton gave him the news: "We completed our investigation. Both the CIA and FBI did an excellent job. It's clear it was directed against you. I've ordered a cruise-missile attack."

"It's clear it was directed against you. I've ordered a cruise-missile attack." The paradox of presidential power distilled into two sentences. Few people live as precarious a life as an American president. Every day, someone, somewhere, is plotting an assassination scheme — and the scary truth is that even the most effective Secret Service is no guarantee against a killer willing to die. But along with the vulnerability comes awesome power: the ability to move global markets with a single statement, to obliterate an entire country by ordering the turn of two keys, to avenge an attack on his predecessor by firing cruise missiles under his command.

Clinton closed the conversation by assuring Bush that he had done everything he could to minimize the loss of life. Maybe that's what Bush needed to hear most; maybe his bred-in-the-bone patrician modesty made him a little embarrassed by all the trouble everyone was going to for him, or maybe a tiny thought he wasn't proud of whispered that if he'd only ordered our military to march on Baghdad in 1991, Saddam would be gone, he'd still be president, and this wouldn't be happening today. All I know is that when Clinton put down the phone, he seemed to be convincing himself that

Bush was behind him, instead of the other way around. "I think he thinks we did the right thing," he told me. "Thought it was a tough call."

Clinton wanted and needed Bush's approval as much as Bush needed — although he may not have wanted — Clinton's protection. Bush may have been the only man in the country, with the possible exception of Colin Powell, who could have singlehandedly stopped the attack. All it would take was a well-placed leak to the press, or a sotto voce call from Brent Scowcroft to Tony Lake. The message would suggest, perhaps, that Bush would publicly criticize Clinton for a hollow, opportunistic gesture — a hasty retaliation, based on shaky evidence, that was more about propping up Clinton's political fortunes than punishing Saddam Hussein. But that wasn't Bush's style. Whatever made him diffident at the prospect of having a military strike ordered in his defense, he kept it to himself. Presidents, especially gentleman presidents, didn't do that to each other.

It's a small, select club, a peerage, the few men alive at any one time who have served as president. What unites them, ultimately, overwhelms partisan differences or even the bitter memories of past political battles. Only they know what it's like to be president — to order troops into battle; to hate the press; to sacrifice privacy in return for power; to face the nation from the West Front of the Capitol and swear to defend the Constitution against all foes, foreign and domestic, so help you, God; to sit alone in the Oval Office late at night and contemplate the imperfect choices that are the stuff of history. Just that week, I had watched Clinton make a condolence call to Richard Nixon after his wife's death. "Nixon's so awkward" was Clinton's only comment; but it sounded less like a judgment than a wish — that somehow, someday, his fellow president would find some inner peace.

Presidents scrutinize each other across the ages as well. Not only do the White House walls have ears, they're packed with presidential eyes. Everywhere you turn, another president is staring down in silent judgment. Thomas Jefferson overseeing the cabinet table, the Roosevelts in a room of their own, John Kennedy brooding in brownish gray by the Red Room. A marble bust of George Washington stood guard on a pedestal outside the ceremonial door to the Oval Office; inside, a tiny bronze of Lincoln watched Clinton work from a small alcove carved into the wall.

Clinton returned their gaze by reading their histories. A new biography was always in his leather satchel or in a stack on the table behind his desk. A whole wall of his study was devoted to the lives of the presidents. At times it seemed as if his predecessors were the only people who could understand him. He railed at the scandal mongers in the press with Jefferson; sympathized with Wilson, whose body broke under the burdens of the office; envied Lincoln his enemies, knowing that it takes a moral challenge to create a memorable presidency. JFK inspired intense jealousy. "The press always covered up for him," Clinton said. Ike's daily rounds of golf just made him laugh. "George," he told me, "if I had won World War Two, I'd be able to play golf in the middle of the week too."

Later in the term, Clinton did learn to relax like Ike. But immediately after the Bush call, he became nervous. Tony Lake entered the Oval to report that twenty-three out of twenty-four missiles had cleared the ship cleanly. But we wouldn't know where they had landed for at least an hour. The president went upstairs to shower and change. He was scheduled to speak to the nation around seven.

At 6:20, he was back on the phone, this time to me. "What's going on?" he asked. "I can't go on without confirmation." I relayed the president's anxiety to Lake, who checked with Powell at the Pentagon. We'll know when we know, Powell said. Lake dryly reminded Powell that "the president's not into existentialism. He can't go on without confirmation." Powell knew that too, but there was nothing he could do. So Tony returned to my office and told the president that we would have to be flexible on the timing of the speech. "I think this is a sign we failed" was Clinton's superstitious reply.

Although our intelligence sources wouldn't confirm the attack, the news was starting to break all around the world. CNN went live from Baghdad and Bethesda, with Wolf Blitzer broadcasting over a cell phone in his car as he drove to the White House from his home in the Maryland suburbs. A flashing red dot superimposed on a map of the beltway tracked Wolf's progress. "Pretty pitiful visual," quipped the vice president, who had come to my office to watch the coverage and wait for Clinton with Tony and me. Soon enough the talking blip was replaced by talking heads. In a case study of preemptive punditry, CNN's *Capitol Gang* assessed the political impact of Clinton's military strike before we even knew where the missiles had landed.

But that was somehow appropriate, because CNN served as the president's intelligence agency that night: David Gergen got word from CNN's president, Tom Johnson, that several missiles had hit the target, which General Powell was then able to confirm from official sources. The president delivered his speech, and his first military attack was a qualified success — small, self-contained, ultimately inconclusive, but still a short-term victory. Relieved at the outcome, the president stood by Betty Currie's desk before heading home and told me that he had just had a "great" talk with Colin Powell. "He said our process was great. All of the options were properly explored."

A welcome coda. Someone who'd been there before had given us his seal of approval. But I detected more than gratitude and pride in Clinton's eye as he recounted the conversation. He was looking ahead. By telling me of Powell's praise, Clinton was also taking out a kind of insurance policy. Only a few months into our first term, what remained of the old Georgetown salons were already buzzing with the rumor that the chairman of the Joint Chiefs could be a president on horseback like Washington, Grant, and Eisenhower. The president and I understood without saying that every Clinton decision endorsed by Powell was another potential campaign issue denied. The general might one day enter the club of presidents. If and when that happened, Clinton would welcome him with open arms. But not yet, not without a fight.

Me neither. I made a note of the call.

HAMLET ON THE HUDSON

"I can't believe you've descended to this level of groveling exploitation."

Mario Cuomo's words look harsher now than they sounded then — the morning of March 30, 1993. Gene Sperling and I were standing over my speakerphone, but for all Cuomo knew we were on our knees. The two of us were begging him to take a seat on the Supreme Court, and he seemed to be loving every minute of it.

Earlier that morning, I had drafted talking points for the call, all the reasons Cuomo had to take the Court:

- This will be the fulfillment of your career.
- You could read and write on the big issues.
- No other job leaves a longer legacy.
- Look at history: Frankfurter, Holmes, Brandeis.
- One hundred years from now your words will still be changing people's lives and protecting their rights.
- You've been training for this all your life.

Gene and I were trying to convince Cuomo that joining the Supreme Court was both his destiny and his duty; that he owed it to himself, his president, his country — and to us. Although Cuomo's regular reprises of Hamlet were exasperating, he was still our hero. The possibility of having Clinton in the White House and Cuomo on the Court was too good to be true. From the day Justice Byron White had announced his retirement two weeks earlier, Gene and I had done everything we could to make it happen.

That morning, Cuomo was still ducking the president. Clinton had called him the day before, but Cuomo's secretary didn't put the call through, saying that the governor was in the middle of budget negotiations and couldn't be disturbed. *Yeah. Cuomo didn't take the call because he couldn't decide what to do — again.*

Clinton was ready to appoint Cuomo, assuming (as we did) that the background check didn't reveal anything disqualifying. He was the only person Clinton had publicly cited as a possible Supreme Court nominee, and Clinton's criteria — "A fine mind, good judgment, wide experience in the law and in the problems of real people, and someone with a big heart"— had been enunciated with Cuomo in mind.

But Clinton hated how Cuomo always made everything so difficult. Despite Cuomo's rousing nomination speech, despite the fact that Clinton had appointed Cuomo's son Andrew to a top administration post, the two of them were still an uncomfortable couple. Cuomo thought Clinton should consult him more and be more enthusiastic about Cuomo and his causes. Clinton thought Cuomo should defer to him a bit more; after all, he was president. Seeing them interact was like watching porcupines mate.

Andrew also wanted his father to take the Supreme Court — for all the same reasons we did, plus one more. A tough-minded political pro who'd managed his father's previous campaigns, Andrew knew that getting Cuomo reelected to a fourth term as governor the next November would be an uphill fight. Better to leave the voters begging for more, and what could be a better exit strategy than accepting a seat on the Court? Like Earl Warren before him, Cuomo would be making the historic switch from big-state governor to justice of the United States.

But the father didn't share his son's ambition or foresight. On Thursday, April 1, Clinton finally reached Cuomo from *Air Force One*, and Cuomo told him that he was leaning against being considered but would think about it. Although Clinton's patience was threadbare, he let the matter rest while he went on to the Yeltsin summit. By the next week, however, various versions of their pas de deux started to leak; the clock was running out. On April 7, I called Andrew. "We have to pull the trigger one way or another," I told him. "It can't go on like this. It's not fair to the president. We need an answer."

Andrew called his father, and he told me later that they spoke for two and a half hours. We needed a decision by day's end, and Mario finally told Andrew: "If you want me to, I'll call Clinton and take it." But an hour later, the governor faxed the president a letter saying that his duty to New York outweighed his desire to be on the Supreme Court. Another chapter in the saga of Clinton and Cuomo had drawn to a close.

The president, however, still had to fill a vacancy on the Court.

Inside the White House, we compiled semipublic lists of the most credible candidates, but everyone had a private dream pick. Clinton's favorite was Richard Arnold, the scholarly friend he had passed over for attorney general. Harvard Law's Laurence Tribe was the heartthrob of liberal lawyers who wanted someone with a pen as sharp as that of Justice Scalia. We brainstormed "outside the box" by tossing around the idea of appointing a brilliant political philosopher instead of a practicing attorney. (The Constitution does not require a law degree for service on the Supreme Court.) Professor Stephen Carter of Yale fit that bill, as did Harvard's Michael Sandel. Both had the added bonus of being younger than Clarence Thomas; they could write opinions for forty years. The wildest fantasy hit closest to home: *Wouldn't Hillary look great in a black robe?*

But the "advise and consent" clause of the Constitution prevented the selection process from becoming a mere exercise in high-concept politics. Clinton's choice had to be ratified by the Senate, where Republicans hadn't forgotten the rejection of Robert Bork, and Democrats were reeling from their recent encounters with Zoe Baird, Kimba Wood, and Lani Guinier. Sexy was good, but safe was better. We simply couldn't afford another failed nomination.

April and May passed without a decision. The president was preoccupied and unsatisfied with the candidates presented to him. He wanted a "big, bold" choice and kept asking for new names. By June, we were up against a wall. If the president didn't nominate someone very soon, there wouldn't be time for confirmation hearings and a vote before the Senate recess, and we'd run the risk of starting the October term of the Court one justice short. June 15 was the new internal deadline.

The final candidates fell into three categories. A "politician" — someone who could use formidable people skills to forge a progressive coalition on the Court. Interior Secretary Bruce Babbitt, the former Arizona governor and presidential candidate, was at the top of this pile. A "brain"— someone with a superior legal mind and literary bent who could match Scalia and Rehnquist brain cell for brain cell, brief for brief. Federal appeals court judge Stephen Breyer, a former top staffer to Senator Edward Kennedy, was the favorite here. Or a "first"— someone whose personal story would make a powerful statement, like Washington attorney David Tatel, who would be the first blind man on the Court, or Judge Jose Cabranes, the first Hispanic. But the demand for diversity was less fashionable in June than it had been in December, and there was no obvious favorite. Judge Ruth Bader Ginsburg emerged near the end of the process. Like Breyer, she would be the first Jewish justice since Abe Fortas, and the first woman to be appointed by a Democrat. More important, she was a pioneer in the legal fight for women's rights — a female Thurgood Marshall.

On Friday night, June 11, a group of us met in the Oval to review the final bidding. Babbitt and Breyer were the front-runners, but both had drawbacks. The interior secretary's aggressive attempts to reform grazing fees and mineral rights had enraged many Senate Republicans and more than a few Democrats, who had accused him of waging a "war on the West." Even Babbitt's home-state Democratic senator, Dennis Deconcini, called Clinton to advise against Babbitt. Choosing the interior secretary would also create another high-level vacancy, an unwelcome prospect given our overloaded appointment process.

Babbitt could probably have prevailed in the Senate, but the confirmation battle would have been bloody. Nominating Breyer in June of 1993 was politically impossible. He was well qualified, and he had the backing of Senator Kennedy and key Republicans like Orrin Hatch, but he also had a "nanny problem." Like Baird and Wood, he hadn't paid social security taxes for his housekeeper, and the fact that he hadn't fully reimbursed the IRS until after Justice White announced his retirement would be difficult to explain to a skeptical Senate committee.

Some of Breyer's supporters made the perverse argument that we should take a stand on Breyer precisely because he was a white man with a nanny problem. He's the best-qualified candidate, they argued, so by fighting for him we'll stick it to the diversity police and the good-government "goo-goos" in a single blow. *Yeah, that'll show 'em, you morons. Let's beat our bloody head against a brick wall one more time just to prove to the world we can take it.* The argument I made in the Oval, along with Howard Paster and Vince Foster, was slightly more restrained, and it persuaded the president. "I agree with them," Clinton said. "We don't need another gang-that-couldn't-shoot-straight story."

That left Ruth Ginsburg, but the president hadn't interviewed her yet. She was invited for a meeting in the White House residence on Sunday morning. The seat was hers to lose.

I walked into work Saturday slightly deflated. *It's not so bad. Ginsburg will get confirmed. She'll be a reliable liberal vote. At least we won't have to eat another round of nanny stories.* Ruth Bader Ginsburg was a solid choice, but she wouldn't set the world on fire like my man Cuomo.

Then Cuomo called. Andrew, that is, although it was hard to tell the difference over the phone. "Is Stephen Breyer a done deal?" he asked. "No. Why?" I replied, hoping that I already knew the answer. "Because that means this is Mario's last chance. If you pick a white male now, you can't pick a white male next time."

I couldn't believe it. Andrew was trying to put his father back in the race! What I should have done was tell him right then that Ginsburg had it, even though that wasn't yet true. But I still wanted to see Cuomo on the Court, and now there was a new inducement: If Andrew's call to me somehow led to his father's appointment, I would be the go-between who made it happen, an agent of history. *Stay cool. Hear him out. Make sure you nail him down.* In a moment, *I* would become the moron beating my head bloody against the wall.

"So, what are you getting at?"

"Did you see Mario on Evans and Novak?" Andrew continued, encouraged by the fact that I hadn't hung up the phone. "They asked him what he would do if the president called, and he said, 'I would not say no to the president.'"

I hadn't seen the show and didn't know that Cuomo had been more equivocal than Andrew led me to believe. But I had been burned enough before to be skittish. "Are you *sure* your father will accept if the president calls?" I asked. "We can't go down this road again. Before the president even thinks about picking up the phone, we have to be absolutely sure that the answer will be nothing but yes."

"Let me check." He put me on hold. Seconds later, Andrew was back on the line. "I just asked him. The answer is yes."

Well, it's out of my hands now. The Democratic governor of the state of New York has an important message for the president of the United States. Who am I not to pass it on?

"I'll get back to you."

My finger reached out to the White House operator's line with Cuomo's message still ringing in my ear. Clinton came on the line. "Mr. President, may I come up and see you for a minute? It's important," I continued, pausing for dramatic effect, "but I don't want to talk about it over the phone."

"Sure," he said. "Come on up. Are you OK?"

I was already on my way. I didn't tell Mack or anyone else, because if the president was understandably reluctant to reconsider Cuomo, it was best to let the idea die a quiet death. And if he did like it, I didn't want it diluted by other advice. When I reached the second floor, Clinton was changing from his suit into one of the Day-Glo polos he wore for golf. He was in an expansive mood; his class of Rhodes Scholars had come to the White House that morning, and later in the day he'd be heading to the British embassy to celebrate the seventy-fifth anniversary of the scholarship. Maybe that affected how he took my news. Instead of rejecting the idea out of hand, Clinton rolled his tongue behind his lower lip like a pitcher adjusting his chaw — a sign to me that he was listening, intrigued, thinking ahead to his next move. Then he asked me what I thought.

"Well, you know me, Mr. President, I'm biased. But I still think Cuomo's the best choice."

"Let me think about it."

That meant he wanted to talk to Hillary. I returned to my office and waited. A few minutes later Hillary called. "George, we need to talk about this," she said. "Can you come back up with David Gergen and Mack?"

Two weeks into my new job, I had settled into a relatively comfortable working relationship with Gergen and Mack, and I was sensitive to the fact that my news could upset the equilibrium. Gergen had been for Breyer, Mack didn't want Clinton to pick a liberal, and they both would likely perceive my collecting them for a meeting with the president as a power play. So I went out of my way to emphasize that I had "received" a call from Andrew and that I was simply passing on a message from the president.

But Clinton and Hillary seemed to be on my side. A liberal like me, Hillary had been warm to the idea of Cuomo on the Court ever since the convention. Clinton was getting positively lyrical about the prospect: "Mario will sing the song of America. It'll be like watching Pavarotti at Christmastime." Music to my ears: Clinton wanted to take the next step. He told me to tell Andrew that "the president was interested in his proposal" and that someone would get back to him after he returned from his round of golf.

That was all Andrew needed to hear. I reached him at his sister's wedding, but that didn't stop him from feeding me more talking points. Don't worry about the background check, he said. "Every tax return since 1974 is public." He also tried to reassure me about his father's psyche. "Mario will do it because the president wants him to. . . ." What came next should have made me pull the plug. "But the president really has to put it to him. Unless he puts it to him, he won't do it. He needs to use strong language, has to tell Mario that he has to do it."

Here we go again. Andrew and I were caught up in the world's oldest courtship ritual. He was telling Cuomo that Clinton really wanted him; I was assuring Clinton that Cuomo really wanted *him.* Andrew worked his father over all through the wedding, asking him four times if he was sure. I didn't have to work that hard with Clinton. Putting Cuomo on the Court seemed even more attractive to him after eighteen holes. At the British embassy that evening, he pulled me into his limo before he left. Talk about pulling rank at a reunion. All our fellow Rhodes Scholars saw me singled out for a private consultation. Even better than how it looked was what Clinton was saying. He'd thought about it and still wanted to see Ginsburg tomorrow, but Cuomo was now his top choice.

At 11:30 that night, Andrew called me one more time from a rest stop on the New York State Thruway. Mario was on board. I relayed the message to the president at 9:30 the next morning, just before his meeting with Ginsburg. After that, Clinton told me to call Andrew again and to let him know that Cuomo should expect a call around six P.M. At five o'clock, the full Supreme Court selection team was scheduled to meet in the Oval. Clinton, who liked to pull strings on secret parallel processes, would tell the Ginsburg group then that he was going with Cuomo.

Clinton didn't actually arrive in the Oval until around 5:30. Before he called in the others, he told Mack, Gergen, and me that he liked Ginsburg but was ready to go with Cuomo: "It's the right thing to do." I was so excited I could barely sit still when Bernie Nussbaum and his team entered the Oval and Clinton started to talk about his meeting with Ginsburg. He liked her, he said, but was afraid that her positions on public funding of abortion would "push her out on the cultural left. Given the fact that we're in a hole, that's a pretty clear argument to call Cuomo and reconsider." Cuomo on the Court, he added, would make "a big, powerful statement. If he doesn't say yes, we'll announce Ginsburg tomorrow."

There, he had said it. It was really happening. But before anyone could even begin to make a counterargument, Nancy Hernreich walked into the Oval with a note for me: Mario Cuomo was on the line.

My stomach sank to my knees. This couldn't be good news. It was 5:45, and Cuomo knew that Clinton was scheduled to call at 6:00. I picked up the phone in the dining room, and Cuomo started a soliloquy: "George, Andrew's been trying very hard to bring me to change my view, but I feel that I would be doing a disservice to the president. I feel that I would not be able to do what we all need, including supporting the president politically. I surrender so many opportunities of service if I take the Court. I feel that I would abandon what I have to do. I don't want the president to think that I might say yes.

"It's important to do what you believe you can do. The only two times I didn't were disasters. That's what I'm afraid of. It would be untrue to myself. It's wrong to enter a marriage that you don't feel. I don't want to be in a position to say no. The president shouldn't call me."

While I was listening to Cuomo in disbelief, Andrew called. "This is a one-hundred-eighty-degree turn from yesterday," he said. "I'm sorry."

I was too. Just to make sure, I got back on the line with the father: "I have to see the president. Let me be clear: If he calls you, you will not accept. Will you turn the president down?"

"Yes."

The game was over. Now I had to walk back into the Oval and own the failure. So much for being an agent of history. Instead, I was the master of another disaster — embarrassed, angry, disappointed, and defeated. Cuomo would never be on the Court, and I looked like a fool. My colleagues would revel in my loss, and Clinton would have a hard time trusting me again on a matter like this. On that late Sunday afternoon, however, he took it in stride, shaking his head with a slightly bemused smile that said this was what he had expected and was probably for the best. I imagined him replaying that line from the stump speech in his head: "My wife, Hillary, gave me a book that says, 'The definition of insanity is doing the same thing over and over again and expecting a different result.'"

The next afternoon, the president stood in the Rose Garden and introduced his new Supreme Court nominee to the country. The sun was shining, and a tear rolled down Clinton's cheek as he listened to Judge Ruth Bader Ginsburg accept her nomination with a tribute to her mother, ". . . the bravest and strongest person I have known, who was taken from me much too soon. I pray that I may be all that she would have been had she lived in an age when women could aspire and achieve and daughters are cherished as much as sons."

Brit Hume of ABC News broke the spell with a pointed but respectfully phrased question to Clinton about "a certain zigzag quality in the decision-making process here. I wonder, sir, if you could kind of walk us through it, perhaps disabuse us of any notion we might have along those lines. Thank you."

President Clinton: "I have long since given up the thought that I could disabuse some of you from turning any substantive decision into anything but political process. How you could ask a question like that after the statement she just made is beyond me." (Applause)

But not beyond the pale. Brit just didn't know how right he was.

"WHAT'S LOVE GOT TO DO WITH IT?"

When August turns Washington into a ten-square-mile steam bath, the best place to be is the U.S. Capitol. Its marble columns and polished stone floors throw off a chill like ice blocks in an old Frigidaire, and the air-conditioning is cranked up high for the comfort of members of Congress chafing under the perennial prerecess pressures — all-night sessions, cliffhanger votes, and nonrefundable airline tickets for the family vacation.

But on August 5, 1993, even the Capitol wasn't cool enough for Senator Bob Kerrey. It felt more like a pressure cooker. Gaggles of reporters pursued him through the halls. Republicans were reaching out to him, Democrats were trying to reel him in, the White House was bearing down on him. Governor Clinton's bullshit buddy in 1991 and candidate Clinton's bitter rival in 1992, Senator Kerrey was the final undecided vote on Clinton's economic plan — the legislation that would make or break Clinton's presidency. Would he be the fiftieth yes or the fifty-first no? Would he save the man who had beaten him? Or let him choke on the vote Clinton called "the bone in my throat"? It was Kerrey's choice.

With official Washington watching his every move, "Cosmic Bob" played to type. He went to the movies: *What's Love Got to Do With It* — the life story of Tina Turner.

Back in my office, I got word of Kerrey's walkabout and shook my head in disgust. *Figures. Same flaky shit he pulled in New Hampshire, watching videos in his van while Clinton was out shaking hands. That's how we beat him. But now he's got us by the balls.* In May, Kerrey had been with us on the first Senate vote, but he was going south. That morning, the president called him from the Oval. I didn't hear what Kerrey said, and I didn't need to. Clinton's increasingly heated responses told the whole story:

"If you want to bring this presidency down, then go ahead! . . .

"Maybe I ought to just pick it up and go back to Little Rock. . . .

"My presidency's going to go down. . . .

"Fuck you! . . .

"Fine. OK! If that's what you want, you go do it."

By then, Clinton's temper was my daily companion. I'd felt the blasts and watched them pass, seen other staff startled their first time, and mended fences with reporters who'd touched a presidential nerve. But I'd never seen him yell at a senator before, especially a senator who could cripple his presidency with a single vote. *Man, is he losing it? Maybe we'd better keep him off the phone.* But when Clinton hung up the receiver, he wasn't red at all, and his voice was flat, matter-of-fact, almost shell-shocked. "It's going to be no" was all he said.

I didn't believe it. Besides, Friday's Senate vote was a lifetime away. If we lost tonight's House vote, tomorrow wouldn't matter. So while Kerrey sought inspiration in the lyrics of Tina Turner — "I've been thinking of a new direction. . . . I've been thinking of my own protection"— Clinton and I spent the afternoon in the Oval, working the phones.

From my chair pushed up against the president's desk, I was the link between Clinton and the House Democrats — between my old life and my new. But there was one huge difference: This time, we weren't looking for enough nays to defeat a president's program or enough yeas for a symbolic show of force before the inevitable veto. Passing this economic plan, with all of its compromises and imperfections, was what we were elected to do. The opposite of Reaganomics, it reduced the deficit by raising taxes on the wealthy while cutting them for the working poor and preserving social programs for the poor and middle class. If it worked, interest rates would keep coming down, the economy would continue to grow, average Americans would be better off, and Clinton would get reelected.

Counting votes was something I knew how to do. When the day began, my five-column tally sheet (Yes/Lean Yes/Undecided/Lean No/No) showed us 30 votes short. Getting to 218 would take a

lot of hand-holding and hard dealing. The Democratic leaders —
Speaker Tom Foley, Majority Leader Dick Gephardt, and Majority
Whip David Bonior — did their part with Howard Paster up on the
Hill. Bob Rubin, Lloyd Bentsen, and Mack McLarty called everyone they knew too. But Clinton would have to get the final few
votes himself. In the end, this was his plan and his presidency. He
was commander and crew.

I was the coxswain. My official function was to get the right people on the phone, to record the deals and ensure they got done, to
pass bulletins back to the Hill and relay the responses back to Clinton. But I also served as coach and companion, prompting the president during his calls with handwritten notes, gingerly urging him
to do a little less listening and a little more demanding, helping
him decipher the hidden meanings in a member's words: "I'll be
there if you need me. . . . Don't worry about me. . . . I won't let
you down. . . . I won't let it die." With the Republican attack —
"Biggest tax increase in the history of the universe"— already ringing in their ears, the final holdouts repeated variations on a theme:
"I've been thinking of my own protection." They didn't want to say
no to the president, but they couldn't bring themselves to say yes; so
they stalled for time, hoping the president would get enough votes
without them. Some solved the dilemma by simply disappearing:
Congressman Bill Brewster spent the afternoon tooling around
Washington in his car, with his cell phone turned off.

By early evening, we'd hit a wall. Two hundred eight hard yesses,
ten short. We had to decide: Do we call the roll and count on party
loyalty and personal honor to carry us over? Or do we pull it? No
meeting had to be called, and there was no real debate. If we post-
poned the vote, it would take months of negotiation to build a new
coalition based on new compromises. Delay was the functional
equivalent of defeat. But all of the main players — Gore, Bentsen,
Rubin, Panetta — came to the Oval anyway, the way everyone grav-
itates toward the kitchen at family reunions. It's the place to be
when there's nothing left to do — except worry. They paced around
the president's desk and chomped on cookies. Clinton's nerves
showed on the shredded butt end of the unlit cigar he'd been chew-
ing all afternoon. My bloodred cuticles betrayed me.

But for the first time in our entire relationship, I was more optimistic than my boss. Usually, I was the dark one; he was Mr. Lucky. Now our roles were reversed. Maybe it was because I knew the House and its rhythms, knew that the body needed a victory even if its members didn't want to vote for it. Maybe it was the fact that Bonior, Foley, and Gephardt were taking early credit by calling the president with their vote counts. Maybe I'm more of a mood balancer than a true pessimist. Or maybe I was just fooling myself. But the more Clinton fretted over the final vote, the more I was convinced we were going to win.

We watched the roll call in Clinton's study off the Oval — a room even smaller than my office and packed with stuff. Clinton's collection of wood-shafted golf clubs leaned up against one corner, surrounded by sleeves of golf balls with the presidential seal. A rough-hewn rocking chair of light pine anchored the other corner. Kenny G. and Barbra Streisand CDs were stacked on the table under the window, next to the wall of books. A soft-focus black-and-white portrait of Hillary and Chelsea hung above the desk. To its right was the tiny Sony that commanded all our attention.

I was sitting in the leather desk chair. Clinton stood directly behind me, cigar clenched in his teeth, steadying himself like a captain on the bridge with his left hand on Mack and his right hand on me. All his tension seemed to be pulsing into me through the knot of my left clavicle. I focused my energy on the little screen, trying to will the yeas up to 218. With no time left on the clock, we were one vote behind, 211–212. I still thought we were OK, but the hand on my shoulder was growing heavy. The leadership wouldn't close the vote until there was no hope left, and I was on an open line to my old colleagues in the House cloakroom, who said we had a couple of safe votes holding back. One came in: 212–212.

Then Dave McCurdy voted no. *Bastard. He still can't stand the fact that Clinton's president while he's just another member of Congress. Trying to bring us down.* We were in the danger zone now: 212–213. We'd either win by two or lose by twenty. Close votes in the House follow the laws of political physics. You have all those guys hanging back who said they'd "be there if you need me." But they're desperate not to be needed, and everybody is watching everybody else. By voting no with six votes to go, McCurdy was trying to start the dominoes tumbling down at the last moment, so a member could reasonably say, "I was ready to vote yes, but you weren't going to win anyway." McCurdy was hoping the final holdouts would follow his lead and give him a seat at the table in the follow-up negotiations. I was certain it was an act of treachery.

Our guys hung in there: 213–213, 216–214. Two votes ahead, with four votes to go. No one remaining wanted to vote yes; the "no" column is almost always the safest place to be in a political storm. Ray Thornton of Arkansas should have volunteered first. *For godsakes, he's the president's congressman. Even if he hates every line in the bill, he should follow the lead of his constituent in chief. Coward.* When we saw another "no" flash on the screen and I told Clinton who it was, he was more incredulous than angry: "I made him president of Arkansas State. I can't believe he's doing this to me."

But Thornton did, so it took two small profiles in courage to save the day: Pat Williams, a loyal Democrat whose home was Montana, where the gas tax would really bite; and Marjorie Margolies-Mezvinsky, a freshman Democrat from Philadelphia's Republican Main Line. Her wealthy constituents would surely remember who raised their taxes. Both had a lot to lose by voting yes; neither would return to the next Congress — because they turned in their green voting cards, and the Speaker's gavel came hammering down. The final vote was 218–216. Not a vote to spare.

The president's study erupted in a riot of hugs that soon subsided into sober relief. Clinton wasn't ready to celebrate. We had lived to fight another day but learned another painful lesson in the limits of presidential power. After all of the threats and promises, after all of the carefully crafted compromises and absurdly trivial deals ("I'd really like to play golf with the president"), all we could do was watch on TV with the other C-Span junkies. Our fate, in the end, was out of our hands.

Tomorrow, it would be in Bob Kerrey's.

A little after eight, Clinton walked into the Oval dripping wet from his morning run in a driving rain. This was usually my favorite part of the day. The monitor behind my desk that displayed the Secret Service's tracking of the president's whereabouts would beep and flash "POTUS — OVAL OFFICE" in tiny green letters, which was my cue to head for Betty's desk. I knew the president's morning routine as well as I knew my own: After stretching on the patio, Clinton would walk through to the pantry for a bottle of water and a cup of coffee, then cool down by puttering around his desk or flipping through the newspapers on Betty's credenza. We staffers from his personal office would hover around him with a little light business: Betty would show him his call sheets from the night before; Nancy might hand him a stray piece of paperwork that couldn't wait, or ask him again whom he wanted to sit next to at the formal dinner that night; I would deliver my patter on the morning papers, serve up a piece of political gossip, and fill him in on the morning staff meeting. The heavy work could wait until after he showered.

That Friday morning, Gergen and Mack joined our little group. After yesterday morning's explosive phone call, they had met Kerrey for a prematinee lunch and feather-smoothing session. Now they wanted to brief the president before his final meeting with Kerrey. "Don't make it personal," Gergen said. "Talk about your shared principles." I knew it was the right advice, but I also seethed for Clinton's sake. *Spare me another Kerrey speech on principled sacrifice. Yes, he's a war hero and always will be. But he's also getting pounded on taxes back in Nebraska. That's what's going on here: He wants credit with the voters back home for no new taxes and credit with Capitol pundits for having the "courage" to stick it to the middle class even more. Give me a break.*

Clinton just nodded — "I'll be all right" — and went home to change. I returned to my office to find Howard Paster on the phone, trying to convince Kerrey not to back out of the meeting with the president. Howard and Kerrey both knew that it would be harder to vote no after a visit to the White House. Kerrey came, of course, and spent an uncomfortable but calm ninety minutes with Clinton on the Truman Balcony. But in the end, the meeting didn't really matter. Kerrey would vote for the bill because he had to, even if he didn't know it yet. Like Clinton, he couldn't afford to make it personal.

Even if Kerrey didn't respect Clinton, even if a side of him still sought revenge for 1992, or even if Kerrey sincerely believed that

the bill wasn't good enough, he couldn't vote no. He may have held
Clinton's fate in his hands, but he didn't fully control his own. It was
too late. If his conscience truly called him to vote no, he should
have said so — clearly, unequivocally, publicly — before the Democrats in the House walked the plank the night before. *Kerrey may be
a little flaky, but he's not crazy. There'll be a lynch mob in his office if he
votes no. He'll be finished as a Democrat.* Once the House hit 218, Kerrey's decision was made for him. A "no" vote after that wouldn't just
be a blow to Clinton, it would betray the bulk of the House
Democrats. They'd have the worst of both worlds: a damaging vote
on taxes and nothing substantive to show for it.

But there was still a chance, however slim, that Kerrey could pull
a Gadhafi, commit a senseless, irrational, self-destructive act. Thank
goodness for Liz Moynihan. She and her husband, Senator Pat,
were Kerrey's close friends and early campaign supporters. Like the
Cuomos, the Moynihans kept their politics in house. Liz ran all of
her husband's campaigns and was his chief political strategist. That
Friday, she convinced Kerrey that loyalty to both the Democratic
Party and his own future ambition to be a Democratic president demanded that he vote yes.

That did the trick. But the drama had to play itself out, and talk
of high principle gave way to hard bargaining. In return for his vote,
Kerrey wanted Clinton to make him chairman of a new Presidential
Commission on Budget Discipline. While this horse-trading seemed
more high-minded than the deals cut by other senators (Deconcini
traded his vote for a mention in the president's Oval Office speech,
fund-raising help, and a job for a longtime aide), it still required
bare-knuckle negotiating.

I didn't like the idea because I feared that a commission could
lock us into a long-term strategy of cutting even more government
benefits for people who needed them. But I also knew Kerrey had
us over a barrel. The vice president was apoplectic at the thought of
Kerrey's trampling on his turf. He thought the commission would
overshadow the Reinventing Government initiative he was scheduled to launch in the fall, so his chief of staff, Jack Quinn, and I were
deputized to edit Kerrey's draft in a way that would reduce the potential conflict with Gore. In the end, we managed to weaken Ker-

rey's mandate by expanding it, renaming the group the White House Commission on Economic Priorities. A commission that broad would inevitably become nothing more than a debating society.

But Kerrey didn't budge, and the negotiations shifted to Majority Leader George Mitchell's office in the Capitol. We followed the faux debate on C-Span (every senator already knew how every other senator was voting) and waited for Kerrey to announce that he'd made up his mind. The call finally came to the Oval at 8:20 P.M.

Clinton was silent. He just chewed his lip and nodded his head to the rhythm of the upright thumb he was pumping in my direction. It would be OK. Less than a minute later, the phone was back on the desk, and Clinton was dumbstruck from yet another strange encounter with Cosmic Bob. After forty-eight hours filled with screams, threats, promises, and demands, Kerrey had just called to tell the president, "This one's for free."

Free, my ass. Kerrey went to the floor and delivered a broadside against Clinton, calling him "green and inexperienced," and followed up with a few self-righteous shots about how "my heart aches with the conclusion that I will vote yes for a bill which challenges Americans too little." Not five minutes later, Kerrey was in Mitchell's office, closing the deal on his commission, but for appearance's sake, he didn't want it announced until a decent interval had passed.

Howard called me from the majority leader's office to let me know that Kerrey was still negotiating, and I relayed the message to the president up in the residence. I also told him about Kerrey's speech, which irritated him, but he didn't let it spoil the victory. He and Hillary were having too much fun. "You know what my wife just said, George?" He chuckled. "'Every woman in the Congress voted for you. They've got more balls than the men.'"

So we won — and our plan did work. The Republican party line that Clinton's plan would be a "job-killing poison" for the economy was flat wrong. At the time, we couldn't have imagined how right we were, but we did know that we'd be in a world of hurt if we lost. A failed vote would mean a failed presidency. Winning meant redemption, and a second chance. *Forget about Zoe, Kimba, Lani, Waco, Haircut, Travelgate, Gays in the Military; we passed our economic plan — did what we were elected to do. The economy, stupid. Remember?*

But we didn't just dodge a bullet; we did some good. An über-wonk with a heart as pure as you'll find in politics, Gene Sperling gave a speech to the staff in the Roosevelt Room that put the whole ordeal into perspective. "People say I'm too obsessed with numbers," he said while glancing down at a sweaty scrap of paper. "Well, let me tell you some numbers — one hundred thousand poor mothers and their babies will be healthier because of the child nutrition program; one hundred thousand more poor kids will get to go to Head Start; fifteen million working families will get a tax cut with our earned-income tax credit; and twenty million more young people will get student loans at better rates." Reducing the deficit was what we had to do, but we also did a little of what we wanted to do — what we cared about when we started.

After the president's victory speech, a bunch of us went to Bice, an Italian restaurant near the Capitol, to celebrate the final act of the 1992 campaign. It was the old War Room gang: Carville, me, Mandy Grunwald, and Stan Greenberg — Sperling showed up late, as always. Halfway through our postmidnight supper, a tray of drinks arrived at our table, from the gentleman in the far corner — Senator Bob Kerrey.

We nodded our thanks and wondered out loud about what it meant. The gesture, like the man, was graceful, awkward, and ironic all at the same time. What was he saying? *"I forgive you for pressing me so hard"*? *"It's you who should be sending me the drink"*? *"I'm glad I did it"*? *"Congratulations. You guys won"* (it didn't feel like "us guys")? or maybe just *"Let's hope this works"*? On the way out, we stopped at his table, but no one knew what to say. We shuffled our feet, mumbled our thank-yous, and went on our way.

The moment wasn't right. But I would have loved to pull up a seat for a real talk with our former adversary and reluctant ally. Kerrey's detachment, his cool, his intellectual curiosity, his ability to do what he needed to do while letting you know that he understood it might not mean much in the end, appealed to the part of me that was afraid to believe too deeply in anything. He was frustrating in a fascinating way.

I was still grateful, however, that Clinton was my president. He may not have had Kerrey's ethereal, ice blue charm — he was too

"out there" for that. He may not have been a hero like Kerrey —
Vietnam wasn't his finest hour. But with all his raw, naked, intelligent, profound, and profane humanity, Clinton really did feel other
people's pain, and he was determined to do something about it.

Courtesy of Bob Kerrey, he still could.

MYSTERY

"Webb, it's George; I'm afraid I have some bad news."

"What is it?"

"Vince killed himself."

"What?"

"Vince killed . . ."

"No. Whaaat?"

"Vince, I'm sorry, Vince . . ."

"What? I don't believe . . ."

Seven times he asked; seven times I answered. It was a little before 9:30 on the night of July 20, 1993. I found Webb from a phone
by the map room on the first floor of the residence. Minutes before,
Bill Burton, an assistant to Mack McLarty, had crashed in from the
colonnade with the news: Vince Foster's body had been found in a
wooded area off the GW Parkway. Early signs pointed to suicide.

Mack looked stricken, but he quickly clicked into checklist
mode. "I'll call Hillary," he said. "You call Webb." We couldn't tell
the president; he was on the air, chatting with Larry King in the library across the hall. At the next commercial break, Mack fixed the
president with a stare to signal that our reluctance to extend the
show wasn't just our usual fear that an overtired Clinton would say
something we'd all regret later. When King said good night, Mack
ushered the president to the elevator with an arm on the back of his
elbow. Clinton's head dropped, and he seemed to steady himself on
Mack's arm as they rode upstairs.

A few minutes later, I went up to the second-floor kitchen to get
Clinton's guidance for a presidential statement we'd have to issue
before the evening ended. But he had no head for official duties that
night. In shirtsleeves, with red eyes but still no tears, the president

was thinking about his boyhood friend and the family he had left behind, about his private grief, not public relations. "You know what to say," he said, not unkindly, just preoccupied. "I have to go see Lisa" (Foster's wife).

When Clinton left for Foster's house, I returned to my office, reviewed the brief statement Dreyer had drafted, read it to Clinton over the phone, and left. Jennifer Grey was in town, and I needed to talk to someone who wasn't immersed in our closed world. At a time when I probably needed them most, my hyperreactive political instincts were shutting down. Jennifer poured me a drink and drew me a bath as I struggled to make sense of what had happened. I didn't know Vince well; he wasn't a friend. But he was my colleague, and he'd killed himself. *How could that be? Is the pressure more intense than we know?*

By the next morning, official Washington's highest-ranking suicide since Secretary of Defense James Forrestal in 1949 was fast becoming a political scandal. Inside the White House, we were captured by grief, confused by the inherent inexplicability of suicide, and convinced that we had a duty to preserve as much privacy as possible for both the Fosters and the Clintons. Focused on ourselves, we walked through the halls with careful looks, huddled in corners and consoled one another with a touch on the shoulder or a hug: "Are you OK? Are you sure? Do you want to talk?" If this could happen to Vince — Clinton's "Rock of Gibraltar"— maybe it could happen to anyone.

Trying to comfort us, the president called the staff together in room 450 of the Old Executive Office Building. He urged us to understand that what happened to Vince "was a mystery about something inside of him" and reminded us "that we're all people and that we have to pay maybe a little more attention to our friends and our families and our coworkers." At his press conference, Mack echoed the theme: "Try as we might, all of our reason, all of our rationality, all of our logic, can never answer the questions raised by such a death." Somewhat less elegantly, I told the *Post:* "The fundamental truth is that no one can know what drives a person to do something like this. Since you can't ever know, it's impossible to speculate on it. In the end, it is a mystery."

This was the White House line, and I believed it was true. But it made sense to the world only if you understood what we were feeling inside, only if you were part of our family. To more skeptical ears, Clinton's refusal to speculate on Vince's psychological state and our preemptive insistence that Vince's suicide could not be explained by examining his White House work sounded as if we were trying to shut down a legitimate inquiry — which guaranteed, of course, that this was just the beginning. At a White House briefing a week after Vince's death, Dee Dee was asked 139 questions about the Foster case. Over the next month, the *Times* and the *Post* each published six front-page stories on the suicide, and William Safire used his column to make it a cause célèbre.

Combine the predictable press interest with Vince's involvement in the travel office imbroglio, with our claim that the White House counsel had to control Vince's papers to preserve his attorney-client privilege with the Clintons, with the confusion over who had been in Vince's office and what had been done there, with the belated discovery and release of a torn-up note from the bottom of Foster's briefcase, and you have the circumstantial seeds of a full-blown scandal. By trying to preserve a measure of Foster's privacy, we invited more invasive scrutiny. By thinking like lawyers, we risked being questioned like criminals. By emphasizing the "mystery" of suicide, we appeared to be manufacturing a cover-up. Our human reactions were read through the prism of post-Watergate politics: Every president is Nixon until proven innocent.

On July 21, the park police said that Foster's injury was "not inconsistent with that of a self-inflicted wound." By August 11, that was their official finding. Subsequent investigations by two independent counsels, congressional committees, and countless investigative reporters may not have convinced ardent conspiracy theorists, but they have confirmed beyond a reasonable doubt that Vince Foster shot himself in Fort Marcy Park, Virginia, on July 20, 1993. Why he did it, we still can't really know.

"Suicide," writes A. Alvarez, "is a closed world with its own irresistible logic." The same can be said of a Washington scandal. When Vince Foster — White House lawyer, president's friend, first lady's confidant — took his own life, the two closed worlds collided like smashing atoms, setting off a chain reaction that Vince would never have wanted and could never have imagined. His suicide raised suspicions; the suspicions spawned scrutiny; the scrutiny sparked resentment and resistance; and the inevitable "cover-up" charge that followed, in the "irresistible logic" of a modern Washington scandal, led to the appointment of an independent counsel. The rest, as they say, is history.

How history will eventually judge Vince Foster and the president we both served is not yet known. But a few weeks before his death, in an interview with Margaret Carlson of *Time*, Vince may have revealed what he feared. His achingly laconic lament is a fair warning for those who aspire to high White House service: "Before we came here, we thought of ourselves as good people."

The pressures were getting to me too. So much had happened in the two years since I met Clinton. . . . And now this. A few weeks later, I started to see a therapist. All of the usual reasons — relationships, family, work — motivated me, but they were magnified by the shock of Foster's suicide and the hothouse aspects of my job. Even this most personal decision seemed to have a public component, which made me hesitate. *Will it get out? How will it look in the* Post? *What if my therapist is subpoenaed? Will she talk?* In the wake of Foster's suicide, White House staffers were vaguely encouraged to "get help," but admitting to mental health treatment was still a political taboo. The memory of Reagan's "invalid" smear of Michael Dukakis in 1988 stuck in my mind. I wondered if I might one day be victimized by a similar allegation, and what would happen if I couldn't deny it. Although I wasn't ashamed of seeking treatment, I instinctively calculated the political fallout.

Then there was Clinton to think about. (*"Is there anything at all, anywhere in your background, that could ever come back to embarrass the president?"*) I knew he wouldn't veto my decision, but I thought he had a right to know. When I entered the Oval to tell him, he responded perfectly — with a shrug of his shoulders that said it was no big deal for him and a look in his eye that said he was concerned about me.

So every Friday evening, shortly before seven, I would leave the White House. Early on, even that one hour away at the tail end of the week felt like stolen time. *What if the president needs me? What if he discovers he doesn't?* But my therapist, a woman who didn't say much but understood that I had to be weaned from my work, had two rules: Failing to show was forbidden except in case of extreme emergency, and I had to say whatever was on my mind — no censoring, no spin.

I did my best. For all the ups and downs, working in the White House was still the greatest privilege of my life. I wanted to do well at it, and enjoy it, and do some good. I wanted to stay, but I needed some help.

8   DOING THE JOB

The night before the most inspiring day of his presidency, Clinton rose at three A.M. to read his Bible — the Book of Joshua, with its tale of Jericho's fall and the Israelites' conquest of Canaan. He was searching for words as meaningful as the impending moment. In a few hours, at eleven A.M. on Monday, September 13, the three thousand folding white chairs on the lawn below his study's window would be filled with witnesses to an unprecedented event. Israeli prime minister Yitzhak Rabin and Chairman Yasir Arafat of the PLO were going to shake hands and pledge to return the ancient lands of Judea and Samaria to a time when "the land had rest from war" (Joshua 11:23).

The concerns that woke me were less lofty. *What time should we open the gates? Will everyone get in? Who did we leave off the list? What if it rains? Did Safire's column screw us or play it straight? What if it falls apart and everyone blames us?* The president was doing his job, and I was doing mine — a job I first learned in my father's church. That morning, Clinton would preside at a kind of liturgy on the White House lawn. I was his altar boy, hoping to serve peace by serving my president — sweating the details.

A few days earlier, the good news had arrived without warning. Tony Lake picked me up on the way to the Oval to tell Clinton that

Arafat had signed the mutual recognition agreement between Israel and the PLO. Clinton responded by repeating what Rabin had said to him on the phone in the Israeli's throaty bass monotone — a sneak preview of the resigned resolve Rabin would later show the world: "After all these years of fighting with Arafat, I can't believe I'm doing this. But after all, you don't make peace with your friends. You make peace with your enemies." That didn't mean he was ready for a celebration. But the president had nudged his new friend privately and publicly, and when Rabin was convinced that a ceremony would cement the agreement, he accepted Clinton's invitation to the White House.

We had seventy-two hours to make it happen.

Mack asked me to manage the process with Rahm Emanuel — not the diplomatic negotiations, of course, but the ceremony surrounding them. Starting Friday, we convened two "countdown" meetings a day in the Roosevelt Room with staffers from every White House office: the National Security Council, the social office, press and communications, public liaison, legislative affairs, and the Secret Service. All hands on deck asking every conceivable question: *Who's on stage? Who signs? On what? Can we get the table Carter used in Camp David? Who speaks? For how long? Where do the Russians fit in — and the Swedes? How do we make sure we hit prime time in the Middle East?*

Where should the ceremony be? Rose Garden? Too small? South Lawn? Whom do we invite? Former presidents? Secretaries of state? How about members of Congress — they'll all want to come. At least the Arab and Jewish members? Big contributors? Sure, but how many? How do we screen them all in through security? Do we do a dinner? Too festive? What about the press? Anchors on the lawn? What do we say? How do we encourage the peace process without appearing to take credit for something we didn't really do? How do we seize the opportunity without seeming opportunistic?

We all knew that a successful ceremony on the White House lawn would be a political boon to Clinton, but we were careful not to say so: Taking credit wouldn't only be crass, it would backfire. I was responsible for judgment calls, asking the right questions and anticipating the appropriate answers, making sure to preface every decision with "If it's going to help the diplomatic effort, we should . . ." This wasn't just camouflage. All of us were awed a bit by the moment's potential. We didn't know if peace would last, but the possibility that it might made us more conscientious and humbled us. Getting everything right was now a higher obligation; getting the *chance* to get everything right was a gift.

The joy of my job often bubbled up in unlikely moments. Like Saturday morning, the first time we practiced the handshake. This was just a dry run: four guys in jeans around my desk, trying to figure out how to make this diplomatic tango flow. First came the signatures, with multiple copies of the treaty, all needing multiple signatures. Then the president would turn to his left, shake Arafat's hand; turn to his right, shake Rabin's hand; take a half step back with his arms slightly lifted from his sides and hope that Arafat and Rabin reached across his belt for the picture of the decade. I had helped plan hundreds of photo ops before, but this time the stagecraft wasn't just spin. The handshake really would happen, and the whole world would be watching. And if we got everything right, and were lucky, the moment might have just enough magic to make a difference.

Monday morning the sun was shining. The Safire column was perfect. ("Why am I getting to see the president?" he had asked me. "I'm not going to bullshit you," I replied. "We don't think you've been fair on Vince [Foster], but we're trying to build support for the agreement in Israel, so we have to build support among American Jews, and a certain segment of American Jews is going to take its cue from you.") A phone call from the president pulled me out of the staff meeting. "George, I feel really good about the speech. I've been up since three working on it, and I think I got it down. I'll be down in ten minutes with the changes."

Which meant I had at least half an hour. In the final countdown meeting, Rahm and I thanked the team and tried to make sure everyone went out of the way to be deferential. "Imagine that you're ushering the guests into a church or synagogue," I told them. Rahm, who had served as a volunteer in the Israeli army, went even further: "You have to understand that even if we do this perfectly, there will be a lot of people leaving this ceremony today whose feelings are going to be unfinished. This isn't pure happiness for all of them, and you have to respect that as well."

The president entered the Oval in an effervescent mood with an iridescent tie — shiny gold horns against a deep blue background, a nod to the trumpet blasts that felled the walls of Jericho. He joked about how he liked Joshua because the only person he left standing in Jericho was Rahab, the prostitute. We finished editing the speech, adding an excerpt from the Koran suggested by Prince Bandar of Saudi Arabia, and I was happy that my one-line contribution —"Throughout the Middle East, there is a great yearning for the quiet miracle of a normal life" — had survived. Everyone was buoyant, but every few minutes Martin Indyk, our liaison to the Israelis, would walk in with a note signaling another diplomatic snag. ("The Israelis aren't coming if Arafat wears a uniform." Tony replied on the back: "Tell him to take the medals off, say it's a safari suit, and see if they'll accept that.")

By now, almost all of the nits had been picked. Arafat wouldn't wear a gun, or a uniform. Clinton was confident he could coax Rabin and Arafat into a handshake, but there was still the matter of the hug. What if, at the decisive moment, an exuberant Arafat upset the fragile diplomatic equilibrium by embracing the president? We had to show enthusiasm but not exuberance, and Clinton's a hugger by nature. The national security adviser devised a defensive strategy — a modified elbow block augmented by a bicep squeeze. Now for the implementation: Lake played the president; Clinton was Arafat. If Arafat leaned in for a kiss, Clinton would reach his left hand above Arafat's elbow, hook his thumb around his bicep, feel for an artery, and squeeze. If that didn't work, we joked, the president would resort to that time-tested, last best defense against an unwelcome advance — a knee to the groin.

We all laughed, but nothing was left to chance. The last thing I said to Clinton was, "Think about your face." He knew enough not to have a big grin at the big moment, but if he overcompensated, it might look glum, and most people's faces in repose look blank, almost dumb. "The one thing you have to be careful of, I'm embarrassed to say it," I said haltingly, "is your expression when you step back and they shake hands. It will be a permanent picture." And I *was* a little embarrassed to bring it up, but I was even more worried that a perfect moment would be marred by a tiny oversight. We practiced a closed-mouth smile.

During the preceremony reception in the Red Room, I felt as if I were watching an elaborate quadrille in an intrigue-ridden Russian court. Little cliques revolved around the room, eyeing their counterparts, whispering under their breath, waiting to see what would happen when Rabin and Arafat arrived. Shimon Peres, the Israeli foreign minister, was the happiest man in the room, his dark and deeply lined face now brightened by a constant smile. Not Rabin. A warrior, more conservative than his foreign minister, he had the air of a man who wanted to be somewhere, anywhere else. When the Palestinian entourage approached, Rabin's scrum slid silently toward a corner of the room. The rest of us pretended not to notice by discussing Arafat's attire: safari suit or soldier's uniform? "I think it's a safari suit." Hillary laughed. "Don't you?" But Martin Indyk was still nervous. He ran my way with the latest potential crisis. The single medal Arafat kept on his chest was the Jerusalem Insignia, a subtle reminder of the disputed Palestinian claims to the city. What if the Israelis demanded that he take it off?

They didn't, but there was one final snafu. Peres had promised the Palestinians that they could sign the document "for the PLO." But the text said "for the Palestinian delegation," and they wouldn't sign. Saying, "It doesn't really matter," Peres offered to pencil in "PLO." Then they went to clear it with a reluctant Rabin. More delay. But with the clock ticking toward eleven, with three thousand people waiting on the lawn and a billion more watching on television, there was no turning back. "For the PLO" it was. I scurried out to the lawn seconds ahead of the honored guests and took my seat next to Rahm in the back row.

The ceremony floated by like a dream. Rabin still looked fretful; his improbable partner, Arafat, was ecstatic, and at the climactic moment Clinton seemed more a president than ever — calm, confident, and fully in control as he took his half step back with his half smile in place and gently cleared a path. The crowd took a collective breath. Then Arafat and Rabin grasped each other's hands and pumped them up and down, and the entire lawn exploded — Arabs and Jews, Christians and Muslims, Republicans and Democrats, joined for a moment in joy.

Soon we were sober again, listening in silence to the eloquent pain of Yitzhak Rabin. "It's not so easy," he said, almost to himself. But his scarred voice gained strength when he said, "Enough of blood and tears. Enough!" And as he accelerated through the seasons of Ecclesiastes to declare that "the time for peace has come," I put my arm around my sobbing friend Rahm — and cried too, thinking of those who'd fought by his side and those who might not have to fight again, believing this moment might last. When the prime minister closed with a line from the Hebrew prayer book — "May He who brings peace to His universe bring peace to us and to all Israel"— we all exhaled our hope: Amen.

After church, my dad was always in a cheerful mood. He would pinch us altar boys on the cheeks as we threw off our robes, and laugh over a lunch of avgolemono soup before taking his nap. Some of it must have rubbed off on me, and I sensed the same mood in Clinton. As he ushered Rabin back to the private dining room by my door, I rushed through hugs on the lawn and worked my way back to peer through the peephole in my office. I almost never invaded the president's privacy like this, but now I couldn't resist. I had to see the two of them sitting there, statesmen at lunch. When they finished, I waited by Betty's desk to walk Clinton home for an hour's rest. He couldn't wait to hear the early reviews and invited me to elaborate: "Do you really think I did OK? I couldn't tell from up there." He reciprocated with an anecdote from the moment before he was called to the lawn with Rabin and Arafat.

"You wouldn't believe it," he said, setting the scene. "It was just the three of us." Then he slipped into Rabin's voice and uttered a single word: "Outside." Again, "Outside." Arafat had reached over for a private handshake, but Rabin shook his head and said, "Outside," which meant, I imagined, *I know what I have to do, but I'll be damned if I'm going to do it until it's absolutely necessary.* Rabin then softened the rebuke by filling the silence: "You know we have a lot of work to do." Arafat answered in kind: "I'm willing to do my part."

Clinton let me feed the press Rabin's and Arafat's final private words without the part about the refused handshake. It was a delicious detail, but it was too raw to use. Why risk misinterpretation? Not that anything could spoil this day. Official Washington's cynicism was suspended, and everyone was caught up in the spirit of reconciliation. On the way to the residence, we ran into Barbara Walters, who asked for a quick interview with Clinton. It was soft and brief, and when the cameras were off, she approached Clinton with one more request: "Is it proper to ask a president for a hug?"

Later that afternoon, we convened Jewish and Arab American leaders for an unprecedented White House working session. When Clinton finished his brief remarks, the dignitaries stormed the stage like teenyboppers, holding up their programs for autographed mementos. I relished calls from the same reporters who often ruined my day. Bill Safire: "The best speech Clinton's ever given." Brit Hume: "I have no questions. You did a helluva job, and it's the best thing you've ever done." Tom Friedman: "Today Clinton made me proud to be an American, and Rabin made me proud to be a Jew." Ann Devroy: "Even I can't think of anything negative to say; it's just too good to be here." *Yes, it is.*

It seemed like a day when all was forgiven and anything was possible. At the president's private reception on the Truman Balcony, I told former Secretary of State Cyrus Vance, "I hope we can do the same in Bosnia," before Zbigniew Brzezinski, his Carter administration nemesis, interrupted: "George, why don't you go down and get some library books for me?" At Columbia, I had been his research assistant, an exalted title for someone whose two main duties were delivering library books (Napoleon's memoirs in French) and lunch (pastrami on brown bread with mustard). Now we traded war stories: "It takes two terms to learn how to do these jobs," he said, reminding me one more time that the last three Democratic presidents hadn't had that chance. Colin Powell walked in. "Hey, superstar," I said, a teasing reference to the general's cover photo on that day's *U.S. News and World Report.* "Give me a break." He laughed. "I've only got sixteen days left in this business." *Sure, until you run against us.*

Well, I'd almost made it — an entire day without a dark political thought. But as much as I admired the general, he was still the potential opponent I feared most. The *U.S. News* article, entitled

"Colin Powell Superstar: Will America's Top General Trade His Uniform for a Future in Politics?" was the mother of all puff pieces:

> Powell could become another Eisenhower, a military hero who floats above partisanship and taps into mankind's oldest myths about the virtues of the warrior-king. . . . Powell is a political tidal wave waiting to happen. . . . By almost 3 to 1, respondents think Powell . . . would do a better job than Clinton in foreign affairs. . . . By more than 2 to 1, Americans think Powell would do a better job than Clinton in fighting crime and drugs. . . . A Republican Powell would defeat Democratic President Clinton by 42 percent to 38 percent in a head-to-head election held today.

As Powell enjoyed his final days as chairman of the Joint Chiefs of Staff, we engaged in a series of quiet talks on a "Colin Powell strategy" with Vernon Jordan, the Clark Clifford of the nineties, as our wise man. Though Powell had rebuffed earlier feelers from Jordan, we still held out hope that his role model was George Marshall rather than Dwight Eisenhower — that over time he wouldn't be able to refuse the chance to be America's first black secretary of state.

Our immediate concern was what honor to bestow on Powell as a retirement gift. Our goal was to offer a prestigious appointment that would show respect without signaling weakness or appearing to pander. Mack asked me to secretly research the procedure for awarding a fifth star to a general. What I discovered from the Pentagon pretty much ended the discussion. Only five generals in American history had achieved the distinction, and the last one was World War II hero Omar Bradley in 1950. Despite the Persian Gulf victory and his earlier service in Vietnam, it would be hard to argue that Powell had a comparable battle record. That obstacle, combined with the fact that the honor would require an act of Congress, was enough to kill the idea.

When I reported my findings to Clinton, he said that he had reached the same conclusion from a different angle. Had it been a clear-cut case, I'm sure Clinton would have recommended the award for Powell. But since it was a close call, Clinton reasoned that rewarding Powell would be a political trap. If Powell did challenge Clinton, the fifth star would forestall criticism of the general's military record. Instead, we discussed something politically innocuous, like asking Powell to chair the American Battle Monuments Commission, but nothing came of it.

In his more optimistic moments, Clinton convinced himself that Powell wouldn't challenge him anyway. We discussed it on the evening of Tuesday, September 21 — the end of another good day. That afternoon, the president had signed the Americorps national service program into law, and I had just handed him a draft of the health care address he'd deliver the following night. Betty Currie and the president's valet, Glen Maes, were standing in the outer office, hoping that I'd hurry him along so they could go home and he could get some rest. But on my second trip back, he was still packing up his desk. Without looking up from his open briefcase, he said, "I think things are starting to come together." It was nice to hear, because despite a few good days, the president had been in a funk since August. Now he talked brightly about bringing in his old friend and our 1992 convention manager, Harold Ickes, to shore up our political operation. Next he brought up Powell. "You don't think he's going to run, do you?"

"I don't know. I still think he might, but I'm not sure."

"I don't think he's going to run. He's going to pull an Eisenhower and sit one out," Clinton declared, punctuating the point by snapping his case shut and asking me to walk him home. Strolling through the colonnade, we discussed the new Richard Reeves book on Kennedy's White House years. Not wanting to spoil the mellow mood, I went for a full suck up, saying that reading about some of Kennedy's early trials made me feel better, because "he made a lot more mistakes than you did, Mr. President." Clinton turned the conversation to how debilitated JFK had been from Addison's disease, saying he was amazed to read about how Kennedy's cortisone treatments supercharged his sex drive. As John, the white-tied operator, held the elevator door, Clinton disputed Reeves's claim that JFK was the first president to run from outside the system and urged me to read the Vidal and Oakes books on the man who was his favorite president — a one-term congressman from Illinois who had created his own base and captured the presidency. Clinton didn't mention what he also knew. In 1864, a general named George McClellan had failed to wrest the White House from President Abraham Lincoln.

But that night, no president was more present to Clinton than Franklin Delano Roosevelt. America's longest-serving chief executive, FDR had secured his place in history during his first term, when he convinced Congress to create Social Security. Clinton almost seemed to regret the fact that he didn't face Roosevelt's challenges: not even a cold war to contend with, much less a world war, and the economy, thank goodness, was going strong. The president was determined, however, to forge another New Deal, to succeed where FDR, Truman, Kennedy, Johnson, Nixon, and Carter had all failed, to be remembered as the president who made basic health care, like a secure retirement, the birthright of every American.

On the second floor, Hillary was waiting for him — Eleanor to his Franklin. Health care was her baby, a sweeping program that would save lives and prove to the world that a first lady could be a fully public presidential partner. Working with Ira Magaziner, she had established a wholly owned subsidiary within the White House, with its own staff, its own schedule, and its own war room, called the Intensive Care Unit. She devoured briefing books, pored over polls, presided at public hearings, schmoozed with senators, buttonholed representatives, and barnstormed the country preaching (without notes) the virtues of preventive care, cost control, and the peace of mind that comes with national health care that's "always there." The public loved it, rewarding her with standing ovations and sky-high poll numbers. (By September, the president had fought his way back to statistically equal favorable/unfavorable ratings, while Hillary's margin of approval was two to one.)

But inside the White House, she must have felt like a single mom raising a problem child in a hostile neighborhood with a weekend daddy who loved his baby but was never there when you really needed him. First he flirted with the New Democrats, who pushed welfare ahead of health care. Then came the screwed-up stimulus bill. The whole summer was lost to the battle over deficit reduction. Now her husband's economic team (when they weren't surreptitiously trying to smother her baby in the cradle with endless questions about the accuracy of Ira's economic assumptions or the efficacy of his cost controls) insisted that NAFTA was the most important presidential project of the fall. Meantime, Clinton's buddy Gore wanted to steal him away so they could "reinvent government" together. To top it all off, on the night before he would deliver the health care address that was the biggest speech of her career, the president was late coming home — again.

But for all the tension that constantly crackled between them, they were compatible. I imagine that they were truly at home working through the speech together on Tuesday night. And whatever their past disagreements over health care strategy, they now shared a passionate opinion: The speech was terrible; it needed a total rewrite.

On Wednesday morning, a group of us went to the residence to survey the wreckage. The oak table in the family dining room was covered with crossed-out pages. As Clinton scrawled over the text with his left hand while gnawing on the thumb of his right, Hillary stood behind his chair and massaged his shoulders. Jeremy Rosner, the speechwriter with the hottest hand after his highly praised draft of the president's Middle East speech, was sent off with David Dreyer to complete the rewrite. I was late for a round of interviews with the radio talk-show hosts we had invited to broadcast from the North Lawn, and the president and first lady had to get dressed for their joint lunch with journalists downstairs in the old family dining room. With less than ten hours until airtime, we were back to bungee jumping without a rope.

All through the afternoon, I checked in with Rosner and Dreyer. They were the speechwriters; I was more like a shepherd, herding the text through its final stages — from the final draft to the dress rehearsal, from the prereleased text for the press to its final placement in the TelePrompTer facing the president's podium. At seven, we were still assembled in the folding seats of the family theater, watching him at the podium, shouting ideas back and forth, typing revisions directly into the TelePrompTer. Clinton never knew exactly what he wanted to say until he heard himself say the words. Shortly after eight, when the president went upstairs to shower and change, Dreyer printed out copies of the text, handed one to me and one to the president's personal aide, and headed to Capitol Hill with the backup computer disks in his briefcase. I stayed behind to ride with the president. I loved the intimate grandeur of these motorcades to the Capitol. While the cars lined up outside, we would wait for the president and the first lady in the foyer off the South Lawn. Seconds before they descended, the Secret Service agents would glide into action and the rest of us would start to hustle. I waited by the back door of the limo until the president and Hillary got in, then scrambled into the jump seat — my hands clutching his text, my knees brushing up against hers — just as the agent gave the order to roll.

As we rode down Pennsylvania Avenue, Clinton kept working. "I'm tightening it up," he chattered. "It's better now." I had my patter down, pumping him up — "It's a good speech; you really fixed it" — and pointing out where to pause — "Be sure you hold the card up long enough for everyone to get it. That's the picture." Hillary became quiet. The fear in her face was masked a bit by the heavy makeup she wore for the cameras, but I had seen it before. The tight smile, the fixed gaze, the hands folded firmly in her lap, holding everything inside — it was the look of a wife who always had to worry for two. During the campaign, she'd hide until the debate was over, retreating with a book to an empty room. But that wasn't possible now. She'd be front and center in the House balcony, the architect of the plan she hoped would be her husband's legacy.

When the president went to the Speaker's office to greet the congressional leadership, I veered off to the Speaker's lobby to give his car-ride revisions to the military aide manning the TelePrompTer. Standing over the operator's shoulder, I made sure he word-searched to the appropriate spots and inserted the proper edits. But I couldn't wait to get to the floor.

Out there, it was like being home again, only better. I headed straight for my old spot by the podium — the place where I learned to count votes and feel the will of the House. It was also the place where, seven months and several political lifetimes ago, I stood waiting for Clinton's first State of the Union. The economic plan Clinton presented that night was now law. But by the time we had squeezed out the deciding vote, our dreams had been squeezed too. At its heart, reducing the deficit was still about cleaning up an old mess, playing defense. Health care was our real chance to achieve a grand ambition.

"Mr. Speaker, the president of the United States."

Clinton ambled down the aisle, shaking hands, absorbing the nourishing cheers, picking up his pace only as he reached the well of the House, circled the three-tiered dais, and bounded up the steps to deliver his speech.

I knew something was wrong when I saw Clinton squint into the distance and slide his head from side to side as if he were trying to find a face in the crowd. Then he turned to the vice president, who turned straight to me, motioning with his index finger for me to approach the podium. *No way.* I shook my head. *There's no way I'm going up there in front of a hundred million people; it'll look like I'm going for the clutch of the century.* Gore motioned again, more insistently, widening his eyes and nodding his head. I shook my head again but started to worry. *What could it be? Is Clinton sick?* Then Gore took two steps down from his seat, and I took two steps up, still out of camera range. "The speech, check the speech. It's the wrong one."

I sprinted off the steps and rammed through the swinging doors, heading straight for the corner where the TelePrompTer operator was staring implacably into his machine, poised for the president to begin. What I saw next literally took my breath away. *This can't be. My eyes are lying.* They weren't. The electronic text is still branded on my brain:

"A NEW DIRECTION"

ADDRESS TO JOINT SESSION OF CONGRESS

BY

PRESIDENT WILLIAM CLINTON

FEBRUARY 17, 1993

Good thing Dreyer was there. I'm a computer illiterate, and the TelePrompTer operator wasn't as composed as I first thought; he was in mild shock. (Only later did he realize what had happened. Testing the TelePrompTer's hard drive earlier that afternoon, he had called up the earlier speech. Then he made a simple mistake: pressing Save instead of Delete. When the new speech arrived, it was tacked onto the tail end of the old.) As Dreyer studied the screen, the president opened with a moment of silence for the victims of an Amtrak train crash earlier that day. *Pray long and hard; we need the time.* Then he had no choice but to begin: "My fellow Americans, tonight we come together to write a new chapter in the American story. . . ."

As Clinton spoke, the old speech was scrolling down the screen. The thought of the president trying to concentrate on his delivery as gobbledygook whirred by his eyes made me sick with worry — for him and me. This screwup might not have been my fault, but it was my responsibility. "This is the worst thing that's ever happened," I muttered. "I dunno," replied Mike Feldman, the vice president's aide, "the Holocaust was pretty bad." *Very funny.*

After a moment that felt like a month, Dreyer fed a new floppy disk into the machine and scrolled furiously to catch up with the president, slowing down only as he reached ". . . talented navigator — someone with a rigorous mind, a steady compass, a caring heart. Luckily for me and our nation, I didn't have to look very far." Seven minutes into the speech, with the right words finally in front of him, the president looked to the balcony to thank his wife.

I wondered if Hillary knew something was wrong as she returned his grateful gaze and accepted her standing ovation. The crowd had no idea, and Clinton had already hit his stride. But I was still a wreck. Only returning to the chamber to actually watch Clinton at work made me feel a little better.

When he was "on" before a live audience, Clinton was like a jazz genius jamming with his pals. He poured his whole body into the speech, swaying to the rhythms of his words, losing himself in a wonky melody, soaring from the text with riffs synthesized from a lifetime of hard study and sympathetic listening. If he sensed a pocket of resistance in the crowd, he leaned its way, determined to move them with raw will if sweet reason didn't work. It wasn't a hard sell that night, especially when Clinton pulled the card from his pocket and pushed it toward the cameras.

It was a vibrant blue plastic square embossed with the United States seal and bordered by a white stripe with two gold stars on the bottom and a red bar with the legend "Health Care Security Card" across the top. A prop, sure, but it was more than that. When this battle was over, everyone in America would have one of these cards, and the guarantee that came with it — just like Social Security. Forgetting about the TelePrompTer for a moment, I recalled the New Hampshire campaign, when I had first met people like Ron Machos, who worked two jobs but still couldn't afford to pay for the open-heart surgery his two year old, Ronnie, needed to survive. The card would mean we kept our promise to them and everyone inspired by their story. Then I imagined a dusty lecture hall in the distant future. Once every semester, I would bring in the original card, pull its flaking edges from my pocket, place it on the table before me, and tell the tale of the time we lost the speech but won the war for health care.

In real life, I worried that my retirement might be coming a little sooner than I had bargained for. As Clinton concluded his speech, I worked my way to the lobby and prepared to face his wrath. But by the time the president reached the back of the House chamber, so many members of Congress had gushed their congratulations that he couldn't be upset.

"You saved us again, Mr. President," I said. "I'm sorry for the screwup."

"Yeah, what happened there?" he asked, as his right arm rested on my shoulder. But before I could answer, he had a follow-up. "I think I did OK, don't you?" Of course he did; the speech was a home run, and the way he asked was proof that he knew it. Relieved, I left to meet the press. The TelePrompTer mishap was certain to get out, so we might as well spin it our way. *"Clinton's amazing, isn't he? Can you imagine what Reagan would have done without a text?"* Too bad it would be the high point of the health care fight.

■　■　■

"What? What did you say?"

Busted. Every eye in the living room of Hickory Hill turned my way. But what really made me squirm was the arched eyebrows and brittle smile of the man who was questioning me — Vice President Al Gore.

It was Friday night, a week after the health care speech, and several dozen cabinet officials and White House staff members were gathered at Bobby and Ethel Kennedy's estate to celebrate the passage of the urban empowerment zone legislation that Vice President Gore had honchoed with HUD's Andrew Cuomo (Ethel's son-in-law). For me, this night was a welcome break from a week of battles over the vice president's Reinventing Government initiative (REGO). But as Gore rose to close the evening, after several toasts in which the speakers joked about Gene Sperling's rumpled appearance and workaholic habits, he caught me whispering to Dee Dee: "Go ahead, George, share it with all of us."

C'mon, it's Friday night. Gimme a break.

"Oh, sorry, Mr. Vice President, I just noticed that Gene's become Washington's Joey Buttafuoco. Say his name, you get a laugh."

Fortunately, everyone did laugh, including Gore. But that exchange was just some slight turbulence in an increasingly tense relationship.

I had never met Gore before 1992, although I did interview for a job in his Senate office after the Dukakis campaign. I ended up working for Dick Gephardt instead. Strike one with Gore. Gore and Gephardt ran against each other in the 1988 presidential primaries, emerging from the experience as political enemies. Gore also knew, I suspected, that after my Cuomo bid failed, I had made a last-minute bid to get Gephardt on Clinton's ticket. Although Gore and I went on to work well together during the campaign, his suspicions of me often surfaced in the White House. At the close of a particularly heated NAFTA meeting, Gore turned to me, exasperated: "George, I'm going to have to find some scientific procedure to get that Gephardt DNA removed from you."

Most of the time, though, the teasing was lighthearted. Gore is quick witted behind closed doors; he likes to make fun of himself and everyone else around him. In my case, that meant taking shots at my celebrity profile. Once, when the gossip columns were covering my relationship with Jennifer Grey, I was late from the gym for a Sunday-afternoon budget meeting, and Gore caught me trying to slip into the Roosevelt Room, my hair still dripping wet: "Where've you been, George? (Beat) Dancing?" The Lorena and John Wayne Bobbitt saga was another one of his running gags; for weeks, Gore would amuse Clinton before morning briefings in the Oval with a detailed bulletin on Mr. Bobbitt's surgical condition. The vice president was also the only person inside the White House who could really poke fun at the president. At press conference preps, he was the designated deflator. If Clinton responded to a practice question with a self-pitying rant, Gore would clap his hands and spike his fist from across the cabinet table. "Great answer, Mr. President. You got that one down!" Clinton got the message.

Clinton relied on Gore's disciplined intelligence, and from the very beginning he was sincerely committed to making him a full partner in his presidency. But Gore, wisely, took nothing for granted. Right after the election, he booked a suite at Little Rock's Capitol Hotel and solidified his place by the president's side during the cabinet selection process. He had a say in every key appointment, and Clinton gave him free rein with a few positions: Carole Browner at the Environmental Protection Agency; his college roommate Reed Hundt to head the Federal Communications Commission; and his brother-in-law Frank Hunger to run the Civil Division at the Justice Department.

Gore also went out of his way to cultivate those of us who would be on the White House staff. A few weeks after the election, he invited me to lunch. Aware of the fissures that could develop between a vice president and the White House staff, he told me that his door was always open, that he wanted my advice, and that I should come straight to him if I ever sensed a problem between him and the president or anyone else in the White House — like Hillary.

The high-level attention was heady but intimidating. Instinctively, I reverted to my subservient humble-staffer mode and told him that he was the one who'd been elected, so he was my boss as much as the president. Both of us were being simultaneously sincere and disingenuous. We liked and respected each other, wanted to get along, and knew that a harmonious White House would help us get more done. But Gore's kind words also carried an implicit threat — *"Don't even think about trying to shut me out; if it comes down to you or me, I'll cut your nuts off."* My obedient pose obscured my overconfident overprotectiveness — the belief that my close relationship with Clinton was all I would need, and that the president needed people like me to think only of him.

Our first clash came early — over the energy tax. Although I had reconciled myself to dropping the middle-class tax cut for the sake of deficit reduction, I believed that adding an energy tax to the mix was a political double whammy. Not only were we breaking our campaign pledge to cut middle-class taxes, we were raising them. Imagining future Republican campaign commercials, I kept replaying the line I'd heard Clinton repeat a thousand times: "I will not raise middle-class taxes to pay for my programs." *It'll be "Read my lips" all over again.*

Gore was the chief advocate of the energy tax, arguing that it was good for both the economy and the environment. He was backed up by the big guns — Bentsen, Rubin, and Fed chairman Alan Greenspan — and in hindsight I know he was right. But then I believed he was treating our early campaign promises cavalierly, and that he failed to appreciate how, for Clinton, middle-class taxes had become a character issue. Through the spring of 1993, Clinton would vent privately that Gore was pushing him to raise taxes too much. I knew Clinton well enough to assume he wasn't saying this to Gore at their weekly lunches, but I took it as an indirect order to keep on fighting for a lower gas tax in our internal deliberations.

On June 29, Gore and I finally had it out in front of Clinton. The question on the table was our negotiating strategy on the energy tax as the congressional conference committee prepared a final plan for floor votes. I argued for a little elbow room at the negotiating table, saying that we should adopt the lower Senate-passed gas tax rather than defend the broader energy tax backed by Gore and passed by the House. "We should be seen as reluctantly accepting a tax increase," I said. "But it's beginning to look to the country like we're in love with taxes." Gore lashed out. I was used to being yelled at by the president, but this was something new and oddly more chilling: "Damnit, George, we can't just go for a good night on the news. Think of the long term. This is the right thing to do." The president just sat there. Emboldened by his silence, I pushed the etiquette envelope. I didn't quite yell back, but my voice strained the cords of my throat and forced its way through my clenched teeth. "It's not going to do anyone any good if it doesn't pass," I seethed, "and the plan . . . can't pass . . . with this . . . high . . . a *tax*."

I won that battle, but my problems with the vice president were just beginning. We clashed again over Reinventing Government.

REGO was to Gore what health care was to Hillary — a worthy goal that grew out of control, another White House within a White House. I had no problem with the idea of saving tax dollars through better management, but I was frustrated by the fact that Gore's task force was generating ideas in a vacuum, often without regard for political reality or the president's competing interests. A small but telling example: The REGO task force recommended that the president eliminate the selective service registration system. *Of course. The president who dodged the draft now wants to do away with it. How come I didn't think of that?* No, I don't think so, particularly when it would save a grand total of $15 million — approximately 0.00001 percent of the federal budget.

I was much more worried about what REGO would mean for the rest of the president's policy agenda. Gore wanted to make a big splash by claiming that his proposals would produce $108 billion in savings. Leon Panetta, our budget director, argued that the real number was probably closer to $30 billion. If he was right (as I suspected), or even close to right, the Republicans would demand that we find other cuts to fill the gap. Which meant that the government programs we'd promised to protect — student loans, worker training, Medicare, Medicaid — would become vulnerable. I feared that our self-imposed goal would become a straitjacket, forcing us (as the president used to say) to be more like Eisenhower Republicans than Roosevelt Democrats.

I lost that battle, and late in September, a couple of days before the Hickory Hill party, I had my worst fight ever with the vice president. The REGO task force had called a meeting to review its proposed government procurement reforms. I was so busy, and the subject sounded so boring, that I wasn't even planning to attend. But I started to get calls from people like Sperling and Chris Edley, associate OMB director, lobbying me to attend. They had heard that the task force was about to set off a political firestorm by proposing to abolish the affirmative action guidelines that helped blacks, women, veterans, and other minorities break into the business of government contracting.

Affirmative action was one of my core issues, and it's nice to feel needed, so I went to the vice president's ceremonial office, a cavernous room with ceiling murals and an inlaid marble floor, and took a seat in the second tier of chairs ringing the conference table. A deputy from the Domestic Policy Council handed me a letter from the Civil Rights Commission opposing the proposal, and several other staffers stopped by with more information. I realized I had a network of support in the room if I was willing to make some noise. After a few minutes, I raised my hand and asked a question: "Has there been a political vet on this?"

"Yes, everyone's signed off on it."

"What about the Civil Rights Commission? Have they checked it out?"

"No."

Hmm. Why are they lying about this? Hold back.

Then Gore walked in the room, and the conversation heated up. After a few minutes of debate, I made what I hoped would be the decisive intervention: "Listen, I don't know a thing about procurement reform, so I can't make an argument on the merits. I apologize. But I do know politics. Veterans already hate us, and after the problems we've had with the women's groups over abortion coverage in the health care plan, and the problems we've had with African Americans over Lani Guinier, and this bloody battle with labor over NAFTA, and the troubles we've had with the disability community because they think we've been silent on their issue, after all that, I just know it's going to be very difficult to do away with these requirements. I mean, it's like throwing a cluster bomb into the middle of our base."

The half smiles I got from my silent supporters in the room felt like a standing ovation. The vice president was compelled to respond, and he was angry. No yelling this time, but he did pull rank. "Now wait a second," he said. "Let's start off on the premise here that the president has already made this decision. . . ."

What the hell are we doing here if that's the case? The vice president had invoked divine authority — a powerful but perilous tool. Once he said that, the meeting was essentially over. But as Hotspur reminds Glendower in *Henry IV, Part I*, any man can call spirits from the "vasty deep" . . . "But will they come when you do call for them?" If you claim to be speaking for the president, you'd better be on solid ground. Something told me that the decision couldn't be that clear-cut. After letting a few minutes pass so it wouldn't seem as if I stormed out in a huff, I went to find out.

The president was taking a break, relaxing in shirtsleeves by rearranging the books in his study before a meeting with the Russian foreign minister. "By the way," I said after updating him on the news of the day, "I just left some meeting. Did you ever approve waiving all of the affirmative action requirements on government procurement?" He turned around, put the last books down, removed the unlit cigar from his mouth, and took two steps in my direction.

"No, no, no," he said, shaking his head and laying the tips of his right hand on my forearm. "I mean, Davis-Bacon [a prevailing wage requirement] I knew about, but never affirmative action."

Three nos and fingers on the forearm. He promised Gore something, but he doesn't want to kill affirmative action. The vice president wasn't lying, but he must have snookered Clinton a little. They had probably discussed the issue briefly during lunch. Maybe the president had been daydreaming for a moment; maybe Gore had couched the decision in technical terms and left out the red-flag words *affirmative action;* maybe Gore had rushed right through it. Whatever the case, it was clear to me that the president didn't want to kill affirmative action. So I closed the loop with Bob Rubin, who as director of the National Economic Council had the institutional heft to force a review of the decision. "I went to the president," I told him. "He doesn't remember making the decision, or even discussing it in a clear way." The proposal eventually died a bureaucratic death.

Which meant that I was in big trouble. I may have won this preliminary skirmish over affirmative action, and I believed the issue was important enough to risk creating hard feelings, but I knew that I could never prevail in a prolonged war against the vice president. When I went home that night I was as discouraged as I'd been in months. *Gore hates me. He'll get me fired. The worm's going to turn again, and I'm going to pay the price.*

But at that point, doing the president's bidding was my reason for being; his favor was my fuel. Not long after the fight, my assistant Heather Beckel pulled me out of the morning meeting because Betty needed help getting Rosie Grier, the former football star, out of the Oval so Clinton could go upstairs to change out of his jogging clothes. Once Rosie left, the president pulled a folder from his desk and fixed me with a serious look. "I know you've been worried about the credibility of Reinventing Government," he deadpanned. "Now *I'm* really worried that the vice president has gone over the line."

Smiling, he handed me the folder, which contained a Xerox copy of "REGO Action #39," a $2 million government project to clean the air by cutting bovine flatulence. Two million bucks to fight the cow-farting crisis. I left the Oval laughing, convinced I wasn't crazy to keep an eye on REGO.

I always wore a beeper on my belt. Just in case he needed anything — anything at all, at any time. One Sunday evening, Chelsea was having trouble with her homework, a project on immigration, so Clinton paged me. From the restaurant pay phone, I tracked down the information on border guards she needed and passed it to Chelsea through her dad. But when my belt buzzed at ten minutes to midnight on Saturday, October 2 —"PLEASE CALL 628-7087 FOR PRES US"— I assumed it was more serious.

So much was going on. American troops were searching the streets of Mogadishu for Aideed, the Somali warlord. Old-line Communist foes of Boris Yeltsin had barricaded themselves inside the Russian parliament building. Back home, we had spent much of the morning in the Oval discussing the case of Admiral Frank

Kelso — the chief of naval operations during the Tailhook scandal. The president wanted to ensure that Kelso got a fair shake without interfering in the Pentagon review process, but he seemed most intrigued by exactly what happened at Tailhook: "What do you mean, *leg shaving?*"

Could it be about Woodward's letter? Bob Woodward was writing a book about the economic plan and had passed on a written interview request to the president through me. All Clinton said then was, "Maybe I should do it to get him off our ass for the next four years." *Maybe he wants to discuss it some more.* Whatever he wanted, it's hard to be blasé about a midnight call from the leader of the free world, especially when you're walking home from dinner with your best friend as a witness to the welcome intrusion. Although I was only three blocks from home, I stopped at the pay phone by the Twentieth Street Safeway and held for the president.

"Hey, you doin' OK? I'm sorry to bother you, but I'm really worried about this Red Mass tomorrow. I don't think I should go."

Each year, on the Sunday before the traditional first-Monday-in-October opening of the Supreme Court term, the John Carroll Society sponsored a mass at St. Matthew's Cathedral to seek "God's blessing and guidance for those who administer justice." Every president since Eisenhower had attended at least once, and it had been on the Clintons' schedule for weeks.

But now Hillary wanted out, a conclusion I reached from hearing her in the background, coaching Clinton. She had picked up a rumor that anti-abortion activists were planning a protest, and that Cardinal Joseph Bernardin of Chicago might take the occasion to criticize the president from the pulpit. But a last-minute cancellation would create an even bigger story — "CLINTON SNUBS CATHOLICS" — and from the tone of Clinton's voice, I sensed that he knew he couldn't cancel but needed some answers to calm her nerves.

"I can't imagine that Cardinal Bernardin is going to do that, Mr. President," I said. "He's got a good reputation. You might get some protesters, but what matters is how you handle them. It doesn't hurt to show respect and stand up for what you believe." We went back and forth awhile, and he agreed to attend before he said good night. I was concerned enough, however, to skip Sunday services at my own church and go with the Clintons instead. If anything happened now, it would be my fault.

As I walked to the residence the next morning, the television hanging in the corner of the lower press office caught my eye. CNN was going live with pictures of anti-Yeltsin protesters poised to seize the state television station and storm the Russian parliament. I called the situation room for Tony Lake, and they connected me to his home so I could get briefed before seeing the president. He assumed I was calling about news that hadn't broken yet: Several American soldiers had been killed a few hours earlier in Somalia. But the first he heard about Moscow was from me. Once again, CNN beat the CIA. As soon as he stopped cursing our intelligence, Tony and I quickly agreed on a "we're monitoring the situation" placeholder response for the president, and I sprinted to meet the Clintons.

They were already downstairs, and the president was engrossed in his red folder from the situation room — a bulletin on the fighting in Mogadishu.

"Are you ready for the questions?" I asked.

"About Somalia?"

"No, Russia."

He didn't know either. So we decided it was best to say nothing now. I would get an update from Tony during the mass, and after the service Clinton would take a few questions from the reporters staked outside the cathedral.

The mass was blessedly uneventful. Cardinal Bernardin did address the sanctity of life from conception to death, but his homily's theme was the "common good" and the need for virtue in American life. Only a few silent protesters held signs by the cathedral steps. In Moscow and Mogadishu, however, things were deteriorating. Riot police were firing on the Russian protesters, and more American soldiers had been killed or captured in Somalia. Tony beeped me just before the end of church, and I left my pew for "Roadrunner" — the mobile communications van in the president's motorcade.

The press still didn't know about the firefight in Somalia, but reporters were clamoring for a Clinton comment on Russia. Tony and I didn't think it was smart, however, to address a volatile crisis on sketchy reports from the steps of a church, so I pulled the president aside after he thanked the cardinal and said we needed to return to the White House for a briefing before he faced the press. He nodded and guided me to the limo, where Hillary was waiting.

Her worries of the night before had been wiped away. Sitting in the backseat, sipping from a bottle of water, Hillary was bubbling with ideas, refreshed from the morning's worship. On the ride back, as Clinton offhandedly waved to the small groups who stopped on the sidewalks at the sight of the presidential motorcade, Hillary tied the lessons of Bernardin's homily back to her work on health care. Clinton talked about how it related to the rest of his agenda and instantly started to compose a speech he now wanted to give on "common ground and the common good."

As we rode, Clinton recalled that the Catholic Church hadn't always taught that human life begins at conception, and I responded with what I remembered from my theological studies. The morning crises faded as we discussed Augustine and Aquinas, and their debates over when the body was "quickened" by being joined to a soul. "Garry Wills wrote a good article on this in the *New York Review*," I said, promising to get him a copy. The president then asked me to dig up some statistics on abortion and adoption as he slid into a moist-eyed reflection on their overnight guest from Arkansas, Connie Fails, who had "brought home a beautiful little girl" from Korea who had been born without arms. Without interrupting, Hillary illustrated his commentary with a photo from her purse, and Clinton wrapped up the conversation by observing how brilliantly Congressman Barney Frank had captured the hypocrisy of those conservatives who acted as if they believed that "life begins at conception and ends at birth."

Tony joined us in the private sitting room between the kitchen and the Clintons' bedroom, and the president played host. "Would you like some coffee?" Normally, the waiters offered it on their own, and I almost preferred to be taken for granted. But today I took Clinton's solicitous gesture as a thank-you for how I had handled last night's phone call. It was also a way to avoid the matter at hand, if only for a moment.

Tony was having a terrible morning, and it showed. He was normally restrained in the president's presence, but now he complained bitterly that he couldn't get straight answers from our embassy in Moscow, and he suspected that our sources in Mogadishu were deliberately keeping information from the situation room. I had hoped to keep the conversation focused on Russia because the press had been waiting for the president's response all morning. But although the situation in Russia was critical, early signs indicated that Yeltsin could handle it, and it didn't pose an immediate threat to American lives. Six U.S. soldiers were already dead in Mogadishu, and the firefight was still raging.

"We're not inflicting pain on these fuckers," Clinton said, softly at first. "When people kill us, they should be killed in greater numbers." Then, with his face reddening, his voice rising, and his fist pounding his thigh, he leaned into Tony as if it were his fault: "I believe in killing people who try to hurt you, and I can't believe we're being pushed around by these two-bit pricks."

I couldn't tell whether this outburst was the product of forethought or pure frustration, but I understood the president's anxiety. Since August, the situation in Somalia had been creeping out of control. What had started out as a humanitarian effort had become a futile manhunt. Now the president felt trapped between two bad options: accepting failure by abandoning an ill-conceived operation, or avenging today's losses by going in with "decisive force" to defeat the Somali warlords. Once today's casualties were public, neither course would be easy to pursue. Congress would vote to "bring the boys home" while attacking Clinton for causing a humiliating American defeat. Retreating under fire would also end a humanitarian intervention that had saved thousands from starvation.

So far, the public had supported our presence in Somalia, but Clinton believed opinion would turn fast at the sight of body bags. "Americans are basically isolationist," he said then. "They understand at a basic gut level Henry Kissinger's vital-interest argument. Right now the average American doesn't see our interest threatened to the point where we should sacrifice one American life." By the end of that Sunday we were beyond that: Eighteen Americans were dead and seventy-four were wounded. All day Monday, CNN showed footage of a dead American soldier being dragged through the streets of Mogadishu, along with the videotape of a captured American pilot.

By Sunday afternoon, the president had decided to go ahead with a scheduled trip to California, but the entire week was consumed by the crisis in Somalia. On conference calls from the road and behind closed doors at the White House, Clinton complained mercilessly about being blindsided by his national security team, insisting that he had never been fully briefed on how the original mission had evolved at the UN and on the ground. He never forgot Defense Secretary Les Aspin's failure to approve the military's September request for more tanks to protect the troops. But in public, the president accepted full responsibility, resisted congressional calls for an immediate pullout, and announced instead a plan for a temporary troop buildup followed by a March 31, 1994, deadline for disengagement. In an October 7 Oval Office address, he struck a defiant note: "We started this mission for the right reasons, and we're going to finish it in the right way."

In quieter moments, Clinton questioned himself, wondering whether he had been tough enough. One Friday evening late in the month, he walked into my office looking exhausted, the bags under his eyes bunched up like the skin on a chicken's neck. "This is what I'm worried about," he said, dropping a red folder on my desk. It was a report on renewed interclan fighting in Somalia that was threatening the food supply. "I hope I didn't panic and announce the pullout too soon."

"Listen," I said, "you had no choice. You got six more months. If you had tried for more, Congress would have forced a vote to end it now, and they would have won. You did the best you could."

As we talked, Clinton spied a copy of former Secretary of State Dean Acheson's memoir, *Present at the Creation*, on my desk, so I told him why I had it. The night before, taking the shuttle to New York to campaign for Mayor Dinkins, I had sat next to R. W. "Johnny" Apple of the *Times*. Our talk had turned to books, and I mentioned that the president and I had both recently read Reeves on JFK. Apple said that Clinton should really be reading Acheson's classic account of post-WWII American diplomacy because "it's much more like what he's going through right now." That morning, I had asked Heather to order it from the White House library.

Pushing out his lower lip, Clinton nodded twice as he picked up the book and headed back to his office. Halfway through the dining-room door, he swiveled around with a sudden thought. It was his turn to comfort me.

"We'll figure this out, George. Good night."

Somalia, Bosnia, Haiti — foreign policy was a mess. In each case, we were caught between critics who said we should use American power for humanitarian purposes and those who insisted that "we can't be the world's policeman" so we shouldn't even try. Safire captured the predicament in a rare defense of the president:

> We, the media, hoot at the president for demeaning American power by entering the arena with such puny pugilists. We fault him for narrowly limiting the missions; for not foreseeing setbacks before we do; for making the American military look like a pitiful helpless giant; or for putting the flower of our youth needlessly "in harm's way."

Clinton shared Safire's conclusion that part of America's "new impotence is the unwillingness of too many Americans to expend blood and treasure" beyond our borders. But in his study, as he waggled an old wooden-shafted niblick (a gift from President Bush), he told me to call Safire and remind him that "even though we're a volunteer army, we're not a mercenary army. That's the big difference." In public interviews, he joked about the good old days —"Gosh, I miss the cold war"— when our foreign policy was filtered through the anti-Soviet framework. But in private he railed against liberal critics, like *Times* columnist Anthony Lewis, who were making his life miserable by pushing him to send troops to Bosnia and Haiti: "Lewis has to accept the fact that he's been against every American intervention for thirty years, and now he's the biggest hawk in world." Sometimes he just exploded in frustration: "What would they have me do? What the fuck would they have me do?"

My first brush with fame was as an altar boy with Archbishop Iakovos. This picture appeared in the *Daily News*. *(Costa Hayden)*

The first comeback. After Gennifer and the draft, sitting with Clinton on New Hampshire primary day as he does interviews.

On the road during the 1992 campaign. Riding shotgun with Paul Begala and reporters. *(P. F. Bentley)*

Clinton scores a direct hit. Backstage at the first Bush-Clinton debate. James Carville, Tom Donilon, Mandy Grunwald, Dee Dee Meyers (obscured), Stan Greenberg (behind Grunwald), Vicki Radd, Wendy Smith, me, and Paul Begala. *(P. F. Bentley/Time)*

Waiting for the win. Presiding with James Carville at one of our last War Room meetings. *(David Burnett/Contact Press Images)*

Savoring the win. Inauguration eve 1993, with my parents.
(George Stephanopoulos)

Clinton's first meeting with the Joint Chiefs of Staff. Subject: gays in the military. Me, Defense Secretary Les Aspin, General Colin Powell, General Gordon Sullivan. *(Official White House Photograph)*

After the raid on the Branch Davidian compound in Waco, I advised the president — badly — not to face the press. With Bruce Lindsey and Mack McClarty. *(Official White House Photograph)*

Facing the music. The press conference the morning I was fired as communications director. Vice President Gore, President Clinton, me, David Gergen, Mack McClarty, Dee Dee Meyers. *(Official White House Photograph)*

By his side. The final run-through before the presidential address announcing the bombing of Iraq in June 1993. *(Official White House Photograph)*

Sharing a light moment with General Colin Powell in the cabinet room.
(Official White House Photograph)

While the president is on the phone with Boris Yeltsin in his private residence study, I am wondering how we are going to finish the health care speech. *(Official White House Photograph)*

The president as usual rewriting his speech minutes before the 1994 State of the Union address. *(Bob McNeely/Official White House Photograph)*

My first trip to the grand jury. Hailing a cab to avoid the message sent by riding in an official White House car. *(Associated Press/Worldwide)*

The infamous *Time* magazine cover photo, before they cropped out Dee Dee Meyers and David Gergen (extreme right). *(Official White House Photograph)*

"You did great, Mr. President." Congratulating Clinton after his performance at a White House Correspondents dinner. *(Official White House Photograph)*

Much of my day was spent taking notes on the president's phone conversations for follow-up and informing the press. *(Official White House Photograph)*

Opposite, top: On the European trip to commemorate the fiftieth anniversary of D day, with Wendy Smith and presidential aide Andrew Friendly. *(Diana Walker/* Time*)*

Opposite, center: September 1994: Two months before the disastrous midterm elections, the president revels in an article attacking the press for not giving him enough credit. With Rahm Emanuel, Dee Dee Meyers (obscured), and Bruce Reed. *(Official White House Photograph)*

Opposite, bottom: Helping the president go through his in-box after a Saturday morning radio address. *(Official White House Photograph)*

Watching every word. Mark Gearan, Leon Panetta, Woodrow Wilson, Tony Lake, and I keep an eye on the president as he revises a speech on Haiti. *(Official White House Photograph)*

The first lady and I compare notes. *(Official White House Photograph)*

Still inside but feeling out. Reacting to another midnight policy flip engineered by Dick Morris. *(Official White House Photograph)*

A happy moment at the final affirmative action meeting, July 1995. I had grown a beard to cover a stress-induced skin condition. *(Official White House Photograph)*

The president about to blow. Gene Sperling (to my left), Erskine Bowles, and I try to persuade Clinton to retract his "I raised your taxes too much" statement. *(Official White House Photograph)*

An Oval Office tableau. On the eve of the first government shutdown, November 1995. Left to right: White House photographer, Don Baer, Erskine Bowles, Mike McCurry, Gene Sperling, Michael Waldman,

Plotting strategy with Erskine Bowles (left) and Harold Ickes during the government shutdown. *(Official White House Photograph)*

Vice President Gore (foreground), Laura Tyson, President Clinton, Leon Panetta, and me. *(Official White House Photograph)*

Saturday morning before Christmas 1995, preparing the president's radio address. The second government shutdown turned out to be Newt Gingrich's Christmas gift to the president. *(Official White House Photograph)*

"What?" Clinton, who hated to be left out of *any* conversation, tries to find out what Leon Panetta and I are talking about. *(Official White House Photograph)*

The president's ire wasn't reserved for pundits. He was plenty angry at his own team, particularly after the *Harlan County* debacle in Haiti. As part of the pact to return the democratically elected President Aristide to power, the United States had agreed to send 600 troops to Haiti with a UN force that would help reform the military and rebuild schools, roads, and hospitals. But the Haitian dictators who had deposed Aristide weren't ready to leave. When the USS *Harlan County* arrived in Haitian waters with the first contingent of lightly armed U.S. troops, it was blocked from landing by armed demonstrators directed by the Haitian security forces. After a day of deliberation, we pulled the ship back. So soon after Somalia, no one had the stomach for another fight.

David Gergen — who knew the president was upset with Aspin, Christopher, and Lake, and sought an enhanced position on the foreign-policy team — saw this setback as an opportunity. On Tuesday, October 12, he boarded *Marine One* with the president for a trip to North Carolina and made his move.

Whatever Gergen said to Clinton had its desired effect. Minutes after takeoff, the president was on the phone to Tony Lake, screaming about our screwed-up foreign-policy team and demanding to know why Gergen was being cut out of the decision making on matters like the *Harlan County*. Never mind that Gergen had been the loudest voice in the White House for turning the ship around. "I want Gergen working on this," the president yelled. "The Reagan people were much better at the politics of foreign policy than we are. Look at Lebanon. They went into Grenada two days later and fixed it."

A few minutes later, as I listened with Sandy Berger to Tony's account of the president's tirade, I couldn't believe what I was hearing. *Grenada? That's how we should handle things? Like Reagan? The answer to losing 250 marines in a terrorist attack is to stage the invasion of a tiny country? If you really believe that, then why'd we turn the damn ship around?* It was bad enough to hear Gergen talk about the good old Reagan days, but to hear it parroted by the president was too much. I made excuses for him instead, almost whispering in disbelief: "He's so angry he doesn't even know what he's saying." Sandy focused on Gergen's backstabbing maneuver: "It's despicable; it's the Nixon White House." Tony wondered where it would lead.

My first loyalty was still to the president, but I wanted to protect Tony too. The next morning, the president's aide Andrew Friendly pulled me out of a health care meeting because Clinton wanted to see me. I asked him for a mood check, and Andrew said, "It's not so bad, just tired." When I entered the Oval, Clinton was reading an interview Tony had given to *USA Today*. "This makes it look like we weren't paying attention to Somalia," he grumbled.

Often, the best way to deal with Clinton's anger was to divert it. "Mr. President, I talked to Tony about the interview, and I'm sure he defended the Somalia decision. You know *USA Today*, they cut those transcripts to pieces." But I also took the opportunity to address my deeper worry. The president's displeasure with his foreign-policy team was bleeding into the press. This wasn't only disheartening; it diminished their effectiveness, and it made Clinton look like a weak and disloyal leader who wouldn't accept responsibility for his decisions.

"Mr. President, you just have to . . ." I started, not quite knowing how to begin. "I know that it's hard now, but you really have to, around other people, you have to stand by your people. You have to communicate confidence down the ranks." He seemed to hear me, but I didn't push it. After a couple of minutes, we both turned to dumping on the press. When Tony arrived for a briefing a few minutes later, the president greeted him by saying, "Boy, you sure got screwed by the editors over at *USA Today*."

The rest of that week was spent deciding what to do in Haiti. The dictators were defiant, and the UN peacekeepers were preparing to evacuate. The president was torn. He understood why the military opposed an invasion and knew there would be no public support. But he wanted to keep our word and enforce the agreement, and he hated the appearance of being pushed around by two-bit dictators. Late Thursday afternoon, as the final cabinet room meeting with the national security team approached, he was thinking of nothing else. I was standing in front of his desk, running through some routine paperwork. The president glanced at each sheet, silently marking them one by one with his backward check.

Then he suddenly looked up and asked me the question that was agitating him: "So you think I should go in and take them?"

I normally wasn't shy about giving advice, even when I wasn't asked. That's why I was there: I wanted the ball at the buzzer. I was also sane enough to know that I was only one small voice among many. *But what if I say yes and he goes in and it's a disaster? I like the idea of taking out terrorists like François and Cedras. But the whole Congress is against us, Aristide's a flake, and like Senator Dodd said, the last time we sent marines to Haiti they stayed thirty years. Whenever we invade a small country we change it, and not always for the better. Half the people hate us automatically, and we never know how to get out. That's the clincher, I guess. Unless we have a plan to get out, we can't go in.*

"I'm just not sure, Mr. President," I said. "We don't have an endgame. Maybe later, if nothing else works. But it's definitely too early right now."

It *was* too early, even for President Aristide. After the vice president called Aristide to talk him through the president's decision to reimpose economic sanctions rather than return him to power by force, Gore returned to the Oval. "He's ecstatic," Gore reported, shaking his head in disgust. Clinton, relieved to hear some evidence reinforcing his decision, responded in kind: "See, I told you. What would *you* rather do? Go back to Haiti, or sip champagne in Harry Belafonte's apartment?"

But a week later, Clinton revealed something closer to his true feelings about the man he would eventually help return to the Haitian presidency. We were in the Oval, discussing CIA leaks to Congress of psychological profiles concluding that Aristide was an unstable manic-depressive. "You know, you can make too much of normalcy," Clinton said. "A lot of normal people are assholes." Then his mind leaped from the present-day freedom fighter Aristide to a memory of one of the greatest. Abraham Lincoln often boarded in rest houses where the guests shared beds divided by wooden planks, Clinton recalled, suddenly distant. "The people who slept next to him said that Lincoln would just sit up in bed . . . staring into the night.

"Well." He shrugged, snapping to. "Lincoln might have been crazy, but he was a hell of a president."

By the end of the year, Clinton was looking like a better president than he had been. Our fortunes started to turn after November's victory on the North American Free Trade Agreement (NAFTA). Not that I can take any credit for NAFTA; I was against making the fight. Maybe Gore was right: It was that Gephardt DNA. Working for Midwestern Democrats who represented communities hit hard by the loss of manufacturing jobs had shaped my thinking, and I believed that we should go forward with the agreement only if it included our promised protections for labor and the environment, which would be a spur, I believed, to higher wages and safer working conditions. I didn't think we could win the NAFTA fight. It was a stick in the eye of our most loyal labor supporters, and our base in the House had been through enough already this year. Why put them through the wringer one more time for a Republican trade treaty?

After I lost the argument, I had the uncomfortable task of trying to prove myself wrong. I was sure we were headed for a defeat that would divide the Democratic Party and divert us from the health care fight. But we needed to win more than I needed to be right, so I threw myself into the battle, working on the undecided members I knew best and trying to keep up a good front.

I didn't always succeed. On October 19, less than a month before the congressional deadline, we were still dozens of votes short, Newt Gingrich (our unlikely ally on this) was publicly calling the president's effort "pathetic," and the House Republicans were resisting a small border tax to pay for worker training. In an Oval Office meeting on NAFTA, I was chafing at the indignity of being beholden to Newt, nearly bouncing on the president's couch as I opposed more concessions. "Newt's trying to have it both ways," I argued. "He's setting up a situation where he gets the credit if NAFTA wins and we get blamed if it loses — because 'we're not trying hard enough' or 'because we have taxes,' whatever. We can't keep caving to these guys."

"We have to," Gergen responded. "The Republicans won't be held accountable. After all, this is President Clinton's treaty; this is *our* treaty."

Gergen's political analysis was essentially correct, but hearing him say "our" just set me off. *Not only do I have to hear Newt Gingrich call the president pathetic. Not only do we have to give up the worker training that makes NAFTA marginally palatable to Democrats. Now I have to listen to a guy who worked for three Republican presidents tell me that an initiative drafted by President Bush is our treaty.*

"That's *bull*shit."

Unleashing an obscenity in a formal policy meeting was the most indiscreet thing I'd ever done in the Oval Office — and it had an effect. For a moment, no one said a word. But then the president took my side, agreeing to call Gingrich and demand some concessions. He wasn't as tough as I'd hoped, but when Clinton put down the phone, he did his best to brighten my mood by taking a shot at Newt: "Dealing with that guy is like hugging an eel."

Caring too much about an issue can cloud your political judgment. In the end, that's what happened to me on NAFTA. I underestimated President Clinton's persuasive powers and the power of the presidency on foreign-policy matters. I also misjudged how crushingly effective Gore would be in his televised NAFTA debate against Ross Perot on *Larry King Live*. Being so wrong made me the butt of gentle jokes inside the White House. Rahm drafted, and the president signed, a "Statement by the President" that read, "While still officially undecided, George's personal pledge to save my presidency and be the 218th vote if needed, demonstrates his loyalty, convictions, and moral compass."

On the day we won, I tried to be graceful in defeat. Walking through the West Wing after a victory press conference, I caught up with Gore, who was strolling a step or two behind the president. "You know, Mr. Vice President, I have to eat some crow. You were right about NAFTA; I was wrong."

"No, no, no, George," he said with a smile. "*You* were right. We *were* going to lose — until I debated Perot." Then, just before ducking into the Oval, Clinton cut in with an exit line: "I like that: win . . . win . . . spin."

On the day before Thanksgiving 1993, the White House was in a playful mood. At our morning briefing in the Oval, we discussed what to do if the turkey Clinton was "pardoning" became incontinent in his arms, and Gore offered to demonstrate his skill at hypnotizing chickens. The president mentioned John Kennedy Jr.'s upcoming birthday, and I told him that gossip columns were reporting that Kennedy had split with actress Daryl Hannah. Bob Rubin seemed so bemused by the banter that the president told him to relax: "C'mon Bob," Clinton joked. "We're just trying to set George up."

I was more interested in setting the president up — with Salman Rushdie, the writer condemned to death by Ayatollah Khomeini for his novel *The Satanic Verses.* On November 24, he was in Washington to speak at the National Press Club, see Tony Lake and Warren Christopher, and secure something that had been denied him in the past — a meeting with the president of the United States. Although the Bush administration, through Marlin Fitzwater, had dismissed Rushdie as simply an author on a book tour who didn't merit any "special interest," I believed that a presidential meeting would demonstrate that the U.S. would stand up to terrorism, provide Rushdie an added measure of protection, and remind the world that tolerance and free expression are values we hold dear. But the State Department advised against a meeting, fearing that it would increase the risk of terrorism against Americans, disrupt the Middle East peace process, and alienate the Muslim world.

In a hurried Oval Office meeting later that morning, Tony Lake and I lobbied hard. Thankfully, the president sided with us, mentioning that he had received a message from an old Arkansas lady friend, Norris Church, Norman Mailer's wife. We hurriedly fashioned a compromise: no Oval Office, no photographer; Clinton and Rushdie would shake hands in the Old Executive Office Building after the president finished taping some interviews — an "accidental" encounter that recalled stories I'd heard about how the Kennedy White House had arranged for JFK to drop by Harris Wofford's office so he could "happen" to meet Martin Luther King.

The meeting itself was anticlimactic. As Tony Lake and I watched Rushdie and Clinton shake hands in a remote corner on the fifth floor of the Old Executive Office Building, I wondered if the setting had somehow diminished what we were trying to do.

The president was unusually uncomfortable, unsure of what to do with his hands; and the two of them together seemed like a pair of old lovers who had bumped into each other by chance — sticking to safe subjects like their mutual friends Norman (Mailer) and Bill (Styron) as if they were afraid of what might happen if they lingered too long or said too much.

No matter. I returned to my office to leave a message — "The eagle has landed" — on the answering machine of Rushdie's friend and advocate the journalist Christopher Hitchens. Rushdie hurried to the Press Club to tell the world about the "real friendship and warmth" he felt from Clinton. That was all that mattered; the meeting was the message.

While we were striking a small blow for free speech on one end of Pennsylvania Avenue, Senate Majority Leader George Mitchell was announcing a victory for public safety on the other. After seven years of trying, the Brady Bill was about to become law. Named after James Brady, the Reagan press secretary shot and paralyzed by a bullet meant for his boss, the bill would require a five-day waiting period and background check for handgun purchasers. Despite Reagan's eventual support for the bill, President Bush had vetoed it twice. But on Thanksgiving eve 1993, the National Rifle Association's Senate filibuster of the bill crumbled, and we immediately invited Jim and Sarah Brady to the Oval for a public celebration. For me, this victory was especially sweet. Seven years earlier, I had sat with Sarah Brady in the office of my boss, Congressman Edward Feighan, to help draft the original bill. Now my new boss would sign it into law, and I was certain it would save lives.

I knocked off early, and as I walked home through an Indian summer mist that afternoon, I couldn't believe how much I had to be grateful for that Thanksgiving. I had the job of my life, and I was doing better at it. The whole administration was getting the hang of governing, and we were getting things done. The next morning, I'd be on a plane to New Orleans for another celebration. James Carville and Mary Matalin were getting married — another incongruous couple, another lavish public ceremony. Republicans and

Democrats flew down to the French Quarter to march in the Dixieland wedding parade led by trumpeter Al Hirt. A "second line" of Thanksgiving tourists joined in, toasting the new couple with plastic cups of beer.

Many toasts later, Mary introduced me to a man who'd often made my life miserable over the past year. Whenever Rush Limbaugh had mentioned me during his new television show, he superimposed my face on the body of a baby. Enough was enough. "Rush," I joked, "don't you think it's time to get me out of the diapers?"

He chuckled nervously, naked without his microphone, and mumbled something about seeing what he could do. By year's end, I was a toddler in short pants, riding a rocking horse.

9   HOOFBEATS REDUX

The hoofbeats were closing in.

This time they came from the Ozark home of the busted land deal that began when I was a senior in high school and Bill Clinton was attorney general of Arkansas. Whitewater. After an early 1992 flurry precipitated by a *New York Times* investigation, the issue had faded when our campaign commissioned an audit that documented how much money the Clintons had lost on the investment. The Republicans couldn't effectively exploit the issue because President Bush's son Neil Bush had come under fire for his own involvement with a failed savings and loan. But late in 1993, the Resolution Trust Corporation (the government agency established to manage the aftermath of the 1980s S & L crisis) asked the Justice Department to open a criminal investigation of Madison Guaranty, the S & L managed by Jim McDougal, the Clintons' Whitewater partner. David Hale, a former judge and business associate of McDougal's who was trying to worm his way out of a fraud indictment, offered prosecutors and the press a new hook by alleging that Governor Clinton had pressured him to lend McDougal money.

These new developments, coupled with the miasma of mystery surrounding Vince Foster's suicide, piqued the interest of the *Times* and the *Washington Post*. They asked again to review all the White-

water documents, and a series of faxed questions from the *Post* sat in
the White House for weeks without a formal response. Busy with
NAFTA, Somalia, and the crush of other business, I didn't attend
the few October and November meetings on the matter. To me
Whitewater was old news, the obsession of a few conspiracy theorists. But by early December, the *Post* was convinced we were hiding
something sinister. Executive editor Leonard Downie made a series
of extraordinary personal requests for the documents, and Ann
Devroy warned me that the paper would go on the warpath unless
we answered their questions and released the documents.

I wish we had. If a genie offered me the chance to turn back time
and undo a single decision from my White House tenure, I'd head
straight to the Oval Office dining room on Saturday morning,
December 11, 1993. The night before, Bernie Nussbaum, David
Kendall (Clinton's private attorney), and Hillary had persuaded the
president to stonewall the *Post*. All three were tough trial attorneys
who were determined to follow a close-hold strategy more appropriate for corporate litigation than presidential politics. The possibility that the Clintons would be implicated in wrongdoing by any
investigation of Madison Guaranty was extremely low, but the
lawyers were taking nothing for granted. Hillary also feared that the
Post inquiry was an invasive fishing expedition that would only create more inquiries. They all underestimated, however, the media
reality that reporters want most what they're told they can't have,
the political reality that a president's right to privacy is limited by
the public's right to know, and the cultural reality that the country
probably wouldn't care about the ins and outs of an old land deal as
long as it didn't look as if the Clintons had something to hide.

On Saturday morning, just after the radio address, Mack gave
Gergen and me one last chance to convince Clinton the only way to
kill the story was to cooperate with the *Post*.

The president was sitting at the head of his small oval table, sipping a mug of decaf, with a pile of folders in front of him. Gergen
and I were on either side. For once, though, the two of us were arguing the same case. Although we often clashed on policy matters,
we both insisted now that turning over the Whitewater documents
was the only way to manage the story. The president seemed to

agree. "I don't have a big problem with giving them what we have," he said, almost apologetically, his mind elsewhere (that weekend, he was preparing to replace Secretary of Defense Aspin). "But Hillary . . ."

Saying her name flipped a switch in his head. Suddenly, his eyes lit up, and two years' worth of venom spewed out of his mouth. You could usually tell when Clinton was making Hillary's argument: Even if he was yelling, his voice had a flat quality, as if he were a high school debater speeding through a series of memorized facts. The antipress script was familiar to me by now. "No, you're wrong," he said. "The questions *won't* stop. At the Sperling breakfast, I answered more questions about my private life than any candidate *ever*, and what did *that* get me? They'll *always* want more. *No* president has ever been treated like I've been treated."

Gergen did his best to calm Clinton down. Having worked for Nixon, Ford, and Reagan, he'd seen what happens when a president is accused of covering up. He also tried to make the case that the *Post* would treat Clinton fairly. "Mr. President," he replied, "in twenty-five years, I've never seen better first-year coverage of a president." Gergen was doing exactly what he'd been hired to do — serving as a kind of emissary from the Washington establishment to the outsider from Arkansas. Still battle scarred from the campaign scandals and the snafus of our first six months, I tried a different tack, hoping to convince Clinton by invoking our shared experience. "Mr. President, you're right," I said. "You *have* gotten a raw deal from the press, and the stories they write *will* be unpleasant. But they can't really hurt you because they're all about the past, and you didn't do anything wrong. If we don't give them what they want, they'll say we're covering up. The pressure will build, and we'll end up answering the questions later anyway. Better to flush it out over the holidays when no one's paying attention."

For a moment, I thought our rare double-team effort had worked. Clinton didn't make a counterargument; the pol in him knew we were right. If only we'd dialed Downie right then and handed the phone to Clinton. But even that might not have worked. On this issue, Clinton wasn't commander in chief, just a husband beholden to his wife. Hillary was always the first to defend him on bimbo eruptions; now he had to do the same for her. Gergen and I didn't know what was in the Whitewater documents, but whatever it was, Hillary didn't want it out — and she had a veto. The president ended the meeting by saying he wanted to think about it some more. Later that afternoon, Mack called Gergen to tell him we were standing firm.

Needless to say, Hillary's strategy failed. Over the next week, successive stories began to suggest that the White House was orchestrating a cover-up. *Newsweek*, 12/15/93: "The White House strategy last week appeared to be to try to contain the story by treating it with contempt." The *Washington Post*, 12/19/93: "But the full financial history of Whitewater may never be known. White House officials have declined over the past several weeks to answer detailed questions about Whitewater's finances." The *New York Times*, 12/20/93: "Based on what's publicly known, there's probably not a crippling scandal here. But the White House is behaving as if there were." *Exactly right.*

A few days before Christmas, the controversy approached critical mass. Then two successive disclosures triggered an explosion. First, the *American Spectator* and the *Los Angeles Times* reported that as governor of Arkansas, Clinton had used state troopers to procure women, and that he had recently called some of those troopers in an attempt, the articles suggested, to offer them federal jobs in return for their silence. When I asked Clinton about the rumors a few days before the stories broke, his abrupt shift to fast-talking, lawyerly, hyperexplanation mode convinced me something was up. "I never offered anyone a job," he insisted. But he didn't deny calling the troopers (and as I soon learned, he had discussed the subject with at least one of them), which gave me a sickening sense of déjà vu. I was back in Little Rock, hearing Clinton's voice on the Gennifer tapes. *How could he be so reckless? He's so sure he can talk his way out of anything that he doesn't even think about the consequences. What if they have a tape? Why can't he just leave these things alone?* A few stupid presidential phone calls now threatened to transform an old Arkansas story into an Oval Office scandal.

The press was still queasy about sex stories, however — especially with Hillary defending her husband surrounded by mistletoe and holly. But when the *Washington Times* reported that in the hours following Vince Foster's suicide a Whitewater file had been removed from Foster's office and given to the Clintons' private attorney instead of the investigators, the repressed energy stirred up by the trooper story was sublimated straight into the "Whitewater cover-up." Republicans jumped on the revelation and began to agitate for an independent investigation, and the editorial pages escalated calls for public release of the potentially incriminating files. Backpedaling, we agreed on December 23 to hand over what we had to the Justice Department but not the press, which only raised more suspicions. The drumbeat for full disclosure continued through Christmas.

On the first Sunday of the new year, I appeared on *This Week with David Brinkley*, and the first question Sam Donaldson asked me was, Would the White House oppose an independent counsel to look into the Whitewater Land Development Corporation affair?

Mr. Stephanopoulos: "This is being investigated by the Justice Department. The president has turned over all the documents to the Justice Department. It was exhaustively looked into during last year's campaign. The president was part of a real estate deal many years ago where he lost a lot of money. Those are the facts. No laws were broken. The Justice Department investigation will show that, but there's no need at this time for an independent counsel."

Four follow-up questions later, George Will finally changed the subject, but by the next day both Newt Gingrich and Bob Dole had publicly called for the appointment of a special prosecutor, and the White House press corps was pressing Clinton for his response. A mistake I had made on *Brinkley* made matters worse. When I said that we had turned over the Whitewater documents to the Justice Department, I thought I was telling the truth. I assumed it was true because we had previously pledged to turn over the files between Christmas and New Year's. But as Felix Unger used to say on *The Odd Couple*, "When you assume, you make an ass of you and me." We hadn't delivered the files yet, because the lawyers were still cataloging them. Dee Dee had to spend the morning cleaning up my mess. Harold Ickes, who had just joined the White House staff to work on health care, was tasked instead with managing damage control on Whitewater.

All day Tuesday, we held a rolling Whitewater meeting in Mack's office. Although I had delivered the party line against a special prosecutor on *Brinkley*, inside I was arguing that we had to request a special counsel before it was forced on us. Ever since Watergate, whenever a president or other high-level government official was accused of wrongdoing, an outside counsel had been appointed. (In January 1994, the independent counsel law had expired. So we were arguing for the attorney general to use her authority to appoint a special counsel as was done under President Carter when questions were raised about his peanut warehouse business.) After the first couple of hours, we reached consensus; only Nussbaum was holding out. Joel Klein, his deputy, was dispatched to broach the matter with Hillary, but she shut him down. Two hours later, Harold and Mack tried again. The answer was still no.

When they returned with the news, about a dozen of us were scattered around Mack's office. Some sat at the conference table in the far corner, some by the fireplace; I was folded over the wing-back chair by Mack's desk, facing the door, griping openly about the magnitude of our mistake. Then she walked in. The whole room dropped dead silent.

"Well," said Hillary crisply, taking a seat on the couch by the door. "I think this is a meeting I ought to be at."

Because I had been talking, I felt as if everyone was looking at me. The old Life cereal commercial passed through my head: Two older boys don't like the looks of their new breakfast, so they pawn it off on their little brother — "Let Mikey try it. He'll try anything." I prided myself on not being afraid to make a tough argument to the principals, and I'd look like a wimp now if I didn't continue.

"Well, I might as well go on with what I was saying," I said. Sitting up straight and staring right at Hillary, I made my case: "Assuming we did nothing wrong, the best thing is to have a special counsel say so. There's an air of inevitability to this. If we don't ask for one from the attorney general, we're going to get an independent prosecutor. Congress will keep the drumbeat going; they'll pass the Independent Counsel Act, and the Appeals Court will appoint one. I know we didn't do anything wrong, but it looks like we did because we're not being forthcoming. More important than anything else, this is going to kill health care if we don't get it under control. This debate will sap us for the next thirty, sixty, ninety days — as long as we keep up the fight. If you want us to fight, Hillary, we will. We can beat this back. But it will take all our time, all our staff resources, and, most important, all our political capital, which we need every bit of to pass health care."

I thought the final argument was the coup de grâce — the killer point that she couldn't counter. Instead it struck at her deepest fear — that after all of her hard work, after all her sacrifice, after all the indignities of the campaign and the frustrations of the first year, the project that would make it all worthwhile would be crippled by scandal. Cornered, she struck back: "What do you mean, the Congress won't stop? You told me that if we gave everything to the Justice Department that would *end* it. It *didn't* end it. Now the Congress wants them? If we were as tough as the Republicans, we'd band together and beat them back."

I tried to stay calm, answering point by point.

"The Democrats are still holding firm." (Republican senators Alfonse D'Amato and Bob Dole had demanded Whitewater hearings, but Democrat Banking Committee chairman Don Riegle was holding them off.) "But I can't promise that they'll be with us in a month. It's beyond the Congress now: It's in the editorial pages; it's everywhere. We don't get the benefit of the doubt because we're not being forthcoming, and we *are* being defensive."

Whatever I said was exactly wrong. Tears stung the corners of her eyes, and I imagined Hillary's fear-induced fury — at the Republicans for trying to destroy health care by destroying her, at the press for its small-minded, obsessive scrupulousness when issues affecting real people were at stake, at her husband for getting her into this stupid land deal with his shady friends in the first place and then expecting her to clean it up, at her best friend, Vince, for killing himself, at herself for letting the situation spiral out of control. All of that fury, for a moment, was directed at me.

"You *never* believed in us. In New Hampshire, it was just me and

Susan [Thomases] and Harold [Ickes] who believed in us. If we wouldn't have fought, we would never have won. *You* gave up on us. . . ."

She paused, her voice fell, and Hillary started to cry. "We were out there alone, and I'm feeling very lonely right now. Nobody is fighting for *me.*"

We all seemed stuck to our chairs, not knowing whether to be unnerved, afraid, or consoling. I was too stunned to respond. Harold, who had been explicitly absolved from the accusation of disloyalty, tried to rescue me with one final plea for reconsideration.

"I don't want to hear anything more," Hillary snapped, back in control. "I want us to fight. I want a campaign now." Looking back at me, she took one last shot: "If you don't believe in us, you should *just leave.*" Then she walked out the door.

A dead moment passed. I fixed a crinkly smile on my face. Once I was sure Hillary was long gone, I rose to leave. "Nice try," Dee Dee whispered. I walked the few steps to my office, closed the door behind me, and broke down.

"*You gave up on us.*" *How could she say that? Nobody's fought harder for them. I'm the most loyal staffer they've ever had. I went out there every day. On Gennifer. And the draft. And Whitewater. Sacrificed my credibility. I went out there on faith, without the facts, and would get killed, just humiliated. No matter what I thought inside, I went before the whole country like a crazy person, even said I believed he never had sex with Gennifer. People would laugh at what I would say. Then to get attacked — not for being wrong but for being disloyal, for abandoning them. Fuck her. I'm arguing for what's best — for her, for him, for all of us and everything we're fighting for. Fuck her.*

But I also knew why Hillary's words wounded me so deeply. They were true. I never showed it to the world, but I did give up in New Hampshire — on the floor of the yogurt factory when we received the forgotten draft letter, in the Nashua laundry room when I was accused of conspiring to get Gennifer Flowers a job, in my Little Rock office when I heard Clinton talking to her. Remembering all that made me feel sorry for Hillary. She'd had to listen to those tapes too. She'd had to gulp hard on prime-time television when Sam Donaldson read back her husband's farewell to Gennifer:

"Good-bye, baby." She'd had to pull it all together every single day — for him, for Chelsea — and she never really knew what was coming next either. And all for what? Not just to be first lady, but to do big things. Now her integrity was being questioned; everything she'd worked for was imperiled, and no one was there for her.

The West Wing is a small place. Later that afternoon, the vice president pulled me aside as we gathered for a meeting in the Oval: "How are you doing?"

"What do you mean?" I replied, trying to stay cool.

"Sometimes it gets pretty rough around here," he said, putting his arm on my shoulder. "But it will be OK."

It was a thoughtful gesture, and I needed the encouragement even if I couldn't admit it. But a phone call I'd received early that evening had already startled me out of my self-pity. Ann Devroy, urgent, on deadline: "George, I just want to be clear on this. We're hearing lots of rumors, but you guys haven't heard anything about Bobby Inman and any possible homosexual activity, right?"

"No, Ann," I said. "What are you talking about? No. Nothing. Not even a buzz. Zero. . . ."

In December, after a secret courtship led by Strobe Talbott, President Clinton had nominated Bobby Inman, a retired four-star admiral, to replace Les Aspin as defense secretary. Having served as deputy director of the CIA and head of the National Security Agency, Inman was a darling of the defense establishment, with a reputation for independence. At the time, I had argued against announcing Inman so precipitously, without giving Aspin adequate notice — not because I imagined what would happen next, but because I thought that Les had been loyal to the president and deserved a graceful exit rather than a public humiliation. But Inman, true to form, played hardball, demanding an immediate decision. His appointment was met by a chorus of bipartisan praise from both the Senate and the political establishment. The *New York Times* called Inman "a safe and smart choice." After a year of troublesome nominations, it looked to the world as if we finally had a winner.

I wasn't so sure. Inman's failure to pay social security taxes for his maid, coupled with his refusal to resign from an exclusive, all-male club called the Bohemian Grove, meant that he'd face some prickly questions during confirmation hearings. Our administration would be accused of having a double standard when it came to "nanny problems," and Inman would be scored for insensitivity to women's rights. Even worse was Inman's arrogance. When the president announced his appointment, the admiral acted as if *he* were commander in chief, saying that he had agreed to be defense secretary only after reaching "a level of comfort" with Clinton.

Devroy's call worried me even more. After hanging up the phone, I headed straight to Tony Lake's office. "Tony," I said, taking a seat in his rocking chair, "I just got the strangest call from Devroy." But before I could finish the sentence, Joel Klein — the counsel supervising Inman's background check — stuck his head in the room and said, "I gotta talk to you guys."

"Funny," I replied, "you were my next stop." Joel let me go first: "Ann Devroy just called me and asked if I knew anything about Bobby Inman and homosexual activity, and I completely denied it. Said it was absurd, the stupidest thing I'd ever heard. Over the course of the conversation, she said that there were people in the gay community in Austin [Inman's hometown] who were saying things. She didn't really believe it, but she wanted to make sure I hadn't heard anything about it."

"It's really funny that you bring that up," Klein replied, a wry smile on his face. He had heard the same rumors, but Inman had flatly denied the allegation to Klein, adding that he'd been dogged by these allegations ever since an incident at the National Security Agency when he refused to follow established practice by firing employees who were found to be gay. (Since then, Clinton had rightly overturned the intelligence community guidelines that classified homosexual orientation and activity as prima facie security risks.) After hearing about Devroy's inquiry, Joel said he'd call Inman again just to be sure.

If the rumors of Inman's being gay could be proved true, there was no way he'd be confirmed as secretary of defense. He'd get hit from both sides: by conservatives who believed that homosexuality was a disqualifying condition and by gay-rights advocates who would argue justifiably that it was hypocritical to have a homosexual defense secretary when gays and lesbians were prohibited from serving openly in the military. Meantime, I faced a dilemma: Do I tell Devroy what Joel just told me? I didn't think it was fair for un-corroborated rumors to worm their way into the paper. On the other hand, if Devroy later discovered that information had been provided to the White House and believed that I had deliberately lied to her, there'd be hell to pay on the front page of the *Post*. She'd never let the story go. If Ann were less trustworthy, I might have taken that risk and kept the information to myself. But I knew that she would honor an "off the record" conversation. So, with the pro-viso that the information was "only for her" (which meant so off the record that not only could it not be published, but she couldn't share it with any of her colleagues inside the paper except, maybe, a single supervising editor), I told her that we had heard some sketchy rumors, emphasizing that Inman had denied them and that they were hearsay, not hard information. Devroy said that the *Post* was hearing the same stories, but they weren't going in the paper with-out more proof. For a night, we'd dodged another bullet.

But now we were in a box. Although Inman had categorically de-nied the gay allegation again in a following conversation with Klein, he understood that the rumors were likely to surface. Before the hearing, some sort of spectacle might be staged by Act Up, the rad-ical gay group that had threatened to out public figures suspected of being secretly gay. Or perhaps the Republican senators and their staffs would find a way to air the allegations, either by leaking in-vestigative files to the media or by calling a surprise witness — the way Democrats did with Anita Hill during the confirmation hear-ings for Supreme Court Justice Clarence Thomas. After the Thomas, Robert Bork, and John Tower hearings, where Republican nomi-nees were publicly pelted with embarrassing details from their pri-vate lives, they would be seeking payback.

For the next twenty-four hours, Inman swung back and forth be-tween depression and defiance. In a second conversation with Klein late Wednesday night, Inman seemed increasingly distraught but still insisted that he wanted the job. We wondered whether Inman's vacillation was some sort of ploy, conscious or not, to get us to make the decision for him. Everyone agreed that at a minimum, Joel had to look Inman in the eye and assess his stability. He booked a late-morning flight to the admiral's vacation cabin in the Rocky Mountains.

Preoccupied with his own sadness, the president didn't know the details of our deliberations. Earlier that morning, his mother had died in her sleep; he spent the day accepting our condolences and preparing for the funeral. Around noon, he wandered into my office, where I was sharing a quick sandwich with the writer Joe Klein, and we spent a few minutes reminiscing about the mother who had given him the gift of unconditional love and a sunny fighting spirit. Then Clinton left, and the lawyer Joel Klein walked in my door.

"What are you doing here?" I asked. "I thought you were going to Vail."

"I have to see you."

I told Joe I'd be back in a minute and walked down to Gergen's office with Joel. Two hours later, we were still there. Just before his plane took off, Joel got an urgent message to call Inman. "Listen," Inman told him. "You don't need to fly out here. Let's just talk. When the president was first considering my appointment, I told you only ninety percent of the truth. Here's the other ten."

While consistently and convincingly denying the gay rumors, Inman next disclosed more about his private life that he had withheld during the initial background check. Had we known the full story a month earlier, the president would not have chosen Inman — and it would be risky and wrong for us to stick with the nomination now in the face of this disclosure. Once the Senate investigators finished digging through Inman's life, everything would be public, and Inman would not be confirmed.

Inman had a corresponding obligation not to place the president in that predicament. The only option was for him to withdraw quietly, but the flinty and flighty admiral wasn't ready for that. His most ardent administration advocate, Strobe Talbott, called in to make his case. According to Talbott, Inman had explained away his behavior as "a way to get attention." The rest of us rolled our eyes, but Talbott continued, arguing correctly that it would be grossly unfair to dump Inman because of some uncorroborated rumors. Then Joel told Talbott about his most recent conversation with Inman. Even if you made the dubious assumption that Inman's private life would remain private during the confirmation process, we had a problem: the fact that Inman had misled the White House at the outset of his background check. By coming clean now, he was basically begging to be cut loose. The more we talked about it, the more we all agreed Inman had to withdraw.

The only question remaining was how. Mack left to call the president. While he was gone, the rest of us brainstormed about Inman's replacement. We kicked around all of the usual suspects — senators like Sam Nunn, John Warner, and David Boren; a business executive like Norm Augustine, chairman of Martin Marietta. But the idea we liked best was to shift Treasury Secretary (and WWII fighter pilot) Lloyd Bentsen to Defense and appoint Bob Rubin to Treasury. Then Mack returned to report on his call to the president, who generally agreed with our judgment but added that Inman's behavior "wasn't quite disqualifying." We dutifully went over the details of the case one more time. Finally, I couldn't take it anymore: "Wait a second, it's just not discussible. We can't do it."

"It may not be discussible," Gergen quipped, "but it's damn interesting."

Once the nervous laughter died down, we had to decide what to do. The president was scheduled to fly overseas on Saturday, and Gergen worried that announcing the withdrawal either right before or during the trip would send the wrong message and drown out news coverage of the president's first visit to Russia. After giving Joel the job of working with Inman to postpone any action for ten days, we adjourned.

It turned out, though, that Whitewater alone would overshadow the president's trip. The morning after my confrontation with Hillary, the *Post* had published another breathless but mind-numbing 2,018-word front-page story going over all of the details. At 7:15 A.M., a good hour and a half before the president usually arrived in the West Wing, Clinton burst through the back door of my office holding a newspaper. I braced myself for another blast. But it never came. Maybe Clinton was trying to compensate for Hillary's broadside by keeping me close; maybe he saw something in the article that I had missed. Whatever the reason, the president was bubbling with excitement.

"Mr. President, I know you think the story's great," I said, puzzled. "But I don't get it. You really have to explain to me *why* you think it's great."

"Oh, don't you see," he said, showing me the paragraphs he'd underlined and starred. "It's full of factually untrue stuff. And it shows that even career attorneys from the Justice Department saw no reason to pursue the case."

The article did, in fact, make that point, adding that "there was no conclusive evidence that the Clintons had done anything illegal." But it also repeated the suggestion that the involvement of the first couple had impeded the progress of the investigation. Putting these two arguments together, I made one last plea: "You may be right, Mr. President, and I know you guys didn't do anything wrong. That's why I think it's best to turn this whole thing over to a special counsel so we can get back to work."

"Hmm, that makes some sense," he said, before going back upstairs to change. When he returned to the Oval an hour later for another meeting with me, Harold, and Mack, Clinton said he knew it was the right thing to do. But a little later, we were back in Mack's office — the same group, going over the same ground — when first Harold and then Mack got called to the Oval. They returned chastened and pale, and it didn't take a detective to figure out what had happened.

"You all can keep talking about this if you want," Harold said. "But it's useless. We're not doing a special counsel."

I knew I was in big trouble again. The president hadn't called me back for the follow-up discussion, and Harold looked at me as if he'd just discovered I had a terminal illness. At the first lull in the meeting, he signaled me out with a shake of his head. We whispered in the hallway.

"Boy," he confided in me. "She's really angry. Blames you for getting him all ginned up again this morning."

"Well, I guess I have no choice," I replied. We'd been discussing how to organize a campaign to get our side of the Whitewater story out, and I asked Harold to engineer the meeting so that I would be appointed spokesman for the damage control effort. "I'm so shot up and bloody that the only way I can recover with them is to be the spokesman."

"George, you're absolutely right."

So I stepped up my contacts with the press and put up an aggressive front. Just before the president's lunch with columnists to brief them on his upcoming trip to Russia, Safire pulled me aside to pound me on Whitewater. "How come it takes two weeks to catalog a box of documents?" he asked, taunting me. "What are you guys doing — tearing them up? Throwing them out? How are you doing, George?" he continued. "Are you doing OK?" "Why shouldn't I be doing OK?" I replied, afraid he might know something. "You're like my old Jewish grandmother in Brooklyn," he said, letting me off the hook. "Every time I ask a question, she answers with a question." With the president, Safire asked only about NATO expansion, but his next day's column on Whitewater was another killer.

Whitewater was everywhere. At the Italian embassy that night, I was seated between Mary McGrory, the longtime Washington columnist, and Katherine "Kay" Graham, doyenne of the *Washington Post*. We were the three unattached people at the dinner. In normal times (if there was such a thing) it would have been a terrific evening. Mary was an old friend, and both women are engaging dinner partners, with something funny and sharp to say about everyone in the room. But that night, all the talk was about Whitewater, and I couldn't give an inch.

"George," Kay said, "I think this Whitewater thing is really trouble, don't you?"

"No, Kay," I replied. "It's not trouble because the Clintons didn't do anything wrong."

"But if they didn't do anything wrong, why don't you just release the documents or ask for an independent counsel to clear their name?"

Good point. But I knew I couldn't even wink — not even betray the hint of distance hidden in an opening like "Well, the president believes . . ."

"Well, Kay," I replied, "that might be good politics, but it would set a horrible precedent. The standard hasn't been met. It would be an invitation to irresponsible allegations if all you have to do to get an independent counsel is level a charge. It's just wrong. It devalues the institution of the special counsel and demeans the presidency."

All that might have been true, but blocking a special counsel was an unwinnable battle. Over the next few days, our defenses completely crumbled after the *Post* reported that our delivery of documents to the Justice Department was not, as we had claimed, strictly voluntary. When David Kendall had first contacted Justice to discuss the matter, he had been informed that the department was already drafting a subpoena for the documents. Kendall subsequently negotiated with department lawyers to broaden the subpoena for the purpose of shielding more documents from the press, another fact we failed to reveal at the time. Although this sort of maneuver was routine and appropriate in private litigation, it reinforced the cover-up charge and raised a new allegation of improper presidential interference with an independent investigation. By Tuesday, January 11, nine Democratic senators — led by Pat Moynihan and Bill Bradley — had joined the Republican calls for an independent investigation, which demolished our claim that this was just a partisan witch-hunt.

The television coverage of the president's trip was dominated by Whitewater. We couldn't go on like this, and Clinton wanted the issue resolved. On Tuesday evening, January 11, Hillary called a small group of us into the Oval for a conference call with the president, who was plugged in by speakerphone from Prague. It was an odd scene, the only time I can remember meeting in the Oval Office without the president present. We stood around the president's desk as if he were there, staring at the small black box in front of his chair. Harold Ickes structured the debate, assigning me to make the case for requesting a special counsel. Nussbaum would oppose.

I made the argument I'd been making for days — that we had no choice; that if we didn't ask for a special counsel now, one would be forced on us later; that the press would keep hounding us until we surrendered; that Whitewater was killing the rest of our agenda. Bernie countered, correctly, that special prosecutors take on a life of their own, but his only answer was to release the documents. *Now you tell us. Where were you a month ago, when releasing them might have made a difference? It's too late now.* But I didn't replow that old ground aloud because it was unnecessary. There was a pro forma quality to this final debate. Clinton had already made up his mind; or, more accurately, he believed that he no longer had a choice. After several minutes of discussion, Hillary asked everyone except David Kendall to leave and concluded the decision with the president.

The next day, Nussbaum sent a letter to Attorney General Reno saying that President Clinton had directed him to request a special counsel "to conduct an appropriate independent investigation of the Whitewater matter and report to the American people."

I went to the White House briefing room to explain our reversal. My internal victory (if you can call it that) had come at some cost, so I went on the offense, using the public forum to challenge our accusers: "Despite their total and voluntary cooperation with the current investigation, the Clintons have been subjected to a barrage of innuendo, political posturing, and irresponsible accusations. . . . We still don't think that the evidence is there to require a special counsel. At the same time, we want to make sure that nothing interferes with the president's agenda."

Toward the end of the briefing, someone asked about reports that Hillary was among the most resistant to naming a special counsel. I didn't want to lie, but I couldn't tell the whole story. Evasion was my only out: "I think that there is a general reluctance throughout the White House." Mercifully, no one asked a follow-up.

Shortly after Clinton returned from Moscow, on Tuesday, January 18, Bobby Inman put on a mesmerizing and manic performance for the Washington press corps. Looking like a man who was broadcasting instructions transmitted through the fillings in his teeth, he railed against "modern McCarthyism," he criticized the White House for "spinning" his failure to pay social security taxes, he attacked the *New York Times* for how it covered his work as a defense contractor and the *Washington Post* for how it depicted him in an editorial cartoon. His diatribe also cited critical columns by Ellen Goodman and Anthony Lewis, but the bulk of his bile was reserved for William Safire. Inman falsely accused him of plagiarism and added that Safire was conspiring with Senator Dole to derail his nomination. After raising the allegations about homosexuality himself and volunteering to take a lie detector test to prove they were wrong, he denied that there was any other damaging information about to emerge and expressed his firm belief that he would have been "handily confirmed" by the Senate.

Official Washington was transfixed, watching and talking at the same time. Minutes after he first appeared on CNN, Andrea Mitchell called to say, "This guy's a nutcase." Brit Hume observed, "You guys dodged a bullet on this one." "At least I take my medication," joked Bob Boorstin, who often spoke publicly about his struggle to overcome manic depression. Hillary and I had exchanged apologies since our confrontation the week before, and she called to ask if we should "be giving psychological tests to our nominees." The next day's coverage described Inman's performance with adjectives like "breathtaking," "bizarre," and "baffling." Not since Ross Perot cited an alleged Republican conspiracy to disrupt his daughter's wedding as his reason for quitting the 1992 presidential race had the political world seen such a public display of delusion.

We didn't know that Inman was going to act out at his press conference. No one guessed that he would be so brazen, and we probably couldn't have stopped him if we tried. Accepting that the motives of others are inherently obscure, I believe there was a method to Inman's apparent madness — just as his prime target intuited at the time. "I think Inman is not crazy," wrote Safire in response to the admiral's attack. "That was the old disinformation specialist in full manipulative mode, screening his final evasion in a newsy concoction." On this weird episode, he deserves the last word.

Two days after Inman's withdrawal, six months to the day after Vince Foster's suicide, one year following President Clinton's first inauguration, Attorney General Janet Reno appointed a Republican former prosecutor and Wall Street lawyer named Robert Fiske to be the Whitewater special counsel. That morning's *New York Times* poll found that President Clinton had a higher approval rating than either Reagan or Carter on their first anniversaries in office and that the American public had more confidence in the economy than at any time since 1990. The pattern of the Clinton presidency was set.

10   THE WEEKEND I WAS HALDEMAN

C linton loves giving presents. All year long he compiles lists and stuffs his closets with gifts for Christmas and special occasions. On February 10, my thirty-third birthday, he walked into my office holding a tiny brass battleship with an alligator clip attached to the back. The front was etched in black: "PT 109." It was a rare souvenir from the 1960 campaign, one of those tie clips that marked a Kennedy man.

That same night, ABC News evoked memories of Nixon and Watergate. Eighteen minutes of *World News Tonight*'s twenty-two-minute broadcast were dedicated to Whitewater, echoing the time in 1972 when anchorman Walter Cronkite startled the political world by devoting nearly an entire CBS evening news broadcast to the still-unfolding Watergate scandal. But in those early months of 1994, ABC wasn't alone. By mid-March, the three major network newscasts had spent 220 minutes on the fallout from Whitewater — three times what they gave to health care.

The saturation coverage reinforced our bunker mentality, which only made matters worse. The tighter we crouched, the harder they hit, and the stories just kept on coming: Clinton accuser David Hale cut a deal with Special Counsel Fiske; congressional hearings were held on whether the administration had tried to derail the Whitewater investigation; a *Post* story revealed previously undisclosed White House/Treasury "contacts" about the inquiry, precipitating a raft of subpoenas to the White House and the resignation of White House Counsel Bernie Nussbaum.

The *Times* also discovered that Hillary Clinton had parlayed a $1,000 investment into a $100,000 profit in the late 1970s commodities market, which provided a plausible theory as to why she had been so adamant about refusing to publicly release the Whitewater documents. The only real "news" in the documents, which would have included the Clintons' 1978–79 tax returns, would have been Hillary's windfall. Other Rose Law partners who had come to Washington with Hillary faced personal ethical problems. Associate White House Counsel Bill Kennedy, who had been responsible for doing background checks on administration nominees with "nanny problems," had to resign after belatedly admitting that *he* had failed to pay social security taxes for his household help. Webb Hubbell resigned from the Justice Department over a billing dispute with the Rose Law Firm that later became the basis for a fraud and embezzlement conviction.

Whitewater became the catchall term for any allegation of unseemliness or impropriety against anyone anywhere near the Clintons or the White House — and it stuck. Health care and the rest of our legislative agenda were stalled, and the president's approval ratings drifted down. With the fire coming in from so many different directions, I was almost nostalgic for New Hampshire — especially when, for the first time, I had to confront a White House scandal of my own.

It began with a heated phone call on a harried day.

February 25 was not a casual Friday at the White House. I woke to a 5:45 bulletin from my clock radio: An Israeli fanatic had walked into the courtyard of a mosque in Hebron and massacred several dozen Muslims observing their day of prayer. Minutes later, I got a fill from the situation room and fed the latest facts to the television reporters preparing their morning stand-ups from the North Lawn. To make sure the president wasn't blindsided, I left a message at the usher's office for him to check in before his morning jog.

Our morning staff meeting focused on Hebron and health care,

but we also spent a few minutes discussing the coverage of a tumultuous Senate hearing into the Resolution Trust Corporation's investigation of Madison Guaranty and Whitewater. The RTC reported
to Deputy Treasury Secretary (and old Clinton friend) Roger Altman, but Republicans had demanded that Altman remove himself
from supervising the investigation because his close ties to the president created a conflict of interest. Here was another needless fight:
I argued that Roger couldn't, wouldn't, and didn't need to do anything improper to shield the Clintons, so why risk the appearance of
impropriety caused by having him oversee the investigation? But
Nussbaum cut me off, saying that Altman's recusing himself would
be a sign of weakness. I didn't pursue it because I had to help brief
the president for a nine A.M. meeting on the Aldrich Ames spy case
with members of the Senate Armed Services Committee. At 9:45, I
hopped into a White House car with Harold Ickes for a health care
strategy session on Capitol Hill. By 11:30, I was back at the White
House to help brief Clinton for his press conference on the Hebron
tragedy.

The crisis had scrambled everyone's schedules. White House
public liaison Alexis Herman asked me to fill in for Ickes at a meeting with business lobbyists on health care, which made me late for a
long-scheduled lunch with two reporters writing a political history
of the deficit. But after half a sandwich and a few minutes of conversation, Heather popped in with a request from the White House social office. Could I do an emergency "grip and grin" over in the East
Room? A hundred party activists from Iowa were waiting for a reception with the president, who was running an hour late. Hillary
and the vice president had already come and gone, and they needed
another body to keep the crowd warm. Since the Iowa caucuses
were our first barricade against a 1996 primary challenge, I headed
to the East Room.

By the time I returned to my office, a few dozen phone messages
had piled up. One of them was from Josh Steiner — an old friend
from the Dukakis campaign who was now chief of staff to Treasury
Secretary Lloyd Bentsen. He was calling to let me know that Roger
Altman had told Howell Raines, the editorial-page editor of the
Times, that he would recuse himself from the Whitewater matter

after all. That pissed me off — not because I disagreed with Altman's decision, but because the White House was still publicly defending his original stance. It would have been nice to know about the reversal before the *Times* did.

Already upset by the Altman news, I got something else off my chest to Josh. I had heard that Jay Stephens, a former U.S. attorney, might have been appointed by the RTC to investigate the financing of Whitewater, and I couldn't believe it was true. When Clinton took office, he had followed the practice of his predecessors and asked each U.S. attorney, including Stephens, to submit a pro forma resignation. Instead of quietly submitting his resignation letter like his colleagues, Stephens had called a press conference and gone on *Nightline* to accuse Clinton of "obstructing justice," saying that the president was trying to derail his investigation of Democratic congressman Dan Rostenkowski. *How could a Clinton hater like Stephens possibly conduct an impartial investigation? This is unbelievable! He has a clear conflict. How could it happen?* I blew up at Josh and demanded to know how such an unfair choice came to be made and whether the decision was final. Doing his best to calm me down, Josh kept his cool and checked the facts. Later, he said that Stephens had been approved by an independent board of career RTC officials, adding that there was nothing we could do about it. When I heard these details, I knew he was right.

But I was still mad. A little while later, Harold was in my office when Altman called to explain his conversation with the *Times*. We yelled at each other over the speakerphone about Howell Raines and Jay Stephens until I concluded by suggesting that Roger write the president a note explaining his actions. Later in the Oval, I reviewed the day's events with Clinton as he packed up his desk, including a mention of Roger's recusal and the Jay Stephens decision. Hearing these two annoying pieces of information at the end of a long day that began at dawn with the news from Hebron, the president responded with a weary shrug. That was it — four encounters totaling about ten minutes over the course of a fourteen-hour period during which I had more than a hundred conversations. I didn't expect to deal with either Altman's recusal or Stephens's appointment again.

Until I got subpoenaed. Special Counsel Robert Fiske's grand jury requested that the White House turn over documents and testimony about any "contacts" between White House and Treasury Department officials concerning the investigation into Whitewater and Madison Guaranty, and my February 25 phone conversations with Steiner and Altman constituted "contacts." By the end of my White House tenure, receiving a subpoena was a routine matter, another item in the in-box. But when news of these first grand jury requests was splashed in bold type across front pages all over the country, the whole West Wing was rocked. We looked like the Nixon White House now. Although I didn't think I'd done anything wrong, I understood how my phone calls to Altman and Steiner could be made to look like sinister interference with an independent investigation.

Carville was my first call, and he could tell from the sound of my voice that this wasn't just one of my run-of-the-mill bouts of darkness. He jumped in his Jeep, picked me up at the Southwest Gate, and calmed me down by driving around downtown Washington before dropping me back at the White House with a parting piece of advice: Get a lawyer. James then called his own attorney, Bob Barnett, a friend of the Clintons' who had played George Bush in our 1992 debate prep, and Bob offered to meet with me Saturday afternoon.

Over fresh fish at a little place off Dupont Circle, Bob explained that he couldn't be my attorney because his wife, Rita Braver, was covering the White House for CBS News. But he left the table and placed a call to the best political defense lawyer he knew. A few minutes later, I was heading to Stan Brand's office on Fifteenth Street. There are certain events — like my phone call to Josh — that acquire meaning only in retrospect. Others seem significant as they happen: your first kiss, your college graduation, your first house.

The first time you hire a criminal lawyer.

I remembered how my father had teased me by asking when I was going to stop playing around in Washington and get a real job. Now I understood finally and deeply what I should never have let myself forget: that I wasn't a precocious kid playing at politics, that my job wasn't just a game. Walking down Connecticut Avenue as a top White House official about to hire an attorney to represent me in a criminal investigation was a rite of initiation.

For my new lawyer, it was a routine Saturday. A former counsel to House Speaker Tip O'Neill, Stan had carved out his niche in the Capitol by defending political figures facing high-profile investigations. Brand was the perfect attorney for me because he specialized in cases at the intersection of politics, criminal law, and communicating in the Washington echo chamber. He answered the door himself in baseball cap and jeans and asked me to tell him everything. "Don't worry," he said. "It's all privileged, and I can't defend you if I don't know the whole story." After hearing me describe the phone calls with Roger and Josh, he was even more reassuring: "George, losing your temper may look bad, but it's not a crime. You didn't do anything wrong. The only way you can get in trouble now is if you don't tell the truth — and that's not going to happen."

A few days later, a phone call from Stan rekindled my anxiety. "I have some bad news," he said. "Josh kept a diary, and there might be some bad stuff in there." *Bad stuff?* I knew my phone call hadn't been the finest few minutes of my career, but nothing else had happened — how bad could it be? For two nights, I barely slept. Then Stan put me out of my misery by calling back with the specifics, which he had finally received from Josh's lawyer. "It looks bad, George," he said. "But in the end, the diary is exculpatory." Here's what it said:

> After Howell Raines from the *New York Times* called to say that they were going to write a brutal editorial, RA decided to recuse himself. Harold and George then called to say that BC was furious. They also asked how Jay Stephens, the former USA, had been hired to be outside counsel in this case. Simply outrageous that RTC hired him. But even more amazing when George suggested to me that we needed to find a way to get rid of him. Persuaded George that firing him would be incredibly stupid and improper.

That penultimate sentence was tough. I didn't remember using those words, but it wasn't a wild inference given how angrily I had questioned Josh about how Stephens had been selected and whether anything could be done about it. The last sentence was my legal salvation, corroborating the fact that once I received the details from Josh, I didn't pursue the matter any further. According to Stan, the diary might make for a few unhappy headlines, but as a matter of law, it helped establish that my anger was rooted in a proper concern about whether Stephens had a conflict of interest and that I hadn't pressed for any improper act.

Now all I had to do was convince the grand jury that I hadn't taken steps to force Stephens out. My appearance was scheduled for the afternoon of Thursday, March 24.

A little before noon, I walked to Stan's office for a final review of my testimony. Finding myself on the other side of a crucial prep, I realized why Clinton always seemed so subdued just before a big debate or press conference. You zone out when you're concentrating so intensely. Stan was keyed up. He did exactly what I would do with Clinton, peppering me with tough questions like the college coach who used to push me onto the wrestling mat with a parting whack to my head.

"Remember the ground rules," Stan said. "Tell the truth, but don't say more than you know. If you don't remember what happened, say so. Don't speculate, don't wonder, don't muse, don't imagine — don't try to be 'helpful.' "

I was ready for the grand jury, but the court of public opinion still had me worried. Above all, I didn't want to look like a crook. That morning, after considering my options in the shower, I had picked out a suit that was dark but not too funereal, offset by a vibrant blue tie flecked with red and silver. I decided to take a cab to the courthouse instead of a White House sedan because I didn't want anyone to say that I rode in an "official limousine, paid for by the taxpayers." I also didn't want to look like a mobster being arraigned with a raincoat over his head, so when I arrived, I waded right into the riot of reporters and walked to the front door of the courthouse with my head held high. No perp walk for me. If I looked guilty, I would lose power, it would hurt the president, and I wouldn't be able to do my job.

Inside, the white buzz of the fluorescent lighting was a soothing relief from the clamor on the street. With its institutional green walls, molded plastic chairs, and linoleum floors, the third floor of the Federal Courthouse felt like any other government building, and I tried to act as if this was just another part of my job. As we waited for Bruce Lindsey to complete his testimony, I repressed my anxiety and anger at being in a situation like this by methodically returning phone calls from the lone pay phone down the hall. *I'll show them. Their attacks can't stop us from doing our work.* Stan tried to keep my head in the game. He couldn't join me inside the grand jury, and he didn't want me to get sloppy. "If they throw you a curveball," he reminded, "ask for a break and come talk to me."

"Oh, I'll be OK," I said, as if I knew what I was talking about. But my stomach was churning. Despite my bravado, I just wanted this to be over, to be back in the West Wing, prepping the president for tonight's prime-time press conference. Then one of the prosecutors called me into the room.

It was set up like a small theater. The jurors sat three deep against two walls, looking down on a table in the middle of the room. Two prosecutors sat in front of thick three-ring binders on one end of the table; on the other sat a court reporter with a microphone strapped to her mouth like an oxygen mask. The empty seat in the center was mine. But before I sat, the foreman asked me to raise my right hand, just like I'd seen in the movies a thousand times before. Except it was real — and it was *my* right hand. I hoped it wasn't noticeably shaking.

As the prosecutors organized their papers, I tried to make eye contact with the jurors. The majority were black women; most had probably voted for Clinton, and I could tell when I entered the room that many had seen me before: *"Hey look, it's that guy with the hair."* Their reaction calmed me down and increased my confidence. My phone call to Josh wouldn't be the only thing they knew about me. Maybe it was an illusion, but I imagined that my celebrity status forged a bond between us, made me part of their world outside this room. They would judge me, I hoped, by more than my worst moment. The prosecutors were still asking the questions, and I still had to answer them. But now I felt better.

The prosecutors began by reviewing my résumé and asking what my job entailed. When I described my life in the West Wing — the meetings, the crises, the pressures, and the people, making sure to mention that I routinely spoke to the president anywhere from five to twenty-five times a day — I felt as if I was revealing an exotic and exciting world to a captivated (if captive) audience. Sure, one juror was asleep and another in the back kept shaking his head with a sneer, but most of them seemed to be on my side. Only at the very end did I get rattled. The prosecutors asked if I remembered saying to Josh, "This conversation never happened." "No," I said. They asked again; again I said no. Then they told me to leave the room for a minute. "Where did that come from?" I asked Stan. This was the only surprise of the day. "Relax," he said. "They might be bluffing." When I returned, they asked me again. After one more no, I was free to go.

Before I left the third floor, Stan and I huddled in the corner so he could take notes while the session was fresh in my mind. There was still a chance that I would be called back to the grand jury or receive a subpoena from Congress, and an accurate record was added protection against a perjury trap. But by the end of the day, we were sure the worst was over. I told the press assembled on the courthouse steps, "It was very good and very refreshing to be before a tribunal that cared about the facts." Then I walked to the corner encased in a bubble of cameras and took a taxi back to work. It was time for the president's prep.

FRIDAY, MARCH 25

The morning's news was dominated by reviews of the second prime-time press conference of the Clinton presidency, which was dominated in turn by questions about Whitewater. But we were encouraged by the tone of the coverage ("Often at his best when his back is against a wall," wrote Ann Devroy, "the president looked at ease and displayed none of the temper or blame placing he has shown in other forums on this issue") and the hope that we could put the matter behind us. "Cooperation, disclosure, and doing the people's business are the order of the day," Clinton said. "I and my administration will not be distracted."

That's what the country loves about him. No matter what happens, he just gets right up and gets back to work. I did my best to follow his example and was beginning to feel that it might actually be possible. The coverage of my grand jury testimony was minimal and straight, and the accompanying photo of me hailing my own cab added a lighthearted touch. For the first time in a month, I spent an entire morning on health care and other legislative issues — and planned a few days off during the president's upcoming vacation. Then I returned from lunch to a phone message from Ruth Marcus of the *Post*.

"What can you tell me about your conversation with Josh Steiner about Jay Stephens?"

How does she know about that? Grand jury proceedings are supposed to be secret.

"I'll call you back," I said. Then I called my lawyer.

I knew the story about my phone calls would get out eventually, but I had hoped it would be after Fiske had concluded that I hadn't broken the law. As a grand jury witness, I was permitted to talk freely about my testimony, but the prosecutors and jurors are sworn to secrecy. Apparently, though, someone with access and an agenda was leaking on me. While Stan and I considered how to handle the *Post* inquiry, Michael Duffy of *Time* called with the same story, slanted in an insidious way. Confronting me with questions I'd faced in the grand jury, he demanded my reaction to the most damaging quotes in Josh's diary. Though Duffy didn't say it directly, I could tell from his tone that *Time* was preparing a major story — perhaps a cover.

Appearing on the cover of *Time* was even more terrifying than facing a federal grand jury. Stan often reminded me that a determined prosecutor could convince a grand jury to indict a ham sandwich, but I also knew that Fiske had a reputation for fairness and was bound by the federal rules of evidence. Ultimately, the grand jury was required to put my conversations in context — to assess all of the facts, examine motive, and address the clincher argument that nothing had come of the phone calls. *Time*, however, wanted to sell magazines and make an impact on the political world. For them, the fact that Fiske was "investigating" the charges was enough justification to raise the most lurid allegations and print the darkest quotes in their most damning light. A full cover package would read like an indictment. If I failed to rebut the charges swiftly and convincingly, I might face Bernie Nussbaum's fate — resignation under a cloud to save the president political trouble.

On Friday afternoon, *Time* had the article they wanted to write. Duffy was just calling to plug in my quotes. Ruth Marcus seemed more reasonable to me. As a lawyer who had covered the Supreme Court, she knew that my phone call wasn't a felony. After reviewing Stan's notes of my grand jury appearance, I called both reporters back with a statement saying that although "I don't remember exactly what was said," I did have a conversation with Josh Steiner on February 25 in which I asked how Jay Stephens had been hired to investigate Clinton and "blew off steam" over the "unfairness" of the decision.

That statement effectively summarized my grand jury testimony. But now the whole world would read about it, which would humiliate me and harm the president. Although I had been advised not to discuss my grand jury testimony with Clinton, I had to tell him about the press calls and give him the option of asking me to step aside.

He was on *Air Force One*, heading to San Diego for his vacation. I called the White House signal corps from the secure phone console behind my desk, and they patched me through to the *Air Force One* operator. My voice was shaky and the line was scratchy, but the president's message was clear: "George, don't go weak on me," he yelled into the phone. "You didn't do anything wrong. You didn't do a damn thing wrong!"

The sound of Hillary's voice shouting encouragement strengthened me even more. I was about to take a public hit for my overzealous defense of the Clintons, but with both of them behind me, I felt protected — drawn into the select circle of those who bore a scar for the sake of the cause. Now I was a true Clinton man. Before signing off, the president, aware that I might confront an enemy within, issued a final command: "Don't let anybody in there tell you that you did something wrong," he demanded. "If anyone in that White House wants to say that you did, you tell them to come to me."

It was more than I had hoped for and just what I needed to hear. The White House had been asked for an official response, and we'd been discussing what to say all afternoon. I went back to the meeting to make my case, but before we settled on the final wording, I had to leave for my therapist appointment. *I need it more than ever this week.* But driving up Connecticut Avenue, I checked in with Devroy and told her, off the record, that we were considering a statement from the chief of staff expressing his "full confidence" in Harold and me.

"Don't do *that*, George," she said. "It's going way too far; you'll pop this story out of control."

Of course she was right. "Full confidence" is often code for "They did something wrong, but we'll stand by them as long as we can, like until tomorrow." I was so caught up in the controversy that I'd lost my cool, and so had everyone else in our increasingly shell-shocked White House. Ann's spontaneous response crossed a journalistic line, but it was a human reaction — she felt for me, and our ineptitude offended her sense of how a White House should work. It was also sound advice that I wasn't about to ignore. When we finished our conversation, I called back into the meeting I had just left. Harold put me on the speakerphone, but I told him to pick up. "Kill the statement," I said. "Don't ask me why, just kill it."

"What are you talking about, George?"

"Just kill it." Then I whispered. "I talked to Devroy. She says the 'full confidence' line will blow this out of control."

"Fine. Good-bye." The line was dropped.

Now there was nothing to do but wait for the first edition of the *Post.* So I kept a long-scheduled dinner with old friends, knowing full well that the calls would start as soon as the story hit the wire. Like clockwork, my beeper went off shortly after ten, just in time for dessert. I excused myself to return the first call — to Gwen Ifill of the *Times,* who had to match the *Post* scoop in her second edition.

Gwen had started covering the campaign back in the early days of 1991. If she hadn't been covering us, I'd have considered her a friend. I didn't mind getting yelled at by Gwen, or yelling back; that was part of my job. But there was one emotion I never wanted to hear in her voice, or the voice of any reporter, and that was pity. Pity meant, to borrow a Clintonism, that I was "bleeding like a stuck pig."

"George," Gwen said, her voice soft, "you're going to have to tell me about this."

I did, and returned to my cake after hearing Gwen say, "You hang in there, OK?"

But dinner was over. The wires were calling now; I had work to do. On my way home, I stopped at the 7-Eleven by my house to pick up the *Post*. Above the fold, in the right-hand corner, was Saturday's lead: "RTC Lawyer Drew White House Ire: Clinton Aides Questioned Hiring."

I sat in my car and scoured the story, thinking it wasn't so bad. The headline was about anger, not illegality; the subhead didn't suggest that Harold and I had demanded that Stephens be fired, just that we "questioned" his "hiring." The rest followed the same pattern — not fun to read, but fair. It gave my side of the story, with no mention of "full confidence" from the White House. I never imagined that I'd reach a point in my career where my rage would be front-page news, or that I would one day read a story like this and consider it relatively good news. But I went to bed that night thinking things could have been worse.

SATURDAY, MARCH 26

The second I woke up, I reached for the *Post*. Still there. Reading it under the covers, I continued to believe this was survivable. Next I checked in with James, Stan, and my friend Eric to be sure. They all agreed: so far, so good.

But there was still *Time*. When I arrived at the office, Duffy was calling with a final question: "Did the president direct you to call Treasury about Stephens?" "No, absolutely not," I answered. An hour later, *Time*'s advance press release on the Monday edition started to whir through my fax machine:

GRAND JURY INVESTIGATING WHITE HOUSE EFFORT
TO HINDER WHITEWATER INVESTIGATION

The most incriminating charges popped right out of the page. "Special Counsel Robert Fiske and a Whitewater grand jury are weighing charges that White House aides tried — though unsuccessfully — to force the firing of Jay Stephens." *Bullshit. I'm not a target. We asked how he got hired and if anything could be done about it. "Force the firing" is precisely what we didn't do.* "The charges involve the actions of George Stephanopoulos, the president's most trusted political adviser outside of his wife and the vice president." *Yeah, right. The only reason they're saying that is because they're trying to kill me. Might be true, though? Nah, just building me up to tear me down.* "An administration official tells *Time*: 'Based on the facts we believe Fiske has developed during his grand jury session, it's possible that at least one and perhaps several Section 1505 indictments could issue.' Section 1505 of Title 18 in the U.S. Code brands any attempt to 'influence, obstruct or impede the due and proper administration of the law,' a crime punishable by imprisonment of up to five years."

Section 1505 indictments? Obstruction of justice? Five years in prison? What are they talking about? It was a phone call. You can't go to jail for yelling at your friend. Or can you? Maybe Stan's wrong; maybe I am in real trouble. Nah, those bastards are just trying to take me out — turn me into a junior H. R. Haldeman. And how could they get this from an "administration official"? Nobody inside would say that, would they? Or would they? I guess you never really know who . . .

My real friends, though, were already there. I didn't have to call; they just came.

Begala and Sperling, Dreyer and Boorstin, and Tony Lake took a break from real matters of state to join me in the foxhole. Brand plugged in by speakerphone, and we put the skills we had honed in defense of Clinton to work for me. Our strategy was inspired by the daredevil firefighter Red Adair. When I was younger, I had read magazine ads about how Red would creep up close to a blazing oil well, a Rolex strapped to his wrist, and blow out the fire with a blast of dynamite. By writing that I was being investigated for a Watergate felony, *Time* had ignited a political firestorm that I had to extinguish with a mini-explosion of my own. The *Post* story was a good start, but we had to do more. Instead of waiting *Time* out, I had to create my own story. Today.

Smothering the obstruction-of-justice angle was most crucial. That was my lawyer's job. He started calling White House reporters to make sure they understood that someone who asked a question about an official investigation without demanding action could never be charged with obstruction, especially if there was no corrupt intent. He gave the same briefing to the Sunday show hosts and to the legal experts most likely to be called by CNN and other networks. It wasn't enough for my lawyer to claim I was innocent; credible third parties had to back us up.

But I still had to take the lead in my own defense. I couldn't have my lawyer speak for me. If I didn't answer the charges myself — aggressively, immediately, on television — I would look guilty, which was almost as bad as *being* guilty. As always, CNN was the first stop. Their tape would run all day, color the network coverage that night, and influence the talking heads slated to appear on Sunday morning. ABC was also planning a story, so we decided to give them an interview too and then release these two transcripts to the rest of the press. After rewriting my notes three times and walking around the White House grounds with my friends to calm down, I sat in the Roosevelt Room for the interviews.

My script was perfectly consistent with my grand jury testimony. It had to be — any material discrepancy could lead to a perjury charge. I also tried to elaborate on my anger, emphasizing my gut reaction to what I thought was the outrageously unfair appointment of Jay Stephens. He had to be a vivid adversary, someone whose appointment Clinton partisans could attack and objective observers could question. People tuning in to this story for the first time would understand that it was wrong for a partisan opponent of the president to be conducting the investigation; they might even react as I had in the same situation. Mine was an instinctive response to a perceived injustice — a point that was echoed by our new White House counsel, Lloyd Cutler. Finally, I had to give viewers permission to suspend my political sentence and put me on parole instead. That required contrition. "Do I wish now that I hadn't lost my temper?" I asked ABC. "You bet I do." I then apologized and said I'd learned my lesson. In his background interviews, Stan even tried to make my relative youth part of my defense by describing my outburst as a "temper tantrum"— immature but not illegal.

That night I attended Mary McGrory's annual St. Patrick's Day lasagna dinner. Another Clinton lesson: Don't get thrown off track. If I hadn't gone as expected, everyone would think I was ducking because of that morning's *Post*. At dinner, I had to demonstrate that I was taking the allegations seriously without appearing guilty. The first person I saw was NBC's Tim Russert. He was cordial but professionally correct; most of his *Meet the Press* broadcast tomorrow would focus on my story. Republican congressman Jim Leach, Clinton's chief congressional nemesis on Whitewater, would be a guest, but thankfully for me, the show's other panelist would be Speaker Tom Foley. He was also at Mary's that night, and halfway through cocktails he rehearsed an impassioned speech in my defense. Columnist Mark Shields chimed in with a supportive argument he had already made that night on CNN's *Capitol Gang*. Saturday had gone as well as possible.

SUNDAY, MARCH 27

My mood took a slight dip when I saw the Sunday *Times*. Mack McLarty had asked Lloyd Cutler to look into my phone calls, and the *Times* was playing that up on page one as one of two "New Inquiries." Not helpful. But all that mattered now was the talking heads — how they interpreted my story would set the conventional wisdom on whether I could survive. Unable to do anything about it, or even watch, I went to church.

"Your prayers have been answered."

David Dreyer's text message lit up my beeper at the close of the liturgy. Within minutes, I was working the phones. Everyone reported the same good news — a clean sweep of the Sunday shows.

After talking with Mary Matalin, Marlin Fitzwater got my morning off to a good start on C-Span's *Sunday Journal:* "I have to admit that if you stand in George Stephanopoulos's shoes, it would be a little difficult not to be surprised and outraged by that appointment." Chris Matthews made my case on CNN: "I find it very hard in reading the account of George Stephanopoulos that he was doing anything more than I would have done, which is to try to protect the president legally."

On *Meet the Press,* Speaker Foley emphasized my bottom line ("The fact of the matter is that Jay Stephens was not removed") before taking a swipe at *Time.* Then Congressman Leach weighed in. When he said, "I think the White House may have made a mistake," but added that "some of it is pretty natural, and one of the figures in the White House is a young man, and I hope we don't make too much of this part of the story," it felt as if the foreman had appeared to announce the jury's decision, a consensus verdict of Democrats, Republicans, and pundits: not guilty on all felony counts; misdemeanor violation settled by time served.

After celebrating my reprieve at lunch with Eric, I wanted to go home, but that was impossible. My building was surrounded by videocams and sound trucks, and my apartment had become a tourist attraction. For weeks, I'd been trying to unload my one-bedroom without even a nibble, but that afternoon's open house drew sixty-five alleged house hunters. So I circled the city in my Honda, monitoring my situation by cell phone. Leach's sound bite had set the story, and I had no intention of giving any more interviews. But I did want reporters to remember that I had been courteous and accessible under siege, so I returned their calls and explained that I had nothing more to say. Of course that didn't stop them from trying. Adam Nagourney of *USA Today* was most persistent. "C'mon, George, c'mon," he insisted. "I need something new for my story. I need something new. Something fresh."

"Fresh" was exactly what *I* didn't need. Anything inconsistent with what I'd already said could put me in jeopardy. I knew Adam well enough to be as straight with him as he was with me. "Fuck you, Adam," I yelled. "Who cares about your story? This is my life."

After deadline, I joined my old friends Dan and Karen for a movie, *The Paper*, that seemed to be based on this particular episode of my life. The film follows a day in the life of a New York City tabloid whose star writer is trying to trump up a scandal with several columns accusing the city's sanitation commissioner of various misdeeds. Finally, the hapless but not corrupt city official goes berserk and pulls a gun on the writer. As they cart the commissioner away, he asks the columnist why he made him look like a crook.

"You work for the government," replies the columnist. "It was your turn."

In the way that every pop song seems to have deep meaning when your girlfriend dumps you, this insight, I was certain, was the cutting edge of cultural criticism. *Yeah. That's exactly what's wrong with the press today. Don't really care if they're right as long as they're first. Sell the scandal now, settle it later. Accuse you on page one, acquit you on page twenty-three.* But by the end of the night, I was more relieved than bitter, and a check-in call from the president ended my hellish weekend on a high note. Reaching me as my friends and I finished dinner at our favorite Indian restaurant, he joked about the incident that forty-eight hours ago had seemed like a political death sentence. "So who did you in," Clinton asked, "old Josh?" "No, Mr. President, I don't think so," I replied with a weak laugh at the thought of how Josh would squirm if he heard the president talking about him like that.

MONDAY, MARCH 28

The *Post* headline was pleasantly muted: "Stephanopoulos Call Played Down." The *Times* was even more satisfying, playing up the "man bites dog" angle of a Republican's coming to my defense: "Top Clinton Aide Gains Defender in Odd Quarter." Never mind that both accounts were inside the paper; they were the official trial record. By 6:30 Monday morning, before a single subscriber had even received the magazine, the *Time* story was dead.

But when I got to the office, there it was. There *I* was, looking like the punch line to a bad joke. *I wanted to make the cover of* Time *in the worst way — and I did. Ba-dum.* The photo appeared to be a hidden-camera shot of the president and me secretly plotting another Watergate — a grainy black-and-white image of me, haggard and shifty eyed, standing over a seated Clinton, his fingers pressed grimly to his brow. In fact, the *Time* editors had cropped several others out of a file photo of an Oval Office scheduling session, the kind where Clinton would complain about being treated like a pack mule instead of a president before adding five more events to his schedule. Even more disturbing was the headline: "Deep Water: How the President's Men Tried to Hinder the Whitewater Investigation." Nothing nuanced there; indictment and conviction were conflated into a single phrase.

After a weekend on full alert, seeing the cover shut down all my defenses all at once — as if I were emerging from shock and feeling an injury for the very first time. *Nothing else will matter. The picture says it all. Guilty as charged. Four million* Time *subscribers will see my mug shot, and I'll never be able to wipe the image away.* A wave of vertigo swept through me, and I shook with anger — and shame. All weekend long, I'd been fueled by the sense of being wronged. But alone in my office, I also had to admit that I'd *been* wrong. If I hadn't made that unthinking phone call, there wouldn't be a cover photo. If I hadn't lost my temper, maybe I wouldn't have been called to testify. In the heat of the moment, I had forgotten the first rule of White House work: Never say, do, or write anything that you wouldn't want to see on the front page of the *Post*, or the cover of *Time*.

I skipped the morning staff meeting, but that evening I had a commitment that I couldn't avoid. Three thousand Greek Americans from all over the country were at the Washington Hilton for the thirty-first Biennial Congressional Banquet of the American Hellenic Educational and Progressive Association, and I was listed in the program as master of ceremonies.

I was exhausted by the weekend's fight, and the last thing I wanted to do was put on a tux and announce three hours of dinner speeches. But failing to show was the only offense this audience wouldn't forgive. The Greek community had always been there for me. Just that morning, for example, I had received a fax from Mount Athos, where the monks on the Holy Mountain of Orthodoxy wanted me to know they had celebrated a liturgy for my protection. Tonight, I had to return that spiritual favor and recognize the countless others I'd received from my extended family. But it would take more than loyal support and special prayers to get me through my night as toastmaster. I needed some jokes, so I called Mark Katz.

Mark and I had shared an office during the Dukakis campaign, where he served as chief joke writer. Hoping to coin a phrase as memorable as "Where's the beef?" or "Read my lips," Mark, Andy Savitz, and I spent several afternoons crowded around a single computer screen, collaborating on dozens of possible debate lines. But the only one Dukakis actually used was one of mine ("If I had a nickel for every time you called me a liberal, Mr. Bush, I'd qualify for one of your tax breaks for the rich"). Given the fact that Katz was the only real comic in our group, that didn't seem quite fair. So when Mark was interviewing for advertising jobs, we made a trade. He could claim my line as his in return for a mild form of indentured servitude. For the rest of my life, whenever I needed a joke, Mark had to write me one:

"As you can imagine, my mom was quite upset with *Time*. 'George,' she said, 'you really should've gotten a haircut if you knew you were going to be on the cover.'"

Hm. I thought that was pretty good. Better hurry to the next one.

"Jay Stephens has nothing to worry about. I don't get even, I just get mad."

My banquet jokes didn't even draw scattered giggles — just nervous silence. Only then did I realize how badly I had misread my audience. Although we were in the basement of the Washington Hilton, this wasn't your standard Washington roast — where political figures are expected to treat scandals with a dose of self-deprecating humor. Tonight was more like a family reunion, a celebration of clan pride. The AHEPAns who hugged me in the receiving line or approached the dais with Instamatics in hand either didn't know about my predicament or didn't care. To them I wasn't

Nixon's Haldeman or Clinton's young man. I was their boy George. I'd made it to the top and made them proud — the highest-ranking Greek in the White House.

Catching my mistake, I pushed aside the rest of my prepared remarks and spoke from the heart about gratitude and responsibility, about how much I valued my Hellenic roots and how much I owed the Greek *omogeneia*. AHEPA had awarded me my first college scholarship; ever since I'd started to work in politics, the Greek community — Democrats and Republicans — had been my stalwarts. That night, they demonstrated their support again by pretending that the weekend's events had never happened. Reassured and humbled, I returned the favor by pledging to them that I would never let them down.

A few weeks later, Richard Nixon died. On the morning of the funeral, I went to the Oval with Clinton's new communications director, Don Baer, for a final review of Clinton's eulogy. The draft was OK, but one line made me squirm. The president wanted to conclude his remarks by declaring that "the day of judging Richard Nixon based on one part of his life alone has finally come to a close."

It was a generous line — too generous, I feared. For Bill Clinton to issue such a new and sweeping, if only rhetorical, presidential pardon of Nixon would be both presumptuous and provocative. Nixon-hating liberals (who already felt betrayed by Clinton) would see the gesture as a hollow pitch to appease the right wing and would feel that only Nixon's victims — the "enemies," the Cambodians, the framers of the Constitution — had the right to forgive him. Clinton-hating conservatives (who would never trust Clinton, no matter what he said) would suspect that it was a self-referential plea for personal absolution, a slick maneuver aimed at closing off criticism of Clinton's own conduct. To the punditocracy, this would be the line that launched a thousand columns comparing the characters of Clinton and Nixon. Although the comment might possibly have passed without notice, the risk wasn't worth the reward.

But how do you tell your boss that he's insufficiently self-aware, or too altruistic for his own good? Very carefully. I didn't mention the misguided comparisons that Clinton critics were making between Whitewater and Watergate — that would just rile him up. Instead I wondered aloud if we were going a "little too far. I know what you're trying to say, but people might misinterpret what you mean," I suggested. "What if we soften it a bit by saying, '*May* the day of judging Richard Nixon based on one part of his life alone finally come to a close'?" By transforming the draft sentence from a presidential directive into a personal wish, I thought we could preserve the spirit of Clinton's expression without provoking a partisan backlash.

"Yeah, that's good," Clinton said, getting it immediately. Seeing and hearing a liberal like me make this suggestion reminded him of the many people who harbored such strong feelings about Nixon. As I walked Clinton out to the South Lawn, he reminisced about running for Congress in the wake of Nixon's 1974 resignation. Clinton was defeated in that Democratic year, and he never forgot the words of an old man on the campaign trail who was more prescient than the polls: "You're not going to make it, son," predicted the codger. "Hammerschmidt [the Republican incumbent] doesn't have enough stink of Nixon on him to lose."

The taint of scandal hadn't stuck to me either. But two days later, on Friday, April 29, Clinton called me into the Oval to ask about a rumor he'd picked up on the way back from San Clemente. "I don't have any inside information," he told me. "But you're not worried about getting indicted, are you?"

I was now. Clinton picked up lots of information from lots of different places. Sometimes the message was garbled because of his poor hearing; sometimes he couldn't read the notes he had scribbled to himself for follow-up later. But if this rumor was even close to right, I couldn't just blow it off. Excusing yourself from a personal audience with the president of the United States isn't easy, but right then, the only person in the world I really wanted to talk to was my lawyer.

After checking with "sources close to the independent counsel," Stan called back with reassurance and a reminder not to believe everything I heard. That same afternoon, however, a long-running rumor *was* confirmed. Mike Isikoff of the *Post* called to tell me that after months of speculation, Paula Jones had finally decided to file a sexual harassment suit against Clinton. "Do you have any comment?" That was Clinton's call. I checked with him in the Oval Office study.

"Mr. President, I've got some good news and some bad news: The good news is that we heard from the Fiske people that the indictment story is bullshit," I said. "But the bad news is that Paula filed."

"Well," he said, a resigned smile on his face. "I guess I'd rather be sued than have you indicted."

I could've hugged him, but neither one of us could have imagined how fateful Ms. Jones's decision would turn out to be.

When the *American Spectator*'s "Troopergate" story was published in December 1993, the details about a woman named Paula who wanted to be Governor Clinton's "girlfriend" hadn't made a particular impression on me. Set against the potentially more serious charge that President Clinton may have offered the troopers federal jobs in return for their silence, it seemed inconsequential. Even if it was true, who cared if Clinton made a pass at a young woman when he was governor? Only on February 11, 1994, when Paula Jones disputed the account and accused Clinton of sexual harassment, did I begin to pay attention.

Paula leveled her charge from the epicenter of anti-Clintonism — the annual convention of the Conservative Political Action Committee. No network covered the performance live, but from every report that reached my desk, it sounded like a farcical turn on the original Gennifer Flowers circus — minus the incriminating tapes. Though I didn't relish reliving that experience, I couldn't have scripted it better for us. The whole scene screamed "setup job." Paula's chief handler, Cliff Jackson, had been making a cottage industry out of attacking Clinton ever since his involvement with the draft story in 1991. We also heard that Paula had put out feelers for book and movie deals, and that a lawyer close to her had even approached associates of Clinton to ask about a job. By now, I had more experience than I ever would have imagined with situations like this — and it looked and smelled like the kind of "cash for trash" transaction we had beaten back before.

The president's initial reaction reinforced my instincts. When I went to the Oval to get his response, he said he didn't remember her: "What does she look like?" he asked. As difficult as it may be to believe, I was convinced. I had seen Clinton dissemble in the past, but this time he seemed genuine. There was no nervous chatter; he didn't overexplain; he didn't recount a rehearsed story at high speed; and, unusual for him when under siege, he even joked about the trooper angle: "I may be a fat old man now, but in my younger days I never needed any help getting women." I left the Oval believing that he might have met Paula, possibly even flirted with her. But I was also convinced that he didn't harass her, and that she was remembering whatever consensual encounter they had as a crime in order to make a buck.

My belief in Clinton, coupled with contempt for his enemies, was motivation enough to mount his defense. Paula's cause was being promoted by the same people who were trying to block everything we believed in. They were threatening to sue Clinton not because they had a strong case, but because that was the "hook" they needed to get press attention and drag Clinton through the mud. I also still believed that the president deserved some statute of limitations on past conduct that wasn't criminal. *It's just not fair for him to be treated this way. No other president has ever had to put up with as much crap as they throw at him. Even if you believe the worst about him, her story's just not credible. He's not a predator; he'd never pull down his pants unless he knew what was coming next.* Armed with my arguments, I went to work.

My goal was to put Paula Jones in the same category as Connie Hamzy — women whose stories were so suspect that their accounts shouldn't be dignified by the media. Most important, I wanted to keep reports of Paula's press conference off television. So I made my case directly to Tim Russert at NBC, Dotty Lynch of CBS, and Tom Johnson, the president of CNN. It wasn't a hard sell, and ABC was even less inclined to sensationalize a supposed sex scandal because of their twenty-two-minute Whitewater extravaganza the night before. Although we couldn't quash all coverage, our goal was to bury a one-day story inside the Saturday newspapers. Asked to comment, I called the performance a "cheap political fund-raising trick."

Initially, the strategy was effective. The coverage was relatively scanty and slanted our way. But a few days later, Ann Devroy called to say we had a problem with the *Post*. "Downie thinks it's like a Packwood problem," she said, which was a statement with two meanings: first, that executive editor Leonard Downie felt an obligation to investigate the womanizing charges against Clinton because the *Post* had pursued similar allegations against former Republican senator Bob Packwood. Second, Downie thought it was legitimate to look into the Paula Jones episode on the grounds that it may have been part of a pattern of compulsive sexual behavior that still defined Clinton's character. When I reported the conversation to Clinton, he was dripping with contempt: "This is sick, man."

According to Ann, the story was being debated intensively inside the *Post*. Not every editor agreed that the Jones episode was relevant to Clinton's presidency or that there was sufficient rationale to pursue the story. Ann reported that there was a "real back and forth," among her, Downie, the editors Bob Kaiser, Bob Barnes, and Karen Deyoung, and the reporter who was pushing hardest to get Paula's story (*his* story) into the paper, Mike Isikoff. Ann also said (ironically, I thought) that she and Karen Deyoung were the "most dubious" about the story. The other editors didn't think it was ready for the paper, but they were more inclined to give it major treatment if it checked out. "Isikoff," she added, "totally believes this." After talking to Ann, I knew that the only way to kill the story was to convince Downie that it wasn't credible or relevant to Clinton's conduct in the Oval Office.

But first I had to talk to Isikoff, because he was the beat reporter. Before I called him, Bruce Lindsey and I compiled all of the facts — even reviewing Clinton's May 8, 1991, gubernatorial schedule to see if we could prove that Clinton could not have met with Paula when she said. It appeared that Clinton had left the Excelsior Hotel by the time of the claimed encounter, but the people accompanying Clinton that day said he had made an unscheduled afternoon return. We didn't have our silver bullet. But even if we couldn't convincingly disprove her claim, it still came down to a "he said, she said." "Doesn't the president of the United States deserve the benefit of the doubt?" I asked. Isikoff didn't think so, and we squared off over the validity of various contemporaneous accounts. But it was a dialogue of the deaf: I believed Clinton; he believed Jones.

But the most credible testimony came from Danny Ferguson, the trooper alleged to have escorted Paula to Clinton's courtesy suite. Betsey Wright was in contact with him, and what he was saying was problematic for both sides. Ferguson told Betsey that yes, he had indeed introduced Jones to Clinton, but that Jones was ecstatic after the brief meeting and wanted to be Clinton's girlfriend. That made me more skeptical of Clinton's claim that he "didn't remember" being in a room with Paula, but it also disputed Jones's claim that Clinton had harassed her. An additional tidbit helped us: Betsey told me that Paula had approached Ferguson after the publication of the *Spectator* story and asked, "Do you think I can get some money out of this deal?"

So the situation was messier than I first hoped, and I was angry about the fact that Clinton had let me go through the charade of trying to prove he wasn't in the room when in all probability he was. It reminded me of one of the worst moments of the 1992 campaign — the day during April's New York primary when we had to deal with Clinton's draft-induction notice from 1969. Ever since New Hampshire, we'd been denying that Clinton had ever been drafted, but when John King of the Associated Press handed me a copy of Clinton's draft notice, I was shaken. *How can this be? How come Clinton didn't tell us?* "I forgot about it," Clinton had said then. By the time the draft notice reached him at Oxford, he explained, his local draft board had told him to ignore it, so he did.

Forgetting about getting drafted was a hard story to swallow, and now I was more skeptical on this story. But I still believed that his amnesia was closer to the truth than her allegation, that Clinton's private behavior as governor wasn't necessarily relevant to his performance as president, and that it wasn't fair to treat a flirtation as if it were a felony. That was the core of the argument I would make to Downie.

On February 17, we met over crab cakes in the dining room of the Jefferson Hotel. On the understanding that everything I said would be off the record, I came prepared with notes sketched on a long yellow pad — a political brief for why the *Post* shouldn't run the story. Despite the sordid subject matter, I felt like a man on a noble mission. Not only was I serving my boss, but I was also taking a stand against the tabloid culture. I imagined myself in the tradition of presidential advisers called to solemn deliberations with barons of the fourth estate over how to balance the public's right to know with the president's responsibility to govern.

I began by flattering the *Post*, emphasizing that our extraordinary efforts to keep Paula's account out of the paper demonstrated our respect for the *Post* and our belief that whatever appeared on its pages would rightfully be taken seriously by the rest of the world. Then I turned to Paula's credibility. Her three years of silence, her refusal to rule out book and movie royalties, and her association with CPAC, I argued, all called her story into question. People who worked with her in Arkansas, I added, had also told Isikoff that she was an unreliable employee who seemed to have a crush on Clinton.

Next, I served as Clinton's character witness. I told Downie about the moment when I had told the president about Paula's press conference. When I mentioned her name, I recounted, Clinton had drawn a blank, and he didn't seem to be faking when he claimed that he didn't remember meeting her. Omitting my subsequent doubts, I added that I had seen Clinton fudge before and had believed him this time. Then I went even further, saying that even if you believed that Clinton was a womanizer, it wasn't credible that he had acted this way with this woman at this time. That's just not his style, I said. Why I thought I knew that is hard for me to figure out now, but it made sense then.

I also tried to use Ferguson's testimony to our advantage. Sure, he puts Clinton in the room with Jones, I argued, but you can't take half his story and throw away the rest. If you believe Ferguson, then you also should believe that Paula Jones didn't feel harassed at the time. And if you believe that, then you have no justification for printing her charges three years after the fact, when she has dozens of reasons to embellish her story. Assume Ferguson's story is true: The fact that Clinton flirted with someone when he was governor of Arkansas does not belong on the front page of the *Post*. By printing Paula's charges against a sitting president, no matter how many qualifiers are hidden beneath the headline, the *Post* is reaching a provisional judgment. You're telling the world, I concluded, that her story is true — and we're put in the nearly impossible position of having to prove a negative.

Downie hardly said a word. Polite but imponderable, he heard me out, asked a few questions, took some notes, and thanked me for my time. He was doing his job, and I was doing mine. And though I don't know what role our conversation played in the decision, I was proud of the fact that Isikoff's account didn't appear in the *Post* until May 4, the day after President Clinton retained attorney Bob Bennett to represent him in the impending civil suit of *Jones v. Clinton*.

With the statute of limitations for Jones's legal claim set to expire at the end of the week, Bennett had first tried to negotiate a preemptive settlement with Jones's lawyers. In the initial phone call, Jones's lead attorney, Gil Davis, took a hard line, saying that Ms. Jones was all but certain to file suit and that she was "prepared to discuss the president's private parts." But when the settlement talks heated up on the afternoon of May 5, Bennett camped out in my office so that he could personally consult with Clinton on the final details.

The president was in the Oval, working the phones for the House vote on an assault weapons ban. Despite intense lobbying by the National Rifle Association, we were within a few votes of victory, and Clinton was doing all he could to put it over the top. I shuttled between the two sets of phone calls, but I should have known after our cliff-hanger victory on assault weapons that Paula Jones would surely file suit. In Clinton's world, good news rarely arrived without a shady companion.

Early in the afternoon, Bennett thought he could buy more time. He called Davis from my easy chair and said that he couldn't "get an answer by today. It's a busy day at the White House, and this is not a decision I can make." The offer Jones had on the table was for the president to read a public statement confirming that they had met and apologizing for any defamatory statements about Ms. Jones from him or his staff. Although it would later seem like a small price to pay, at the time it appeared unacceptable. We couldn't agree to subject the president to such a public spectacle over an incident he had denied. In addition, the Jones attorneys were asking us to sign a "tolling agreement." That meant we would agree to suspend the statute of limitations for Jones's sexual harassment claim, and they would reserve the right to file a lawsuit at any time. That was a nonstarter for us; if we agreed to a settlement, it had to be final. We couldn't run the risk that as Clinton's reelection campaign approached, they would concoct a reason to refile the lawsuit.

In his conversations with Davis, Bennett used me as a foil. He said that the president's "political advisers will go nuts" about any settlement, and that we were adamant about holding the line on a public apology by the president. Davis responded with a joke: "You know about the Stephanopoulos bond, don't you? It doesn't mature." It rankled me a little, but I was happy to play bad cop. The president adamantly denied harassing Jones. I believed him, and with reelection only two years away, I thought it was perilous to admit to a boorish act like that, especially if it wouldn't eliminate the threat of a lawsuit. But Bennett and I did draft a counterproposal that he read to Davis over the phone:

> I have no recollection of meeting Paula Jones on May 8, 1991, at the Excelsior Hotel. It is entirely possible that I did meet with her on that date.
>
> If such a meeting occurred, neither she nor I did or said anything of a sexual nature. I regret the untrue assertions which may have been made about her.

I was willing to propose to Clinton that this statement be issued as a written release from the White House press office, provided that Ms. Jones would publicly agree with the statement that the president hadn't said or done anything inappropriate and that the statute of limitations would expire on schedule. I thought at the time that we couldn't admit any more than this: It satisfied Ms. Jones's public complaint that she had been defamed by the *American Spectator*'s claim that she had sex with Clinton without forcing the president to admit to behavior that he had denied.

But the tolling agreement was a bottom line for the Jones team, and it wasn't clear that Paula would agree to publicly confirm the president's claim that he hadn't done anything wrong. These conditions fueled my suspicion that Paula would see if she could sell her story and then concoct an excuse to refile the lawsuit as the 1996 election approached. Bennett, while preferring a settlement, was also convinced that he could win the case in court. Within hours, the debate was moot. The Jones team pulled out of the negotiations with the excuse that they needed a tolling agreement because they couldn't trust the White House not to trash Paula.

The next morning, as we prepared for a prolonged legal and public-relations battle, we joked about which one of us would have the privilege of talking to the president about his "distinguishing characteristics." It wasn't the kind of subject that had come up before in the confines of the West Wing; I didn't remember reading anything like it in Clark Clifford's memoirs or Haldeman's diaries. That the president was in a fighting mood made it all easier. When Bennett and Cutler reviewed the details, he reacted vehemently, without hesitation, and offered to have a urologist examine him and file an official affidavit on the spot. Later, when we were alone in the Oval and he seemed more dejected, I tried to buck him up by saying that we would make history when he was reelected despite all this garbage.

"You *may* be right," he responded with skeptical hope. "Andy Jacobs [Democratic congressman from Indiana] told me that I'd be remembered with Adams and Truman as a great president who was vilified while in office because he was doing tough things."

Clinton understood how fierce his enemies were, and he was willing to pay the personal price for advancing his public agenda. He also knew that he had no "distinguishing characteristics," but he failed to comprehend the complexity of his own character. Had he been able to predict how he would react as Paula's case made its way through the legal system, Clinton would have never permitted it to go forward — if only for the harm it would do to everyone and everything he cared about. Me neither; in retrospect, the risk of a tolling agreement seems painfully small.

But who knew? In May of 1994, Monica Lewinsky was still in college.

11 THE LONGEST SUMMER

The Japanese prime minister had the American president on hold, and Clinton wasn't happy. But his impatience on the morning of May 24, 1994, had more to do with domestic politics. A few hours earlier, the polls had opened in Kentucky for a special election to replace the late William Natcher, a courtly Democrat who had cast a record 18,401 consecutive roll-call votes over a forty-year congressional career. Although no Republican had been elected from Kentucky's Second District since 1865, the president was worried about the race. Shielding the phone with his right palm, Clinton said he wanted to be campaigning: "It's Nazi time out there. We've got to hit them back."

Afraid that Prime Minister Hata would overhear and misinterpret the president, I talked him down, suggesting that the Republicans' harsh campaign tactics could backfire. "They might," he replied. "But not if we don't stand up to them." Then, seamlessly, "Thank you, Mr. Prime Minister, I think you've found your voice in more ways than one. . . ." Minutes later, after jump-starting trade talks with Japan, Clinton felt better. "I like Hata. Speaks more English than he lets on; caught himself answering my questions before they were translated. But he's a good politician."

High praise, like Joe DiMaggio's calling someone a "pretty good ballplayer." Clinton's feel for electoral politics extended abroad; he intuitively calculated the domestic pressures facing his counterparts like Hata, Helmut Kohl, or Boris Yeltsin. Since his biorhythms were tuned to election cycles, he usually knew when to push and when to hang back. Campaigns, he always said, were his "best friend." But that morning he was blind to his own political predicament. Our Democratic House seat was imperiled all right, but letting Clinton campaign would only have made matters worse. In 1994, the voters just didn't like their president. Republican polls showed that only 30 percent of the voters in that Kentucky district thought Clinton deserved reelection, and even half of the Democrats polled thought it was time to send him a message by voting Republican.

Whitewater, Paula Jones, and other missteps like gays in the military weren't our only problems. By the spring of 1994, even our legislative successes were working against us. The Brady Bill and the assault weapons ban had enraged and energized members of the National Rifle Association, but the general public didn't know yet that crime was down. Voters heard Republicans call our economic plan "the largest tax increase in the history of the universe," but they had yet to feel the benefits of lower interest rates and stronger growth. Our labor base was depressed by the president's all-out effort on the NAFTA agreement they considered a job killer, but the corporate interests profiting from the pact showed their gratitude by attacking our health care plan. Rush Limbaugh and other talk-show hosts were fanning all of this smoldering resentment into an angry flame, and Republican strategists had crystallized the intense anti-Clinton mood into a single, devilishly clever campaign commercial: the "morph ad."

Thanks to digital technology, voters in Kentucky's Second District saw a photo of Joe Prather, the Democratic candidate, slowly dissolve into an image of the president as an off-screen announcer ominously warned, "If you like Bill Clinton, you'll love Joe Prather." Sending a Clinton clone to Congress was about the last thing voters wanted in 1994. Prather lost by ten points, and the Republicans had a road-tested strategy for November's midterm elections.

Turnabout *is* fair play. In 1992, our campaign had exploited voter anger at President Bush for breaking his "Read my lips" pledge by broadcasting a series of commercials consisting entirely of video footage of Bush promising "no new taxes" or discussing the dismal economy. But neither Clinton nor I was in a philosophical mood when we received the early returns from Kentucky. A little before 7:30 that evening, I accompanied the president to a working dinner on our upcoming European trip to commemorate the fiftieth anniversary of D day. He yelled the whole walk through the Rose Garden colonnade. "I told you," he said. "We have *no* strategy. We shouldn't be getting beat this badly. Nobody has our talking points. Nobody knows what we've done."

Better distribution of our "talking points" wouldn't have helped much, but the president was right. With the country at peace and the economy improving, we should have been in better shape — and those of us on the political team deserved our share of blame. But I instinctively depersonalized the outburst and refocused the president by lapsing into jargon. "We have real opportunities coming up with D day and the G-7 trip," I said. "Our numbers will rise to match the fundamentals if we have a good performance."

Another irony. We had defeated President Bush, in part, with the charge that he spent too much time and attention on foreign policy. Now I counted on escaping our domestic difficulties by going abroad. Having President Clinton on the world stage, surrounded by fellow statesmen and cheering crowds, would help the country see him in a new light. It had to. Our legislative agenda was floundering, and our poll numbers were plummeting. At a Memorial Day weekend strategy session, Clinton complained that the "American people hired me to get things done, but I'm becoming a prisoner of Congress." I was starting to take it all personally. The American people were rejecting the Congress I worked for, the president I helped elect, and the policies I cared about most.

But they couldn't take away *Air Force One*. To climb its back steps was to enter a world even more rarefied than the White House itself. Inside the huge cabin are all the comforts of home and office combined: couches flanked by bowls of fresh fruit and candy in the corridors; a conference room with two TVs in the wall and a library of first-run movies; offices with computers, fax machines, copiers, and phones; a full kitchen crew serving hot meals and cold drinks around the clock. Up front, the president has a one-bedroom apartment with an office, full bath, and king-sized bed.

Once we were airborne, Clinton changed into jeans and a flight jacket and patrolled the halls like the captain of a cruise ship. After reviewing his itinerary in the conference room, he joined us for a movie over baskets of tortilla chips and salsa, while Hillary and her staff lounged on the couches outside the door. The president wandered over to catch up on White House gossip and tell tales about how he learned his trade in tiny Ozark churches where they charm snakes and speak in tongues. Hillary had heard it all before, but she seemed to enjoy it anyway, letting him ramble on with an indulgent smile.

From the moment we touched down in Rome, I felt enhanced, like more than an embattled presidential aide or a member of the Clinton team. Here in Europe, half a century after the battles that defeated fascism, I was an emissary of both my country and my generation. My main responsibility on the D day trip was to monitor the home front, but like the rest of our entourage, I was seized by a sense of history and humility. Sure, we hoped the president would get a political bounce from the trip, but we wanted even more to honor the generation that had made our world possible. At every ceremony, with every speech, in every detail, we wanted to express how grateful we were to be "the sons and daughters of the world they saved."

President Clinton spoke those words across a field of marble bordered by cypress and pine — Nettuno's American cemetery. This speech and every other D day ceremony included a variation on our theme —"We are the children of your sacrifice"— along with heart-stopping gestures of remembrance: At Nettuno, a fighter squadron roared low over the crowd, the jets ascending in unison until a single plane suddenly vanished, like a silver bird plucked to heaven by an invisible, almighty hand. Its mates soared on, an empty space their silent tribute to "the lost flyer." Over the moist, mown lawns of Cambridge, bagpipes pierced the fog with a haunting "Amazing Grace." At dawn, from the deck of the USS

George Washington, fifty years to the hour after D day's first landing, a single wreath was tossed into the sea. Off the cliffs of Pointe d'Hoc, a lonesome gull hovered at attention for a lone bugler playing taps.

I absorbed these moments from the edges of the crowds, assessing Clinton's performance with one eye, appreciating its meaning with the other. At Colleville-Sur-Mer, I sat behind a sunburned man with a snow white crew cut. When Clinton spoke of Corporal Frank Elliott — one of "the fathers we never knew, the uncles we never met, the friends who never returned, the heroes we can never repay" — the veteran started to cry. His wife reached over to rub his back, and I was acutely aware of being two people at the same time. My human side was moved by the sight of an aging soldier being consoled as he remembered his youth, his mission, and his fallen comrades. My political twin was jumping out of his skin. *Perfect. It's working. Clinton rose to the moment again. Even the sun broke through when he started to speak.*

Just as Clinton finished, the man turned around, thinking he would find Dee Dee, whose place card had been on my seat. He had a message for the president: "My name is Frank Callahan. I didn't vote for your man, but I'm a veteran of Omaha Beach. And as a very staunch conservative Republican, please convey to the president how very proud I was of him today. Frank Elliott was with me . . ." He couldn't go on. The tears were back, unbidden, and he tried to stop them by tapping his fist to his chest. Then he smiled. "Where's that Dee Dee? She's cute as a bug."

The trip was filled with little thrills. Like standing on an aircraft carrier in the Atlantic and hearing the loudspeakers bellow, "AMERICA LANDING" as your boss's helicopter touches down on the deck. Or jogging by his side through the stone streets of Rome, with Secret Service agents on bicycles clearing the path ahead and kids on sneakers yelling from behind, *"Cleen-ton, Cleen-ton."*

In Paris, François Mitterrand more than matched his reputation. I couldn't wait to meet him. The moment came just before a joint interview with Clinton on French television. Wendy Smith, the president's trip director, and I were heading to Clinton's holding room when we saw the French president strolling our way, with his head down and his hands clasped behind his back, apparently deep in thought. As we crossed paths, he looked up abruptly and blocked our way — and not (as I fantasized) to make the acquaintance of the young presidential adviser he'd heard so much about.

"Bonsoir, madam," he said, bowing slightly as he locked eyes with Wendy, a statuesque beauty with luxurious hair. He took her in from head to toe and back again, lingering in appraising silence. I got a nod.

At the state dinner that night, the dining room was a scene from Versailles. Every table had a name (I was at "Begonia"). Candles were the only light for a meal of lobster topped with caviar, followed by quail stuffed with truffles the size of chestnuts. The champagne was tinted dusty rose, matching the linens and walls. After Mitterrand's closing toast, a few of us joined the Clintons for a midnight tour of the Louvre's new wing. "What a shame you can't be here during the day to see the sunlight play," apologized our guide, the wing's architect, I. M. Pei.

That last night in Paris was a festival of wonderful excess. I stayed up all night, staving off the bad news back home, ignoring for a few more hours the tensions beneath the surface splendor of our European trip.

The trouble had begun on the Saturday before the anniversary of D day. We had just finished lunch at Chequers with Prime Minister John Major, and Clinton was meeting for the first time with Tony Blair, the Labour Party leader. Back at the White House, a small group coordinated by David Dreyer was quickly reviewing advance copies of Bob Woodward's new book, *The Agenda*, and faxing us summaries with suggested responses. The next day, all of Washington would read an excerpt on the *Post*'s front page, and the rest of the country would see Woodward in person on *60 Minutes*. We were in for a media blitz.

That was the power of Woodward. What he wrote, people read. His apparently omniscient accounts of how Washington works had toppled a president, exposed the cloistered corridors of the Supreme Court, unveiled the clandestine operations of the CIA, and revealed a White House at war in the Persian Gulf. Now his sights were set on us. For more than a year, he'd been chronicling the economic policy wars inside our White House. His book, as he predicted in the letter I had hand-delivered to President Clinton eight months earlier, would be "the most serious contemporaneous examination of your administration's economic policy."

In the summer of 1993, several months into his project, Woodward's first call to me had sparked two simultaneous thoughts: *Oh, no!* and *I have arrived.* His books invariably created embarrassing headlines for their subjects, but his sources were assumed to be the most important, connected, and knowledgeable people in Washington. I was wary of Woodward but flattered and curious too. I also considered it part of my job to know what he was up to and make the best of it. We met for a late dinner at his Georgetown town house, where I received the full Woodward treatment.

The polished wood of his dining-room table was topped with neatly stacked, typed notes and a pocket tape recorder. Over home-roasted chicken, he hit me with memos from one of our first economic meetings, then some handwritten notes from another, followed by word-for-word transcripts of what I had said at a third. Woodward's technique is no less effective for being so obvious: He flashes a glimpse of what he knows, shaded in a largely negative light, with the hint of more to come, setting up a series of prisoner's dilemmas in which each prospective source faces a choice: Do you cooperate and elaborate in return (you hope) for learning more and earning a better portrayal — for your boss and yourself? Or do you call his bluff by walking away in the hope that your reticence will make the final product less authoritative and therefore less damaging? If no one talks, there is no book. But someone — then everyone — always talks. The deadliest initial response was my instinctive one: "Well, it wasn't like that exactly. . . ."

"Really? . . . *Innn*teresting. . . . I didn't *know* that. . . . Tell me. . . ."

Our dance had begun, the mutual seduction of reporter and source. Woodward's calculated charm was custom tailored to my intellectual vanity, professional pride, and personal loyalty to the president. I knew that Woodward always beguiled sources into saying more than they should. But like so many others who had supped at his table and spoken into his cassettes under the cover of "deep background," I was arrogant enough to believe that I could beat him at his own game, that my spin would win. I thought it was possible to soften Woodward's negative slant with context and perspective, or overwhelm it with up-close and personal accounts of the president's public-spirited fortitude, intelligence, and empathy.

I knew that there was a risk in openly cooperating with Woodward, but at the time, I accepted it as the price of loyalty. It would *appear* more loyal to ignore Woodward, I reasoned, but it would actually *be* disloyal because it would cede the book's battleground to those who didn't have Clinton's best interests at heart. I was so sure the book was going to be damaging, so sure I knew how to prevent it, and so sure my motives were beyond question, that I took it on as my personal project.

What I couldn't fully admit to myself, of course, was what I surely also knew: that even spinning you think is selfless is an act of self-aggrandizement — especially with a reporter of Woodward's stature. Talking to him in an authoritative way demonstrates that you were in the room and in the know. Working on Woodward's book was my job, but it also fed my ego. Relishing the role of fixer, I encouraged friends and allies like Carville, Sperling, Begala, and Greenberg to cooperate with Woodward. I also urged Hillary to do an interview, gave three interviews myself, and handed Woodward's private letter to the president without telling anyone else about it.

The interview request was masterly; Woodward knew his subject and his potential source. He opened with bland understatement:

> I believe you are aware that I am writing a book on government economic policy-making. The book already has a heavy and growing emphasis on your administration.

Followed by intimidation:

> I already have accumulated more than 100 pages of typed notes, memos, recollections, charts, and tables on just one of

the pre-Inaugural meetings (January 7, 1993, in Little Rock) you had with your economic team. . . .

Obligatory humility:

But I have wondered many times, what am I missing? A lot, no doubt — too much. My reporting has yielded enough that I am definitely humbled by what I don't know. . . . Though much of what I have comes from the inside, I've written enough about government and Presidents to know that the most powerful inside account is still really from the outside. It lacks the perspective of the President. . . .

An appeal to history:

Richard Reeves, in his remarkable new book on President Kennedy, *Profile of Power*, poses the graphic and compelling question: What is it really like to be President? . . . Reeves was forced to rely on substantial documentary records and the testimony of others near, but not at, the very center. He never interviewed Kennedy. . . .

A civic-minded slap at the press:

Just in eight months, it's clear you've been on a singular journey. But the published and broadcast accounts of it miss far too much. Public dialogue is at too low a level. Aren't the problems of governing connected to the shallow discourse? Don't Phil Donahue and Rush Limbaugh and the twenty-second update dilute understanding and short-change the public? People ought to know, or at least have the chance to know, as authoritatively as possible, the truth. . . .

Fair warning and reassurance:

Might it involve some loss of control and some risk? Yes. . . . [But] I don't intend a how's-he-doing assessment. . . . No cheap shots. No cheerleading . . .

And a big, flattering, irresistible finish:

> In my last book, *The Commanders* . . . I ended the introduc-
> tion with this idea: "The decision to go to war is one that
> defines a nation, both to the world and, perhaps more im-
> portantly, to itself. There is no more serious business for a
> national government, no more accurate measure of national
> leadership."
>
> I wrote that in the spring of 1991. About that time, you
> made the point to friends and associates that the battlefield
> had shifted. National self-definition, seriousness, and lead-
> ership would next be measured by economic and domestic
> policy. You were right.

Clinton secretly met with Woodward, and *The Agenda* largely
lived up to the promise of that hand-delivered letter. Taken as a
whole, in the fullness of time, it is a comprehensive and basically accurate account of how we developed and passed an economic plan
that worked. But that's not how it played in June of 1994. Appearing on *60 Minutes*, Woodward boiled the whole book down to a
less-than-twenty-second sound bite: "Chaos. Absolute chaos." *The
Agenda* was marketed as the most persuasive proof yet that Clinton
was an undisciplined and indecisive president leading an inexperienced, out-of-control White House. The repercussions were
immediate.

Mack McLarty was the first casualty. Woodward's book crystallized the conventional wisdom that Clinton needed a stronger chief
of staff from the Washington establishment. Mack was a good man,
a successful business executive, and a close Clinton friend, but he
had never worked in Washington — and Clinton never gave him
real authority. When Clinton was first considering Mack, I encouraged the choice, myopically thinking that my relative wealth of
inside-the-beltway experience would increase my power within the
West Wing. But even before *The Agenda* was published, it was clear
we needed a change, and even I wanted a tough chief of staff who
could corral the president and keep his headstrong independent operators (like me) in line.

During the flight to the D day ceremonies, Leon Panetta and I spent a few minutes alone in the empty back passenger section. I knew Leon from the Hill, where he was chairman of the Budget Committee and a close friend and ally of Dick Gephardt's. A former Republican, he was a bit too much of a fiscal disciplinarian for my taste, but he had a big heart, first-generation immigrant values, and an infectious laugh. When he said that Clinton wanted to talk to him about replacing Mack and asked for my advice, I was encouraged. Leon's indefatigable, disciplined leadership was exactly what we needed. I handed him the book I was reading, *The Haldeman Diaries*, with a placemark on page 309, an entry recounting a 1971 Nixon speech to his cabinet. "Here," I told Leon. "You need this, this ultimate control":

> From now on, Haldeman is the Lord High Executioner. Don't you come whining to me when he tells you to do something. He will do it because I asked him to and you're to carry it out. . . . I want discipline. It's up to Haldeman to police it. . . . When he talks, it's me talking, and don't think it'll do you any good to come and talk to me, because I'll be tougher than he is. That's the way it's going to be.

"You need a broader mandate than Mack's," I continued. "You need the power not to be overridden, not to have to deal with three different White Houses. You need to be a dictator."

Leon thanked me and took the book. If he appreciated the irony in the exchange over the diary excerpt, he didn't mention it. (Nixon had tried to fire Panetta from the Office of Economic Opportunity for disloyalty. Leon resigned.)

I didn't realize the joke was on me. Everyone has a blind spot; mine was on the issue of loyalty and leaks. I was trying so hard to stop bad stories that I thought I was immune to being blamed for them. I assumed I was part of the solution, but the president and Hillary were beginning to think I was part of the problem, and *The Agenda* became their proof. The overall impression left by the book was bad enough. The quotes attributed to me were even worse:

"You've got to always keep in mind," Stephanopoulos said to one of his closest associates, that watching Clinton "is like a kaleidoscope. What you see is where you stand and where you're looking at him. He will put one facet toward you, but that is only one facet." . . .

Leon Panetta was up next. Campaign aides had told him that Clinton was deadly slow to make decisions. "The worst thing about him is that he never makes a decision," Stephanopoulos had said.

Woodward's attribution clearly indicates that he didn't get these quotes from me. But I had said things like this in the White House when I was trying to explain Clinton to my new colleagues. These "closest associates," or one of *their* "closest associates," then passed the anecdotes on to Woodward. Whatever their provenance, the words appeared far more damning in the black-and-white type of a number one bestseller than when they evaporated into a West Wing hallway. And my unvarnished assessments combined with my earlier advocacy of Woodward's project enraged Clinton.

Which means I didn't hear about it directly at first. I rarely took Clinton's outbursts personally; more often than not, they passed right through me. But I did worry about his silences. As I was still learning, there were many dimensions to Clinton's anger, and he was a virtuoso at expressing them.

The most common and least virulent strain of Clinton's anger was the morning roar. He's not a morning person. He wakes up cranky and moves slowly. The morning roar was a way of clearing his throat before breakfast, like a rooster greeting the dawn, but with an edge. It rarely signified any deep seething, just irritation at an outside event that he couldn't control, like an overcrowded schedule, a speech draft he didn't like, or almost any story in the morning paper. Typically, he'd be at his desk in the Oval, surrounded by little piles of notes that he'd just removed from his briefcase, holding the offending article at arm's length. He'd push the paper toward me, his voice rising in staccato bursts to emphasize his point: "This . . . is . . . just . . . *wrong*. . . . It's just not honest. . . . I don't . . . have time . . . to *think*. . . . I try . . . and try . . . and try . . . to tell you . . . but they never . . . get it . . . *right!*" As long as Clinton stayed seated at his desk, there wasn't much to worry about. I'd promise to fix the problem, explain the reasoning behind the day's event one more time, sympathize with him on press bias, and change the subject.

A close cousin of the morning roar was the nightcap, which I rarely witnessed. I generally heard it over the phone, but I could imagine him in jeans and a sweatshirt at the kitchen counter, surrounded by his ubiquitous piles, with the television on in the background. The trigger event was usually a conversation with Hillary, a phone call from a friend in Arkansas about some new right-wing outrage, or a critical Senate floor speech that he had just seen replayed on C-Span. Like the morning roar, it usually wasn't too serious. Again, a promise to fix it in the morning, coupled with some reassuring words or a tidbit of gossip, usually worked like a glass of warm milk. The nightcap was a problem only when the evening upset didn't fade with a good night's sleep. That was a sure sign that more serious trouble was brewing.

The slow boil could develop during a single meeting or over the course of a couple of days — or even weeks. Unlike the first two variations, the slow boil wasn't sparked by a single precipitating event. It was, instead, the eruption of a resentment that had been churning inside him, and every external event became new evidence that the underlying condition wasn't being addressed. Certain recurring phrases were sure signs of a serious slow boil: "These leaks are killing us. . . . Al From is right; all we are is a bunch of yuppie elitists. . . . You lashed me to the Congress like Captain Ahab. I'm *president*, not prime minister. . . . The Senate is full of wimps. I raise them money, get them reelected, but one word from Howell Raines or the Republicans and they fold." The slow boil built like a baroque concerto, with intricate variations on a theme, repeated and repeated at increasing volume until the crescendo ended in a crash of exhaustion. Slow boils were the product of deep-seated structural problems, not trivial matters. Although the outbursts were unpleasant, they were usually justified.

Two other types of outbursts were more calculated: the show and the last gasp.

The show was Clinton's way of making himself mad for the benefit of someone else in the room, usually Hillary. Over the course of the health care fight, he often exploded in legislative strategy meetings as a way of protecting Hillary and telling us to take her seriously. The last gasp was generally reserved for those times when Clinton suspected that he had made a mistake but didn't want to admit it. It would also contain elements of counterattack and a little preemptive blame laying. "I'll do this if you want me to, but I have to say, I think it's *wrong!*" A good example was Clinton's earlier-described performance on the conference call to decide which ads to run over the final weekend of the 1992 campaign.

The worst of all was the silent scream. No yelling, no finger in your face, nothing. Just silence. I would walk into the office, and he wouldn't look up; the slightly formal "Hello, George" would sound more like an irritating obligation than a greeting. He wouldn't automatically turn to me to gauge my reaction to his new idea or his proposed answer in a press conference. He wouldn't stop by. He wouldn't call. And worst of all, he wouldn't mention what had made him so mad — because it was me.

Toward the end of the D day trip, I knew Clinton was raging about Woodward — he had to be. But he didn't discuss *The Agenda* in my presence. The only inkling I got of how angry he was came below the decks of the USS *George Washington.* As we walked toward a makeshift television studio for the president's interview with NBC's Tom Brokaw, I warned Clinton about a new *Newsweek* poll that rated Colin Powell and Bob Dole ahead of him as "role models" for America's young people. Both were potential rivals, and if Brokaw blindsided Clinton with the news, it could make for a petulant interview.

Dozens of times before, that kind of last-second intervention had saved the day. But not now. Clinton seized up and stared straight down at me, his clear blue eyes clouded with suppressed rage. "I didn't need that now, George. I didn't need you to bring me down." I perceived the rebuke as an outburst, but he wasn't yelling at all. He was all control, and his words had a metallic tone. It was the first manifestation of a resentment that would last for months.

Hillary didn't mask her anger. Over the next several weeks, *The Agenda* became her single-bullet theory for our summer troubles. "The whole problem with this administration is the Woodward book," she said at one July strategy session. "It's hurting us overseas, and it's the reason all our numbers are down. There are people who go out there with no loyalty to the president, no loyalty to the work we have to do for the country, just seeking to aggrandize themselves. And I hope they're *satisfied!*"

I wasn't — disloyal or satisfied. Deciding to grant such broad access to Woodward was a mistake — a naive lapse of judgment. Had I been more mature and disciplined, I might have seen that there was no way to win with Woodward; a less authoritative account would have been less damaging to our agenda in the short term. My open cooperation, however, was not an act of treachery. Nor was it the sole source of our political turmoil in the summer of 1994.

After forty years of dominating Congress, our party had become a complacent feudal kingdom no longer bound by fervent belief or fear of the king. Each member was master of a barony, each chairperson, lord of a duchy. Our majority was more a tactical alliance of autonomous factions than a political movement based on shared values and a coherent governing philosophy. Striking at our weakest seams, Republican strategists pitted North against South, suburb against city, a capitol controlled by liberal career politicians against the America where real people lived. They understood how populist anger that had worked for Clinton in 1992 would work against him in 1994, and they coalesced around a strategy that political analysts Dan Balz and Ron Brownstein labeled "the politics of 'no' — 'no' to Clinton, 'no' to the Democrats, and 'no' to bipartisanship." In August, as we confronted rapid-fire Republican attacks on Whitewater, the crime bill, and health care, our fragile coalition broke apart.

The summer had opened with some uncharacteristically welcome news on Whitewater. Special Counsel Fiske disappointed conspiracy theorists by finding that Vince Foster did indeed commit suicide in Fort Marcy Park, and that the various White House–Treasury "contacts" over the Whitewater investigation (including my phone call to Josh) were ill-advised but not illegal. A separate inquiry by the Office of Government Ethics reached a similar conclusion. But these findings didn't stop the Republicans. Although ringleaders like Senators Al D'Amato and Lauch Faircloth had praised the appointment of Fiske, saying that "he's the kind of person who will bring out the truth for the American people," they maneuvered to have him replaced once he started to clear the administration. They also held full-scale hearings to cultivate the full electoral potential of Whitewater come November.

We knew that sequential inquiries in the House and Senate would hurt us, but we hoped the Republicans would overplay their hand and appear obsessed with a small-bore scandal at the expense of substantive issues. Our talking points for the hearings attempted to turn the "character" issue on its head:

> Whitewater is about the character of the president's foes —
> lacking a positive program of their own, they simply engage
> in attack politics. Meanwhile, the president is determined to
> fix the economy and health care, and attack crime — to do
> the work the people elected him to do.

The Republicans were willing to take that risk, hoping that a focus on Whitewater would weaken us and make it easier to kill our legislative agenda. Here they were helped by the media. Major newspapers and the television networks were invested in proving serious White House wrongdoing, if only to justify all the time and money they had spent on Whitewater. Conservatives reinforced this predisposition by repeating the charge of "liberal media bias." A Democratic scandal, they argued, deserved exactly the same treatment as Watergate and Iran-Contra. All this guaranteed two weeks of gavel-to-gavel coverage on C-Span and CNN, combined with several minutes a night of negative spots on the network news.

Which meant more trouble for me. Although I had already been smeared by *Time* and cleared by Fiske, the hearings would bring my phone call to Josh back into the spotlight. The word on the Hill was that D'Amato had targeted Harold and me: We were both from New York, and he knew that we'd worked to defeat him in the past.

The Republicans also banked on the fact that distracting senior staffers like us was half the battle. If we were busy with our lawyers or testifying in the hearing room, we couldn't be working on health care and crime. I also worried that with the president and Hillary still upset about Woodward, I couldn't count on the same reservoir of support I had received when the *Time* story first broke. If I slipped up now, Clinton might not be there to catch me.

The opening tableau of the House hearings wasn't pretty: a long table of mostly youthful White House staffers, all with right hands in the air, like a well-dressed version of the Little Rascals in a police lineup. At first, we were nervous; none of us had testified to Congress before on a matter of policy, much less as witnesses before an investigating committee. But the hearing turned out to be a partisan political food fight. Halfway through, Barney Frank sent me a note: "Relax, we're beating the shit out of them." He was right. The hearing didn't help us, but it didn't do any more damage.

The Senate was a different story. To me, the House was home, but I had never worked in the Senate and didn't have the same feel for it. Everything about it seemed imperious — from the senators to their staffers to the setup of the hearing room. I knew D'Amato was out to get me, and the Democratic senators weren't as encouraging as my old friends in the House. Our legislative liaison, Pat Griffin, called me up to his office for a cup of coffee and confided that the Democrats were worried that I would be "arrogant" at the hearing and fail to show the committee proper respect. "You gotta be humble, George," he said. "I know it's hard for you, but you have to." Pat and I had become close friends over the course of countless car rides back and forth to Capitol Hill; I knew he was giving me good advice. But I also wondered what was happening to me. *"Before we got here, we thought of ourselves as good people."* Have I changed? Am I as bad as they say? A punk? I promised Pat that I'd do my best.

But I also didn't want to be pushed around, or give the Republicans the satisfaction of making me look like a criminal again. My job was to defend myself without demonstrating contempt for the process. I consulted with Clinton's speech coach, Michael Sheehan, who advised me to: 1) look studious by jotting notes at the witness table; 2) start out every sentence with phrases like "As I've said before . . ." and "The facts are . . ."; 3) above all, "Be boring. No vivid language." I thought about my appearance for days, but only the night before did I realize what the crucial moment of the hearing would be. Sitting at my kitchen counter in front of a carton of moo shu chicken, I tried to think like a Republican. *What would I do to me if I were them? Of course! The __diary__. They'll make me incriminate __myself__.*

If you're a Senate staffer preparing for a hearing like this, your job is to get your boss on television. The best way to do that is to develop a camera-ready prop, and the most embarrassing prop for me was a blowup of Josh's diary. Have the senator hold it toward the cameras and order me to read the damning words: guaranteed sound bite on the evening news. I was determined not to give it to them. Under no circumstances was I going to read that diary on national television. Once I figured it out, I would have been almost disappointed if they hadn't asked.

No need to worry. Senator Orrin Hatch followed exactly the script I had imagined. Halfway through my questioning, he held up a laminated poster.

Senator Hatch: "I would like you to read from page two of the Steiner diary transcript where it begins 'after Howell Raines.' "

Mr. Stephanopoulos: "Sir, it's not my diary."

Senator Hatch: "It's not your diary, but I'd like you to read it. 'After Howell Raines' and just read down through the sentence which ends with 'stupid and improper,' because this is what he says."

Mr. Stephanopoulos: "It's not my diary. I'm not going to read it."

Senator Hatch: "I just want to see if we can refresh your recollection with this. If you can't say you don't . . ."

Mr. Stephanopoulos: "I'm looking at it, I've heard it several times. I'm not going to read it."

The chairman: "Senator Hatch, I don't know that he should be expected to read somebody else's diary. I think he can read it off a piece of paper to himself or you can state it to him."

Chairman Riegle had awarded me a tiny moral victory, but I couldn't fool myself into thinking that this gamesmanship in the hearing room was good news. Being sworn in at a witness table made me look like a defendant, and every hour spent sparring with Republican senators was an hour stolen from what I was supposed to be doing. Just being up there made me a problem to be handled rather than a person handling a problem.

At eight the next morning, I saw the president. He waxed on about how well Bernie Nussbaum had done before the committee but didn't even ask how I had done, which made me even more paranoid. And in a final Kafkaesque twist, a three-judge Federal Appeals Court panel announced that afternoon that it was replacing Special Counsel Fiske with a new independent counsel, Kenneth Starr, who would reopen the entire investigation. Chief Judge David Sentelle's opinion argued that Fiske had a conflict of interest because he had been appointed by Attorney General Janet Reno — a decision he reached after lunching with Republican senators Lauch Faircloth and Jesse Helms. We thought this decision was outrageous, but unwisely (in retrospect) failed to challenge it. So just when it looked as if Whitewater were finally over, it was starting all over again.

A week later, as Starr geared up his inquiry into Clinton's supposed crimes, our crime bill fell apart — a defeat I memorialized with a midnight note to myself:

> So it's Thursday, August 11, and I guess today we had our first big legislative loss. I felt like kind of an idiot because for the last two weeks I've been walking around saying I'm sure we're going to win. Rahm's been gloomy. Usually it's the other way around.
>
> He had a bad feeling about it all along. Felt the Southern Ds couldn't shake NRA on this one, and it turns out he was right. But even as we went to the vote, I thought we would win. I set up TV in P's study and prepared to sit through routine ritual: watch the vote, know it's a nail-biter, see it come out over the top. I got P just before Speaker Foley's

closing speech. He sat in his chair; I sat in mine, with open line to the cloakroom.

We got six Republicans right from start; good sign. I told P that we have to make sure we thank the Republicans when we win this thing. "Thank them? We'll build monuments to them." Democrats were holding too, but P barking out negative thoughts. "Looks like we're going to lose. Looks like they've got us beat." Right at the end of vote, clear things weren't going to break our way. The "nos" hit 200, then 206, and then it tumbled out of control. Finally hit 225 — the exact number I'd predicted the day before, except I thought they'd be "yesses."

In 1993, we'd won the big votes by cobbling together a bare majority with begs, bribes, belligerence, and appeals to conscience. But by the time we got to the crime bill — with the president's approval ratings in the tank and an election less than three months away — we couldn't make good on our threats, and we had nothing left to promise. Normally loyal Black Caucus members abandoned us over our decision to delete a section of the crime bill that would enable death row convicts to challenge their sentences with statistical evidence of racial prejudice. We didn't have a choice; in a rabidly pro–death penalty Congress, the "Racial Justice Act" was a poison pill. But neither did they: Voting no, they felt, was the only form of protest they had left. Meanwhile, conservative Democrats, mostly from the South, opposed the bill for being too tough on guns. The National Rifle Association was still smarting from its 1993 loss on the Brady Bill and vowed not to get beat on the crime bill's ban on assault weapons. The gun lobby's grassroots network flooded congressional offices with postcards and phone calls, which did the trick. Southern Democrats had already defied populist sentiment in their districts by supporting the president's policies on taxes and trade; an antigun vote, they feared, would be their third strike.

Despite these understandable desertions, we could have made up the difference with the votes of moderate Republicans who supported the assault weapons ban. But the NRA had devised a clever advertising strategy that never mentioned the word *guns*. Instead, the campaign called the bill a $30 billion barrel of "pork" and highlighted its funds for inner-city programs like "midnight basketball." The fact that the NRA refused to mention what it cared most about revealed an underlying weakness and predicted future defeats; but at the time, this fiscally conservative stance with a racist subtext played well even in suburban districts that favored the assault weapons ban. Unfortunately, our congressional leadership played right into the NRA's hands. They approved a "rule" governing floor consideration of the bill that protected the pet projects of powerful committee chairmen like Jack Brooks of Texas. (The chairman had slipped $10 million into the bill for a "crime institute" in his district named after, you guessed it, Jack Brooks.) This heavy-handed tactic was the last straw. Doing exactly what we would have done in their shoes, the Republican leadership publicized the offensive provision and secured moderate Republican votes against the rule by appealing to their resentment at being an oppressed minority in an institution corrupted by forty years of Democratic control.

With liberal Democrats, moderate Republicans, and conservative Democrats all against us, there was no center left to hold. The defeat itself was anticlimactic. We sat in the president's study for a few minutes, silently shaking our heads. But within minutes, the crime bill's collapse began to feel oddly liberating. Leon and Pat went up to the Hill to confer with the Democratic leadership on legislative strategy, and Mark Gearan called a meeting at the White House to prepare a communications plan. I was a conduit between these two worlds and the president, and for the first time, I truly understood the difference between president and prime minister.

Up until then, I really believed that passing legislation was the measure of our success. It was what I had been waiting to do for twelve years, and I was usually the first to argue for cutting the deal that would get us the votes. *You can't do any good if you don't get anything done.* But when Leon and Pat called in from the Hill with a recommendation from the Democratic leaders in Congress — to drop the assault weapons ban so the rest of the crime bill could pass — I rebelled against my past. I knew that was where the deal was (once the assault weapons ban was gone, conservative Democrats would vote yes, and we'd have a majority again), but I didn't want to do it. Yes, the ban was largely symbolic, but it was a valuable symbol. And I couldn't bear the thought of caving to the NRA — especially when pundits were always accusing Clinton of expedience. Better, I thought, to keep the assault weapons ban and let the deal go. We could put together a new coalition and woo back moderate Republicans by dropping some of the pork and picking a principled fight with the gun lobby. Even if we lost, we'd make a point. Rahm agreed, and we came up with a plan to have the president fly to Minneapolis with Republican Rudy Giuliani for a fighting speech before a national convention of police.

The president was with us. He was tired of being "lashed to the Congress" and frustrated by the fact that we hadn't made common cause with moderate Republicans more often. He was also furious at the NRA. All through his career, they had tried to defeat him. He loved to tell the story about how he almost got into a fistfight with the NRA's Arkansas lobbyist on the steps of the state capitol in Little Rock. But he had never backed down before, and he wasn't about to start now. Clinton signed off on our campaign plan and went to the briefing room to rail against "a procedural trick orchestrated by the NRA." Although the correspondents' commentary focused on our devastating defeat, it was exhilarating to see all three network news broadcasts (a "roadblock" in the parlance of spin) show Clinton fighting again after months of taking licks on Whitewater. That night, I closed my note in a mostly hopeful mood:

> We're at a turning point, because it seems like there's nowhere to go but up from here. I do feel good tonight. I was working out at around ten when the president called after talking to Jim Ramstad [Republican congressman from Minnesota who had agreed to host Clinton the next day]. Trying to figure out why I feel so lighthearted inside. Don't know what it is. Maybe it's just that losing turned out to be better for us than winning in some way. I also do feel that we're going to pull this off — that we're going to come

back, the pendulum will swing, and the president will achieve a great deal for the American people. Unfortunately, I know that's not what the papers are going to say tomorrow morning.

I was wrong about "nowhere to go but up." After two weeks of negotiations with the moderate Republicans, the crime bill eventually passed. But that was time and political capital that needed to be devoted to our health care effort, which was languishing after a series of summer setbacks: Memorial Day came and went without a bill from Moynihan's Finance Committee, and Chairman Rostenkowski's indictment for abusing his congressional accounts cost us an ally with the heft to forge a deal. With every day that passed, Republican opposition hardened. No amount of compromise could save us now. The few potential allies we had, like Senator John Chafee of Rhode Island, lost influence as their more partisan colleagues realized that defeating health care was their ticket to victory in November.

As defeat seemed inevitable, all of us were disheartened. But Hillary soldiered on and tried to keep our spirits up. Seeing that I was fluey from fatigue, Hillary sent me some preventive care, a carton of homeopathic cures accompanied by a note: "We need you healthy for health care! H." The message was even more important than the medicine: Although her anger about Woodward would occasionally flare, I was still part of her team.

But Hillary's echinacea and goldenseal wouldn't cure the severe case of insomnia I had developed. Ten to twelve times a night, I'd wake up to check the clock. *Phew, it's only two.* At 5:55, I'd beat out of bed before the alarm, alert but unrested. My eyes were red, and the underside of my skin felt like it had been scrubbed with steel wool. Once I got to work, the morning papers brought my first adrenaline fix of the day, and I would be cruising by the time I finished our staff meeting and a second cup of coffee. But as my exhaustion deepened, I finally went to see a doctor. She couldn't really help either. My problems weren't physical.

Over the course of 1994, the uneasiness I felt the summer before had deepened into a real depression. The pressures created by the

Whitewater investigations, the disappointment that came from watching our legislative agenda go down the tubes, and the sense of professional insecurity and personal estrangement from the Clintons that followed from the Woodward book all contributed to my dark mood. But it was more than that: The power and celebrity I had craved were also exacting their price. Certain that every move I made would be reported and every word I said would be repeated, I rarely let my guard down. Even home was no refuge. A troubled young woman repeatedly appeared at my door and followed me around my neighborhood. She sent me several rambling letters a week, studded with insight into me beyond what she could have known from reading the newspapers. Only after studying them did I realize how she'd learned so much: by commuting to my dad's Bible study group in New York and asking him seemingly innocent questions after class. The Secret Service confronted my stalker, but the intense scrutiny was shutting me down. Increasingly, my therapist's office felt like the only place I could store my frustrations and sort out my feelings without any fear of disclosure.

I couldn't even imagine how Hillary handled the personal assaults she had to weather. Health care and Whitewater made her hate radio's favorite target — G. Gordon Liddy even suggested using cardboard cutouts of Bill and Hillary for target practice. Her late-July bus trip, the "Health Security Express," encountered intense crowds carrying incendiary signs: "Go Back to Russia," "Bill and Hillary are immoral homosexual communists." In Seattle, Secret Service agents confiscated two guns and a knife from the crowd. Hillary was a tough politician, a veteran of her husband's often gothic campaigns, but nothing had prepared her for this. In public she tried to hide it, but inside the White House, her guard was down. Her husband looks soft, but his accommodating nature cushions him; Hillary looks hard, but her often brittle exterior masks a more vulnerable core.

On July 28, we met with Hillary to discuss how to counter our opponents' guerrilla tactics. Not surprisingly, she favored massive retaliation. Our best weapon, she argued, was for the president to go on prime-time television with a fiery speech — preferably before a joint session of Congress. Although I wanted the president out there as much as anyone else, I was back in the position of apostate, arguing hard realities to defenders of the faith. "Congress won't agree to another joint session," I replied, trying to be neutral. (What I didn't say was how offended they would be at the idea of even being asked. To grant a president one joint session for a single legislative initiative was exceptional; to request a second was a self-indulgent insult.)

"Well, what about an Oval Office address?" she tried, slightly more exasperated.

Again, I was Dr. No. "We should try, but we're probably not going to get it." The networks had become increasingly parsimonious with prime-time slots. Short of a national emergency, they weren't going to grant the president ten minutes of free airtime. "We should call a press conference in the East Room instead," I countered. "That's our best hope. But if we do it, it will probably have to be on the day Maggie [Williams, Hillary's chief of staff] testifies, so the president will have to take a lot of Whitewater questions."

"Who cares about that?" she shot back. "We have to do it. We can't care about that stuff anymore." With all of us in vehement agreement, the press conference was set for eight P.M. the following Wednesday, August 3.

On Tuesday afternoon, I was in the office of Alice Rivlin, the new director of the Office of Management and Budget, for a preliminary meeting on next January's budget, when Hillary paged me: "Need to speak to you urgently, please call." I called the White House operator. After a brief pause, the operator announced, "Mrs. Clinton on the line." She didn't mention that Mrs. Clinton was sobbing.

"George," she gulped, her voice falling in utter frustration, "how did this happen? How can it be that we're having a press conference the night that Maggie and Roger [Altman] are testifying?" Then she echoed the speech patterns of her husband, or perhaps he had learned the litany from her: "I try and I try and I try. I don't get involved. I stay out of your decisions. But people never think; they *just never think.*"

If it hadn't been for the agony in her voice, I might have laughed at the absurdity of it all. But the first lady was crying, and I knew she didn't remember biting my head off just a few days before. Reassurance was all I could offer: "I know exactly what you're saying, Hillary. All I can tell you is that we spent dozens of hours discussing this point. It's not without risk, but we think it's an opportunity. We're trading off a six-minute opening statement — a six-minute commercial, really — for twenty-four minutes of questions. The president is good at this. He can beat back the Whitewater stuff, and we have a chance to really sell what we're trying to do on health care. I don't think we can get out of it now. It would be a worse mistake if we did."

After twenty minutes, she conceded that going forward was our only option. But I knew that in her eyes I now owned this press conference, so it had better be a success. Thankfully, Clinton turned in a stellar performance, combining passion on health care with cool responses to all of the questions on Whitewater. But I didn't take anything for granted. After gauging the initial press response from Ann Devroy and Andrea Mitchell, and getting the preliminary focus group results from Stan Greenberg, I set up a phone bank to Hillary. First *I* would call, then Stan would follow with his research, and Carville would come in behind with his gut. Buzzing the operator, I waited for her to say:

"The first lady."

"Hillary?"

"Hi, George, how did we do?"

"Pretty well, I think. My first press calls were positive, and Stan . . ."

"Oh, there's Stan now . . ."

"Really? Take it. I'll talk to you later. Bye."

But even a month of boffo press conferences wouldn't save health care, which had already fallen victim to the forces that had defeated every other president who had tried. Corporate America, the insurance industry, and small business pooled their enormous resources and invested millions in lobbying and advertising to preserve the status quo. The Republican Party coupled sincere ideological opposition to our approach with pure political opportunism.

When they saw, in the words of future Speaker Newt Gingrich, that health care was "a springboard to win Republican control of the House," they pounced. Democrats were basically united around the goal of national health care, but our various factions didn't trust each other, and we were deeply divided on matters of tactics and strategy.

All of these obstacles might have blocked health care reform even if we had run a perfect legislative campaign from the White House. But we didn't. Presenting a detailed bill to Congress (on the theory that it could be pared down by horse-trading as the legislation worked its way through Congress) turned out to be a serious tactical mistake. While the provisions that threatened a segment of the health care industry became targets of laserlike lobbying campaigns to remove them, all the costly benefits of the bill became effectively locked in once they were printed. We couldn't compromise without cracking apart our coalition.

Besides, compromise didn't come naturally to Hillary. She was driven by the righteous and intellectually sound conviction that only a comprehensive solution would work, but that was more than the political system could bear. In a way, her leadership was more than the political system could bear. It's difficult to escape the conclusion that having Hillary run health care was a mistake.

At the time of her appointment, however, I was convinced it was a masterstroke. By choosing his wife to head the effort, we believed, Clinton was showing how much he cared about health care, and Hillary had all the right tools. She knew the subject cold, she was a tough-minded political tactician who could organize a national campaign, and her public advocacy was brilliant. But the approach she developed reflected both her strengths and her weaknesses. The plan, like the woman who guided it, was ambitious, idealistic, and highly logical; but it was also inflexible, overly complex, and highly susceptible to misinterpretation. Our standard line after the 1994 debacle was that we tried to do "too much too fast," that "we bit off more than we could chew." Instead of threatening to veto legislation that didn't meet our demands, we should have articulated the long-term goal of universal coverage and negotiated legislation that built up to it in stages. Here is at least one instance where Clinton's sometimes maddening instinct for the political middle ground might have better served their shared cause.

Hillary was also too juicy a target for the enemies of reform. They supplemented legitimate questions about the propriety and wisdom of having a first lady manage a major legislative campaign with more sinister attempts to cripple health care by turning Hillary into a caricature of a power-hungry radical feminist. Which leads to a final question: not what Hillary did to health care, but what health care did to Hillary. It made her vulnerable. The press cited her quasi-official position as justification for more intense scrutiny of her past, which helped fuel the Whitewater mania. The Republicans and their fringe allies felt that it made her fair game. Inside the White House, her position stifled healthy skepticism about our strategy, and Hillary became the object of some quiet resentment because no one was ever quite sure what the rules were in internal debates. Only Hillary can say if she would take the lead again, but my guess would be no.

On August 26, 1994, Congress adjourned without acting on the Clinton plan, and Senator George Mitchell announced that comprehensive, universal health insurance would not pass the Congress that year. By then it was a mercy killing.

12   CRASH

ndrew Jackson was in office when the old magnolia first graced
the South Lawn of the White House. Now, at 1:49 A.M. on
September 12, 1994, that tree was Bill Clinton's last line of defense. A small plane piloted by a depressed veteran was heading
straight for the White House. It skidded across the lawn, hurtled
through a holly hedge, and winged the branches of the old magnolia
before slamming into the wall two floors below Clinton's bedroom.
The agents on duty could only duck for cover.

I didn't learn about the crash until 6:25, when I strolled up to the
Starbucks next to my Dupont Circle apartment and saw the stack of
Posts propped against the still-locked door: "PLANE CRASHES ON
SOUTH LAWN."

No way. How could this happen? How come nobody called me? I
rushed to work, upset at being out of the loop, unsure if this was a
national security crisis or a bizarre prank gone awry. Apparently it
was a little of both. The Secret Service agents managing the situation from their West Wing basement control room said that the
dead pilot, Frank Corder, had boasted about landing a plane on the
South Lawn, but his friends had brushed it off as beer talk. The incident was, however, a severe problem for the Secret Service. Their
effectiveness in thwarting threats against the president stems in part

from the illusion that their protective shield is impregnable, from the unconfirmed but undenied belief that a kamikaze heading for 1600 Pennsylvania Avenue would be blasted out of the sky by a heat-seeking missile.

My immediate concern was ensuring that our snakebit White House avoided blame. The way our luck was running, I half expected to discover that the pilot was a first cousin of Gennifer Flowers's who had stolen one of Harry Thomason's planes from Arkansas's infamous Mena airstrip; or that the failure of the FAA's early-warning system was connected to some REGO budget cut. As Leon Panetta and I walked across the Rose Garden to inspect the damage, our mission seemed both surreal and surprisingly mundane. It's Monday morning, the start of another work week, and we're dealing with another crisis that's cropped up overnight — this time a stolen Cessna crumpled up against the White House like a crushed beer can.

Hours later, hundreds of kids and their congressmen and -women were scheduled to gather on the South Lawn for an event celebrating Clinton's Americorps national service program. Instead of canceling our "news of the day," we moved the rally to the North Lawn, and we did our best to deflect questions by designating that all official press briefings be handled by Secret Service and Treasury Department officials. *Let them take the hit for this one.* Of course that wouldn't stop our press corps from writing the inevitable "ticktock" stories of what the president knew and when he knew it, laced with analysis of what all this said about Clinton. Maureen Dowd of the *Times* pressed me all day for a Reaganesque anecdote — something like "Honey, I forgot to duck," the line President Reagan was said to have delivered to Nancy after being shot by John Hinckley.

"C'mon, George, you never give me anything."

"Maureen, I'm always nice to you."

"But you never give me anything. This is the time."

"Maureen, I'm not going to give it to you."

Still, Maureen may have been right. So we actually had a meeting about whether to leak an anecdote showing Clinton handling the "crisis" with equanimity and a sense of humor. All Clinton said when Dee Dee and I went to the Oval to get his story was that after

Leon called him he "turned over and went to sleep." So far, so good. "Can we knock down the rumor that you're going to stop jogging because of security concerns?" "Hell, yes," Clinton replied. "If I don't jog, I'll get up to two hundred sixty pounds. Be an even bigger target." Nice, but a joke about Clinton's struggle with his waistline didn't seem to strike the insouciant note Maureen had in mind. Our best spin here was the straight story: He turned over and went to sleep. The less said the better. We didn't want this to be a story about Clinton. We didn't have to prove that he was a regular guy with a good sense of humor. We had to show that he was up to the job.

Especially since the president would be ordering military action later that week. Shortly after I left the Oval, John Deutsch, the deputy secretary of defense, dropped by my office and mentioned his misgivings over the impending invasion of Haiti. "The first few days may be easy," he said, "but I'm afraid we might get three or four boys hacked up in a few months."

In the year following the humiliating retreat of the *Harlan County* from the docks of Port-au-Prince, the situation in Haiti had steadily deteriorated. The troika of military dictators, led by Lieutenant General Raoul Cedras, refused to reinstate President Aristide and intensified its reign of terror. Back in May, Clinton had resisted calls for American military intervention, preferring to ratchet up the pressure on the dictators with tightened economic sanctions and a final diplomatic push. But as Haiti's decline threatened to create a new wave of boat people heading for Florida, he felt more pressure to act. In July, after international human rights observers were expelled from Haiti, the U.S. pushed a resolution authorizing force to remove the Cedras junta from power through the UN Security Council. By September, there was no turning back.

The president believed military intervention was morally justified, but he fretted privately that he was being forced to act at the worst possible moment: "I can't believe they got me into this. . . . How did this happen? We should have waited until after the elections." But I knew by then that his scapegoating and second-guessing were just nervous tics, his way of steeling himself for what he knew he had to do. In the broader meetings with his national security team, Clinton was markedly more self-assured than in his early encounters with the military.

On September 7, the national security brass assembled to review the proposed battle plan. At first I wasn't sure they'd let me in. Now that Leon was reorganizing the White House staff, I no longer had automatic walk-in privileges to any policy meeting, especially on military matters, and I was still suspected of being a leaker. But Tony Lake invited me both because he was my friend and because the success of the effort would depend, in part, on how we handled Congress and the public — my areas of expertise. I walked into the cabinet room that afternoon aware that I needed to make a real contribution to justify my presence.

General John Shalikashvili, Colin Powell's replacement as chairman of the Joint Chiefs, opened the meeting. With his straight back, square shoulders, and short haircut, Shali was the epitome of an American military man — an identity reinforced for my ethnic ears by his clipped Polish accent. Listening to the general detail the pathetic state of the Haitian military, I was struck by his supreme confidence — and slightly apprehensive. *Isn't this what they always think before the fighting actually starts?* But his certainty wasn't hubris. The Haitian forces were fierce when facing unarmed women, orphans, and priests, but they'd cut and run at the sight of twenty thousand American troops.

"Thank you for the briefing, General," Clinton replied briskly. Then, without hedging or hesitation, he gave the command: "It's a good plan; let's go."

That was that. The rest of the meeting, however, dealt with the aspect of the invasion he *was* worried about: convincing the Congress and the country that invading Haiti was the right thing to do. First, we had to decide whether to secure a congressional vote authorizing military action. Secretary of State Christopher framed the argument against seeking a resolution in terms of presidential power, saying that if Clinton insisted on going to Congress he would be constraining his successors. Colored by my years in the House, I believed that a president shouldn't send soldiers into combat without congressional support. But that principle was now being tested by hard reality: We didn't have the votes, not even close. Congress wasn't about to give President Clinton political cover for an unpopular invasion, so restoring democracy to Haiti required sacrificing a bit of it here at home. I thought the cost was justified, but Congress would howl, and partisan tensions were so high that a few members might even argue for impeachment if American casualties mounted. To cover our flank, I suggested that the State Department draft a public "white paper" making the case for unilateral presidential action. Like me, Clinton had just read in Doris Kearns Goodwin's new book that FDR had used this tactic when he circumvented Congress on lend-lease. He took the suggestion.

Quit while you're ahead, George. I kept quiet as Clinton discussed marketing the mission to our various audiences: Congress, elite opinion leaders, the Haitian people, and the American public. With two-thirds of the country against military action in Haiti, it wouldn't be easy. And with two dozen people in the cabinet room, it would be just as difficult to maintain military secrecy. All through the session, the president grumbled about leaks coming from so large a group. When we adjourned, General Shali was nose to nose with Tony Lake, heatedly warning that if "one American soldier dies because of some leak, it will be on your head!" As one of the "extras" ringing the cabinet table, I hoped my presence hadn't put Tony in an untenable position. But any guilt I felt was balanced by indignation and anxiety: Those of us on the political team couldn't build public support without the basic facts. Besides, the most damaging national security leaks almost always came from dissenters in the bowels of the Pentagon or Foggy Bottom.

No real secrets leaked, thank goodness, but our political situation didn't improve either. Led by two war heroes, Senators Bob Dole and John McCain, the Republicans pounded Clinton, arguing that returning Aristide to Haiti wasn't worth a single American life and that Clinton was ordering the invasion not to protect national security, but to appease a political constituency. That was the argument that drove us most crazy. Aside from Harry Belafonte and a few members of the Black Caucus, no one was clamoring for an invasion of Haiti. This was our most unpopular act since gays in the military. But although the invasion was not politically motivated, and full of political risk, it could be a political plus. Clinton was constantly being called "spineless" and "wishy-washy" — *Doonesbury* was depicting him as a talking waffle. Paradoxically, the more the Republicans screamed, the more they helped the president. Taking a lonely stand on a tough issue like Haiti was the best way for Clinton to demonstrate presidential character. It was also one of the times that I was most proud to work for him. Defending human rights and democracy was what Democrats like us were supposed to do, and despite his private doubts about the timing, the president didn't flinch.

Which is not to say that he was always pretty to watch. On Tuesday morning, September 13, Clinton was riled up from a night of phone calls from complaining members of Congress. As Pat Griffin, Leon Panetta, and I filed into the Oval Office to brief Clinton for a meeting with other Hill Democrats, the president greeted us with a blast of shared pain: "After those fucking phone calls, I guess we'll have something to show those people who say I never do anything unpopular." I kind of liked Clinton's defiance, but the members we met with feared it would cost them the election. The discussion was dominated by talk of delaying any action until after November. Clinton just brushed the suggestion aside. "We're damned if we do, damned if we don't," he explained. "We get hit for politics by going in now, but the downside dangers of slow-walking until after the election are higher. More people will be killed."

Because the members knew they couldn't dissuade Clinton from going into Haiti, the congressional meeting had a resigned, desultory feel. But as our troops began to mobilize and the president prepared to address the nation from the Oval Office, the White House air was charged. Missile strikes were one thing, but this was the first time in our twenty months in office that the United States was planning a military invasion. OK, the Haitian armed forces weren't exactly a fearsome adversary. But restoring democracy to Haiti was a good cause, and something about watching grim-faced officers with medals on their chests and spy photos under their arms hustle through hushed corridors helped me imagine what it must have been like to be Ted Sorensen during the Cuban missile crisis, or Bill

Moyers when LBJ dispatched troops to the Dominican Republic. I never presumed to question the military plans, but on Tuesday night, the mission commander, Admiral Paul Miller, called me to talk politics. "We need to get a couple of people flying wing on the Hill for us," he said in the can-do cadence of a career military man. As for the speech, "that democracy argument is right on the bull's-eye. People want to hear value and cost. But you have to hit them where they live. Tell them there are nine million Haitians off our shores — and they *all* want to be your neighbor."

Actually, our polling showed that the American people were more moved by altruism than naked self-interest. Since August, we'd been quietly testing various arguments for the invasion. Unlike foreign-policy elites who insisted that the United States should deploy troops only when "vital" economic or military interests were at stake, the general public was more willing to use our power to protect innocent civilians from torture and terror. This was all relative, of course; risking even one American life was unpopular, but a humanitarian argument softened the opposition. How to use the evidence we had — graphic photos of maimed children and mothers with slashed faces — was dicey, and it revealed a subtle shift in the world of spin between the Reagan and Clinton administrations. David Gergen argued that when the president met with wire-service reporters on Wednesday, he should have the photos spread on the table before him for the reporters to see. "That would have worked for Reagan," I argued, "but they'll kill us for it. Just have the photos in a folder. If he hands them out, he hands them out." The Reagan team's success at spin control had conditioned the White House press corps. Elaborate staging only increased the tendency of skeptical reporters to focus on the process rather than the substance of what we were trying to say. The benefits of spin were being canceled out by the press's resistance to it. Often we reacted by spinning even harder, but I was beginning to see the virtue in just letting stories go — Zen spin.

But I still wanted to influence our coverage, which presented me with a dilemma that afternoon. We needed the public to know that our mission in Haiti would be "limited," that the U.S. military wasn't going to become an occupying force, and that we didn't con-

sider America "the world's policeman." But as his wire-service interview wound down, the president still hadn't said it. How could I
get Clinton to make that point without its looking as if he was being
coached? That's all *I* needed — a line in some story noting that the
president's spin doctor was telling him what to say as he sent American troops into harm's way. Sitting across from the president, directly in his line of sight, I worked to get his attention without
being noticed by anyone else. First, I simply stared at him, a trick
that had worked in the past. He'd see my wide-open, worried eyes
and his mind would click back to the points I had emphasized in
the prebrief. When that failed, I mouthed the word *limit* while
moving my hands in front of me as if I were squeezing a small ac-
cordion. That only made him think I had a stomach flu, but now
that I had his attention I wrote "LIMIT MISSION" in block letters
on my notepad and flashed it fast. No luck; his squint told me
that he couldn't read it without his glasses. Finally, I took the risk
of making myself part of the story. Before Dee Dee announced
last question, I wrote out a note, folded it up, and walked across
the room to hand it to Clinton. Nodding his head, he ended his
next answer with a segue into a soliloquy on our "exit strategy,"
starting with "I do want to emphasize this. . . ." Even though I
thought I had done the right thing, I apologized to Clinton after the
reporters left. "No, no," the president assured me. "It's a good thing
you did."

The next day, I wasn't so lucky. Stan Greenberg had conducted a
final poll to fine-tune our arguments before the president's speech. I
had cautioned Clinton against calling Stan himself, because while I
thought it was appropriate to use a poll to help sell a decision that
was already made, I didn't think it would look great to have the
president's pollster on his call sheet the day he was telling the nation
we were going to war. On Thursday morning, Stan faxed me the results, and I gave Leon an oral briefing. The Haiti arguments hadn't
changed, but the president's overall approval rating was the lowest it
had ever been. Several times that morning Clinton asked for the results, which put me in a bind. I didn't want to distract him with bad
news, but if I tore out the offensive pages, he would notice and accuse me, rightfully, of manipulating him. What I *should* have done

was simply give Leon the poll and let *him* deal with it; after all, he was the boss. Instead, I dropped it on the president's desk.

Twenty minutes later, I was facing Leon Panetta in full patriarchal fury. The president had ripped into him about his approval ratings, and now Leon was ripping into me. "Damnit, George, what happened here?" I didn't know, but I did apologize — fast. "I'm sorry, Leon. I told you about the poll but didn't think to give you a copy, and the president kept asking for it. I just didn't think. I'm sorry." One of the knocks against me was that I had a tendency to upset the president with bad news; and although I believed it was an unfair rap (*What am I supposed to do, Leon? Tell the president, "No, you can't have your poll, it'll make you too mad"?*), I knew this incident would hurt me with Leon.

By that evening, however, it was like old times with Clinton. His hair still wet from the shower, he and I stood in the hallway outside his bathroom in the residence, making the final edits on the advance text of his Oval Office address, which would be released to the press. When we got to the central sound bite of the speech —"The message of the United States to the Haitian dictators is clear: Your time is up. Leave now, on your own, or we will force you from power" — Clinton ran his felt tip through the words "on your own." The president didn't say a word; neither did I — sometimes you just know not to ask. But the two phone calls that Clinton had received from President Carter earlier that afternoon suddenly made sense to me.

An hour later, Clinton had finished his speech and was back on the phone in his study. I knew something was up with Carter and Colin Powell, but I didn't know exactly what. As I did my usual round of postspeech press and political calls, Tony, Leon, and the vice president kept shuttling through my office with intense looks and zipped lips. The intrigue continued the next day, Friday, September 16. At nine A.M., Tony slumped into my office and asked, "Do you ever have black moods?"

"All the time."

"Well, I've been working on a very complicated operation," Lake continued. "It went south late last night. What's the earliest I can leave?"

Before I could answer and pump Tony for more info about this "complicated operation," the president called him to the Oval. A few hours later, I got another clue when Clinton wandered, talking, into my office: "I can't figure out why they [the Haitian dictators] don't want to leave. I guess they just think it's their country and we're trying to take it away from them. They have different values, and they think Aristide is a bad guy." Only later did I realize that Clinton was musing out loud on his latest conversation with President Carter about Raoul Cedras. In his post–White House incarnation, Carter had developed a negotiating style that led him to form bonds with strongmen like Cedras, Kim Jong Il of North Korea, and Slobodan Milosevic of Serbia. But even Clinton, the king of empathy, couldn't convincingly work his way into the head of a Haitian dictator. Aware that the president just needed company and reassurance, I stuck to my usual script.

"You ought to feel good about the preparation. You've done everything you could."

"I do feel good about it. The military's impressive, isn't it?"

A few minutes later, Clinton was back on the phone in the Oval, and Tony was back in my office looking chipper. "We're trying another angle," he said. "I think it's going to work." I felt as if I were watching one of those British bedroom farces in which the whole plot is revealed with snatches of dialogue punctuated by slamming doors. Clinton returned to my office after talking to President Aristide, hoping to catch a nap with a John Calvin Batchelor novel he had spied on my desk about a vice president who plots a coup against his boss. But he probably couldn't sleep through the commotion. A few minutes later, I was in the hallway talking to Jesse Jackson and Leon Panetta when alarms started to blare and firefighters ran by in full gear. Apparently, a crossed wire had sent out a puff of smoke and set off a wave of panic on the second floor. But in a White House week that began with a plane crash and was about to end with military action, everyone was jumpy.

Finally, just before four o'clock that Friday afternoon, Clinton let me in on the secret. Before heading to a Capitol Hill ceremony for black World War II veterans, the "forgotten heroes," he pulled me aside in the doorway of the Oval. "I'm sending Carter," he whispered in my ear. "You think it will be OK, don't you?"

"Yeah, it'll be OK," I said, but I wasn't sure. After pressing President Carter not to fly to Haiti on his own, Clinton had agreed to send him as part of a trio, along with Colin Powell and Sam Nunn, to present Cedras with a final offer. If Carter stuck to the talking points, I was all for it — who could be for war as long as diplomacy might work? But there was an even chance that Carter would make it harder to force the dictators out. The former president is a true humanitarian, but his pacifist leanings could have had the effect of undercutting Clinton's ultimatum. He was also a bit of a lone ranger. A year earlier, during a tense diplomatic confrontation with North Korea over its nuclear weapons program, we had learned what Carter was offering the North Koreans by watching CNN. We couldn't afford more freelancing, and Tony and the president had reduced that risk by convincing Powell and Nunn to accompany Carter. But none of them really agreed with Clinton's Haiti policy, and they now had an effective veto over it. I also worried about the appearance of subcontracting our diplomacy to a former president. The draft press release I reviewed in Tony Lake's office would have sealed that impression. It began, "With President Clinton's approval, Jimmy Carter . . ."

"Tony, we can't say this," I said. "It has to be 'President Clinton has requested . . .' "

"Can't. Clinton already agreed to this draft."

"No, he couldn't have meant it. Let me call him."

"Go ahead."

Clinton has political grace; he doesn't stand on ceremony and goes out of his way to share political credit. But in this case, his instincts undermined our central message. Presidents don't "approve" national security missions; they "order" them. We couldn't afford to give the impression that Carter had backed Clinton into a corner (even if he had), or to allow anyone to mistake the president's willingness to negotiate for a failure of nerve. I reached the president in his limo. "Sure, sure," he said. "Make the change."

Carter's team took off early Saturday morning for a final round of negotiations with Cedras, and I made a scheduled fund-raising appearance in New Hampshire. Late Sunday morning, with the deadline for military action only hours away, I returned straight from the airport to the Oval, where the president's national security team was sprawled across the couches, waiting for word from the deliberations in Port-au-Prince. Leon welcomed me back by kicking me out: "George, there are too many people in here; go."

So I spent the afternoon swinging between self-pity and shame: angry at Leon for banishing me, angry at myself for being upset about it. I kept busy by working on an immigration problem that had cropped up in California, but I really wanted to be in on the action in the Oval. The talks had a noon deadline, but at two P.M., Carter's team was still negotiating, and Clinton had to make a decision: Should the 82nd Airborne Division pack their parachutes for an invasion that night? "Pack 'em," Clinton ordered. But the talks continued: Carter told Clinton that Cedras had agreed to leave, but he wouldn't agree to a date certain for the departure, saying that his resignation had to be tied to an amnesty vote in the Haitian parliament (which might never happen). Carter advised the president to accept the compromise.

Around five, I was on the phone with Janet Reno in Panetta's office when the president walked in. "Come see me," he mouthed, motioning toward me with his finger. When I got down the hall, Leon and Strobe Talbott were sitting in Betty's office. Spooked by my earlier ejection and wary of saying the wrong thing, I approached Leon and assured him the president was looking for me. "Go in," he said, flicking his head.

"Here's where we are," Clinton said, as he motioned me toward the seat by the side of his desk. "They've agreed to leave, but we're stuck on a date. Carter says we don't need one; what do you think?"

Not wanting to blow my return to action, I was all business. "No date is not even worth talking about, Mr. President. You'll get killed. You told the country and the world they have to go by noon today, so they have to go. But if you get a date certain, even with a delay, I think it's easy. You gotta go for it."

A few minutes later, Betty cracked the door to say that Colin Powell was on the line, and the rest of the national security team filed in. Wary of overstaying my welcome, I headed for the door. But the president stopped me. "George, stay here. I want you to hear this." The president then told Powell that it had to be a date certain, and Powell agreed. A short while later, with our planes in the air, the dictators agreed to leave Haiti by October 15.

Did Clinton really need me that afternoon? Probably not; everyone in the inner circle agreed that a date certain was essential. I don't know why he came to find me. But whether it was an act of kindness or a vote of confidence, the president had asked for my advice at a critical time. The situation in Haiti might later deteriorate, and Congress would still carp, but for now, at least, democracy was being restored to Haiti without war, President Clinton had a diplomatic success, and I could tell myself I had helped.

The satisfaction didn't last long. Our political situation as the 1994 midterm elections approached was effectively summed up by an encounter I had the week we were preparing to invade Haiti. At a New Hampshire fund-raiser for the Democratic nominee for governor, an ardent and early Clinton volunteer from the 1992 primary approached me near tears. Her nine-year-old daughter had come home from school with a question she couldn't answer: "Mommy, why do we love Bill Clinton so much if he makes so many mistakes and he's taking us to war?"

I stuttered out my practiced spiel about how "change is tough" and "we've made steady progress; people just don't know it." But most of the country had a much simpler answer to the girl's question: "We don't." Despite the diplomatic success in Haiti, our poll numbers were stuck in the mud. The shrinking deficit was fueling a growing economy, but people didn't buy it yet; and the failure of health care overshadowed legislative successes like the Family and Medical Leave Act and the Brady Bill. All this was driving the president to distraction. Although he didn't mind sharing credit, he hated not getting any. His response was to work even harder, to become a hyperactive combination of campaign manager, press secretary, and robocandidate.

Seeing Clinton the campaign animal up close was a new experience for Panetta, whose passion was governing, not politics. One Friday afternoon, after two straight days of presidential bellyaching over the quality of the Democratic National Committee advertising campaign, Leon couldn't take it anymore. He called me in. "Listen," he said, removing his glasses and rubbing his eyes, "the president is all upset about these political ads. Would you just go sit in his office and talk to him, calm him down?" Resisting feelings of vindication (*You see, it's not just us kids who have a hard time handling Clinton*), I walked down to Betty's office and waited. Wendy Smith and Nancy Hernreich were there too, and Clinton's mood must have been even worse than I thought, because they were wondering how to cheer him up. At one point, Nancy was called into the Oval and returned with a question: "What's another word for 'Pavlova's slippers'?" Pulling the *Times* from the credenza, I checked the crossword puzzle and walked into the Oval.

"Toe shoes."

"Oh . . . thanks," he replied, penning in the blanks. I took my seat by his desk, and we went to work. I reviewed the DNC's advertising strategy, outlined the scope of the buy, and received Clinton's suggestions on how to tweak the wording here and there. Most of the discussion, though, was a form of political therapy. A new wave of Republican "morph" ads was taking a toll on Clinton's psyche, and he was having a visceral reaction to being caricatured into a "cardboard cutout of myself." But his answer — a series of ads centered on how he'd kept his promises — wouldn't work. Even if people liked one of his policies in the abstract, support tended to drop when Clinton's name was attached to it. I heard him out and faithfully relayed his ideas to our consultants. That fall, President Clinton was the unfortunate opposite of King Midas — everything he touched turned to lead.

But Clinton was nothing if not persistent. Often that October, I would enter the Oval during his "phone and office time" to find him settled behind a stack of Xeroxed articles, furiously writing notes to editorial writers, friends, and supporters around the country. Journalists like Gene Lyons, Tom Patterson, Richard Rothstein, and Jacob Weisberg had recently written that the press was treating Clinton unfairly or not giving him enough credit for his accomplishments. When the president ran low, he'd summon me for a fresh supply of his favorite articles from the folder that I kept on file.

Clinton's favorite remedy for personal and political malaise was to hit the road. He crisscrossed the country to raise money for the party, and appeared at rallies and fund-raisers for any Senate candidate who would have him. He called in to talk-radio shows and wired up for satellite interviews with local news anchors. If his staff couldn't get the message out, he'd do it himself. With hindsight, it's easy to see that our only hope of avoiding electoral disaster in 1994 would have been a modified "Rose Garden" strategy. In the weeks leading up to the election, whenever the president stuck to official business, whether it was ordering missile strikes in Iraq or helping broker a new peace agreement in the Middle East, his ratings improved. But advising Clinton to stay off of the campaign trail in October was like asking him not to breathe.

I was beginning to understand the impulse. That fall, I was learning what it was like to be a candidate. I had become a "draw." Since I was the best-known staffer in the White House, the party pressed me into service as a fund-raiser for cash-strapped candidates all across the country. Not that I had to be forced. Our agenda would be dead if we lost the Congress, the country had to be warned about Newt Gingrich's "Contract with America," and nothing was more important in the homestretch of a tough campaign than money in the bank.

Besides, I needed to get out of the house. Instead of being a sign of power, celebrity now masked my increasingly tenuous status inside the White House. Our White House operation had improved under Leon Panetta's leadership. He became the nerve center of the West Wing, tightening up decision making, instilling a sense of discipline, and shaking up the staff. But I worried about being eased out. It was already happening to others, like my friends Dee Dee Myers and David Dreyer, and there were rumblings about bringing in Clinton's old friend ABC News executive Rick Kaplan to push me aside. Even if I survived on staff, I no longer knew where I fit in. The power of my position, and the rhythm of my workday, had always rested on my "special relationship" with Clinton. I understood how he thought and knew how to prepare him for public appearances. Others in the administration relied on me to interpret his moods or get decisions made. Clinton, in turn, counted on me to give him accurate information, and he seemed to value my judgment. So he had let me freelance and float. But part of Leon's mandate was to put me in my place (a move that was emphasized on the organization chart by shifting me from the "Office of the President" to the "Office of the Chief of Staff").

Which meant that I needed a job description beyond "by my side." Although I still had strong relationships with my colleagues in the White House, the cabinet agencies, and on Capitol Hill, I was doing poorly with all three principals. On the surface, Clinton was still cordial, and he still sought me out for my advice. But I knew he was constantly complaining to others about how I was to blame for the Woodward book and the liberal drift of the administration. Leon called me in and asked if I was "having any problems with the vice president." The question answered itself: Gore rightly thought we needed a more clear-cut hierarchy, and our relationship had become more steady, but I was still paying a price for our early disagreements and my lingering ties to his rival Dick Gephardt. My situation with Hillary was more mercurial. We had several nice phone conversations a week, during which I would brief her on what was going on and slip into thinking that all was well, but she couldn't forgive or forget Woodward. For days I couldn't figure out why I was being excluded from a round of secret meetings on resuscitating health care, until Harold pulled me into the old barbershop in the West Wing basement and explained that Hillary went into a tirade every time he suggested including me: "Bring George in? *Sure* — if you want it all over the street!"

So the campaign trail was a kind of refuge. Every weekend, I'd pack an overnight bag and head to the airport. For an hour or two on the plane, I could nap or read without being interrupted by the phone. Touching down in another city was like landing on a distant planet, where people were amazed to meet a man who worked for the president, rather than worried about how many minutes a day they met with him. And the audiences at my events were hard-core Democrats, not the skeptical reporters or hostile Republicans I normally had to confront. Their adulation was flattering, and it was fun to be among true believers who just wanted to feel good about their president. Sometimes I had to watch out for the guests who wanted to feel a little more. In the receiving line at one event, I was approached by a pair of hearty nurses on the far side of middle age. Helga wore a brush cut, Rose a beehive. Both had big smiles.

"We just had a raffle, and we're deciding who gets to take you home."

"Great, I haven't had a home-cooked meal in months."

"Who's talking about eating?" They giggled, squeezing me between them. "We're not going to feed you. . . ." Cracking up into the camera, they bid me good-bye by pinching my cheeks — the lower ones.

Doing these fund-raisers helped cover my butt in another way. Attending them was like paying premiums on a political life-insurance policy. The more favors I did, the more political friends I had, and the more friends I had in Congress, the harder it would be to fire me if my stock in the White House continued to fall. But of my twenty-two appearances that election cycle, the most memorable, the most foreboding, and, ultimately, the saddest was an event I did to repay a political debt — the one I owed Mario Cuomo, whose example had inspired me when I was first starting out.

That night in Queens, my worlds converged. The rally was held at the Crystal Palace, Astoria's premier Hellenic banquet hall — the place where, back in 1988, thousands of Greeks had smashed plates and danced in the streets to celebrate the nomination of their favorite son, Michael Dukakis. Now the scene was slightly more subdued. Cuomo was running for governor, not president; and he was Italian, not Greek. But the folding metal chairs were all filled, with my parents in the front row. At the cocktail reception, I chatted with some college classmates and a handful of our volunteers from the 1992 campaign while fending off the entreaties of well-meaning but overeager family friends who wanted to know when *I* was going to run for president. The third time's the charm, they said. We lost Tsongas, we lost Dukakis, but you're going to win!

Their confidence was comforting but disconcerting too: It made me feel like a bit of a fraud, as if I were hiding a secret. *Run for president? I don't know if I'll even have a job next month.* I was also worried about my speech: Speaking before Cuomo was like dancing before Baryshnikov. Cuomo cared about rhetoric; he loved what he had once called the "poetry" of campaigns. I wanted to impress him, and I hoped he would understand that my appearance was more personal than political. Normally, I improvised from jotted notes. But this time, I was nervous enough to work on a prepared text. All through the reception, I kept patting my breast pocket to make sure it was still there.

Then Cuomo arrived, still bigger than life to me, and we waded toward the dais together, shaking hands and leaning over for wet kisses from the older ladies lining the aisles. There was no hurry; this was a dinner organized by Greeks and Democrats — the program was just beginning, and it would take another hour to get through the thank-yous and introductions. Once we reached the head table, someone asked the governor to autograph a copy of the Ken Burns baseball book, which included a scouting report on minor league centerfielder Mario Cuomo ("Potentially the best prospect on the club and in my opinion could go all the way . . ."). But before Cuomo returned the book, he pushed it toward me, opening to the passage he wanted me to see — a vintage Cuomo riff on baseball and community ("I love the idea of the bunt. I love the idea of the sacrifice. Even the word is good. Give yourself up for the good of the whole"). It was lovely — his lyrical best — but Cuomo's head didn't seem to be in this game; the speaker was looking at the governor while the governor was watching me read.

When it was my turn to speak, I nodded to Cuomo, smiled at my parents, and began: "Every generation of Democrats has a leader they look up to. For my grandparents, it was FDR, who in the midst of the depression kept a sign on his desk saying, 'Let unconquerable gladness dwell . . .' For my parents, it was JFK, who fought the 'twilight struggle' for freedom and willed American leadership on earth and in the heavens; for the president and his generation, it was Bobby Kennedy and Martin Luther King, who preached of the need to reach beyond hatred and beyond division. But for someone who started in politics a decade ago, that inspiration, that leader, was Mario Cuomo. . . ." I closed on a confiding, conversational note: "Listen, I've got to tell you, I did everything I could to get Mario Cuomo out of this race. In the spring of 1992, I wrote a memo to Governor Clinton outlining all of the reasons why Mario Cuomo just *had* to be VP; in the spring of 1993, I was at it again, with all of the reasons he *had* to be on the Supreme Court. But each time, the answer back from Albany was 'Don't even think about it; I've got a job to do in New York.' Well, now New Yorkers have a job to do for the man who's done so much for them, for us . . . Mario Cuomo."

My parents were crying, Cuomo was smiling, and I was drenched with sweat but happy with how I'd done. The governor started well, joking easily, praising my parents and the speakers who preceded him. But within a few minutes, I sensed that something was wrong. This wasn't the powerful orator who urged Americans to see beyond the "shining city on a hill" or challenged them to follow the lead of "our new captain for a new century." He wasn't preaching on the "idea of family" or pointing to the future with hope and pride. His voice was tired, and his words were hard — his new favorite seemed to be *vindication*. Thirty minutes after he began, Cuomo was still defending his record, talking about the past, and even this loyal crowd was drifting. When a wild-eyed woman in the back started to scream at him, he didn't ignore her or brush off the ravings with a lighthearted joke. The governor took her on.

I was in pain — worried for Cuomo and more anxious than ever about the coming election. *The governor just had a bad night, that's all. But it sure feels down out there.* As I flew home on the final shuttle, my thoughts drifted beyond the immediate contest. Cuomo was a good man, committed to public service, inspiring at his best, but did the whole game of attack and defend, attack and defend squeeze the soul of everyone who played, even the best? And then what? *So this is how it ends when you miss your chance and hang on too long. Not in the White House, or on the bench of the Supreme Court — but in a Queens social club, debating a heckler who doesn't know her own name.*

On election day 1994, Cuomo lost. So did Marjorie Margolies-Mezvinsky, Speaker Tom Foley, and the old bulls Rostenkowski and Brooks. Senator Harris Wofford, the "Kennedy man" whose special-election upset three Novembers before had foretold our 1992 triumph, lost too. Democrats everywhere were defeated, but not a single Republican incumbent running for governor, House, or Senate lost. The Republicans won back the Senate, captured a majority of governorships for the first time since 1970, and took control of the House for the first time since 1954. Our nemesis Newt Gingrich was now Speaker — two heartbeats away from the White House. If Clinton really were a prime minister, he'd have been out of a job.

A few days after the election, the president kept to a long-scheduled trade mission to the Far East. With Washington in tumult, Leon stayed home, and I was put on the trip to help Clinton answer political attacks and respond to any new Republican proposals. My only task was to keep him out of political trouble, and I failed. At a press conference in Jakarta, the president was asked for his position on the Republicans' proposed constitutional amendment to permit prayer in public schools. Although Clinton had consistently opposed amending the Constitution, he supported statutory efforts allowing "voluntary" school prayer. Aware of his ambivalence and focused solely on avoiding controversy, I told the president to punt. That's exactly what he did ("I want to reserve judgment. I want to see the specifics"), but it had exactly the opposite effect of what I intended. Clinton's kicker ("I certainly wouldn't rule it out") made it look like he was flip-flopping on a matter of bedrock political principle. It took us two days to clean up the mess of stories about how Clinton had lost his political and moral compass.

When the president and Hillary left Jakarta for a short vacation in Hawaii, I dropped off the trip and returned to Washington alone. All through the twenty-five-hour flight, I stewed about my screwup. But my anxiety was about more than a muffed answer at a press conference. The tensions of the past several months were coming to a head. On the long flight over to Asia, the president and Hillary rarely left their cabin. The "silent scream" had descended again, and grapevine rumors (from people who had talked to people who had talked to the president by phone) confirmed that Clinton was privately blaming his trouble on "those kids who got me elected. I never should have brought anyone under forty into the White House."

Even if the reports were only half true, they were nearly impossible to take. I thought for sure that my days in the White House were numbered. My confused feelings — of sadness and anger, despair and defiance, and failure most of all — kept me awake night after night. So hours before Clinton's scheduled return, on a dark Saturday night in a deserted West Wing, I walked into the empty Oval with a handwritten letter — a sheet from a yellow legal pad, folded in three, labeled "To: The President. From: George." Sneaking alone into the Oval was something I had never done. But if I sent the letter through the staff secretary, my colleagues would see it and Clinton wouldn't get it for days. If I delivered it to the residence, the president might show it to Hillary, and I wasn't sure how she'd react. I needed him to read it alone, as soon as possible. When *Marine One* landed, he'd walk to the Oval as usual, and the letter would be sitting by his phone, the only document on an otherwise empty desk.

It was an apology. Taking the hit for the school prayer controversy in Jakarta, I said there was no excuse for such inadequate preparation: "I'm sorry." Then I wrote, "Same theme, different subject," and addressed what was really bothering Clinton. Still the Woodward book. The time had never seemed right, but I should have found a way to have a direct discussion with the president months earlier. Now all I could do was grovel and hope it worked. I defended my motives but apologized for my awful judgment. Unsure of how it sounded, I called Wendy Smith as I was drafting the letter and read it to her. She was my closest friend then, and she understood Clinton as well as anyone who worked with him.

"You can't just write a letter like that," she said. "If you don't close with some constructive advice, he won't pay attention." So I added a third paragraph: "You're going to get a lot of advice over the next few weeks about how to fix your presidency, so let me get in my two cents: 'Be president like you ran for president.'" Back in 1992, I continued, you knew what you wanted to do and how you wanted to do it better than any of us around you. No matter what anybody says now, "do what you think is right. And don't worry too much about what we tell you." In November of 1994, I wanted to be back with the Clinton I had encountered in the autumn of

1991 — in Stan Greenberg's office, at the governor's mansion in Little Rock, at the Navy Pier in Chicago, and at the Church of God in Christ convention in Memphis. I wanted to be inspired again.

But the president was in a funk, spending more and more time alone, talking to old friends for hours on the phone. He and Hillary even went on to invite New Age self-help gurus Tony Robbins and Marianne Williamson to a secret session up at Camp David. He did, however, respond to my note. Sort of. Passing through my office on Monday morning, Clinton seemed somehow surprised to find me there. He nodded hello and kept on, before turning around suddenly. "I agreed with your letter." Zeroing in on the relatively comfortable space of paragraph three, his eyes wandered around the room as he talked distractedly about "returning to my roots. . . . I reread my announcement speech, and that's exactly what we have to do." Then he mentioned school prayer, accepting my apology by saying, "Nah, I screwed that up; it was my fault." Not a word about Woodward.

Until December 3, nearly two weeks later. It was a Saturday morning, and I had just received a call from Peter Jennings, who was filming a special on religion in America at the church of Bill Hybels, one of the president's spiritual advisers. Jennings wanted to interview Hybels about what it was like to be pastor to the president, but Hybels wanted the president's permission. I found Clinton in the Oval, sifting through the paperwork that had built up over the week. He thought it was fine for Hybels to do the interview, but he wanted to talk to him first. When I got up to leave, he said, "Wait.

"I'm really glad you wrote that letter," as if he had never mentioned it before. "That Woodward book tore my guts out, and I didn't handle it completely well," he continued. "We all made mistakes. We hired too many young people in this White House who are smart but not wise."

Pretty fair description of me. Although he couldn't quite do it directly, the president was both acknowledging my errors and absolving me of them. "Mr. President," I responded, "I don't know what to tell you. I saw a bad thing coming and I thought this was the best way to stop it, but I was wrong."

"Yeah, you did your best," he concluded. "But that Woodward's an evil guy."

I left the Oval perplexed but enormously relieved. As always, though, the respite was short-lived. Three days later, on December 6, I hit bottom and felt as if I were hanging on to my job by what was left of my fingernails. It started at 6:15 A.M. in Harold Ickes's office. As Harold sipped Irish Breakfast from a mug with the tea bag still floating on top (whether it was frugality or taste, Harold always used his tea bags twice), we talked about what was shaping up to be a typical Clinton day, one in which the nomination of Bob Rubin for treasury secretary would be balanced off by the news that Webb Hubbell was pleading guilty to charges of mail fraud and tax evasion. Harold also reported on what he knew about the various White House reorganization rumors, and when I told him that I'd had a heart-to-heart with the president, he knew exactly what I was talking about. "Yeah, the president mentioned it. He said, 'George finally fessed up on the Woodward book.'" *Whatever it takes. At least he got the message.*

But I soon discovered that any lingering presidential suspicion was the least of my problems. Looking out for me again, Pat Griffin called me up to his office to fill me in on what he was hearing on the Hill. "George, I feel about you the way I feel about my wife," he said. "When I'm afraid something bad is going to happen to her, I want to protect her, but I feel powerless and it drives me crazy." He then told me that some Republicans on the Hill had decided to make me a target. "D'Amato hates you and wants to bring you down," he said, which he could do by convening more Whitewater hearings now that he was chairman of the Senate Banking Committee. Pat added that their focus groups showed that I was exactly the face Republicans wanted people to think of when they heard the words "Clinton White House." I sent the message that we were too young, too liberal, and too big for our britches, and they were going to do everything they could to reinforce the message. That explained why the new Speaker was gratuitously repeating my name in interviews, saying things like Stephanopoulos "scowls in meetings" and that I should return to my "dacha."

That also explained why, the day before, Leon had been so angry at me when the *Post* quoted me calling the Speaker "irresponsible" for making his outrageous accusation that 25 percent of the White House staff "had used drugs in the last four or five years." I didn't feel I had a choice, because Devroy had called me on deadline when she couldn't get anyone else to respond. When I walked into the staff meeting that morning, I was expecting to be congratulated for a good save; instead I got reamed out in front of the whole room. Pissed, I went right back at Leon, saying that I had checked first with the counsel's office and his deputy. Only after talking to Pat did I realize that, in his own way, Leon was trying to protect me. We worked it out, but I couldn't fool myself into thinking that everything was OK when his instinctive response to getting unfairly attacked was to blame me for defending us. Maybe I *was* becoming more trouble than I was worth.

But my most direct hit of the day came later that afternoon, when the president met with a contingent from the Democratic Leadership Council. I wasn't part of their camp, and now some of them saw an opportunity to correct what they considered a "liberal tilt" in the White House. The ringleader was their outgoing president, Congressman Dave McCurdy, who blamed Clinton for his failure to win a Senate bid in Oklahoma. At the DLC convention, McCurdy called the president a "heavy burden" and said that "while Bill Clinton has the mind of a New Democrat, he retains the heart of an old Democrat." In the president's presence, he wasn't quite as bold. Talking to Clinton but looking at me, he took his shot: "Mr. President, with all due respect to George, you need to have serious personnel changes. The only way the American people are going to believe you've changed is if you show the change."

Pat muttered "cocksucker" under his breath. I couldn't breathe. Clinton just ignored it, which was better than the alternative. Like Clinton, I was lucky in my enemy. If someone was going to call for my head, who better than a bitter, out-of-work congressman who was publicly attacking the president? But this was another first I could have done without: When I imagined working in the White House, I never thought that one day I'd be sitting in the Oval Office watching someone try to get me fired. By the time I returned to my office and heard from Heather that Rush Limbaugh had devoted fifteen minutes of his show to attacking me, there was nothing to do but laugh — and contemplate payback. Later, I found a fragment of a Republican newsletter in my in-box and taped its frayed edges to the center of my desk: ". . . it will take not just a comeback but a miracle for Bill Clinton to win in 1996. . . ."

Just seeing the words made me feel better; they had the power of a lucky charm. Little did I know that Bill Clinton had been reaching into his past to retrieve a talisman of his own.

13   MY DINNER WITH DICK

here is that cocksucker? I knew what Harold was thinking. We were finishing our drinks on the curved banquette by the second-floor landing of Kinkead's, his favorite restaurant. It was 9:30 P.M., and our guest still hadn't arrived. Although this felt like a transparent power play, I didn't have the standing to complain. I needed this meeting, and showing up late was a trick I'd often used myself. Pleading an uncontrollable schedule was one of the perks that accompanied a place in the president's inner orbit (*"You know what he's like, just wouldn't stop talking. . . ."*). On that night, May 17, 1995, no one flew closer to the sun than the man we were meeting.

I sat on Harold's left, by his good ear. What our tardy dinner partner would say didn't much interest him. He'd heard it all before. Not me. Aside from an accidental after-hours encounter in Betty Currie's office, I'd never really met the man. Twenty minutes passed. Harold threatened to leave. I said we should order. Dick Morris then appeared at the top of the stairs and promptly excused himself to find a phone.

He was the dark buddha whose belly Clinton rubbed in desperate times. I didn't really know that then. I didn't know much about Dick at all. When I first joined Clinton's team, Morris was just another unsavory figure from Clinton's past, an ex-adviser with a grudge and a story. A few times in 1992, I knocked down a Morris-related rumor about Clinton's 1990 campaign — something about how Clinton had coldcocked Dick on the porch of the governor's mansion. Aside from a single reference in October 1993 to a poll conducted by his "old friend," Clinton had never mentioned Dick's name in my presence.

In late 1994, however, I had picked up an unfamiliar frequency in Clinton's monologues. Keeping track of the president's information flow was part of my portfolio, and I always tried to decipher what I heard him say through the filter of what he'd read and who he'd seen. If I knew the source of a command or question, I could usually figure out how to handle it. But monitoring Clinton's phone calls was nearly impossible. He called all sorts of people at all hours of the day and night, and would often pass on new thoughts without revealing his sources — a kind of blind market testing. A few times that fall, I could tell that someone new was wiring his way into Clinton's brain. The president would wander through my back door during his "phone and office time," saying, "I was just talking to someone. . . ." He would then recite a fully developed revision of his stump speech, propose a brand-new script for the DNC ad campaign, or launch into an extended critique of the political advice he was getting from Stan Greenberg and the rest of our consultants. His running theme was the need for a "centralized strategic process," coupled with a plan to raise "twenty to twenty-five million dollars" to finance a steady stream of generic Democratic ads on cable television. After the election, as Clinton withdrew from those of us on staff, the clues were silent but still visible, like the boldly inked crib sheets the president slipped out of his folder during meetings. Or the anonymous calls announced by Betty Currie that Clinton would take in the privacy of his study. Or the yellow Post-it notes left by his phone, reminding him that "Charlie called."

"Charlie" was Dick's code name. The president had engaged him to run a covert operation against his own White House — a commander's coup against the colonels. The two of them plotted in secret — at night, on the phone, by fax. From December 1994 through August 1996, Leon Panetta managed the official White

House staff, the Joint Chiefs commanded the military, the cabinet administered the government, but no single person more influenced the president of the United States than Dick Morris.

As Dick's power grew, mine receded. I still participated in White House policy meetings; I still helped prep the president for press conferences and other public appearances. My office wasn't moved, and my title stayed the same: senior adviser to the president for policy and strategy. But I was a presidential strategist in name only.

The estrangement from Clinton that I began to fear in 1994 became more pronounced in 1995. My word could no longer tip the balance of a decision; I was no longer the morning flak catcher, the master interpreter of Clinton's mood, or the ultimate authority on what he would do. Clinton would occasionally take my suggestions on minor tactical matters. But after the 1994 debacle, the president didn't fully trust me or my judgment.

When I was honest with myself, I couldn't really blame him. I was part of the team that had failed. But it still hurt, and I wanted to fight my way back, certain there was too much at stake, both personally and politically, to just pick up and leave. Instead, I picked my spots — working with the Democrats in Congress to run a guerrilla campaign against the Republican budget, the heart of their "Contract with America," and volunteering within the White House to manage a review of federal affirmative action programs. If I was no longer a trusted adviser, no longer defined as "by his side," at least I'd work on the issues that mattered most to me.

Tonight's dinner was part of the president's evolving effort to integrate Morris into the official White House operation. For most of the winter they had met alone. Then Clinton had introduced Morris to the vice president and convened weekly political strategy meetings in the residence with Gore, Leon Panetta, and Leon's two deputies, Harold Ickes and Erskine Bowles. I was excluded, which was killing me and my pride. *Yeah, '94 was a disaster, but it wasn't all my fault. I'm still the only staffer here who's been through an entire election cycle. Besides, how can I even pretend to myself that I'm the president's strategist if I don't attend the strategy meetings?* Both Harold and Erskine let me know that Dick was constantly undermining me with the president, telling him that I was too liberal and too much of a leaker to be part of the team. But although Clinton didn't want me in too close, he didn't want me too far away either. I wouldn't have been there that night if Clinton had wanted to totally freeze me out. If I was worthy of a summit, I still had some juice. But Morris had far more — and it showed.

When he returned from the phone, I got my first good look at Dick. He was a small sausage of a man encased in a green suit with wide lapels, a wide floral tie, and a wide-collared shirt. His blow-dried pompadour and shiny leather briefcase gave him the look of a B-movie mob lawyer, circa 1975 — the kind of guy who gets brained with a baseball bat for double-crossing his boss. But his outfit was offset by the flush of power on his pasty face. I knew *that* look — the afterglow of a private meeting with the leader of the free world. For some reason, however, Dick seemed a little nervous. When he first spoke, his hands fluttered just below his chest and his voice vibrated his saccharine greeting. "I am *soo* happy to meet you. I have been *soo* impressed by your work," he said, bowing into the table. "I know Bill *soo* well, so I know how hard your job was in the last campaign. Watching from the outside, I could imagine how hard it must have been on the inside. And I really want to thank you for winning the last election — so *I* can win the reelection."

Spare me the unctuous bullshit, you insincere prick. You've been trying to get me fired for months. Of course I didn't say that; all I squeezed out was my own false note of thanks. To me, Dick's flattery was a form of condescension, the verbal equivalent of a pat on the head. *Now go away, kid, you bother me.* After all, he was the one who really knew "Bill," who had the intimate, long-term relationship that I couldn't presume to challenge. An hour ago, he was the one in the family quarters of the White House while I was working out in the OEOB's basement gym. That final line said it all: "I really want to thank you for winning the last election, so I can win the reelection." *Oh, so that's why I did it. Thanks for clarifying.*

But beneath Dick's grandiosity was a childlike transparency that might have touched me if I hadn't been so jealous. His greeting betrayed a tendency to say things that political operatives like me might think but not speak because they're not seemly and not really true — like the notion that "we," rather than the candidates, are the ones who really win elections. I noticed at once that Dick was missing a gene: He literally had no shame. At the moment, though, I was focused on the message Morris was sending to me — that my experience was merely a brief chapter in Clinton's political saga, and my time had passed.

For the next forty-eight minutes, I listened to the Morris story. Every last detail. How Dick managed his first student-council campaign in grade school and worked his way up to ward leader races on the Upper West Side, winning every time. How he did field organizing for McCarthy in '68 and McGovern in '72. How he shifted abruptly from urban policy analyst to political gun for hire in 1977, when he lost his job and found a wife. Dick talked nonstop, in fluent, unpunctuated paragraphs. Yet he seemed as disconnected from his own words as he was from us, as if he were reading someone else's obituary from a TelePrompTer; at least until he got to the heart of the narrative — part buddy movie, part perverse morality play: the story of Dick and Bill.

It was a tale of two political prodigies — one from the North, one from the South; one short, one tall; one a consultant, the other the candidate of his dreams. Idealistic, fast-talking baby boomers, they both grew up revering Kennedy, hating Nixon, losing with McGovern, and vowing never to let it happen again. They believed in the power of politics to help people but loved the sport of it even more. When they met in 1978, Dick was a fledgling consultant scouring the country for candidates and Bill was an ambitious attorney general of Arkansas looking to make a move. They bonded by poring over polls and bantering about campaign strategy the way baseball fans study box scores and relive their favorite plays. And together, they won. But it wasn't an easy or equal relationship. When Dick looked up at Bill, he saw a future president; when Bill looked down at Dick, he saw the devil he knew — the part of himself that confused power and popularity with public service and principle. Dick knew how to win, but by the time he met Bill, he wasn't scrupulous about how he did it or whom he did it for. His other clients were Republicans, and his attack ads were the roughest in the business. Word was that he would work for both sides of the same race if he could get away with it.

So after Bill became America's youngest governor, he fired Dick for being, as Morris put it, an "assault on his vanity." Two years later, Bill had become America's youngest ex-governor. Tried to do too much too fast, let his ideals get the better of him. Chastened, he summoned Dick to plot the comeback. They trimmed their sails, tacked to the center, and won — again and again. The only victory Dick missed was the biggest — 1992 — though Morris claimed to me that Clinton's comeback kick in New Hampshire was plotted with him over the phone. The world according to Morris wasn't complicated: Over their sixteen-year relationship, when Dick was by his side, Bill succeeded; when Bill pushed Dick away, disaster.

Just as he reached that conclusion, Morris paused. His eyes widened, his hands fell still on the table, and his voice settled back into his body. For the first and only time that night, he sounded authentically human. "Bill only wants me around when his dark political side is coming out," Morris said, self-aware and sad. "He doesn't want anything to do with me when he's in good-government, Boy Scout mode." Dick knew his client well. Bill might need him, but he'd never be proud of him. They might be soul mates, but it had to be secret. And there would be days and weeks, months and years, when Bill just wouldn't call.

I almost felt for the guy. But the moment passed in the time it took for the insight to flash across Dick's face. Being out wasn't his problem now. Morris was as in as you could be. Hillary had helped bring him back. Although she didn't share Dick's politics, she valued his strategic skills and the magic he could work on her husband's political mood. They had stayed in touch, talking on the phone several times in 1993 and 1994; she knew they might need Dick one day. Shortly before the midterm election, the president joined the conversation. "I told Clinton that he was going to get beat," Dick said. "I tried to tell him not to demonize the Republicans and focus on his smaller accomplishments, like family leave and direct student loans. After the Middle East trip, I told him not to campaign at all, just stay out of the race."

Most of Dick's soliloquy had washed right over me. *Why is he telling me all this? Is he ever going to stop?* But these last few points were different. Not because they were new. Quite the contrary. I'd heard them all before — straight from the president. "I knew that going after the Contract with America was a loser. . . . I should have never let you talk me into attacking it. . . . Should have never let myself get sucked into campaigning so much." Never mind that Clinton had insisted on doing more talk radio, more television interviews, and more campaign rallies in the closing days of 1994, or that when the spirit moved him on the stump, no one loved to rip into the Republicans more. Dick's advice — sound advice, I had to admit — was his ticket to the family quarters of the White House. It had also become one of the stories Clinton told himself to explain his defeat.

"I've been talking to Clinton constantly since the election," Morris continued. *No kidding.* But my resentment was temporarily replaced by fascination. As Dick dictated to me what he'd been drilling into Clinton for months, he morphed into a political version of the autistic math genius played by Dustin Hoffman in the movie *Rain Man.* His voice gained speed but lost all its tone, as if it were being generated by a transistor wired to the back of his throat. His index finger tapped furiously at a slim pocket computer that stored the polls he called his "prayer book." Weaving that data with bits of policy analysis, political science theory, and historical analogies from England, America, and France, Dick spun out an elaborate "Theory of the Race"— that Clinton would win in 1996 if he "neutralized" the Republicans and "triangulated" the Democrats.

Neutralization required passing big chunks of the Republican agenda: a balanced budget, tax cuts, welfare reform, an end to affirmative action. This would "relieve the frustrations" that got them elected in 1994 and allow Clinton to "push them to the right" on "popular" issues like gun control and a woman's right to choose in 1996. Triangulation demanded that Clinton abandon "Democratic class-warfare dogma," rise above his partisan roots, and inhabit the political center "above and between" the two parties — a concept Dick helpfully illustrated by joining his thumbs and forefingers into the shape of a triangle. That meant Clinton had to deliberately distance himself from his Democratic allies, use them as a foil, pick fights with them. Combine these two tactics with a "strong" foreign policy, a reasonably healthy economy, and public advocacy of issues like school uniforms and curfews that would demonstrate Clinton's commitment to "values," Dick said, and Clinton would win in 1996.

Suddenly he stopped. His spine stiffened, and his head dropped mechanically toward his belt. Then it popped back up, as if he'd been snapped out of a hypnotic trance. It was his beeper. "The president." He smiled, followed by a little laugh. *All I need, another reminder of who's in charge.* But at least the interruption as Dick went to find a phone gave me a chance to collect my thoughts and absorb all I'd seen and heard.

It was a tour de force, no question about that. As abstract strategy, Dick's theory was elegant; as performance art, it was mesmerizing. Watching Dick, I began to see what attracted Clinton to him. Beneath the weird veneer, Dick's mind was color-blind. He thought in black and white, a useful complement to Clinton's kaleidoscopic worldview. Stan Greenberg, Clinton's previous pollster, was a former professor with an academic style, analytical and nuanced. He appealed to Clinton's intellectual instincts and synthesizing nature, but Clinton often groused that Stan didn't make definitive recommendations. Dick, however, spoke to the part of Clinton that wanted to be told what to do. He offered clear prescriptions and promised measurable results. His certainty helped cure Clinton's chronic bouts of indecision. I could almost hear his steady drone on the phone with Clinton, calming the anxiety that often came over the president after midnight: *"Remember the theory. If we stick to it, we'll win. Just like we always have. Promise. It's in the prayer book."*

Of course, no single adviser could ever fully own Clinton. He was too smart and too stubborn for that. But after hearing Morris out, I was struck by the degree to which Clinton had integrated Dick's thinking with his own. In strategy meetings, Clinton had been repeating the Morris mantra that I'd heard fully explained tonight: "We have to help the Republicans spend their antigovernment, antitax energy. We don't want 1996 to be about taxes and government." Other scenes now started to make sense as well. Like the time in December when I was up in the residence with Hillary and Clinton as he prepared to address the nation from the Oval Office. "Who came up with this language on the middle-class bill of rights?" I asked. Clinton pretended he didn't hear me; Hillary wore a Cheshire grin, throwing me off. It wasn't her; it was Dick. Or on State of the Union day. Clinton and Hillary retreated to the family quarters to revise the speech themselves, or so we thought and faithfully spun to reporters as a sure sign that the president was preparing to speak from his heart. When I reviewed a late draft and questioned their decision to drop a line opposing Republican "tax cuts for the wealthy," Hillary snapped, "You say what you want to say, Bill." *That's weird. She usually likes a good pop on the Republicans.* I didn't know then that the edit had come from Dick, who was hiding in the family room next door.

Repeating Dick's rhetoric was one thing; what really worried me was the possibility that Clinton would actually act on it. Dick explained his theory in elaborate terms, but it boiled down to a relatively simple proposition: Steal the popular-sounding parts of the Republican platform, sign them into law, and you'll win. The fact that it would anger Democrats was not a drawback but a bonus. The fact that it would contradict Clinton's past positions and professed beliefs was barely relevant. Dick made obligatory references to avoiding "flip-flops," but his cardinal rule was to end up on the right side of a "60 percent" issue. If six out of ten Americans said they were for something, the president had to be for it too.

How can Clinton even listen to this guy? He wants us to abandon our promises and piss on our friends. Why don't we just go all the way and switch parties? "Neutralization" sounded to me like capitulation, and "triangulation" was just a fancy word for betrayal. I also thought the strategy wouldn't work. The Morris approach might have polled well, but adopting it in its pure form would eviscerate the president's political character and validate the critique that made him most furious — that he lacked core convictions, that he bent too quickly to political pressure and always tried to have it both ways. Not to mention that it would guarantee a serious challenge in the Democratic primaries — the surest predictor of a single-term presidency.

Preventing that challenge was Harold's job. His official title was deputy chief of staff, but his portfolio was politics, the nuts and bolts — building a campaign organization, watching the money, tending to our Democratic Party base. Harold despised Dick, always had, ever since the late 1960s, when they ran rival Democratic cells on the Upper West Side. He hated even more what Dick was trying to do to the Democrats now. Though he was loyal to Clinton, Ickes revered the party. He had played a role in every Democratic convention and presidential campaign since 1968, usually for the liberal underdog — Gene McCarthy, Teddy Kennedy, Jesse Jackson. It was in his blood. His father, Harold Ickes Sr., had been FDR's confidant and interior secretary, a New Deal legend. Serving a Democratic president was an ambition passed from father to son. Now that Harold was actually in the White House, he was following in his father's footsteps in another way. The stakes were smaller now — we didn't have to contend with a depression or a world war — but Clinton was pitting Ickes against Morris just as FDR had created constructive tension in his inner circle by playing off Harold Sr. against counselor Harry Hopkins. Tonight, though, Harold was too tired to fight. He left the table before Dick finished his phone call.

"I'm glad we've had this opportunity to get together," Dick said when he returned to the table, noticeably relieved to see that Harold was gone. "I want you to know where I'm coming from and what I'm thinking. The president's happy we're meeting too. He wants us to work together."

The sound of Dick's reporting to me on Clinton's state of mind made me cringe, but I said, "We have to try," my first full sentence of the night. In a weak attempt to establish my own bona fides as a Clinton expert, I added, "He hates open fights. Hates being presented with personal confrontation."

But I wasn't worried only about the president's psychological comfort. The whole White House had become dysfunctional. Faced with an aggressive Republican Congress, we were floundering, unable to formulate a coherent response to their ambitious agenda. The day shift, led by Leon, would push the president toward a confrontational stance. We had studied Harry Truman's 1948 campaign against the "Do Nothing" Republican Congress and hoped that Clinton would follow that fighting example. But that wasn't the president's style or Dick's strategy. On the night shift, Morris would pull Clinton back. Every presidential event, each radio address, had become a battleground. One draft would be prepared by the staff, a second would whir through the president's private fax. Clinton would take a little from column A, a little from column B, depending on the day, his mood, and whom he had talked to last. As Newt Gingrich was orchestrating House passage of the Contract with America, we were responding with a symphony of mixed signals.

By the symbolic "100 day" mark of the Republican Congress, we had reached a point of crisis. The entire administration had been mobilized for a weeklong series of events highlighting the president's commitment to education and the threat posed by the Republican Congress, which would be kicked off with a presidential address to the American Society of Newspaper Editors. Two days before the event, at an Oval Office meeting meant to lock him in on the strategy, Clinton signed off on the speech draft and the rollout plan, including parallel events by cabinet secretaries and other administration officials. The next night, in the residence, Dick convinced him to scrap the speech and deliver instead a point-by-point commentary on the Republican contract — a decision that was announced at the senior staff meeting the morning of the speech. Dick actually had the right idea, but it was done in the wrong way — and it wreaked havoc in the White House. Panetta confronted the president and demanded that the situation be brought under control.

After our plates were cleared, Morris and I retreated to the back of the bar to discuss the terms of our engagement. I ordered a scotch, Dick a cognac. The maître d' delivered them personally, compliments of the house. "Oh, it's so good to be here with someone famous," Dick said. "But I don't want any publicity. Being a man of mystery helps me work better. I just want to do the job." Aware of his own frailties, Dick was basically talking to himself. But the unspoken subtext wasn't lost on me: *"You have fame, but you lost your power. Celebrity is double-edged. I have the power now — and I'm not going to blow it."*

The more I listened to Morris, the more I sensed that his position with Clinton was slightly more precarious than I had imagined. The president wanted Dick's ideas, but he couldn't afford open rebellion in the White House. Dick was essentially under orders to play nice. He knew that Harold was his mortal enemy, and that Leon could barely stand to be in the same room with him. I was part of their team, but the underlying purpose of tonight's dinner was to determine whether I could be a bridge between the two camps. Trying to draw me in, Dick started our private conversation with a stab at making me feel sorry for him, explaining that his Republican clients were furious at him for agreeing to work with Clinton: "You have no idea how much trouble I'm in with the people on my own side."

You have no idea how little I care. It was maddening enough that Clinton was relying on a consultant whose publicly stated professional goal was to "help the Republicans govern successfully and become a majority party." Even worse were all the rumors we kept hearing from the Hill about how Dick was still feeding inside information from the White House to his most prominent Republican client, Senate Majority Leader Trent Lott. As Dick reeled off his woes of financial risk and lost friendship, I just stared back at him.

So he tried a new tack: veiled threat. Twisting his neck and working his jaw in a nervous tic that made him look like a cut-rate Cagney impressionist, he lowered his voice to a sotto voce hiss: "Now listen, George, I know you leaked all those stories on me in April. Don't say that you didn't. I don't care what you say. I know you did."

"All those stories" consisted of a brief "Talk of the Town" piece in *The New Yorker* and a passing mention in the "Washington Whispers" section of *U.S. News and World Report.*

I wasn't their source, but it didn't matter. Dick had me cornered here. *"Screw with me,"* he was saying, *"and I'll screw with you."* I felt compelled to respond for the record: "Dick, you may not want to hear it, but I'll tell you anyway: I didn't do it and I wouldn't do it. Not because I care about you, but because I don't want to hurt the president."

Nice-sounding sentiments, but they wouldn't do me much good if Dick continued to press this complaint with Clinton. Given the president's attitude toward me and leaks, an accusation was tantamount to a conviction. Back on solid ground, Dick outlined his view of the power equation in the White House. "Your basic power is the administration. They all look to you. You also have good ties to the press. But I have the president. We should work together." He then started to list a series of policy proposals and presidential decisions that he wanted to "take off the table" by securing my agreement.

Though it was typically overstated, Dick's analysis wasn't far off. I could frustrate his night thoughts by raising questions in the morning senior staff meetings, or by getting a cabinet member or member of Congress to weigh in against one of his schemes. But he could do the same to me by working the president directly, and it was emotionally exhausting and politically debilitating to develop a strategy, build coalitions inside the administration, consult with the Congress, and prepare the ground with the press, only to have the whole approach upended in a late-night meeting where you didn't have a say. Dick needed me, and I needed him. Now we really started talking.

His big idea that week was a "national crusade" against domestic terrorism. In the wake of the Oklahoma City bombing, Morris didn't think that, politically, you could be too tough on the militias. While Dick's read of public sentiment was unassailable, his proposals re-minded me of the advice his late cousin Roy Cohn used to give Joe McCarthy. Morris wanted to require militia groups to register their guns and their membership with the FBI, and he wanted the Justice Department to publish the names of suspected terrorists in the newspapers. I raised a civil liberties argument. "Oh, people don't care about that," he said. So I countered with process, saying that if the attorney general wasn't on board (which she'd never be), Dick couldn't achieve his goal. Leaks from the Justice Department would only make Clinton look weak, and the paperwork would never emerge from the bowels of the bureaucracy unless the president typed it himself.

Next on his list of potential presidential targets was immi-grants. Basically, he wanted to create a background-check system that would turn your average traffic cop into a member of the U.S. Border Patrol. If, say, a police officer spotted a suspiciously brown-skinned person driving a car with a busted taillight, Dick's scheme would give him the ability to dial into a computer and order imme-diate deportation if the driver's papers weren't in order. Though he brushed off my fears of potential abuse and political harm to our Hispanic base, I persuaded him to hold off on the practical grounds of prohibitive cost.

As we worked through his list, Dick became more and more excited. He didn't seem to mind having his ideas shot down; there were always more where they came from. More important to him was the fact that he thought he had figured out a way for the two of us to work together. "I got it, George, I got it," he said as he began reeling off various metaphors for our relationship. "I do strategy, you do tactics. Together we have twenty-twenty vision: I see long, you see short. I'm the playmaker, you're parked under the basket."

Whatever. I still didn't trust him. Dick would get me fired if he could and would try to own me if he couldn't. I'd do the same to him. Meantime, I knew we had to work together. Whether I liked it or not, the president wanted Dick to be his strategist. If I didn't like it, I could leave. But that felt like surrender, and vaguely disloyal — a betrayal of the ideas and ideals we had fought for in the 1992 campaign. To serve the president I helped elect, I had to fight the president Dick was trying to create. If Clinton didn't like that, he could fire me. But that felt less likely now.

There must be a method to his madness. Clinton is pulling an FDR. He wants Dick's energy and ideas, but he wants us to check him too. He wants us to get along, but he doesn't want me to give up.

That's what I told myself, anyway. I knew I wouldn't win every battle, but I was glad the shadowboxing was over. Dick and I were finally in the ring together. Still ahead were the biggest bouts with the broadest political consequences and the most direct conflict between us. As Dick prattled on about our new partnership, I finally told him to stop. "The two things we need to talk about," I said, "are affirmative action and the budget." After a few minutes of debate, it was clear that these issues were still very much on the table. "Oh, I'm going to beat you," he said with a dismissive shrug that made me even more determined to prove him wrong. But it was 1:30 A.M., the tables were bare, the lights were up, and our waiter was giving me a bleak look. Dick and I parted with a handshake and a promise to talk in the morning.

14   A TALE OF TWO SPEECHES

Two days after my dinner with Dick, I was in the Oval to help prep the president for an interview with New Hampshire Public Radio. (With the first primary of Clinton's final campaign only nine months away, we weren't taking anything for granted.) Wendy Smith, who covered New Hampshire for the White House, briefed Clinton on local issues like the Portsmouth Naval Base, while Gene Sperling and I stood by in case he needed some fresh budget facts. Not likely. At a cabinet room event earlier that morning, Clinton had already delivered our standard critique on the Republican budgets — that they cut too much from Medicare, Medicaid, education, and tax credits for the poor "to pay for tax cuts for upper-income Americans." Our "message of the day" was set; all the president had to do was repeat it. When Wendy handed Clinton the phone, I left for lunch. Twenty minutes later, my beeper went off. It was Gene. "George, we got a problem. You gotta get back here."

I knew I should've stayed. He stays on message when he's being watched. Clinton hated repeating himself, and he was ambivalent about our budget, which continued deficit reduction but wasn't projected to reach balance. Morris was pushing him to scrap it and to match the Republicans with a balanced budget of his own, preferably on Sunday night in a prime-time televised address from the Oval Office. That wasn't going to happen. The entire economic team was opposed to such a precipitous move — the proposed cuts would eviscerate our commitment to "investments in people," and we didn't even have a new budget to propose. But when the interviewer challenged Clinton's commitment to fiscal discipline, the president gave him the answer he was looking for, replying in a roundabout way that he owed the Republicans and the American people a "counter-budget" that reached balance by a fixed date. "I think it clearly can be done in less than ten years," he said.

Owe it to the Republicans? What about the Democrats? Gene and I were off the wall. Panetta too. The former chairman of the House Budget Committee knew how tough it would be to produce a balanced budget that protected our priorities, and he understood the pace of the negotiating process. We accepted that Clinton would eventually have to compromise with the Republicans, but now was too early. They were just starting to pay a political price for their unpopular cuts; why let them off the hook?

We spent the whole afternoon trying to keep a lid on the story. The only regular White House reporter who'd heard the interview was National Public Radio's Mara Liasson, and I did my best to sell her the line that what the president said wasn't all that new, that it was more analysis than advocacy. It was a Friday afternoon, and the rest of the press corps was preoccupied with the pending Secret Service decision to close the two-block stretch of Pennsylvania Avenue in front of the White House to cars and trucks. No need to distract them; we delayed general distribution of Clinton's New Hampshire interview transcript until after deadline. For another weekend, at least, our budget strategy would survive.

The stakes were high. For as long as I'd been in Washington, the budget deficit had defined the domestic-policy debate. Reducing it had become an economic and political imperative. But as Clinton always said, no good deed goes unpunished. He had defeated President Bush in 1992 largely because Bush had sacrificed his "no new tax" pledge for the sake of deficit reduction. Republicans had defeated Democrats in 1994 largely because, in 1993, Democrats raised taxes to reduce the deficit. The 1996 presidential campaign would turn on the budget showdown of 1995. But how? Would voters, as Morris believed, reward Clinton for cooperating with the Republicans and signing a version of their balanced budget and tax cuts into law? Or would they, as I believed, reward the president for vetoing the Republican budget and protecting core government programs against crippling cuts?

But the budget debate wasn't just about the president's reelection prospects. It also revolved around fundamental questions of philosophy, economics, and politics: What is the proper size, scope, and role of the federal government? What policies are most effective in creating economic growth and ensuring a fair distribution of its benefits? What are the responsibilities of a president in a divided political system? When is compromise honorable — and when is it cowardly? How much ground could we cede to the Republicans and still call ourselves Democrats?

Our initial budget strategy, conceived in December, when Morris was still in the shadows, was unapologetically partisan. It rested on the premise that the Republicans' 1994 campaign was fundamentally dishonest and the hope that we Democrats could make them pay for it. Right up until November, Newt Gingrich and his allies had adamantly denied our charge that their Contract with America pledge to balance the budget with huge tax cuts and higher defense spending would require cuts of up to 30 percent in government programs like Medicare and Medicaid, student loans, environmental protection, and crime prevention. Rather than match their return to Reaganomics, we called their bluff. Our December budget basically extended the deficit reduction policies of our 1993 plan but didn't come close to balance. Deficit hawks derided it as a "slide by" budget; I liked to think of it as a "show me" budget, designed to draw clear lines in the sand and force the Republicans to specify the painful cuts it would take to pay for their popular promises.

At first, Clinton was enthusiastic about the strategy. He felt he had done the hard work of deficit reduction without any Republican help and that they had an obligation to do the same. But as the months passed, he became increasingly uncomfortable — and not just because of Morris. Clinton's a doer by nature, and an optimist;

he believed there had to be a way to balance the budget without abandoning his principles or past promises. He doesn't like playing defense, and he was rankled by the consistent Republican critique that he was AWOL in the balanced-budget fight. "I'm president. I need to be *for* something," he would tell us. "I can't just stand on the sidelines." The New Hampshire interview was Clinton's way of sneaking off the bench.

By Monday, May 22, the press corps was buzzing. Although the president had couched his proposal in conditional terms, the reporters knew they had a story here: The president was breaking with his allies and advisers and striking out on his own. When Sperling tried to spin down the significance of Clinton's new pledge with David Broder of the *Post*, Broder dryly replied, "I hope you don't mind, Gene, but I'd rather use his words than yours on this one." Tuesday morning, the clandestine budget debate inside the White House was front-page news.

At eleven A.M., the economic team filed into the Oval for a damage control session. Everyone was on edge, perturbed by Clinton's unilateral shift and uncertain about what he would say that afternoon at a Rose Garden press conference. Although the players arrayed on the couches flanking the president and vice president held diverse views on budget policy, we thought we had a consensus on the negotiating strategy: that the president should hold off from announcing a new budget until after the House and Senate Republicans had spelled out *their* cuts in a single, specific plan; that we should offer a counterproposal only when we had a credible document that could withstand scrutiny, and only after the Republicans made concessions in our direction on Medicare, education, and taxes. While Morris (who didn't attend the formal policy meetings but was clearly there in spirit) was fighting this approach, even he agreed that Clinton's offhand comment in a local radio interview wasn't the best way to signal a shift in strategy for the most momentous legislative battle of the presidency.

Clinton was both sheepish and defiant. He knew that he'd made a mistake, but he groused with some justification that the press had taken his words out of context. And he chafed at our counsel for patience: "You guys want me to go out and criticize the Republicans, and when they say, 'Where's your plan?' you want me to say, 'Well, who am I? I'm just the president of the United States. I don't have a plan.'" Even though the president still maintained that he was sticking by our strategy, he clearly wanted to produce a balanced budget sooner rather than later. The best we could hope for was to buy some time.

Panetta and Pat Griffin led off the meeting with a report from Capitol Hill. The Democrats were angry and confused. Their disciplined drilling of the Republican plan was drawing blood, and they didn't want the focus to shift from the Republican plan to our counterproposal. Just the week before, in a closed-door session with the leadership, the president had reiterated our commitment to stick with a joint strategy. At a minimum, they thought they deserved to be consulted before such a significant departure.

Alice Rivlin, director of the Office of Management and Budget, followed with a briefing on balanced-budget options — all of them bad. An eminent economist and committed public servant, Alice was a feisty bureaucrat and a sincere deficit hawk. She relished the job of drafting a balanced budget as much as I feared it, which was why we were constantly feuding. As she went down her spreadsheet of proposed reforms, I made a parallel list of broken promises and alienated constituencies: veterans, farmers, senior citizens, college students, police, any middle-class American who'd taken Clinton at his word when he promised a tax cut. In 1995, neither the Office of Management and Budget nor the Congressional Budget Office analysts realized that the American economy would grow far faster and far longer than their forecasts predicted. Given the economic assumptions we had to work with, you couldn't balance the budget on paper without big cuts in programs that affected broad slices of the population.

Gene Sperling and I were the only ones in the room that day (aside from the president and vice president) who had actually worked on the 1992 campaign. Dejected as we watched promise after promise disappear under the budget director's blue pencil and our boss's seemingly blithe indifference to his past commitments, we resorted to gallows humor. Leaning over to me on the couch, Gene whispered, "You know this guarantees a primary."

"I think I'll run," I replied. "Do you have to be thirty-five to enter the race or just to be elected?"

Two years older than I, Gene saw his opening. "Just to be safe, I'll run."

"No way. I may have to miss Iowa, but I'll be old enough when New Hampshire rolls around. Besides, I have better stump skills and higher name recognition than you. I'm running."

"OK, OK."

But we weren't giving up yet. Rivlin's budget review was a reality check for the president — a useful antidote to the happy talk Morris was feeding him over the phone about how easy it would be to propose a balanced budget that protected our priorities. The more he heard, the less ready he was to change strategy. Figuring that a late intervention would be most effective, I waited until the meeting was nearly over to repeat the litany I had drafted in response to Rivlin's presentation. "If you proposed a budget like this, Mr. President," I concluded, "Gene and I could produce a book in three days called *Putting People Last*, showing how it defies the promises you made in 1992. We can't do this." The flip on *Putting People First* was over the top, and though I was trying to strike a lighthearted tone, I knew I was right on the edge of being rude. But I also wanted to break through, and I saw myself as the ghost of campaign past.

Our combined efforts must have made an impression. In the Rose Garden, Clinton came out squarely against a seven-year balanced budget. When asked whether he was going to propose a counterbudget, the president dodged, reiterating our original strategy of waiting for the "reconciliation" process, which "the president has a role in because I have a veto." Of course, Clinton's use of the third person was a subtle hint that he wasn't really sold on our strategy, and you always have to listen for what Clinton doesn't say: He didn't rule out proposing a nine- or ten-year balanced budget.

Morris was still lobbying hard behind the scenes. He opened our end-of-the-day conversation with a flourish —"*Le roi est mort. Vive le roi*" — which was his way of telling me that although I had won this early skirmish over the timing of the balanced-budget speech, I would lose the bigger war.

The next day, the budget dominated our 7:30 A.M. senior staff meeting. As I went through my usual spiel about how disastrous a change in course would be and how we had to make sure that the president *really, really* understood *all the implications* of making a move, Erskine Bowles blew up. "Damnit, George," he said, "the president has made a decision. He wants a ten-year budget. Let's just give it to him and make sure he has a balanced presentation." Treasury Secretary Bob Rubin seconded the motion. Although both knew that Clinton hadn't formally made up his mind, proposing a ten-year budget was clearly the president's desire. Erskine was telling me to get with the program.

This was *my* reality check. I respected Bowles and Rubin. We worked well together, and they generally deferred to my political judgment. Although their faith in the ultimate fairness of ungoverned markets was deeper than mine, I had to concede that Rubin had been dead right in 1993 when he said that the economic benefits of deficit reduction would make up for the costs of scaling back our "putting people first" investments. As successful investment bankers, they were also seasoned and disciplined negotiators. Through the early months of 1995, they had supported the hard-line budget strategy I advocated. But they were looking ahead to the next move. Above all, they were telling me, "The president has made a decision. Deal with it."

They're right. Face it, George, you lost this fight. Grow up and make the best of it. I still believed in holding out as long as possible, and that moving too far and too fast in the Republican direction was too high a price to pay for staying in power. But I couldn't blind myself to political reality. The Republicans had won the last election. The president did have a responsibility to work with them in a reasonable manner, and arguing against the notion of balancing the budget was politically untenable. If people weren't convinced that we shared their commonsense belief that government should live within its means, they wouldn't even listen to the rest of our arguments. Finally, whether I liked it or not, the president wanted to make this decision.

So I made one too — to play ball. After the meeting, Leon, Harold, Erskine, and I huddled for an hour to figure out a rational process for moving forward. The goal was to produce a credible balanced budget, through the normal channels of the Office of Management and Budget and the National Economic Council, as quickly as possible — within a month. But we also needed to account for the irrational. Our best-laid plans could still be ruined by a single phone call from Morris. After clearing it with Leon, I called him.

"Dick," I said, "if the president is determined to come up with a balanced budget, which I'm still not happy about, I think you and I owe it to him to make it as politically prudent a document as possible. We ought to see if we can develop a common position." In victory, Dick was gracious. He said he now realized that I wasn't acting only from "knee-jerk liberalism" or my past ties to the Democratic Congress, but also from a legitimate concern for the president's political positioning and the real-world consequences of further budget cuts. We agreed to meet Friday, the morning after his next session with the president.

Having made my deal with the devil, I tried to get some credit with Clinton. At the end of the day, as we were walking back from a "drop-by" with a delegation of Greek Americans, I raised my dinner with Dick to the president and added that we'd been discussing the budget: "We'd like your clearance to work together." Clinton didn't say anything right away, just looked down at me out of the corners of his eyes, skeptical. *Terrific; now he's worried that we're cooperating* _too_ *much. Or does he think I'm bullshitting him?* But when we reached the Oval, the president pulled a pad from the drawer by his phone. It was covered with his hieroglyphics. "I've been thinking hard about how we can shave the budget without doing too much harm . . . ." he said. Maybe I hadn't been giving him enough credit.

The era of good feeling didn't last long. At 6:15 on Friday morning, Harold slipped into my office and flipped a plastic-laminated folder at the newspaper spread before my face. It was Dick's "neuropsychological profile" of the American electorate, his handout at last night's seance. Harold was my spy at Dick's weekly strategy sessions in the residence, and his report this morning couldn't be worse. "It was pretty tough on Leon last night," he said, looking disgusted, sounding dejected. Morris had responded to our success at stalling a balanced-budget announcement with a furious counter-strike at Panetta and the rest of us on the day team. Calling the White House "a graveyard of speeches," he circulated a list of his brilliant ideas that had been "snuffed out by the bureaucrats" and browbeat Clinton into scheduling the budget speech for Tuesday night — four days from now.

At our morning meeting, the strain of holding two White Houses together showed on Leon. Testy, his normally ruddy cheeks waxy with fatigue, he pulled Press Secretary Mike McCurry and me aside. "Guys, I felt awfully lonely in that meeting last night," he confided. "I need your help." Panetta knew that we had meetings with Morris later that day, and he asked us to do what we could to change his mind about a Tuesday speech. Not only was it bad budget strategy, but the Serbian bombing of another "safe area" in Bosnia the day before meant that we had a weekend of NATO air strikes ahead. To have Clinton slap together a budget and spring it on the country in the midst of an intensified military action in which American troops were at risk didn't seem presidential or prudent.

Morris was unmoved by that argument. He came to our meeting bearing me a gift — a Diet Pepsi — but he wouldn't budge on the timing of the speech. The polls, he divined, dictated next week: "There's been a ten percent drop in the number of people who would vote against Clinton, but no increase in the number of people who would vote for him," he said. "The key to getting that ten percent — the swing vote, the Perot vote — is to give a prime-time speech. It has to be next week, or we lose them forever."

Next week *or we lose them forever? No wonder we're proposing a Republican budget. Our strategist is Nancy Reagan's astrologer. How does Clinton listen to this crap?* Actually, I thought I was beginning to understand. Morris had a strong fix on Clinton's psychology. His focus on swing voters was solid analysis that appealed to the president's intellect; his obsession with the timing was superstition that inflamed the president's insecurities. When he told Clinton, "I can't guarantee that you win if you follow my advice, but I can guarantee that you lose if you don't," he played into the same part of Clinton that covertly consulted New Age gurus. A man blessed with political luck, Clinton usually took precautions to protect it.

Over the course of our two-hour meeting, it was clear that Dick didn't really care about the budget — as long as it was ready by Tuesday and we could claim it reached balance. He didn't understand the numbers, and he was happy to work with me to protect Democratic priorities and preserve lines of attack against the Republicans. We reviewed the Rivlin budget options and agreed that Clinton couldn't scale back his tax cut or propose tax increases, that we needed to maintain a net increase in funding for education and our commitment to a hundred thousand new police, and that we should draw a clear contrast with the Republicans on Medicare by proposing far smaller savings and no new premium increases on its beneficiaries. The problem, of course, was figuring out how to do all that and still produce a balanced budget. Dick was willing to make cuts in welfare and benefits to legal immigrants that I opposed, but it still wasn't enough to fill the shortfall. No matter. "I'll work with Alice over the weekend," he said, concluding our meeting.

I spent the rest of the day reporting to my colleagues. Panetta was busy when I went to his office, but he walked into mine a few minutes later, his sour mood replaced by an air of resignation. I told him that Dick had signed off on most of my substantive objections, but that he still insisted we had to go on Tuesday. Leon just exhaled, slowly shaking his head from side to side. It wasn't just the substance of the decision that offended him; there was plenty of room for honest debate over budget policy. It was the assault on the integrity of our policy-making process, the fact that we were beholden to polls, and the double indignity the night before of being insulted by a charlatan and hearing no defense from the president in return. This wasn't the way a White House was supposed to work. He leaned his elbows into my desk for something of a heart-to-heart. "You know, Leon," I said. "If the president actually does this on Tuesday, Laura [Tyson, director of the National Economic Council] and a couple of other people might resign."

"I don't know that I can stay either," he replied. "I've been doing budgets for a long time, and the way we're going now just isn't right."

"I guess I'd leave too," I said, tentatively. Neither one of us could believe, I think, that the president would actually stick to Dick's schedule. It wasn't really possible to produce a new budget over the Memorial Day weekend, and we didn't think Clinton would propose it over the opposition of his entire economic team. Still, we couldn't be sure. When Leon left, I called Laura Tyson to commiserate over how the National Economic Council process had been corrupted. "No, George," she said. "I feel sorry for you. You went through the whole campaign. Now it's all going down the drain."

My next stop was Erskine, who said he was leaving the White House by the end of the summer. His wife had just been promoted, and it was his turn to take care of the kids. Besides, he added, "this situation can't last much longer." By that, of course, he meant the trouble with Morris. Erskine was Dick's official control officer. But even though he generally agreed with the Morris approach on the budget, Bowles said he felt like "taking a shower" every time he dealt with him. Before I left, Erskine showed me the memo Morris had already faxed him that detailed the agreements we'd reached on the budget. Though overstated, it was a surprisingly fair summary. Just in case, Erskine asked me to speak directly to Clinton.

But the president didn't really want to hear it. While noting my arguments on his pad, he set his jaw when I argued that we wouldn't be ready and it wouldn't be wise to go on Tuesday. "We have to move quickly. We have to move quickly," he insisted. "We're losing the spin war on the budget." Then Harold and the vice president joined us, and the president seemed intent on getting me out of there. "I agree with a lot of your points, but I want the option of going on Tuesday. I want all the numbers." Clinton's impatience was a sign that I was winning the argument; he'd have been more solicitous if the decision were going against me. But we still had to go through the motions. OMB would spend the weekend crunching numbers, and our budget group would meet with the president on Monday, Memorial Day.

A lurid lightning storm enhanced the surreal quality of our late-holiday-afternoon meeting in the Oval. Despite a weekend of all-nighters, the OMB analysts hadn't completed the options paper for the president, but we were still laboring under the fiction that he would present a full budget to the country the next night. Clinton pressed the issue, and Gore joined in, suggesting that the president cancel his Thursday trip to Montana if we couldn't be ready by Tuesday. *There's a plan. We're bombing Bosnia, but we scrap the president's schedule to propose a budget that doesn't exist.* I couldn't resist the bait. It's one thing to cancel a presidential trip for a national security crisis, I responded, but doing it for another flip on the budget would send the signal that this was another knee-jerk reaction and not part of a well-thought-out plan.

"That's fine," Gore shot back, "if all you care about is a news story. We're trying to change our strategy. This is a dynamic process. We've lost the game. The Republicans have called our bluff, and we don't have any cards without a budget."

"It isn't nearly over yet," I said, risking several months of peace with Gore. "All they've done is set goals, not a line-by-line budget. We haven't had enough patience to let the strategy sink in." Even as I made my case, however, I had my doubts. The vice president had been on board all along, insisting that the Republicans had to have a "rendezvous with reality." *Maybe I am wrong here — and it sure looks like I'm going to lose.*

But when Bob Rubin inveighed against an announcement that couldn't be backed by credible numbers, the president retreated. He started rehearsing each side's best case out loud, and our decision meeting became a discussion group. *In his heart he knows we can't go tomorrow. Now he's buying time.* The only decision we made before going home that night was to convene again the next day. It turned out to be a rolling session during which cabinet secretaries Bob Reich, Ron Brown, Richard Riley, and Donna Shalala all lobbied against further cuts. When each secretary's policy concerns were taken into account, we were a good $100–150 billion short of reaching balance. But the most important new voice at the table belonged to Hillary. This was her first appearance at a meeting of the economic team since the defeat of health care, and she had a purpose. The health care reforms of the budget still didn't meet the president's condition of reforming Medicare and Medicaid "only in the context of overall health care reform," and she wanted more time to fix them. But to avoid appearing at odds with the president in this semipublic setting, she made a cagier case for delay.

"If our administration had any message discipline," she argued, "the president could give the speech this week. Instead of getting sucked into a debate on the details, everyone could just say, 'You heard what the president said last night; that's what we're going to do.' But we don't have that kind of discipline, so we have to wait."

Brilliant. She defeated the president's position by playing into his prejudice, echoing his perennial complaints about staff loyalty and our inability to communicate a clear message. As the day wore on, Clinton began to argue the virtues of delay, even asking me to retrieve a newsletter by Republican analyst Kevin Phillips praising our "shrewd" budget tactics. "The spotlight on the GOP's proposals," Clinton underlined, "will be harsher than voter reaction to the president for not compromising." By the close of business, he had agreed to put off any announcement for at least a week — a good day's work for our side.

Of course, if Dick's theory was right, we'd just lost the election. *"It has to be next week, or we lose them forever."* Manic at the setback, he struck back — at me this time. The next morning, Erskine showed me an irate fax that Morris had sent to the president disputing the decision. "P.S.," he had added, "I know who the leak was on the *Time* story," referring to an article that week critical of Morris and, by implication, Clinton. "It is a person I have been talking to of late, and I have tacit confirmation from the reporter."

"Tacit confirmation from the reporter." What the hell does that *mean?* I offered to show Erskine my call sheets to demonstrate that I hadn't even talked to *Time*, but he told me not to worry. "Just hang in there," he said. "Keep standing up like you've been doing in these meetings. If the president wants you to leave, you'll be gone. Until then, do your job." More good advice, but I wasn't taking anything for granted. First I swore my innocence to Evelyn Lieberman, Hillary's deputy chief of staff, who promised to approach the first lady. Then I buttonholed Harold, Leon, and McCurry to do the same. Since Woodward, living under suspicion had become my chronic condition, but I couldn't afford a flare-up. The charge was particularly dangerous right then because we knew that Ann Devroy was working on a big story in which she would label the White House a "portrait of confusion on budget issues." Somebody would take a hit, so Morris had launched a preemptive strike.

But when that story appeared, our artificial crisis in the White House was overshadowed by the real one in Bosnia. Captain Scott O'Grady's F-16 had been shot down by a Serb missile, capping a week in which Bosnian Serb forces had taken more than three hundred United Nations peacekeepers hostage because NATO had dared to retaliate for the Serbian shelling of Sarajevo. In a commencement address at the Air Force Academy two days earlier, the president had said he was prepared to send U.S. ground troops to assist in a "reconfiguration" of these UN forces — a shift from our previous policy that ground troops would be used only to evacuate the peacekeeping forces or enforce a peace agreement. Twenty-three thousand U.S. troops were being redeployed to the region, and the prospect that we'd get drawn into a Balkan ground war looked more likely than ever.

The ensuing uproar on Capitol Hill caused half the National Security Council to run for cover. Secretary of State Christopher and Defense Secretary Perry both complained to the president that Tony Lake hadn't adequately consulted them on the policy change, a charge Tony denied. Morris was apoplectic: "Eighty percent of the country is against sending ground troops to Bosnia!" When he discovered that the president was devoting his Saturday radio address to the subject, Dick faxed in last-minute language that led the president to depart from the approved NSC text and ad-lib twice that the reconfiguration scenario was "highly unlikely." Not surprisingly, the next day's stories emphasized another Clinton flip-flop.

For the next week, we continued our behind-the-scenes budget struggle, but the country was focused on the Balkans. Congress debated the wisdom of sending ground troops, criticized our failure to retaliate for the downed pilot, and passed amendments condemning Clinton's policy. Sketchy reports from Bosnia hinted that Captain O'Grady was still alive, hiding in the hills and sending signals to his rescue team. Morris didn't stop pushing for the budget speech, but with so much else going on, it wasn't hard to stall.

We did, however, make time for *Larry King Live*. In honor of King's tenth anniversary on the air, he was invited to the White House for the "first ever" joint television interview with a sitting president and vice president. It must have seemed like a good idea at the time, but by the night of the show no one on staff was rushing to own it. You couldn't predict what King or his callers would ask, and the way things were going, who knew how Clinton would answer?

Once Clinton and Gore were wired up in the old library, Mark Gearan and I settled on the couch in Mike McCurry's office to watch the show. We toasted the opening with drinks from Mike's corner bar, and the first few minutes went so well that Gearan joked about how glad he was to have proposed the interview. After a sluggish section on the Waco debacle, he reconsidered, suddenly recalling that it had been my idea. But Clinton and Gore were having a good time, and it seemed as if we had nothing to worry about. With a minute to go, Mike asked me what I thought.

"It was pretty good, I guess."

"Pretty good? You're crazy, George, it was a home run," and he proceeded to tease me with a story from election night 1992. As a BBC election-night commentator, McCurry had told the British audience that Clinton's victory speech was the first time during the whole campaign that he'd seen the Clinton people smile.

Fair shot. I do get too dark. But before I could say anything, King was signing off: "Thanks, guys. You don't want to do a Brando close, do you?" Months before, Marlon Brando had said good night by kissing Larry full on the lips. The scene was still being replayed in promotional shots, and we had actually warned our bosses that Larry might try for a kiss. No problem. Gore deflected the request with a simple "Just a handshake," a vice president doing his duty. Then came an offscreen grunt.

We all froze, unsure of our ears. King confirmed it: "Oh, let me — here — President Clinton does Brando. Do it once. . . ." *No, no, don't.* He did. As the camera zoomed in for a close-up, the president of the United States cleared his throat, puffed his cheeks, and plugged *Larry King Live* in the voice of Don Corleone.

"See, Mike, *that's* why we looked so worried all the time."

We walked back to the residence, cracking up but also saddled with a small dilemma. While the overall interview was OK, the clip on the morning news was sure to be Clinton's Brando impression. Not as bad as discussing his underwear on MTV, but hardly a presidential moment, and it would be replayed again and again in future advertisements for *Larry King Live*. How could we warn Clinton without insulting him? If we came down too hard, it would only upset him — and there was nothing we could do about it now. But if we ignored it and acted like everything was great, we'd have no credibility in the morning. As the president cheerfully removed his makeup with a Handi Wipe, he asked me how it had gone.

"Well," I said. "Strong answers on Bosnia. Made news on terrorism like you wanted. Decent on Waco and movie violence. You avoided any *big* mistakes, but, umh . . . you know . . ."

"What?"

"You may get a little too much attention on this Brando thing. It was a *good* Brando, probably too good. The morning shows won't be able to resist it."

Clinton screwed up his face as if I'd just served him sour milk and turned away in search of a second opinion. *Don't sell me out, guys. I need some backup here.* Mike came through, saving me from the charge that I was just being my usual pessimistic self by affirming that Clinton doing Brando would be the news.

It could have been worse. To our relief, when King had asked about the budget, the president made no new promises, saying only that he would address the subject at "the proper time." In the days following the King interview, we arranged for Gephardt and Senate Democratic leader Tom Daschle to make personal pleas for sticking with our strategy. And in their private meetings, Clinton assured them he wouldn't make a solo move. But over the course of the week, our other arguments for delay began to fall away. Another round of policy meetings and some creative accounting *had* allowed us to hammer our counterbudget into reasonable shape, and it wouldn't get any better with time. The gradual release of UN hostages and the dramatic rescue of Scott O'Grady calmed the sense of crisis in Bosnia — at least for us, at least for now. And the praise Clinton received for the bipartisan spirit of a joint New Hampshire "town meeting" starring him and Newt Gingrich renewed his faith in the promise of "triangulation."

Morris finally had his win. At 8:45 on Tuesday morning, June 13, Vice President Gore held a conference call with the heads of the television networks to request a prime-time slot that night for the president to present a balanced-budget proposal to the nation.

The rest of the day we had the usual struggle over the text. But since the networks had allotted us only five minutes and the thrust of the speech was set, there wasn't much to fight about. I focused on reducing gratuitous insults to Democrats, but Morris was triangulating with a vengeance. It wasn't enough for the president to balance the budget; Dick wanted to make our friends howl. He insisted, for example, that the president contrast his plan to the "congressional" rather than the "Republican" budgets; and his draft praised the civility of Speaker Gingrich — acid words to our allies who were campaigning against the Republican budgets and had been burned for years by Newt's scorched-earth crusade against the "corrupt" congressional Democrats.

I lost both fights. As the president reviewed the final draft at the small desk in his study, Dick stood in the doorway and stared at him. Clinton didn't look up; Morris didn't shut up. He was back in machine mode, repeating his rationale in the rat-a-tat-tat of an old stock ticker. Whenever the president touched his pen to the text, Dick would fuss — "No . . . don't . . . not that" — leaning in until his head was hovering over Clinton's left hand. Only after Clinton swatted the air and barked, "Dick!" did Morris back off.

Resigned, jealous, a little amused, I watched them work from the high-backed rocking chair in the corner. *Is that how I acted when I was Clinton's guy? Probably. Nah, couldn't have been that bad, could I?* Shortly before airtime, I left the room to take a call from Lisa Caputo, Hillary's press secretary. "I have an important message to you from Hillary," she said. "She's depending on you to make sure the speech gives something to the Democrats."

A little late for that, isn't it? "I'm doing my best," I replied, enjoying the slightly adulterous pleasure of conspiring against the president. I explained to her that Morris saw each of my edits as part of some partisan (Democrat) plot and suggested instead that the first lady call the president herself. Knowing full well that Hillary had a longer memory than her husband for Newt's attacks (not to mention that of Newt's mom, who had referred to the first lady as a "bitch" in a television interview earlier that year), I made special mention of the reference to Speaker Gingrich. But by now, even Hillary could do only so much. After her call, the president agreed to beef up the health care sections of the speech, referring specifically to "breast cancer and AIDS research," but the only other concession he'd make was to drop Newt's surname. The final text praised the "Speaker."

The speech was fine. Watching it on the television in my office, I had to concede that the logic of the argument was compelling. I was still concerned about the policy consequences of the cuts, but Morris was absolutely right about the political power of calling for a balanced budget. It preserved our critique of the "extreme" Republican (uh, congressional) budgets, while denying them the same charge against us. Supporting a balanced budget said that Clinton wasn't a "tax and spend" liberal. Senator Dole's haggard and hackneyed response to Clinton relieved me even more. Instead of accepting Clinton's olive branch, declaring victory, and asking for an early summit where the president would be forced to make further concessions, Dole and his fellow Republican leaders stayed on the attack, saving us from ourselves. Because they insisted on all or nothing, we still had a chance to reunify our troops for the ultimate budget showdown later that fall.

The Democrats, however, were enraged by the speech, which was exactly as Morris intended. A group including Morris, Gene Sperling, and me was with the president in his private dining room when the first reactions came in. Slightly flushed from the stress of speaking to an audience of sixty million, Clinton pulled a chair up to the credenza that concealed a small television. His knees were nearly touching the screen, and his eyes were fixed on CNN's Bill Schneider, who was describing the president's move as a blow to Democrats that left them hurt, angry, and confused.

"That's right," Clinton muttered, sipping his Diet Coke, feeling sorry for them and even sorrier for himself because they were mad at him. "No president was ever rewarded for doing deficit reduction."

"This is just the pangs of the childbirth of transition," Morris assured him from across the small room. But Clinton was silent, drifting into the state of "buyer's remorse" he so often observed in others. Morris was losing him. More agitated now, his postvictory euphoria fading fast, Dick bounced on the balls of his feet and tried to lure Clinton back. "Remember the theory. Remember the theory," he chanted, his voice rising with every syllable. "We have the Perot voters out there, lying in wait. This is the moment to strike — and watch the poll numbers go-o *UP!*" On that last phrase, Morris threw his hands high above his head while wiggling his fingers and standing on the tips of his toes — a political shaman casting a spell, enraptured by his own ecstatic dance.

But it wasn't working. The more Dick talked, the angrier Clinton got. His grip tightened, denting the soft metal can in his hand. His jaw muscles pulsed. His flush became a flare. Ashamed at hearing these private incantations invoked in public, surely embarrassed for the rest of us, Clinton lashed out: "I did this because it's the right thing to do, Dick. I did this because it's the right thing to do."

I wanted to believe him.

Our congressional allies sure didn't, especially after they read Dick's background quote in the *Post* that called the speech Clinton's "declaration of independence" from the Democrats. Pat Griffin and I attended the next day's House Caucus to hear them pile on. "This isn't leadership; it's bullshit," said Black Caucus chairman Donald Payne, summing up the general sentiment. But it wasn't just Clinton's tone and tactics, or even the substance of the budget, that bothered them; in June of 1995, everything we Democrats cared about seemed to be imperiled.

That summer threatened to be the season that swept away the Great Society. In the historic legislative sessions of 1964 and 1965, self-confident Democrats had created Medicare and Medicaid, outlawed racial discrimination and segregation, opened America's doors to millions of new immigrants, and declared a war on poverty. In 1995, resurgent Republicans were bent on reversing their thirty-year-old defeats. Medicare would be privatized, Medicaid sent to the states, immigration blocked, and the federal battle against poverty abandoned because, they said, "poverty won." On top of all this, a Supreme Court dominated by conservative Republicans had already restricted the reach of the Voting Rights Act, and on the day before Clinton's budget speech, the Court's decision in *Adarand*

Constructors, Inc. v. Pena raised the specter that federal affirmative action programs would be found unconstitutional.

Democrats were scared. They didn't know where their president stood. Would Clinton fold or fight? If he fought in 1995, would he lose in 1996? What then?

The question was most acute on the issue that rubbed emotions most raw — race. From January on, Republicans had mounted a crusade against affirmative action. In their early appeals for campaign cash and conservative support, all of their leading presidential contenders attacked what they called "racial preferences." Legislation was drafted in both the House and the Senate to strike down affirmative action programs mandated or managed by the federal government. Activists in California prepared a 1996 ballot initiative that would do the same in their state, including a total rollback of race-conscious admissions in the state university system. Conservative strategists like Bill Kristol (who had mapped out the successful assault on our health care plan) briskly predicted that the "wedge" issue of affirmative action would blow the Democratic coalition "completely apart."

We feared they were right, but we didn't know what to do. Discrimination against women and minorities was still a fact of life, and Clinton had always supported affirmative action, but reforming its excesses and eliminating some flawed programs seemed essential. Our opponents were already circulating killer anecdotes, like the story of the "minority tax certificate" administered by the Federal Communications Commission that amounted to a no-risk, multimillion-dollar windfall for a group of affluent African American lawyers fronting for white billionaire Sumner Redstone of Viacom. Try defending *that* in a legislative or presidential debate. Early in the year, Senator Dole had asked the Congressional Research Service to compile a list of all affirmative action efforts administered by the federal government, and we suspected it would uncover other programs that were functioning more like illegal quotas than legitimate equal opportunity outreach. Our challenge was to find a way to neutralize the Republican threat without abandoning our core principles, defending indefensible programs, or dividing the Democratic Party.

I wrote a memo to Leon volunteering for the job. Although it smacked of a no-win situation — another gays in the military that would end with everyone on all sides upset — I felt that I had nothing to lose. With my services as a general strategist to the president no longer in high demand, I needed something to do, and I still had enough self-assurance to believe that I was the person best equipped in the White House to balance the competing pressures at play. But I had another motivation too. From his Little Rock announcement speech, in which he had promised to stop the Republicans from stealing another presidential election by playing the race card; to his sermons in Memphis and Macomb County, in which he had appealed to black and white audiences alike without pandering to their prejudices; to his meditative campaign interview with Bill Moyers, in which he had vowed that race was the one issue that he would never compromise for political gain, Bill Clinton inspired me most when he spoke about race. Now his words and his principles would be put to a fierce political test. This could be a defining moment for him and our party. I had to be part of it.

Leon scrawled "Set up" across the top of my memo, so I convened a group of about twenty senior staffers from the White House and the Justice Department to begin the process of preparing a recommendation for the president. Although this was a preliminary staff meeting, the deliberations were fervid. For my African American colleagues around the oblong table in the Roosevelt Room that afternoon — Maggie Williams, the first lady's chief of staff; Alexis Herman, director of public liaison; Thurgood Marshall Jr., senior adviser to the vice president; and Deval Patrick, assistant attorney general for civil rights — this wasn't just another exercise in abstract policy making or political damage control. Each one of them had personally confronted prejudice and experienced affirmative action — both its benefits and its burdens. Affirmative action had opened doors of opportunity for them, and they were determined to use their influence to open other doors for millions more. A righteous presidential defense of affirmative action, they argued, was a political and moral imperative.

Just as passionate, however, were the "New Democrats" — Bill Galston, deputy domestic policy adviser; Joel Klein, deputy counsel; and John Schmidt, Webb Hubbell's replacement as associate at-torney general. They argued that affirmative action was a good idea that had gone bad over time: Implemented in a rigid and inflexible manner, it was becoming just another form of discrimination, with severe moral and political costs. Being honest meant that we had to address the legitimate resentments of whites who felt punished for past wrongs that they didn't condone and hadn't committed. Presidential leadership, they insisted, required straight talk about where affirmative action had failed and how it needed to be fixed.

Sympathetic to both sides, I was torn, which made me an appropriate proxy for Clinton. That first meeting was unsettling. The surface debate was charged with suppressed suspicion and hostility, but it was still a relatively mild version of what the president would have to confront in our party and across the country. It was also exhilarating, combining moral urgency and the intellectual energy of a graduate seminar with the intense risk of a high-stakes poker table. We didn't know when, and we didn't know exactly how, but I think we all believed that our deliberations would set the stage for a presidential decision that would matter and be remembered.

All we agreed on that afternoon was the need for a major Clinton speech grounded in his "lifelong commitment to civil rights and equal opportunity." We just couldn't reach consensus on what else to say. My notepad was filled with far more questions than conclusions: "What constitutes affirmative action now? Where has it worked? Where has it failed? What is the evidence? Have any forms of affirmative action done more harm than good? To whites? To minorities? If there are to be modifications, how should they be done?" Without answers, Clinton would never agree to give a speech; I also knew that getting accurate data from the cabinet departments managing the programs was a Sisyphean task. In my single best decision of the process, I recruited Chris Edley to do the job.

A tenured Harvard Law professor and associate director of the Office of Management and Budget, Chris was a brilliant policy analyst who liked to say he "grooved" on complexity and knew how to shake facts free from the bureaucracy. Though not close friends, we'd met during the Dukakis campaign and had worked well together when our paths had crossed at the White House. That he prided himself on facing hard choices head-on and that he was a black man with a sterling civil rights pedigree (his father, Christopher Edley Sr., had served as president of the United Negro College Fund) made him perfect for the job. Any Clinton recommendation for affirmative action reform, no matter how minor, would inevitably raise suspicions, if not provoke an outcry, in the African American community. Edley's presence would ensure and demonstrate that the process wasn't rigged.

Chris was wary of being used but unable to resist the challenge. Legal pad in hand, he prodded our group to ignore the politics, examine first principles, and ground our deliberations in "values and vision." By now, that wasn't my natural inclination. Conditioned in a way I wasn't always proud of, I saw policy debates as political time bombs. My job was to disarm them before they destroyed us; it didn't much matter how. But Edley's academic rigor blew the dust off neglected parts of my brain, and I soon understood that, paradoxically, Chris's wonky idealism was also the most pragmatic approach. The two wings of the Democratic Party were flying in different directions, with Jesse Jackson threatening a primary challenge if Clinton didn't "stand firm" on affirmative action, and Senator Joe Lieberman of the Democratic Leadership Committee declaring that racial preferences were "patently unfair." Whatever the president decided, friends and allies would feel alienated, and critics and enemies would be armed with fresh ammunition. We had to make a plausible case to all sides that Clinton was acting for the right reasons. Affirmative action would be perceived as a test of the president's political character. To pass it he would need to prove that he was being true to the beliefs he had articulated and acted on all his life, and that his conclusions were based not on crass calculation but on principled analysis.

Opaque with both political anxiety and honest intellectual uncertainty, Clinton was in no hurry to address the issue. Since our relations were distant in early 1995, I wasn't even sure if he knew that I was managing the review. So I summarized our first Roosevelt Room meeting in a memo ("As you may know, we have established a working group . . .") and attached a packet of his previous statements on civil rights, race, and affirmative action. The memo closed with a request for "more direction" for our strategy group. But I didn't hear anything back right away.

So, like the rest of the world, I plumbed his public statements for clues to his thinking. The message was clear: He wanted to keep his options open. At an early-March press conference, after surprising me by announcing that our nascent review was "almost done," Clinton sent a shock wave through affirmative action supporters by suggesting that we should move to an "alternative" based on economic need rather than race. But in other appearances he would proudly proclaim to be a "relentless practitioner of affirmative action" and declare that his goal was "to build support" for the programs. At the April convention of the California Democratic Party, he argued both sides in a single speech: "We need to defend, without apology . . . anything we're doing that is right and decent and just that lifts people up," he declared, but he added that we Democrats must also empathize with the "so-called angry white males" and "have to ask ourselves: Are they [affirmative action programs] all working? Are they all fair?"

Unready to answer his own rhetorical questions, Clinton resorted to a relatively noble stalling tactic — study. He became more engaged over the course of the review. As I fed him a steady stream of position papers, monographs, and opinion pieces from various sides of the debate, he'd check them off and ask for more. Our core group would meet with him every week or so, and he seemed to enjoy the Socratic dialogues, asking the right questions ("What are the legitimate worries of those who don't get affirmative action?"), making pithy observations ("The definition makes all the difference: Preferences we lose; affirmative action we win"), and pondering the politics ("The Republicans think this is a silver bullet to destroy Democrats, a bird's nest on the ground. They think they gain either way — win or lose"). But even as he engaged in the internal debate, he was still equivocating. The decision memos stayed on his desk.

As frustrating as it was, I understood his hesitation. By May, the basic draft of our review was done, but the final presidential call was difficult. We were prepared to conclude that affirmative action was an effective tool to fight discrimination and promote diversity, and

that the federal programs that focused on education and employment were generally implemented in a fair way. We had not found
as many horror stories as we first feared, so rather than advocating
wholesale changes, we recommended that the president issue a
directive reasserting the "right way" to do affirmative action: no
quotas, no reverse discrimination, no preferences for unqualified
people. Our ideal model was the military, which aggressively recruited and trained minorities for advancement without sacrificing
standards or resorting to quotas. When people thought about affirmative action, we wanted them to see General Colin Powell.

But we found problems with federal "set-aside" programs, which
reserved a percentage of government procurement contracts for
minority businesses. These programs had "worked" — in the sense
that they had dramatically increased opportunities for minority-
and women-owned businesses — and the overwhelming majority of
government contracts — 97 percent — still went to nonminority
firms. But the programs were often abused by scam artists who won
the contracts by "fronting" for nonminority firms. In addition, as
we wrote in our decision memo for the president, they were arguably unfair because "the practical effect of a set-aside is to take a
contract and hang out a shingle saying, 'Whites need not apply.'"
The question was: Could the programs be reformed in a way that
made them less like quotas or did they have to be eliminated? Our
hope was that showing a principled willingness to jettison flawed
programs would strengthen our defense of affirmative action in education and employment.

Just raising the idea of killing some programs created an uproar.
In late May, an "administration official" leaked a draft of our review
to the *Times*, along with the spectacularly unhelpful (and inaccurate)
comment that "we want black businessmen to scream enough to let
angry white males understand that we've done something for
them." Dozens of people had read the draft by then, and while I was
surprised that we had survived so long without a serious leak, I was
also furious. Now our efforts to put principle above politics looked
like a lie. I figured the leaker was a clever bureaucrat executing a defensive maneuver against our threatened reforms, but the next day I

found myself in a conference room of the OEOB with a group of successful black entrepreneurs who were blaming me.

The leaders of the delegation were Bob Johnson, the head of Black Entertainment Television, and Earl Graves, publisher of *Black Enterprise* magazine, accompanied by several lawyers who represented minority contractors. One by one, they chastised me for the *Times* article, and I tried without success to convince them that I was as upset at the leak as they were. But I really couldn't blame them for thinking it was me; after all, I was the "white boy" running the review. I also knew, of course, that their real worry wasn't the article itself but the potential policy change it reported. What really ticked me off, though, was when one of the attorneys, B. J. Cooper, played victim.

"When this is all said and done," he said, "Chris will go back to Harvard and be a law professor; George will go to Hollywood and make a million dollars." *Cool.* "But where will we be?" *Oh, I don't know. Graves and Johnson will scrape by on their $100 million fortunes. You don't seem to be starving, either. But what's more important? Your contracts or protecting the rest of affirmative action — the part that helps the kids who really need it go to a good school and get their first job?*

I held my tongue, but their distemper was another excuse for delay and deliberation — especially since the Supreme Court was about to decide on a constitutional challenge to minority set-aside programs. Its ruling in the *Adarand* case would trump Clinton's decision anyway, so why take the political heat now? Being principled was one thing, but there was no need to be reckless. Edley and I joked that the president's new task force on affirmative action was now "nine guys in black robes."

The June 12 ruling in *Adarand* wasn't definitive. Although it found that federal minority contracting programs needed to be reviewed and reformed, it didn't explicitly prohibit them. Instead, Justice Sandra Day O'Connor's 5–4 opinion set a tougher constitutional standard, saying that set-asides could survive "strict scrutiny" only if they were "narrowly tailored" and served a "compelling governmental interest." At first, I thought it was the worst of all worlds: The Court had cast doubt on affirmative action without finding it unconstitutional, and it was throwing the problem back to the other branches of government. Bob Dole and other conservatives cited the decision as "one more reason" to eliminate affirmative action, saying that the programs did not serve a "compelling governmental interest" because they discriminated against nonminorities. But echoing the sentiments of the Congressional Black Caucus and our other allies who supported affirmative action, Jesse Jackson argued that the new constitutional standard could easily be met and called *Adarand* a "racist" ruling that had to be resisted. Not surprisingly, views inside the White House mirrored that tension.

The day after the ruling, Edley and I were working on the president's statement along with Deval Patrick, Maggie Williams, and Alexis Herman at the conference table in Chris's spacious, high-ceilinged OEOB office. Deval and Chris had penned a draft that coupled an analysis of the decision with some pointed criticism of the majority opinion. Not quite as strong as Jackson's statement, but a little tougher than I thought prudent. From a brief discussion between budget speech drafting sessions earlier in the day, I could tell that Clinton didn't want to go that far. He didn't say much, just gave me a hassled glare while complaining that he needed more time to read and think. To be safe, I toned down the statement. When I looked up, Edley was in my face, his eyes fired with accusation: "At every point in this process," he seethed, "whenever an African American appointee starts to push for something, George, you take it away."

Oh, now I'm the racist. If you only knew what I'm dealing with back there. Morris is telling Clinton to praise the damn decision. If we go too far in the other direction, the president will discount our advice. We have to take what we can get.

"Listen," I shot back, my voice rising for the first time in our partnership. "I'm just trying to protect the president. He's not ready to go that far." Chris could see that I was stung by his suspicion, and he apologized. Soon we were joking about it. "Every time I bring up affirmative action in front of the president," I said, "he develops this sudden urge to go to the bathroom." "It's true. It's true," laughed Alexis. The rest of the day, all I had to do to relieve the tension was say the word *bathroom*.

After consulting with constitutional scholars like Harvard's Laurence Tribe and Walter Dellinger from the Justice Department, we finalized a relatively neutral presidential statement that praised affirmative action when "done the right way" and added that the *Adarand* opinion "is not inconsistent with that view." We also came to see that our final decision *had* been made by the Court. To comply with *Adarand*, the Justice Department would be required to review all federal affirmative action programs and subject them to a stringent constitutional test; many — maybe most — would not survive. The greater danger now was not affirmative action's excesses, but its potential evisceration. With the Supreme Court mandating sweeping reform of how affirmative action was practiced, the president was now free, indeed obligated, to mount a vigorous defense of its underlying principles. Politically, delay worked — as if Clinton had planned it all along.

Of course Morris wasn't satisfied. High on his budget victory, he saw the *Adarand* decision as another occasion for triangulation — the second half of a one-two punch. His goal was a presidential speech exactly one week after the budget address. His script would have Clinton leap over the Court's ruling by launching a preemptive presidential strike against set-asides and declaring that affirmative action must be replaced by a system based on "class, not race." His hope was to draw Jesse Jackson into the 1996 presidential race. "I want Jackson to run for president as an Independent," he told me.

"What are you, nuts?"

"No, I polled it," he replied. "If Jesse runs it will cost us three points with blacks but open up fifteen percent of white voters" who would never even consider voting for Clinton without Jackson in the race.

Thankfully, the president dismissed this Morris brainstorm. He'd had his fill of triangulation for a while. "I hope the Court decision will make this a less virulent issue," Clinton said a few days later; and he finally authorized us to finish the report and prepare a speech that would say: "Here are my principles . . ." and "Here's what works . . ." We scheduled it for July 19. While Edley polished our official report, I devoted the final month to getting the politics right. In the wake of the double assault of *Adarand* and Clinton's

balanced-budget speech, unifying the Democrats was not only politically prudent, but, at least to me, had become a matter of principle — solidarity. I wanted the president to demonstrate fidelity to
long-held beliefs and loyalty to longtime friends, and I wanted to be
on the side of the underdogs; I wanted the Democrats to praise
Clinton, not rage at him — to feel inspired, not betrayed.

I also wanted Clinton to be reelected. Remembering the rule
that primary challenges almost always cripple incumbent presidents, I was convinced we'd lose if Jackson ran. To feel him out,
Harold and I paid Jesse a courtesy call at the Rainbow Coalition
headquarters near K Street. Maybe it was the daylight hour and the
downtown offices; or the numbing rush of intervening events and
the fact that I was four years older, a little jaded, and more of a principal; but that first Clinton-Jackson summit now seemed like a
scene from another life. This session was cordially corporate, less
dramatic but far more direct. Sitting beneath a huge wall map of the
United States marked with each state's filing deadline for an Independent slot on the presidential ballot, Jesse rehearsed speech riffs
("If we can use goals, targets, and timetables to get fair trade with
Japan, we can use goals, targets, and timetables to get a fair shake
for our own folks. That's what affirmative action is all about"), and
he delivered his bottom line ("I'm not moving one inch on set-
asides"). If we went beyond the *Adarand* decision, he'd be calling
Bob Johnson and Earl Graves to finance his presidential run. Dick
might get his wish after all.

From there I made the rounds, giving briefings on our review
and getting suggestions for the president's speech. Emulating the
style of my old boss Dick Gephardt (who had earned the admiring
nickname Iron Butt for his ability to sit through as many meetings
for as many hours as it took to reach a consensus with his colleagues), I visited all the House caucuses — blacks, women, His-
panics, Asians, and the "Blue Dog" conservatives. I had small group
sessions with cabinet secretaries and one-on-one discussions with
influential senators like Bill Bradley and Pat Moynihan (who told
me how he'd helped draft Lyndon Johnson's famous Howard University speech on affirmative action back in 1965). Outside the government, I balanced our running contacts with the liberal civil

rights community by reaching out to my old adversaries in the DLC. In each meeting, my message was the same: The president would defend affirmative action; *Adarand* would do the job of reform.

Of course, I couldn't be sure that Clinton would actually do what I was saying. Dick kept pushing for daylight between Clinton and the Democrats, and the president was still fiddling with the final decision. Although he didn't relish a Jackson challenge, Clinton was intrigued by one of Dick's decent ideas (developed by presidential assistant Bill Curry), for a system of race-neutral incentives for businesses to locate in poor neighborhoods, which I favored as long as it was clearly a supplement to rather than a replacement for the current system. All my soundings made me more certain than ever that we had to stay within the confines of *Adarand*. If Clinton seemed to be moving to the right of Sandra Day O'Connor by pre-emptively eliminating programs before the Justice Department had analyzed them using the *Adarand* guidelines (a process that would take several months at least), Democrats would fracture.

So in the final days leading up to the speech, I made sure that the president heard from Democrats directly. Personal testimony would affect Clinton even more than Dick's polls. The more meetings he had with civil rights leaders, old friends like John Lewis and Vernon Jordan, cabinet secretaries like Donna Shalala, Henry Cisneros, Ron Brown, and Dick Riley, the more locked in he would get. But I still had to listen closely to every word; he was preserving his options right until the end. At a meeting with the Congressional Black Caucus, D.C. delegate Eleanor Holmes Norton tried to pin him down: "Mr. President, there is considerable anxiety about your views here. We need to know more."

"I don't think I'll cause high anxiety," he replied. "You'll find what I do interesting but not troubling."

"Interesting but not troubling"? Oh, that helps. Now I know what to do: "Edley — the president's decided: He wants a policy that's 'interesting but not troubling.' Call the speechwriters, tell them we need a ringing speech that's 'interesting but not troubling.' "

As the meeting continued, Clinton's responses became more fulsome. His tone was reassuring. His denunciations of discrimination were passionate, but his words were careful. When other members stood up to say that an unequivocal statement of presidential support on affirmative action was essential, Clinton took notes, bit his lip, and nodded his head in vigorous agreement. The members left thrilled, convinced they had a promise from the president. I hoped he wasn't leading them on. Erskine and I approached him after the meeting to call him on it.

"Mr. President," Erskine said, "you understand now that whatever door you think you left open, you didn't."

"What?"

"In *their* minds," I continued, "you have firmly decided to stay within *Adarand*, not to go one step outside it, and to fully support affirmative action."

"I didn't say that."

Maybe not those precise words, but his message was clear — even if he didn't want it to be. Clinton's compassion was involuntary, fully felt yet entirely existential, an instinctive empathy so ingrained that he communicated commitment even when he thought he was creating space. He couldn't control the bend of his neck, the fold of his lower lip, or the earnest curl of his forefinger any more than he could pace the beat of his heart or the blink of his eye. His mind, however, never stopped calculating, playing the angles, figuring the outs. Read him his words, and he'd show you the loopholes.

But this time, he didn't put up much of a fight. By now, he wanted an unapologetic defense of affirmative action. Sensing the changing tide, Morris called the weekend before the speech with the convenient news that a new poll he had commissioned showed that a Jackson candidacy would turn the presidential race from a 38–38 tie with Bob Dole to a 30–38 loss. At least he was consistent. The "prayer book" was an infallible guide; his hands were tied. In the only way he knew, Dick was conceding defeat.

So I had a win — my most satisfying yet. I thought we were doing the right thing for (basically) the right reasons. The more I had studied and learned, the more I had encountered people who knew and cared about affirmative action, the more I had become convinced that embracing the idea and its advocates was a form of presidential leadership. That's what Clinton was going to do, that's what the job was supposed to be about, and I could tell myself that it might have turned out differently if I hadn't been there. Others went out of their way to praise me to the president. After a dinner at Vernon Jordan's house where I previewed the review for a group of African American journalists, Vernon passed the president a note through Erskine: "George was the only white person there. He stood his ground, defended you, and was not afraid. You would have been very, very proud. He was a White House staffer in the best sense of the word." Henry Cisneros did the same, telling Clinton that by successfully managing such a large effort I had shown "a different side" of myself. Morris's replacing me "by Clinton's side" — a form of psychological exile I still hated — had turned out to be good for me, giving me the opportunity to immerse myself in an important issue and to stop defining myself solely as Clinton's flak catcher, defender, and message disciplinarian.

Of course, it was still nice to be needed. On the day before the speech, Clinton walked back and forth from my office, draft in hand, asking for facts, testing a phrase, looking for my advice. Later in the evening, he tracked me down at the gym and called me at home to report on his last-minute consultations with Colin Powell and Jesse Jackson. "Colin's going to be fine," he said, "and I had a good talk with Jesse, but he needs more information. Give him a call." I was Clinton's guy again, and he was in a groove. The basic speech was set: The president would decry the persistence of discrimination, defend affirmative action as a crucial tool in the struggle for equal opportunity, and demand that it be reformed, as necessary, to meet the test of fairness and the requirements of the Constitution. But Clinton still tinkered with it through the night at his kitchen counter, following the advice that Senator Howell Heflin had offered a few hours earlier: "Put a little Bible in the speech."

Which made for a typically chaotic morning in the Oval. The president was late to the office, then he was delayed by calls to the prime ministers of Britain and France — another emergency in Bosnia. Nancy Hernreich and I used the time to try and decipher Clinton's edits, but even our combined experience was inadequate. He would have to dictate them to us. Edley couldn't take it. A major

Clinton speech was always a hazing for some novice who hadn't been initiated into the rite. Chris paced around Betty's office, pressing his fingers to his scalp, tormented by the thought that we'd never make it to the National Archives on time.

But of course we did. Edley and I took our seats in the second row, and the president walked to the podium we had set between glass cases holding the Declaration of Independence and the Constitution to begin a forty-five-minute meditation on "America's rocky but fundamentally righteous journey to close the gap between the ideals enshrined in these treasures here . . . and the reality of our daily lives."

"Rocky but fundamentally righteous journey." Vintage Clinton, an improvisation that condensed the struggle for civil rights into a single phrase. *Rocky but fundamentally righteous journey.* I wanted to believe it captured the essence of our presidency. And at a moment like this, on a day like today, for the first time in a long time — with Clinton preaching in the fervent tones of an evangelist on the basic tenets of the Democratic faith, with our allies ecstatic at the sight of a president taking a stand and challenging their fellow citizens to follow his lead, with our adversaries temporarily flummoxed by Clinton's call to "mend but don't end" affirmative action — I could.

The president asked me to join him on the ride back to the White House. I sat on the jump seat, facing him and the vice president. Clinton handed me a bottle of water from his cooler; Gore congratulated me: "George, you did a hell of a job on this."

"Yeah," the president added. "You really did a good job on this, George."

My reaction to that praise caught me by surprise. I thought I was hardened to political courtesy — the autographed picture, the handshake on a rope line, the handwritten note, the thank-you car ride for a job well done. But I wasn't. I needed a sip of that water now — to clear my throat and keep my voice from cracking. Escaping to safe territory, I reported on the early reviews I had gathered while Clinton shook hands at a postspeech reception. The civil rights guys were crying, they were so happy. Not a single Democrat was complaining yet, Mary McGrory called it the best presidential speech on race since 1965, and even our beat reporters (now *they* were off the record) said they had never seen Clinton better. In the interest of full disclosure, I had to add that California governor Pete Wilson (who was planning to challenge Clinton in 1996) would get some attention with his response: "He should have said end it. You can't mend it." And that Joe Klein was fuming and would probably write a nasty column in *Newsweek* because the speech wasn't tough enough for his taste.

Knitting his brow, the president nodded. "I was walking down the aisle and could see in his eyes that he didn't like it." For a second, I thought I saw regret in Clinton's eyes. A potential foe and an old friend were both on the attack. But his doubt seemed to pass as we entered the White House gates.

"I feel good about it," he concluded. "We did the right thing."

15   ENTENTE CORDIALE

There are these two George Stephanopouloses — Dr. Jekyll and Mr. Hyde. Dr. Jekyll is unbelievable. He's the only staffer in the White House with a brain. The only one who's good. I talk to my wife and I catch myself liking him. We were driving along the other day, and I'm telling her how great you are, how smart you are, how brilliant you are; and she reminds me: 'Dick, he wants to kill you.'"

She's right.

"That's Mr. Hyde," he continued. "The one who tells people, 'Dick Morris lies directly to my face.' Ann Devroy says that Stephanopoulos and Ickes are out to kill Morris. I hear these things."

Late in the afternoon of the affirmative action speech, after a silence of several days, Dick called. It was time to talk again, he said, but in person, not on the phone: "Meet me outside 160 OEOB." So there we were, crouched together in a recessed space off the main corridor, whispering. Why? I didn't know. But Dick's eyes kept darting toward the hallway, and his hands were trembling.

If we don't win in 1996, he continued, "there are only two losers: Bill Clinton and Dick Morris. You'll go on. You'll have a candidate in the year 2000. I have given up my career. I have no home. I have no one left to talk to."

Get a dog. Get to the point.

"I want us to share power — everything. I'll make a deal with you: I'll trade you access for an end to the backbiting. I want you to be my friend and confidant."

He's suing for peace by sucking you in. Knows your weakness, knows you need that place at his weekly meeting with the president. Must think it's going to happen anyway; knows Harold's working on it. Didn't like losing on affirmative action. Doesn't want it to happen again. Knows he needs you. Hang tough.

"Well, Dick, this is a chicken-and-egg problem. I think you're trying to fuck *me*."

"I'm not the one who's kept you out of those meetings," he responded. "The president's kept you out."

Ummgh. He's right. Who am I kidding? Today was great, but how will Clinton feel tomorrow? Dick's still got the real power. The president's ear, his confidence, and those polls. Without him working on Clinton, I'll never get back in.

"So what do I have to do?"

"I'll know when you stop," he said. "A thousand flowers will bloom. I'll be surrounded by sweetness and light. All these people you control will stop fucking me."

"Dick, I'm in an impossible situation. You're blaming me for things other people do."

"Sorry," he said. "That's just life. I'm going to have to see results to make the trade work."

"Fine, but I need direct access. I need to be in the meeting, and it has to be soon. I'm not going through the whole campaign filtering my advice through you."

"I understand."

We parted abruptly, turning in opposite directions like a pair of incompetent spies. I walked back to the West Wing trying to figure out what Dick's terms meant exactly. I made no secret of my dislike for Morris and no apologies for opposing his ideas. But as much as I loathed Morris and his methods, I wasn't leaking on him. As much as I loved the idea of running him out of the White House, it wasn't going to happen. As amused as I was by his delusion that I "controlled" White House troops, I didn't — everyone loathed Dick for his or her own reasons. As angry as I was at being beholden to Morris, I needed to be in those strategy sessions. Exclusion made me feel like a poster boy for downward mobility. The day I started to attend, Dick's power over me would effectively end — and his influence with Clinton would be diluted. I'd have the chance to make my case directly to the president — all you can ask for in the White House; Clinton would hear me debate Morris before he made his decisions, instead of on the fly or after the fact. Morris knew that too. Maybe he couldn't avoid it forever, but Dick wanted to squeeze me and would use any pretext to keep me out of his Clinton meetings. I was determined not to give him one and figured I had nothing to lose. I couldn't be Dick's friend, but I could be his confidant. Five minutes after our encounter, I called him to confirm our deal.

So began a phase that Morris called our "entente cordiale." For a few months, we talked more than a dozen times a day, at all hours, usually on the phone or in the OEOB (Leon had effectively banned Dick from the West Wing). Watching him work was fascinating, almost fun. He could read a poll and compose a five-minute speech on its findings in five minutes flat. We often agreed on the tactical maneuvers, like how to play off breaking news, that are the daily fare of campaigns. Sometimes I felt guilty for enjoying his company — for letting my need to be a player, and the pleasure I took in it, cloud my conviction that even being associated with a guy like Morris was corrupt. So I rationalized, telling myself that I was getting my hands dirty for the sake of Clinton and our cause, that somebody like me had to hug Morris to stop his crazy ideas before they went too far.

Like the time he wanted to fire the attorney general. About a week after we struck our deal, Dick summoned me back to his OEOB hideaway to discuss an "urgent, private matter." He was certain his phones were bugged, and this mission demanded utmost secrecy — never mind that his words caromed off the marble columns and down the open corridor.

"The president," Morris said, "is stark, raving, berserkly mad" at Janet Reno. "I can't divulge why," but Clinton wanted us to "rid him of this priest." He asked me to devise a cabinet shuffle that would include a new attorney general. "I can't do it myself," he concluded. "I don't know these people well enough, but we need to come up with a plan."

What are you, nuts? We couldn't fire Reno if we wanted to. I sure couldn't. Must be a test. No, a trap. He's trying to see if I'll leak the idea, so he can blame me when it goes bad.

Unable to resist his reference to Henry II, I replied, "Dick, maybe Clinton does want us to 'rid him of this priest,' I don't know. But sometimes our job is to talk him out of his politically suicidal impulses."

"Don't worry," he said. "This isn't the Saturday Night Massacre."

Why — because it's Tuesday?

Dick's scheme was so incendiary that I didn't mention it to anyone — and certainly didn't do anything. I wasn't even sure what Clinton was supposedly so upset about until I saw the July 30 Sunday *Times*, which ran an AP story that said Attorney General Reno had filed court papers that Friday arguing that Independent Counsel Kenneth Starr had "the right to pursue fraud and conspiracy charges against President Clinton's successor as Arkansas governor," Jim Guy Tucker.

It all made sense now. The report was perfectly pitched to the mutually reinforcing paranoia of the president and Morris. Dick had another theory. "We have succeeded," he once told me, "in having sixty-five percent of the public blame Hillary for Whitewater." To him that was good news; his only fear was that "Starr will get Jim Guy Tucker to cop a plea in order to nail Hillary. Then Hillary will have to bargain with Starr for disbarment or a critical report in return for no indictment." Unsure of the law, he probably thought a new attorney general could reverse Reno's decision.

Clinton was smarter than that. He understood the decision was a fait accompli, and I'm sure he didn't share Dick's equanimity over the political value of having his wife take the fall for Whitewater. But he didn't like Janet Reno all that much, and he sure did hate Ken Starr. When he heard about Reno's decision, he probably did erupt; he may even have wailed for a new attorney general. But I couldn't believe that he really imagined that he could get away with removing her.

But Morris didn't give up. Two days later, he called me at seven A.M. "Clinton is through the roof," he said. "He just gives me this dumb stare, demanding an answer." Dick was obsessed, pleading with me for a solution; here was one problem he couldn't really poll (at least I hoped he hadn't). "Why can't we replace her with Mickey Kantor or Leon Panetta?" he asked.

I hated even having this conversation. A phone call about Jay Stephens had put me on the cover of *Time;* plotting to get rid of the attorney general would probably land me in jail. (*"Section 1505 of Title 18 in the U.S. Code brands any attempt to 'influence, obstruct, or impede the due and proper administration of the law' a crime punishable by imprisonment of up to five years."*) But like an idiot, I didn't hang up. Instead, I tried to reason with Dick. "The president will get crucified if he picks Mickey," I said. "Everyone will accuse him of trying to save his own skin by replacing an attorney general brimming with integrity with a political crony. Leon's not a close friend, but he would never take the job until the end of the year, when the budget is done." I was learning how to deal with Dick. Instead of raising broad ethical or political objections that he'd simply dismiss, I'd offer relatively narrow but irrefutable rebuttals. He'd bounce off these roadblocks like a bumper car and spin off in a new direction, but at least I could slow him down.

"What about Babbitt?" he tried.

I didn't have a rapid response. The interior secretary's reputation for integrity rivaled Reno's. I told Dick I'd have to think about it. Thankfully, he let it drop after a few more calls. Bosnia had grabbed his attention. Earlier in July, when Harold had shown me an agenda from the weekly residence meeting, I saw that a page and a half were missing from the memo. "What's this ripped-out part?" I asked.

"George, you can't tell anybody," he said. "It was Dick's recommendation for a bombing campaign against Serbia."

Any public exposure of Dick's foreign-policy role would be political death. Bad enough that he was wreaking havoc with domestic policy. On national security matters, ad hoc decisions could be dangerous, and his involvement would open the president up to attack for turning to an amoral pollster on matters of war and peace. In

May, after Morris tried to end run the NSC and rewrite U.S. policy on terrorism and trade with Japan, Tony Lake had gone to Clinton and secured his commitment that Morris would be walled off from the national security policy-making process. But by July, Dick was on a power jag. He was building his campaign empire, and he had the run of the government, foraging through the agencies and pressing cabinet secretaries for new ideas to poll. He claimed that he was "functionally White House chief of staff," and he wasn't far off. As his influence grew, he became more manic and less discreet.

On the same day Morris asked me to remove Reno, at a weekly meeting of about twenty senior White House staffers from the press, politics, and communications departments that Dick presided over in room 180 of the OEOB, we were discussing the need for a presidential statement on Bosnia. "The next statement I want to hear on Bosnia is *brroom!* . . . *brroom!* . . . *brroom!*" Morris started bouncing off his seat cushion while puffing out his cheeks and lips to simulate a bombing raid. Seconds later, like a two year old acting out, he was giggling. We were stunned. All of us knew Dick; most of us were disgusted by him. Sometimes you could suspend your revulsion long enough to enjoy his shtick. Not now — not when the most influential adviser to the president of the United States was discussing an act of war in the manner of a madman.

The next morning, only slightly more calm, he called me with a question: "Why can't Clinton just bomb Bosnia on his own?"

I was sympathetic to the idea of air strikes. The fact that we had failed to confront the ethnic cleansing in Bosnia with punishing force was a black mark on our foreign policy — a shame underscored by the massacres in Srebrenica earlier that month. But as I explained to Dick, our UN and NATO allies had peacekeeping forces on the ground in Bosnia. If we decided to bomb without their consent, they would withdraw their troops — and we were obligated to provide U.S. ground troops to cover their retreat. This posed a dilemma for Morris: Bombing polled well; ground troops didn't. But you couldn't have one without the other unless the allies were on board.

"Then why can't we just launch an attack directly on Serbia?"

The Pentagon will go into open revolt, I explained. If the president essentially declares war on Serbia on his own, Congress will say he's creating another Vietnam, and some will start to talk about impeachment. A little hyperbolic, maybe, but the Morris method was rubbing off on me, and I was desperate to shut Dick up, if only to throw him off track. I knew that Tony Lake was secretly drafting a risky new Bosnia strategy that would include, as a last resort, the threat of unilateral air strikes. Only by convincing Britain and France of our resolve to go it alone, Lake believed, would we keep them on board — a lesson we had learned from our 1993 Bosnia failures. Tony was right, and I wanted the initiative to work. But if Dick kept talking about the idea (he was now covertly consulting foreign-policy experts outside the government and summoning White House reporters to his hotel suite for supersecret "background" sessions) or one of his polling memos leaked, the delicate effort would collapse — dismissed by opponents at home and abroad as pure politics.

Which for Morris, of course, it was. The more we talked, the more frustrated he became. I tried a new tack — taking his side. "Listen, Dick," I said. "I agree with you. Our policy is unsustainable. The killings are horrible. But you have to be patient." Enraged, he cut me off. "Yeah, well, they're slaughtering the Bosnians, but *so what?*" Dick roared in a guttural tone that made me feel I had exorcised a demon from the darkest corner of his soul. "I want to bomb the shit out of the Serbians to look strong."

"So what"? "Look strong"? The candor was chilling. Not only for what it said about Dick, but for what it touched in me. Maybe Dick was right; maybe there were two Georges: I cared about the Bosnians, and I believed bombing was our moral duty, but I also wanted Clinton to look strong, and I believed bombing was a political necessity. Which motive colored my judgment more? Was Morris truly the alien force I imagined him to be? Or just brutally honest? With every encounter, Dick was becoming more than a hated colleague; he was a cautionary tale — even when, especially when, I agreed with his advice. *"The last temptation is the greatest treason: To do the right deed for the wrong reason."* Like the lines of Eliot I kept underlined behind my desk, he was a daily reminder of who I was when I wasn't careful.

How Clinton reacted to Dick's ravings on Bosnia, I can't say. This part of the Morris portfolio was still supposed to be their secret. Another problem in dealing with Dick during this period was trying to figure out when he was speaking for the president and when he was freelancing; when he was anticipating Clinton's demands and when Dick's wishes would later become the president's commands. But I did know that Clinton was anxious, consistently complaining that the status quo in Bosnia "makes everyone look weak and unprincipled. The only thing that has worked is when the Serbs thought we were prepared to use disproportionate air power." The president was also conscious of the politics — international and domestic. Our allies were getting shaky. If they decided to withdraw, American troops would have to go in even without a peace agreement. At home, Senator Dole's resolution to lift the arms embargo on Bosnia was about to pass the Congress by a large margin; Clinton could sustain a veto and avoid a political defeat only by forcing a peace in Bosnia now. We needed "to bust our rear to get a settlement in the next couple of months," he said, "explore all alternatives, roll every die." Otherwise, he feared, the decision would be "dropped in during the middle of the campaign."

The president was now prepared to do what had always seemed unthinkable before: dispatch twenty thousand American ground troops to the Balkans, knowing that any casualties could cost him his presidency. Would Clinton have been willing to gamble if his hand hadn't been forced by the campaign calendar? Was his moral courage now a function of political necessity? I wished I knew. Humanitarian concern, realpolitik, and electoral politics all steeled Clinton in their own way. But the pressure seemed to bring out the best in Clinton, in contrast to Morris. The experience of *being* president appeared to be making him a better president. In a series of early-August meetings with his national security advisers, he was calm and determined, aware of the weight of his decision. "If we let this moment slip away," he said, "we are history." After reviewing the maps, pressing all his advisers with detailed questions, and personally revising the terms of the initiative, he signaled his decision with a glance across the cabinet table at Tony Lake: "How quickly can you get your bags packed?"

"I've got a toothbrush in my office."

With the hole card of Clinton's commitment to strike alone if necessary, Lake secured allied backing for more aggressive bombing coupled with intensified peace talks. By early September, the shelling of Sarajevo finally triggered a massive NATO bombing campaign that forced the Serbs to back down and gave our negotiator, Richard Holbrooke, the leverage he would need to negotiate a diplomatic settlement before the Balkan winter.

Back home, Dick Morris was counting on a similar formula to produce a budget deal with the Republicans. "We'll defeat them in the air war," he said. "Our Medicare ads will turn them into roving bands of hunter-gatherers in search of a home." Morris had discovered Medicare, and he was now planning to force the Republicans to compromise by launching a multimillion-dollar ad showing the president standing up to their assault on Medicare. For Dick, this was a twofer: Not only did he believe that the ads would improve Clinton's poll numbers and help pave the way for his prized budget deal, but he would also get a healthy commission for every dollar we spent on television.

Despite Dick's support, I was all for the ads. The insurance industry's "Harry and Louise" campaign had demolished us during the health care fight; this time we'd beat them to the punch. And Medicare was our best weapon — the only Democratic issue as potent as the Republicans' "less government, lower taxes" mantra. Medicare was more than just another government program; its guarantee of health care for the elderly was a metaphor for our commitment to the middle-class American dream and a political shield for less popular programs for the poor that we were trying to protect. All year long, the Republican leadership had threatened to stop funding the government and financing its debt if the president refused to sign their budget. "We want to force change," Gingrich warned Clinton in a meeting before the August recess. Now the showdown was only weeks away. To prevail, we would have to convince the public that the president was making a principled stand against blackmail and using his power to protect average people. An ad campaign focused on Medicare would help Clinton and the congressional Democrats sustain a presidential veto and survive a government shutdown. Morris didn't want a Clinton veto, and he insisted that the ads, coupled with back-channel negotiations with his former client Trent Lott, the number two Republican in the Senate, would produce a budget deal long before it came to that. In early September, he asked me to help with these "secret" talks, just as I had worked with him when we were constructing our June budget. "Only Lott, Gingrich, Clinton, Gore, and Panetta know about it," he said. "Lott and I will be the negotiators. Gingrich specifically requested that you and Ickes be kept out of the loop, but I need your help with the deal."

To secure my cooperation, he offered two incentives — one old, one new. Two months after our hallway accord, I still hadn't been invited to the weekly strategy meetings, so he tried to resell me a place in the room. It seems there was a new obstacle. "Gore's cut your balls off," he said. According to Morris, now it was the vice president who was blocking me. Dick said that early in 1995, Gore had urged him to make peace with Harold, not me, because "George is your real enemy. He's shrewd, tactically smart, and he runs this place." But Dick was too obsessed with Ickes to follow that advice, assuming Gore had even given it. "I have a list of twenty-three times that Harold has fucked me over," he said. "One of the two of us will have to go, and I don't think it's going to be me." Then he pressed me to join forces with him against Harold. "I had to destroy you so you would know that I could," he confessed. But now he and I could be "the heart and soul of the campaign," he continued. "My team is like the politburo. We work together, everyone has a say, and when we disagree, we submit the decision to the ultimate master of the Western world — the polls." Sweetening the offer with a bribe, Dick later added that if I left the White House and formally joined his team, he would pay me a million-dollar fee — my cut of the ad buy.

What's true? What's spin? What's fantasy? What's pure control? What planet is this guy living on?

I didn't want Dick's money. After telling him that I thought Clinton trusted Harold ("No, it's only because Ickes has something on him"), I agreed to help him only with the budget. He accepted my partial rebuff but added that I couldn't discuss our conversations with Panetta (who complained that Morris was "a spy in our midst"). "OK," I lied. Since Morris was a Republican mole inside our White House, I would be a double agent.

Dick would relay his conversations with Lott, and I would report back to Leon and Pat Griffin. Not that I really needed to. The fact that Morris and Lott were talking was the worst-kept secret on Capitol Hill. Lott was giving detailed debriefings on their conversations to the entire Republican leadership, which would filter back to us through Pat's network of Hill contacts. In turn, I tried to sensitize Morris to what Democrats were thinking and to help him understand the political realities behind the budget numbers that he and Lott were throwing around. For example, I explained that meeting Lott's "bottom lines" of a $200 billion tax cut and a seven-year balanced budget under the economic assumptions of the Congressional Budget Office would require almost $500 billion more in cuts than our June budget. No Democrat would vote for that, I argued; the president would be perceived as caving, and he wouldn't be protecting Medicare as we were promising in our ads.

Morris listened but didn't hear. The truth is, he didn't really care. His theory demanded a deal, so we had to get one. But he feared that once the Republicans "walked the plank" and actually voted for a final budget that included deep Medicare cuts, a subsequent Clinton veto would harden each side's position and make compromise impossible. That was fine with me. I was happy to take the issues to the 1996 election — and even lose — rather than have Clinton sign anything close to the Republican budget into law. I didn't think a good deal was possible. The gap between the two sides was too big, and the consequences of the Republican cuts — particularly for the poorest children and seniors who relied on Medicaid as well as Medicare — were too devastating to contemplate. A Democratic president just couldn't sign them into law. Even if a decent deal were possible in theory, I believed that Clinton couldn't forge it without the sledgehammer of a veto — and his party would lynch him if he tried. "If you force Clinton to make a deal before he has the veto," I argued to Dick, "you're forcing him to commit political suicide."

What the president would do was anyone's guess. He was talking tough in public but itching for a deal. The Morris theory merged in his mind with his natural inclination toward conciliation and a Panglossian faith in his ability to achieve what he willed. To nudge the process along, he supplemented the Morris-Lott back channel with his own quiet phone calls to Speaker Gingrich. We worried about these contacts, fearing that the Republicans would be smart enough to make some quick concessions and lock Clinton into an agreement that wouldn't get Democratic support. But the Republican leaders were hemmed in by hubris and their own restless troops — the freshmen elected in the revolution of 1994 who equated compromise with capitulation. They overplayed their hand and, like me sometimes, underestimated the president.

Unlike Morris, Clinton understood the implications of the budget numbers, especially in programs like Medicaid that he had administered as a governor. "I know a bit about this," he'd say. "Poor kids are going to get screwed; that's what I feel passionately about." While Clinton was willing to give the Republicans a balanced budget with tax cuts, he refused to accept what he called their "below the line" goal: an end to activist government, especially in health care and education. "We're going through Stockman's revenge," he said at a September budget meeting, referring to Reagan budget director David Stockman's insight that even if supply-side economics didn't balance the budget, the deficits created by their tax cuts would create persistent resistance to all government spending. "They're using the deficit to destroy government."

To me, this observation was a sign that we hard-liners had the president's other late-night adviser on our side. "Stockman's revenge" was a phrase I'd often heard Hillary use, and the fact that Clinton repeated it after a morning at home was surely no coincidence. Although she was less visible now, devoting large blocks of time to handwriting revisions of her book *It Takes a Village*, the first lady was still the most powerful liberal in the White House. The combative side of her that had hampered the health care effort and backfired on Whitewater in 1994 was exactly what we needed in the budget showdown of 1995.

My relationship with Hillary was going well. Her Woodward fury had passed, and I had helped myself by how I handled affirmative action. Although she was instrumental in bringing Morris back, she also sensed the need for a liberal counterweight to him inside the White House. Several times a week, she'd call to check in and buck me up — often as she exercised. "How're we doing today, George?" she'd ask, her measured breathing and the hum of the treadmill serving as background for my morning updates. If she called in the afternoon, I might be on the StairMaster in room 11 of the OEOB. The phone by the machine would signal me with its distinctive ding-dong chime, and, trying not to break stride, I'd give her my take on the budget and get hers, tell her what Democrats were saying on the Hill, pass on an interesting story from the television news. She no longer watched — too infuriating, too painful. One late-September day, however, she called to console me on *my* latest bout of bad headlines and revealed how she was coping with her own.

A few nights earlier, I had been arrested in Georgetown. The charge was "hit and run"; the truth was that I couldn't maneuver my car out of a tight parking spot on M Street. When I scraped the bumper ahead of me, an excitable police officer who happened by recognized me and made a scene — patting me down as a crowd gathered around. More bad luck, I had carelessly let my license expire. He cuffed my hands behind my back and called in four cars to take me to the station. Although my car never left the curb, I was cited for leaving the scene of an accident. Several hours later, I was released with an apology from the station chief, and the charges were dropped. But the damage was done: Video footage of my arrest was all over the morning news.

"I'm glad to see you've overcome your problems with the police, George." Hillary laughed. "You know, I've been thinking about what happened to you" (and herself). Both of us got plenty of ink for things we didn't do (like throw a lamp at her husband); both of us made even better copy when we really did screw up (like throwing a temper tantrum at a treasury official). We bonded again — two liberals, two lightning rods, Boy George and Saint Hillary — commiserating about the press and our other shared enemies, musing about how being caricatured drives you crazy and the futility of trying to fight it. Whimsical and bitter, wistful and shrewd, she signed off with praise for how I had left the station house — head held high, a calm smile on my face. "That's what I've learned how to do," she explained. "Whenever I go out and fight I get vilified, so I have just learned to smile and take it. I go out there and say, 'Please, please, kick me again, insult me some more.' You have to be much craftier behind the scenes, but just smile."

It was a lesson we both had learned from her husband — the master of the public smile that masks private rage. That fall, one man was increasingly the source of Clinton's foul moods. His book was a bestseller, his poll numbers were soaring, and his potential presidential run had pundits swooning. General Colin Powell was pissing the president off.

"The press is going to give him a pass." Clinton scowled from behind his desk as he scanned one more fawning clip about his presumed rival.

"I don't think so," I replied. Though I was equally anxious about Powell, I believed that if he ran for president, the press would do its job. "Once he gets into the race, despite the fact that they love him and despite the fact that they may want him to win — and I agree with you, Mr. President, they do want him in the race — they will feel compelled to cover him like any other candidate."

I should have stopped there. Whatever I was saying wasn't working. The president was standing now, staring down at me, unsmiling, both hands pressed on his desk. But since I fancied myself an expert on the media and I had a captive audience, I continued my lecture. "The structure of campaign coverage will override their personal feelings, which I grant, you're right, they like him more than they like you. . . ."

His right forefinger flew off the desktop, heading straight for my face: "You're wrong! You're wrong! You're wrong! They'll give him a ride, even though he wouldn't do half the things I've done as president. They're just going to give him a free ride."

The president tried to hide his frustration. Everywhere he went, he was asked about Powell, and he responded with the requisite pablum ("I've worked with him and like him. . . . He's a very appealing man . . . got a very compelling life story"). But his public remarks also hinted at private resentment (". . . he's gotten a lot of favorable publicity, *much* of it well deserved"). Sooner or later the bile would come spilling out, and I was particularly worried that it would happen at the annual dinner of the Congressional Black Caucus in late September. This was the heart of Clinton's political base, but Powell was family, and he was being honored. C-Span was televising the event live, and our press corps was buzzing because it would be the first head-to-head matchup between the two potential rivals since Powell's presidential boomlet began.

Early that Saturday evening, I went up to the residence to work on the speech with Clinton. Sitting in the second-floor den, surrounded by family photos and his collection of ceramic frogs — with a cigar in his mouth, bifocals perched on the tip of his nose, and papers spread on the card table before him — the president was happy. But he still wanted to take "a little dig" at Powell.

At the Arkansas dinners where Clinton learned his trade, taking "a little dig" at opponents was what you did. But in Washington, a president is permitted to poke fun only at himself. Before ritual roasts like the White House Correspondents dinner, we usually struggled with Clinton's sarcastic side to get him to deliver the self-deprecating jokes in his script. Tonight, he wanted to score a direct hit. Apparently he had heard somewhere that Powell had criticized the Black Caucus for losing "their vision and their way."

"I want to take him on, tell them they've never lost their way," he said, a formulation that would manage to merge a pander and a put-down in a single sound bite.

"Mr. President, if you say one word that looks in any way, shape, or form like criticism, everyone is going to say that you're afraid and obsessed, and they're going to jump on it," I replied. "It will be a huge story. Just be generous, be gracious."

"You're right, I know," he said. "But this draft says too many good things about Colin. We have to shorten it down."

"Fine, shorten it down."

I could tell right then that the dinner would be fine. By the time Clinton got to the podium, he'd be adding praise. It was getting late, though; he had to leave. As Clinton fiddled with the text, we discussed the upcoming Million Man March ("You can praise the values behind the March if you want," I said, "but keep Farrakhan out of it"), and I used my privileged position that night to push my pet project ("If you want to dig Colin, the best way to do it at the Black Caucus is to whack the Republican budget"). The words were new, but the routine was familiar. Just like early mornings during the campaign, with me sitting on a twin bed in a small motel room, reading headlines and reviewing the day's events as the candidate cooled down from his jog.

Except the candidate was president, I was his senior adviser, and we were in the White House. The navy valets who served every president were laying out a fresh tux in the master bedroom. The doorway framed a portrait of Alice Roosevelt, and Lincoln's bedroom was down the hall. Even now, I could be startled by the setting if I stopped for a second to think about it. While the president shaved (using a plastic razor and no foam on his light beard), he started singing scales to loosen his diaphragm and told me that before a big speech John Kennedy "used to go into the bathroom and bark like a dog." Then he barked. Clinton was conscious of being in a stream of presidents. I was conscious of being in a stream of presidential assistants who had listened to their bosses and done their jobs while leaning against that bathroom door.

As I left, I felt like I'd done a good day's work. Clinton was psyched. Confident. He'd left his demons in the locker room and was about to do what nobody — not even Colin Powell — did better: feel a crowd, feed their hope. "I'm gonna give a hell of a speech," he said. "They may take me down, but they're going to say, 'He's not going down without a fight.'"

The fight Clinton was anticipating didn't materialize that night. Both the president and the general took the high road. But for the next month, the "Draft Powell" movement sucked in all the oxygen in the political atmosphere. The broader American public, however, was preoccupied with the fate of another black American. In the

White House, we calculated what the O. J. Simpson verdict would mean for Clinton and the country — and prepared for the worst.

On Monday, October 2, Gene Sperling and I were in my office when CNN's "Breaking News" logo lit up the television that was always on. Caught off guard by the fact that the jury's deliberations had taken less than four hours, Panetta hastily called a meeting in his office. The president would need a statement responding to the verdict, and the Justice Department was preparing for possible riots in Los Angeles. We naturally started out, however, by speculating on the verdict, and each person's guess was a window on his character.

Leon, a former prosecutor and strict disciplinarian, went straight to guilty. Morris went straight to the polls: "Eighty percent of the blacks in the country think O. J.'s been framed or that there was police misconduct. With that many blacks on the jury, I'm telling you, he's innocent." Carville phoned in a prediction from his gut: "He's guilty. I feel it; they'll find him guilty." My own conclusion was more a wish than a prediction. "Guilty," I said. The president refused to play, saying only that he was surprised at how quickly the verdict had been reached. Morris had an answer for that too: "That kind of impetuousness is characteristic of blacks."

Early the next morning, we met with Justice Department officials to review their contingency plans. Their Community Services Task Force reported that African Americans in Los Angeles were on tenterhooks and focused on Mark Fuhrman. They feared a guilty verdict would set off riots in the streets and were coordinating with the LAPD and community leaders to keep the situation under control. Deputy Attorney General Jamie Gorelick told us that once the verdict was announced, the Justice Department would pursue a civil rights complaint against Mark Fuhrman and investigate allegations of misconduct against the police — a move that would be especially crucial if O. J. was found guilty. We all agreed that the president's statement should be as neutral as possible.

When we went to get the president's approval, he opened the meeting with a wan stab at humor: "So, Jamie, are we going to have black or white riots today?" I flashed back to a moment shortly after Simpson's arrest. Clinton was in his dining room, recalling the time he'd played golf with O. J. and reflecting on the anxieties that eat away at a middle-aged man whose greatest achievements are behind him. But now the president was more focused on politics than psychology. The prospect of acquittal made him anxious. He feared it would fuel white resentment and feed the prejudiced notion that "blacks can't be trusted with the criminal justice system." An acquittal would deepen racial divisions; and while Clinton didn't say it then, he knew it could also mean more "angry white males" voting Republican in 1996.

The verdict was set for one P.M. eastern time. At the top of the hour, we arranged for Clinton to sign an appropriations bill so we could legitimately claim that the president just "took a break" from legislative work to watch. But we were as transfixed as the rest of the country. Several of us watched in Betty Currie's office, which had the largest television in the Oval Office suite. Clinton pulled a chair up to the console facing Betty's desk. He was uncharacteristically quiet and didn't look up from the crossword puzzle he was working on. But when cowboy lawyer Gerry Spence predicted a guilty verdict, the president muttered, "Good for you." Then the members of the jury took their seats, and the forewoman announced their decision: not guilty.

Clinton stared at the screen; we stared at Clinton. For us, the suspense wasn't over yet. No one said a word, as if we were waiting for the president's permission, for official guidance on what to think. After all, at some level, Clinton's reaction would become our reaction; that came with the territory. The president knew that too. A year or two earlier, he would have mimicked Spence — analyzing the decision to death and saying everything on his mind. But by this point in his presidency, he was more aware of being watched and better understood the weight of his words — even the private ones. He struggled to remain silent, but a single disgusted syllable slipped out: "Shit."

That was all we needed. As the television displayed a scene of crowds cheering in the streets of South Central L.A., our small room became a babel of anger and invective. Clinton didn't move from his chair, just silently redrafted his public reaction, a single sentence expressing respect for the jury's decision and sadness for

"Ron and Nicole." Mike McCurry took the statement and asked if he had any other thoughts. "Not that I want to say," he replied. Still sitting, he slowly doubled over, lowering his head into the palms of his hands, grinding them into his eyes as if to keep all those thoughts from escaping.

Everyone returned to work, and Clinton retreated to the relative solitude of the Oval, leaving the office to Betty — the only African American in the room. We had first worked together in the Dukakis campaign, then the War Room, now the White House. She was a serene presence, quick to offer a piece of candy or a hug when you looked a little harried. As I returned to my office, I wondered about her. *Boy, it must have been painful for her to watch that scene, even if she loves the president, even if she's friends with us.* Ashamed of my insensitivity, I went back to talk with her about it and asked if she could explain the cheers.

"You mean, what do they think in the 'hood?" she asked, with just enough of an edge to let me know that my outraged reaction to the verdict had been noted. "Most people feel vindicated by the verdict. It sends the message that the police can't screw around with black people."

But Betty, what kind of a message does it send to let a murderer go free? The look on my face gave me away. So Betty brought up a talk we'd had shortly after O. J. was arrested. "Remember, George, when this started, I thought he was guilty and you didn't believe it." It was a gentle reproach, a reminder to be humble in my judgments, and another sign of the gulf between how whites and blacks viewed the verdict. Several of us spent the rest of the afternoon debating whether Clinton should say anything more, but the president wanted to let the matter drop — a decision Morris ratified with another overnight poll, which found, he said, that "eighty percent of the country opposed a presidential statement" on the Simpson case.

Perhaps the most significant presidential statement of the fall, however, was one that wasn't polled because it wasn't meant to be repeated aloud. Morris had indoctrinated Clinton with dogma designed to persuade him that triangulation was his political salvation — a creed the *New Republic* had labeled "The Explanation." The president's original sin, it held, was falling in with the congressional Democrats and their allies like me and Leon Panetta. His first-term mistakes were our fault. Whatever the merits of The Explanation (and there were some), it was a guide for contemplation, not ceremony — stage direction, not script.

But at a late-night fund-raiser in Houston, the president proclaimed his faith with a public confession to a roomful of wealthy contributors. Acknowledging that many of them were "still mad" because "you think I raised your taxes too much," Clinton added, "It might surprise you to know that I think I raised them too much too." Most of the frontline White House reporters missed it because they'd skipped the speech and snuck off to a restaurant. After all, Clinton rarely made news at these events, it was past deadline anyway, and you couldn't get good Tex-Mex in D.C. But a Reuter's wire service correspondent filed some copy when she heard Clinton seem to repudiate the central legislative accomplishment of his presidency.

The next morning, I was startled by the headline on page A-9 of the *Washington Times:* "Clinton Says He Thinks He Raised Taxes Too Much." In his speech, Clinton's quotes were wrapped in a fulsome defense of our 1993 economic plan, but wrenched from their context, they looked like Republican talking points. Holding up a copy of the paper folded over to the incriminating story, I announced to the senior staff meeting that "we have a big problem." But then, I always thought the sky was falling. Pooh-poohing my pessimism was a pretty safe bet, especially when my evidence was a brief wire report picked up only by a conservative rag: "Oh, that's just Clinton being Clinton. . . . What's new about him trying to get a roomful of rich people to like him? . . . It'll blow over."

But timing is everything, and I wasn't the only person reading the *Washington Times.* The Republicans needed to change the subject from their Medicare cuts, so Gingrich and Dole held a gleeful "I told you so" press conference next to a huge poster of Clinton's admission. Already suspicious of the president, wary that he would sell them out in the budget talks, the Democrats ranged from distressed to apoplectic. At a meeting of the Senate Finance Committee, Senator Moynihan incited his colleagues by handing out photocopies of Clinton's latest betrayal. The leadership made livid calls to Leon demanding a retraction. Evicted from Congress thanks to her vote for Clinton's tax increase, all Marjorie Margolies-Mezvinsky could say was "Oh, my."

By midday, McCurry was getting pummeled at his daily briefing. The evening news was a chorus of criticism from Democrats, Republicans, and independent observers, who all agreed on one point: that the president would say anything to anyone to get his or her support. Clinton had to retract his remarks — before the morning papers. But he was resting in the residence after several days of travel, and no one was eager to disturb him with this news. Shortly before the president left the White House again for an evening fund-raiser in Baltimore (those Medicare ads didn't come cheap), Gene Sperling and I implored Erskine Bowles for a five-minute meeting. "I know he's going to yell at us. I know he's going to be angry," I said. "But he has to take it back or it will kill him."

The three of us met Clinton by the elevator across from the map room. He was exhausted; an angry fever blister on his nose flashed like the beacon on a sea buoy. Erskine told him why we were there, and I plunged into my opening argument before he could erupt. "We've been defending you all day, Mr. President, but after talking to the Hill and watching the news, we really feel we have a problem that needs to be fixed." I then outlined a four-part presidential retraction that mixed three parts sugar and one of castor oil: "First, you can definitely say that your words were taken out of context. They were. Second, repeat that you're very, very proud of your economic plan. Third, say that nobody likes to raise taxes. And fourth, we have to say something like 'I shouldn't have said what I said,' or 'It wasn't right to say what I said,' or 'It was a mistake. I was wrong.'"

The forefinger was back in my face before I could finish the sentence. Clinton stepped toward me, glaring down, using every inch of his physical advantage. "I'm *not* going to say that," he declared. "You just want me to go out there and say something that's not true."

He followed up with an intricate, if somewhat convoluted, digression on how the tax increase on the wealthy we had promised in the campaign was marginally lower than the one that passed the

Congress because the bureaucrats wouldn't score our budget proposals accurately, the Republicans wouldn't vote for any tax increase, and the Democrats wouldn't cut spending as much as he would have liked. Never mind that most Democrats had originally opposed the energy tax increase proposed by the president and that we had promised more spending in the campaign than congressional Democrats eventually approved.

After Clinton's first flurry, Sperling took over our tag-team effort. Matching the president line for line with citations from *Putting People First* and our 1993 economic plan, Gene closed like a lawyer. "We just can't litigate the past, Mr. President," he said. "Even if you're right, we just can't do it."

Sensing an opening, I followed up with a modified pander. "Mr. President, what you are saying may have some deep truth to it, but it's not going to help. We can't win the argument." Now he had a way to walk off the plank, I hoped. It wasn't that he was wrong; it was just that he couldn't clearly communicate in an environment where the press was always playing "gotcha."

"So *what* would you have me do?" he said, still testy but on the verge of surrender.

"We need a concession of sorts," I replied. "Can we say something like, you're proud of your plan, and you have no regrets?" It wasn't good enough. Not really an apology, and Clinton agreed only to have me issue a statement, not to appear before the cameras himself. But it would have to do for now. Gene and I drafted a short response — "The president has absolutely no regrets. Period. None. And he didn't mean to suggest otherwise"— and phoned it into the major papers. The "didn't mean to suggest otherwise" fillip was farther than the president wanted to go. But it would be the bare minimum necessary to get us through the night.

After hearing the questions shouted at him on the way to his car, Clinton began to realize that too. He called me several times that night to ask me how the story was spinning. That was his way of thanking me and of apologizing for his earlier outburst. But the next morning, he was still in no mood to make the full mea culpa that Democrats and the press were demanding. The senior staff was unified in its recommendation: Clinton had to go to the briefing room to clean it up. Hillary called me twice to make the same point. But when we met with Clinton later that morning, he was still reluctant to go all the way. Gore, Panetta, Rubin, Bowles, and Ickes all weighed in, but the most the president would agree to was a conditional apology — an "if I said anything that people took the wrong way" statement coupled with a lame joke about how his mother had warned him not to give speeches when he was tired.

Even Clinton's mistakes, however, had a way of working out for the best. To assuage the Democrats, his opening statement was his best blast yet at the Republican budget — "So my message to the Republicans is simple. . . . I will not let you destroy Medicare, and I will veto this bill" — solidifying the intransigent strategy we hardliners preferred. Of course, Clinton still desperately wanted a deal, so badly that later in the press conference he blurted out that we could balance the budget in seven years instead of the nine our budget now called for — which amounted to a unilateral concession of about $200 billion in spending cuts to the Republican side. Watching the television above the entrance to the briefing room, I pressed my forehead silently to the wall to keep from screaming; Gene looked as if he were about to cry. Just when we were cleaning up one problem, another popped out of the president's mouth.

What we didn't know, what we *couldn't* know, was that even that slip would work to our advantage. Force, diplomacy, treachery, and luck were complementing each other in a manner Machiavelli would have appreciated. The hard public line coupled with our advertising campaign was unifying the Democrats and weakening the Republican position. Simultaneously, Morris's secret talks with Lott, Clinton's soothing phone calls to Gingrich, and his distancing from Democratic allies and premature public concessions — all sincere in their own way — combined to create an inadvertently ingenious disinformation campaign. It lulled the Republicans into believing Clinton would cave, if only they waited long enough.

But *they* didn't know that toward the end of October, the confrontation camp (Trent Lott called me, Panetta, and Ickes "the Sandinistas") had a new asset. As Morris became more prominent, he started to get more press scrutiny. The Sunday *Times* ran a front-page story detailing how, in his previous work, Morris had "openly and forcefully ridiculed Mr. Clinton's personal conduct and policy stands — and advised his clients about how to seize on the president's vulnerabilities in their own campaigns." Other reporters started to comb through Dick's record and discover that he'd worked in Republican campaigns that had been roundly criticized for their racist overtones. Morris had bragged, for example, that he had been behind the infamous "white hands" ad for Jesse Helms, in which Helms's black opponent, Harvey Gantt, was accused of supporting quotas for racial minorities. For another Southern Republican candidate, he had developed a radio ad that defended the symbols of the old Confederacy to the tune of "Dixie."

It didn't take long for Dick to realize that these revelations were a threat to his checkbook. Democrats on the Hill were already gunning for him. Given the president's commitment to racial healing, Dick's association with race-baiting campaigns could give them the ammunition they'd need to get him fired. At least I hoped it would. When reporters first poked around on the "white hands" story, I asked Morris if it was true. "Well, not exactly," he began. "I discovered the issue, polled it, advised Helms on it. . . ." Then he suddenly realized that I was laying a trap. He paused, and his voice rose, becoming righteously indignant. "But I didn't write that outrageous, despicable, racist ad."

To me, that was a distinction without a difference. In a meeting with Harold, Erskine, and Leon, I argued that Morris should be fired if the charges were true. "We dump Lani Guinier because of her views on race," I said, "but this guy writes the most racist ad in modern politics, and we say, 'What's the big deal?'" All of us wanted Dick out of there, and Leon asked Erskine to review the rest of his record for potential land mines. But Morris went into damage control mode, orchestrating an effective campaign to obscure all of his past work. When I returned to my office, he was working from my easy chair. "I just got off the phone with Roger Ailes," he said. "He'll take full credit for Willie Horton, which is great — because I wrote it."

When I asked Dick what Clinton knew about the Helms ad, he didn't even blink. "Clinton knew all about it," he said. "I was talking to him through the whole campaign about how great we were doing with this issue." I didn't know how much was true, but this was exactly what I didn't want to hear. *Of course Clinton knew. He just didn't care.* Not the world's worst failing, a sin of association rather than action, but disheartening all the same — and I knew again that Morris wasn't going anywhere.

But the public exposure weakened Morris. With the debt limit and government shutdown deadlines only days away, Panetta, Pat Griffin, and I took the opportunity to confront Dick in a meeting around Leon's conference table. "The next time something happens, these Democrats are going to go after you," Pat told him. "The price for a vote is going to be your head." Now the blackmail was working for our side.

Terrified at the prospect that *he* would be triangulated, Dick experienced a political deathbed conversion: "I have now reassessed everything. It is becoming clear to me that we cannot compromise now, that we cannot reach a deal. . . . I'm not even sure we need to balance the budget anymore. People believe that we wanted to balance the budget, so we don't have to do it. But the only way this strategy of intransigence can work is if we go *heavily, heavily, heavily* into paid media."

Going "heavily" into paid media, of course, meant millions more in commissions for Morris. Pat and I started kicking each other under the table to keep from laughing at Dick's transparent performance, but Morris kept right on talking. "Some people need a shot of vodka for courage," he said. "The president needs paid media. *I* need paid media. I have no courage without it." It wouldn't last long, but at a crucial moment, for the right price, Morris was a liberal like me. We were standing shoulder to shoulder, shaking our fists, saying, "No, no, no . . . we're going to veto." Morris would get his money; we'd prevail in the budget shutdown. I thought it was a small price to pay.

Clinton, however, was still a true believer in the original Morris doctrine of accommodation — an inclination reinforced by the increasingly likely prospect that the United States was about to go bankrupt. The Republicans were refusing to extend the government's credit line unless we made unilateral concessions on the budget. Treasury Secretary Rubin was using creative financing to forestall the day of reckoning, but if Congress didn't grant the government authority to issue more bonds, the United States was, at most, weeks away from defaulting on its debt for the first time in history — on Clinton's watch.

Publicly, the president was resolute; privately, he was wavering. "I'm not comfortable being this hard-line," he said at a Morris residence meeting (yes, in late September, I was finally invited to the weekly strategy sessions). Not only might he bear the blame when 43 million Americans failed to get their social security checks, but the president was understandably afraid that default could trigger a free fall in global financial markets. It might, replied Bob Rubin; but in keeping with his sphinxlike demeanor, he declined to predict the consequences, simply repeating his mantra that default was "unthinkable." But so was capitulation. Steeled by years of weighing probabilities and placing billion-dollar bets in the bond market, the treasury secretary believed that buckling to a congressional blackmail threat would set a terrible precedent, weaken the presidency, and eliminate our leverage in the budget talks. His resolve was consistently our best counter to Clinton's vacillating tendencies.

So when Gingrich called Clinton to discuss the debt limit, we intercepted the message and had Rubin return the call instead — joking that to keep him from calling Newt and trading away the store we would disconnect Clinton's phones, "like they did to Gorbachev during the coup." But the Speaker, correctly, would deal only with the president. An Oval Office meeting was scheduled for Wednesday, November 1.

In the two days prior to that encounter, our budget group spent nearly eight hours strategizing about how to keep the president from caving; and to lock Clinton in more securely, Panetta spoke to the *Washington Post* and the House Democratic Caucus on Wednesday morning to say that the president believed that "no deal is better than a bad deal." As Gingrich and Dole drove down from the Capitol, our Oval Office prep had the feel of a family intervention. All of us — Rubin, Panetta, Tyson, Sperling, Rivlin, Bowles, and Griffin — surrounded the president, bucking him up, telling him how strong he looked when he stood on principle and reminding him of the consequences of retreat. I went negative on Newt. His objective was total victory, I said. "Newt will lie and Newt will leak to force your hand," I told Clinton, adding that he had to be on his guard and willing to let Newt walk away. In this case, I concluded, "a failed meeting is a successful meeting."

"George is exactly right about that." Welcome words from a powerful new ally — the vice president. Over the course of 1995, as our views began to converge on the big issues — affirmative action and the budget — the tension between us had eased. Back in June, Gore had been a strong advocate with Morris of proposing a Clinton balanced budget (a position Morris attributed to a specific deal he made with the vice president in March: "I would fight for his priorities — reinventing government and the environment — in return for full power"), but he believed that we would ultimately reach an acceptable deal only if we held firm against the Republican threats, and he was willing to live without one if necessary. Gore also had a strong partisan streak and wasn't afraid of a fight. When Newt opened the meeting by complaining about our attacks on their "extremist" budget, the vice president fired back: "At least we didn't accuse you of drowning those little children in South Carolina."

The remark referred to a recent Gingrich press conference in which he had cited the case of Susan Smith — a South Carolina woman who had drowned her children — as a reason to vote Republican. Gore's shot rocked Gingrich and fortified Clinton. A president has no real peers, but Gore was getting close. Always respectful in public, he leveled with Clinton in their sacrosanct weekly lunches. Over the course of the budget talks, Gore became Clinton's bad cop. In this initial meeting, however, watching Gore coldcock Newt tapped the competitor in Clinton. As Newt pressed for concessions, the president fashioned a dramatic moment of his own. "If you want somebody to sign your budget," he said, pointing to the remains of the HMS *Resolute* across the room, "you're going to have to elect Bob Dole to sit behind that desk, because I'm not going to do it." The meeting ended successfully — in deadlock.

A week later, Clinton's brotherly rivalry with Gore manifested itself in another way. At noon on November 8, I was in the Oval to brief the president for a fund-raising lunch with minority entrepreneurs who were showing their gratitude for Clinton's stand on affirmative action. Both of us, however, were preoccupied.

"You really think he's not going to run?" Clinton asked.

"Dead certain," I replied. "He's announcing it within the hour."

"It's because of his sense of duty. McClellan was the only sitting general to run against his commander in chief. Ike could have run against Truman, but he waited."

The president returned to his paperwork. Apparently that was his only comment on the happy news: Colin Powell was about to announce that he would not be a candidate for president in 1996. I waited to see if Clinton had any questions. No; but as he handed Nancy Hernreich his homework, he peered over the rims of his glasses with a mischievous grin that revealed a momentary lapse of empathy. "Too bad for Al," he said.

We burst out laughing, and the president broke into a big smile, proud of his joke. Just as quickly, though, he backpedaled, a little embarrassed by our delight in his display of political selfishness: "Al knows it's better for him if we win this time around." But the smile didn't fade. If Powell ran next time, it was Gore's problem.

General Powell's withdrawal also eliminated a key risk of our confrontational budget strategy — that a prolonged, partisan stand-off would create space for an outsider like Powell to run up the middle by attacking both parties for Washington gridlock. But during the two government shutdowns that occurred in November and December, the Republican leaders themselves were our secret weapon. As much as I would love to think that we were the sole authors of our success, their self-inflicted wounds and tactical blunders made the crucial difference.

First, they failed to pass their budget on time. Although "continuing resolutions" (aka CRs — legislation designed to keep the government running while Congress completed its normal budget process) had become standard operating procedure, the fact that the Republicans missed their deadline made it marginally easier for us to blame them for the government shutdown. Even more damaging, however, was their decision to attach the politically poisonous Medicare premium increase to the CR. Hitting that one back was like batting practice. Not only did their maneuver amplify our television ads (which had been recut with fresh footage of Gingrich praising the day when Medicare would "wither on the vine" and Dole bragging about being "one of twelve" senators to vote against LBJ's original Medicare proposal), it proved our blackmail point. Clinton vetoed the CR, effectively shutting down the government. But when he appeared before the cameras to scold the "deeply irresponsible" Republican leaders for cutting Medicare "as a condition of keeping the government open," the president was the picture of stern compassion, America's dad.

Gingrich, meanwhile, looked more like America's brat. At a November 15 breakfast, Gingrich had told a roomful of reporters that he had sent the tougher CR to the White House because of how he'd been treated by the president on the trip to Prime Minister Rabin's funeral. "You land at Andrews Air Force Base and you've been on the plane for twenty-five hours and nobody has talked to you and they ask you to get off the plane by the back ramp. . . . It's petty," he concluded. "But I think it's human."

And not completely crazy. We *did* deliberately avoid any discussion of the budget on *Air Force One* — in part because the president was grieving for the foreign leader he most respected, but mostly because of our continuing worry that Clinton would concede too much in a private negotiation with Gingrich or Dole. I was appearing at fund-raisers in California that weekend, but I made sure to call Erskine and Harold with the warning that we had to find a way to prevent any budget negotiations on the plane ride. One of Leon's responsibilities on the trip was to stop any budget talks before they got too serious. Newt's childish reaction, however, transformed a largely abstract issue into a story everyone could understand; now our plot had a crime (shutdown), a culprit (Newt), and a motive (personal pique).

An hour after Newt's breakfast, my phone was ringing off the hook. By noon, the White House photographer had found a picture of Clinton and Gingrich conferring in the *Air Force One* conference room, a photo we helpfully released to our friends in the media. By nightfall, the beltway was buzzing about the Speaker's temper tantrum; the next morning, the rest of the country would be too.

Democrats displayed the front page of the *New York Daily News* (a cartoon of Newt in diapers under the headline "Cry Baby") on the floor of the House. For Clinton, we scripted a more subtle dig. When asked if he knew of "any reason" that Newt would react so strongly to his treatment on *Air Force One*, the president delivered an unhesitant apology. "I can tell you this," he answered. "If it would get the government open, I'd be glad to tell him I'm sorry."

Despite these gaffes, the Republicans were still in a strong position. On Sunday, November 19, six days into the first shutdown, the White House was functioning with a skeletal staff, and our coalition was cracking. Forty-eight Democrats had voted for a new Republican CR that didn't include the Medicare premium increase but did require the president to submit a seven-year balanced-budget proposal on their terms. Still blackmail, but the threat was less partisan now and especially difficult to oppose given that the president had already said we could balance the budget in seven years. With Thanksgiving approaching, Democrats were bailing out on us by the hour. In the House, we couldn't hold enough Democrats to sustain a veto.

To ward off that disaster, our budget team drove to the Capitol with an offer to meet the Republicans' demand for a balanced budget in seven years "if and only if" they agreed to provide "adequate funding for" the president's priorities: Medicare, Medicaid, education, and the environment. In our minds, the two halves of the resolution canceled each other out; nothing would be agreed to until everything was agreed to. Certain that the Republicans would reject it, we returned to the White House and waited. The president was puttering through the Oval Office suite in his sweatsuit. He stopped by my desk for an update. Sperling joined us, then Panetta and a few others, so we migrated back to the Oval to plan our response to the inevitable override. Clinton was grumpy; the rest of us were grim — until Betty cracked the door and handed Leon the Republican counterproposal, fresh from the fax machine.

Reading over Leon's shoulder, I saw that the only changes were cosmetic, replacing "if and only if" with "and," and adding language praising veterans and citing the need for a strong national defense. "This is it!" Panetta exclaimed. "Yes!" I screamed in his ear.

The president high-fived the whole room. Our fellow Democrats back on the Hill immediately agreed to accept the amendments, and the government was back in business. We Democrats emerged from the first shutdown more unified, while the Republicans fractured. Whether the cause was hubris, naïveté, or a failure of nerve, the Republicans had blown their best chance to splinter our party; from that point on, everything started breaking our way.

The CR gave the Republicans time to pass their overall budget, which Clinton promptly vetoed with the same pen LBJ had used to sign Medicare. Then, while Panetta led our negotiating team to the Hill to see if a deal was now possible, the president floated above the fray. He signed the Bosnian peace accords in Paris and was greeted like a hometown hero in Belfast. Back home, knowing that a second government shutdown was possible when this CR expired on December 15, we devoted hours to keeping the Democrats unified and developing a consensus budget we could all stand behind if the negotiations with the Republicans eventually broke down. The days of triangulation were long gone. Feeling neglected, Morris left for a long Christmas vacation.

While the president still preferred a bipartisan deal, he was getting more comfortable with confrontation. He allowed Leon to hold a hard line in the Capitol Hill talks, which was driving the Republicans rabid. The Speaker also understood that the calendar was working in our favor now: He knew full well that if there was another government shutdown, he'd be blamed — "the Gingrinch who stole Christmas." But by now, he'd lost control of his troops. They refused to reopen the government unless we agreed to their terms, and the second shutdown began. The freshmen had become Newt's Frankenstein monster — and my new best friends. The more they dug in, the better off we were. Even pragmatic veterans adopted their kamikaze spirit. "We will never, never, never give up," thundered Lousiana's Bob Livingston on the House floor. "We will stay here until doomsday."

Not Bob Dole, though. A few days before Christmas, we were in his Senate office, chatting before another round of budget talks. The room was fragrant with pine; a fire was crackling. For the Senate majority leader, this was home. But he wanted the office next to mine, and the government shutdown was preventing him from campaigning for it. Clad in a cardigan, he offered me a Moravian spice cookie and mused aloud about his predicament. "I've got to get to New Hampshire," he confided. "One way or the other, it's over on the thirty-first, because I'm out of here."

Mistake or message? Doesn't matter. All we have to do is hold on one more week. They'll break. "It's over on the thirty-first. . . ."

On New Year's Eve, the budget talks at the White House recessed for the holiday. The two sides were still far apart, and, true to his word, Bob Dole was about to bolt. In two days, he'd announce that Senate Republicans were abandoning their House colleagues and voting with Democrats to lift the government shutdown. The Republicans had finally become the "roving bands of hunter-gatherers" that Morris had predicted we'd see in September. There would be no budget deal.

The president was still in a good mood. He never lost hope, and he was about to make his annual pilgrimage to Renaissance Weekend with some of the highest poll numbers of his presidency. Before he left, he called me into the Oval. "You should know," he said, handing me a piece of paper, "that Dick's blaming this on you."

"Confrontation Is the Key to Clinton's Popularity: Adviser Morris's Strategy Proves Inconsistent." It was a clip from the December 24 *Washington Post*, a story I'd already seen and savored several times. Not only did its detailed analysis of public polls show that Clinton's popularity had actually fallen after the June budget speech; it also concluded that the "only time Clinton's ratings have improved substantially the past year as a result of his actions has been when he adopted a strategy of confrontation, not triangulation."

Without saying anything, the president watched me reread the entire article. I couldn't help myself. Every sentence was sweet vindication. The year that began for me in exile was ending in victory. We'd done the right thing, it was paying off, and now I was getting credit for it. Or was I? *He's awfully quiet. He can't really be mad about this, can he?*

No, Clinton was just being Clinton. For months, he'd been playing me off against Morris, taking the best from both of us and turning it into something better. Dick had been right to push the president to propose a balanced budget. My White House colleagues and I were right to insist on a firm defense of New Deal and Great Society commitments that Morris would have sacrificed in a second. Clinton was right to pick and choose, creating a synthesis that was good for him and good for the country. But in this quiet encounter at the close of the year, Clinton must have sensed how maddening it was to be subject to his mercurial will — and he was making up for it with the perfect gesture at the perfect moment. "Don't worry." He smiled. "Dick's a little paranoid.

"Just keep on doing what you're doing."

16   GETTING OUT

I don't want to stay. . . ."

The words escaped my mouth before I realized what they meant. But Dr. Hyde's smile showed he understood. Around my age, with the short hair and bulky build of a rugby player, he was a specialist at the top of his field — neurology and psychiatry. And he had just explained that if I didn't learn to manage the stress, I wouldn't make it through a second term. When I blurted out that all I wanted was to get through the next year and get out, he applied some gentle pressure: "Can you really walk away from the White House? . . . Don't you feel an obligation to stay?" But his questions didn't make me feel ungrateful for being unhappy or guilty for wanting to go. That's how I knew it was time.

Of course, the decision wouldn't necessarily be mine. It was only 1995, a dark afternoon in mid-December on the brink of the second government shutdown. We still didn't know how that confrontation and the 1996 campaign would conclude. And I was determined to leave on my own terms — after we had prevailed on the budget, after Clinton had become the first Democratic president since Roosevelt to get elected twice. So I bargained with the doctor: Patch me up now, and I'll promise to change my life later. He prescribed

Zoloft, a medication for anxiety and depression — and ordered me to take more walks.

I had been putting off this visit for months. Although the worst of my depression had lifted by 1995, my nerves were shot, and it had started to show. During the June battles on the budget and affirmative action, hives had erupted across my chin. I grew a beard. The rash subsided after an August vacation, but my most pernicious symptom persisted unseen. It was a sound: of fingernails screeching across slate or the tines of a fork scraping a bone china plate. Several times a day, for up to an hour straight, it would loop around my brain and reverberate through my torso like feedback from an over-amplified guitar. I'd blink hard to force the sound out of my ears and compulsively rub the back of my scalp when my hair started to stand on end. But I couldn't control the sensation. My therapist prescribed mind games: Imagine yourself in a warm bath or wrapped in cool sheets. Cook a four-course meal in your head; if you miss a step, start again. We discussed medication. She gave me Dr. Hyde's number. I resisted. The Spartan in me said, *"Suck it up"*; the spin doctor saw future headlines.

By December I couldn't take it anymore; I needed quiet now. So when Clinton flew overseas, I finally drove myself to a nondescript high-rise off Wisconsin Avenue, where I sat on the edge of the sofa as Dr. Hyde told me what I already knew: I was burned out. A serotonin reuptake inhibitor like Zoloft, he then explained, would help stop my nerves from flooding my brain with the chemical fueling my compulsive symptoms. Just hearing the mechanics calmed me down, and the medication helped even more. Soon I slept four hours straight, then I was up to six. I no longer woke up waiting for the sound to start. The feedback cleared, and I could breathe deeply again. Testing myself, I would see fingernails on a blackboard, hear the sound track, then switch it off.

All of the White House stresses were still there, but they didn't affect me so severely. The medication stripped away layers of worry, allowing me to remember what it was like to be *me* — a melancholy nail biter, sure, but not someone consumed by anxiety, not someone who measured himself by his proximity to a president or convinced himself that his words and deeds would make or break a presidency.

It helped restore my sense of perspective, the internal balance my father had taught me to prize. I still worked hard, but I worried less. I cared about what we could do, but I didn't obsess. Calmer, more detached, I prepared to leave.

Even as my health improved, I wasn't tempted by the thought of a second term. Of course, I still wanted Clinton to win. Victory would redeem our failures and validate our successes. Four more years in the White House would mean more Democratic judges on the federal bench, perhaps another seat on the Supreme Court. It would mean that more of our people would be managing the government for more time, making the day-to-day decisions that add up to meaningful change. Legislatively, Clinton would use his veto to prevent the Gingrich Congress from doing too much harm and his bully pulpit to persuade them to do some good. As commander in chief, he'd be more confident; as chief diplomat, more creative. Attuned by experience to the power of the office, freed from the burden of another election, he would become a better president.

But not a bolder one. In 1993, Clinton groused that the bond market was turning him into an Eisenhower Republican. By 1996, with the nation prosperous and at peace, with Republicans controlling the Congress, it seemed that Clinton's second term would be even more like Ike's — and he didn't seem to mind. I couldn't fully blame him for bending with the times. The voters did send us a message, and moderation did have its virtues. But it wasn't all that inspiring. So like my boss, I would play it safe. While serving in the White House, I had survived failure, scandal, and internal exile. The next time I made a mistake or came under attack, I might not escape. Protective of my reputation, less enthralled by Clinton now, I wouldn't press my luck in a second term that promised to be competent but complacent — a second term encapsulated in the slogan "The era of big government is over."

A product of Dick Morris's word processor, that phrase was the heart of the 1996 State of the Union. Dick said it captured a "new national consensus." I thought it proved that we had won some battles but lost the larger war, that we were the prisoners of conservative rhetoric, and that the American people were as full of contradictions as their president. *How would they like it if we said, "The era of*

Medicare is over" — or *Social Security? How would they like it if the "era of disaster assistance" was over the next time they faced an earthquake or flood?* So much of Clinton's comeback had been propelled by a defense of "big government." Even if the phrase reflected reality, even if government had gone too far at times, the triumphalist tone of the declaration felt dishonest and vaguely dishonorable, as if we were condemning Democrats from Franklin Roosevelt to Lyndon Johnson to the trash heap of history for the sake of a sound bite.

But it was solid-gold politics, testing at 80 percent in the polls. And Clinton had paid a price for reducing the deficit, so he might as well get some credit for it. Eliminating the sentence from the State of the Union wasn't going to happen. Instead, a few of us wanted to balance it by adding, ". . . but the era of every man for himself must never begin." Morris, surprisingly, didn't object; but our political-correctness police did. Displaying the same kind of thinking that was behind the attempt to prevent the president from wearing a Cleveland Indians baseball cap on opening day because it might offend Native Americans, they now argued that "every man for himself" was a sexist insult, and they appealed directly to the president. Clinton neutered the sentence: "But we cannot go back to the time when our citizens were left to fend for themselves."

Not the same. In a political speech, it takes a cliché to counter a cliché. Maybe it didn't matter; maybe the man-bites-dog quality of a Democrat's declaring the death of "big government" would drown out whatever words followed. But if Clinton's compromise was too clunky, the editorial decision itself was poetically concise. The fall of a single sound bite to the Oval Office carpet summarized the Democratic Party's journey of a generation: from a party unified by the belief that government could promote the common good to a loose coalition of caucuses alienated from average Americans by a fixation on identity politics. It showed, as speechwriter Michael Waldman said when we left the Oval, "the death of liberalism at its own hands." Clinton's bold and bland synthesis also revealed a secret of his personal popularity in the face of his party's decline. While striking deep into Republican territory, he covered his flank just enough to keep his fragile coalition whole. The centrists got the sound bite; the feminists excised a phrase; the traditional liberals like me couldn't really complain. A remnant of our idea survived even if the rhetoric wasn't ringing.

The country loved it. Not just the death of big government, the whole presentation — with Clinton's patently passionate delivery of issues designed to appeal to suburban moms: school uniforms and curfews, stopping big tobacco from targeting kids, V-chips to block televised sex and violence. Ironically, though all involved government intervention, the proposals were wildly popular, which was at least half the point. Of course, I was no virgin. Taking a poll, to me, was like taking our temperature, and I had advocated the relatively inconsequential middle-class tax cut in 1992 not only because it symbolized whose side we were on, but also because it scored well. But during the Morris era, it seemed more and more as if we were polling first, proposing later.

My only original contribution to the State of the Union was "a little dig" at our most likely opponent. On the afternoon of the speech, as Clinton practiced before a group of us from a mock podium in the family theater, I interrupted when he reached the section on national security challenges. As drafted, it opened with thanks "to our veterans" for providing America with "fifty years of prosperity and security." I suggested that the president stop there and single out Senator Dole and his World War II colleagues for special praise. Clinton smiled and made a note on his reading copy.

The maneuver would rankle the Dole campaign, but what could they say? How could they possibly criticize the president of the United States for taking the unprecedented step of praising his prime opponent during the State of the Union Address? Because it was a body blow wrapped in a bouquet. Clinton's seemingly gracious salute was a subtle reminder that Senator Dole's time had passed — and he was already in a deep hole. With the economy humming and Clinton stealing the political center, even a flawless campaign would probably fall short. The crucial contrasts were working in our favor: Thirty-five years of congressional experience tagged Dole as a Washington insider; Clinton was still a relative newcomer who seemed to be in touch with average Americans. The government shutdown, during which Dole had repeatedly appeared in press conferences (and our television advertising) joined at the

hip with Newt Gingrich, portrayed him as captive to the most extreme forces in his party, while Clinton had shown his backbone by
standing up to them. Clinton had started green, but he was growing
into the job; Dole seemed too old to be president.

Morris was so eager to make sure Dole won the Republican
nomination that he tried to help him out — in his own way. Two
days after the State of the Union, he secretly leaked a polling memo
to the Dole campaign that said Dole could not win in either New
Hampshire or Iowa unless there was a budget deal. Like one of
those aged Japanese soldiers still fighting World War II from deserted island outposts, Dick hadn't surrendered his magnificent
obsession. The Dole people thought the memo was bizarre. The
questions were clearly slanted, and they couldn't figure out what
Morris was up to. But they did take the opportunity to embarrass us
by passing it on to the *Post*.

When Ann Devroy called Mike McCurry for our official comment, McCurry found Morris, and Morris blamed . . . me. On the
spot, he concocted a convoluted scheme in which I had supposedly
stolen a copy of the memo from Clinton's desk and passed it on to
Carville, who gave it to his Republican wife, Mary Matalin, who
funneled it through to Devroy — all to smear Morris. Dick could
prove it, he told McCurry, because the president's copy was missing
a line scribbled on the memo that was given to the Dole campaign:
"You might want to check this with your own pollster."

After informing me that I had been charged with treason, Mc-
Curry called Devroy, whose copy, I knew, included the handwritten
notation that would prove that I had nothing to do with Dick's
scheme. But when McCurry, Panetta, and Ickes presented the case
against Morris to the president, I stayed away. Not only because I
had also been accused, but because I didn't want to watch the charade. I knew that Dick would pay no real price for falsely charging
me with the political equivalent of a capital offense. A few days earlier, I had heard a rumor that the Dole campaign had the Morris
memo, so I went to the Oval to warn Clinton that they were likely
to leak it. "Dick wasn't supposed to do *that*," he said — a rebuke
that was also, I suspected, an inadvertent admission. Morris had
probably told Clinton that he would make another play for a budget

deal by passing his polls to the Dole campaign, but the president must have assumed that Dick was smart enough not to leave a paper trail.

Which Clinton was sincerely furious about. Leon and Harold came straight from the Oval with the verdict: The president had defended me and chewed out Dick. "Whenever something goes wrong around here," he yelled, "you blame it on George." Against my will, my eyes welled up. I guess I wasn't all that detached yet. Although I feared that Clinton didn't fully mean it and knew that nothing would follow from it, the president's spontaneous defense was something I needed to know about. The episode ended with a front-page story by Devroy, a public McCurry wrist slap of Morris, and a Morris apology to me, which I didn't accept. He was sorry for getting caught, and I didn't have to pretend anymore. From now on, no Dick attack on me would stick.

Dole secured the nomination despite ignoring Dick's advice, but he couldn't develop any real momentum. When he tried to use his position as majority leader to pass popular tax cuts and force a Clinton veto, Democrats pinned him down on the Senate floor with amendments on our issues like raising the minimum wage. Then he tried to reignite his run by resigning from the Senate. Although his farewell speech was the most moving rhetoric of the campaign, its political benefits didn't linger. On the campaign trail, he looked lost, almost sad, a man homesick for Capitol Hill. Following our 1992 example, he tried to compensate for his lack of campaign funds by hitting the "free media" talk-show circuit. But Dole's ironic humor didn't always translate well on television; nor did his clipped legislative shorthand, honed over thirty-five years of cutting Senate deals. In the emblematic moment of the preconvention season, Dole argued with *Today*'s Katie Couric about whether tobacco was addictive. Taking on America's sweetheart, he seemed crotchety and out of touch. All we had to do was watch.

But I still worried. Dole couldn't match Clinton as a communicator, but there was still the issue of "character" — the contrast between the straight-talking war hero of sterling integrity and the slippery draft dodger under an ethical cloud. Our internal mantra was "public values trump private character" — a refined version of the formula that had worked ever since Gennifer Flowers and the draft. For us, it was now an article of faith that Clinton could overcome personal attacks as long as he kept addressing the "real problems of real people." That meant, however, that the rest of us had to work even harder to keep the hoofbeats at bay.

In June of 1996, it felt like an entire herd was converging on the White House. Ken Starr won convictions of Arkansas governor Jim Guy Tucker and Clinton's Whitewater partners Jim and Susan McDougal, and he named Bruce Lindsey an unindicted coconspirator in the trial of an Arkansas banker with ties to Clinton. Senator D'Amato issued a scathing report on Whitewater recommending that several Clinton friends and staffers be investigated for perjury. Even worse, we created a mess of our own when two midlevel White House staffers mistakenly obtained the FBI files of nine hundred Republicans from previous administrations, including former Secretary of State James Baker. "Filegate" was a bureaucratic screwup, but with its echoes of Watergate and our 1992 attacks on the Bush administration for examining Clinton's passport file, it had the potential to be our most serious scandal yet.

By now, damage control was a cottage industry in the White House. We had a team of lawyers, nicknamed the Masters of Disaster, whose sole job was to handle Whitewater and related inquiries — responding to grand jury subpoenas, preparing congressional testimony, answering questions from the press. Better them than me. From experience, I'd learned that simply gathering facts to answer allegations could spawn new inquiries and additional avenues of attack, creating a cycle that was the political equivalent of a perpetual-motion machine. Anyone anywhere near the activity risked getting sucked into the swirl and spit out with a tarnished reputation and a ton of debt. At approximately $100,000, my legal fees were already high enough. Though I talked to our Masters of Disaster frequently, I had steadily disengaged from the daily scandal patrol.

At the end of June, however, I took myself out of early retirement for a farewell run at the "right-wing conspiracy." Maybe Jay Stephens made me do it. My old nemesis was now representing

Gary Aldrich, an ex–FBI agent who wanted to document the depravity he supposedly witnessed when conducting security checks on the Clinton White House staff. Stephens steered Aldrich to Regnery Publishing, an established conservative publisher. With additional assistance from the Southeastern Legal Foundation — a right-wing law firm with ties to Newt Gingrich and funding from Richard Mellon Scaife (the reclusive tycoon who had donated millions of dollars to groups promoting conspiracy theories about the Clinton White House) — they created a work of fiction and called it a memoir: *Unlimited Access: An FBI Agent Inside the Clinton White House.*

The prepublication buzz was hot, and the book broke into the news on Thursday, June 27, when ABC reported that Aldrich's book alleged (falsely) that Craig Livingstone — the White House staffer under fire for obtaining the FBI files — had been hired at the direction of Hillary. The *Washington Post* was working on the same story, and we knew that the *New York Post* and the *Washington Times* were planning front-page treatments of the book's most sensational fabrication — that Clinton frequently snuck out of the White House in the backseat of Bruce Lindsey's car for late-night trysts at the downtown Marriott. Although the charge seemed ludicrous on its face, the media was taking Aldrich seriously. Over the next week, he was set to be seen by millions of Americans on shows like *This Week with David Brinkley, Larry King Live, Good Morning America,* and *Dateline.*

To counter the air assault, I first had to read the book. My assistant Laura Capps bought me a copy, and I settled in by my fireplace for a night of study. With a blue felt tip, I underlined each specific charge and ranked it in the margins: "False," "Innuendo," "Fabrication," "Lie." The allegations (that the social office hung pornographic ornaments on the White House Christmas tree; that when the Gennifer Flowers story surfaced, Washington superlawyer Lloyd Cutler brokered a deal in which Hillary agreed to stand by Bill in return for total control over domestic policy in the White House; that the men on Clinton's staff wore earrings and the women no underwear) were either silly, specious, or provably false. The more I read, the more righteously indignant I became. *How can*

they even think about broadcasting this crap before checking it out?
But Aldrich's outlandish account also created an opportunity: His
fifteen minutes of fame would make him the poster boy of the
anti-Clinton conspiracy. If we could destroy his credibility in a
high-profile way, the press might be more skeptical of the inevitable
flurry of allegations late in the campaign.

The next morning, I worked with our team to document
Aldrich's partisan connections and collect affidavits refuting his
claims. Then I called the *Washington Post*'s Howard Kurtz, a respected media critic whose column would be read by the editors and
producers deciding how to handle *Unlimited Access*. Offering him an
exclusive first look at the information we'd compiled, I pitched a
piece about the ethics of airing the Aldrich allegations. The real
story here, I argued, is not Clinton's sex life, it's his sleazy attackers
and the state of journalism, adding for good measure that Aldrich's
tale "couldn't get past the fact checkers at the *National Enquirer.*"
Then I walked to the Washington bureau of ABC News to make my
case to the producers of the *Brinkley* show. Although I didn't expect
them to be particularly moved by my commitment to their First
Amendment responsibilities (and they weren't), I did hope that a
full-court press would help ensure that Aldrich didn't get a free ride.
Brinkley kept Aldrich, but they also offered me a chance to answer
his charges in person on Sunday morning.

I arrived at the studio spoiling for a fight, and the sight of an
Aldrich handler in the greenroom gave me extra ammunition: Craig
Shirley was a paid agent of the NRA and big tobacco, and an unpaid
adviser to Senator Dole's campaign. His presence was all the proof I
needed to charge that Aldrich was part of a "smear campaign conducted by Republican Party operatives." But as it turned out, *my*
presence was largely superfluous. Like a boxer dissing his opponent
in the center of the ring, I whispered "Liar" at Aldrich as I walked
onto the set. But he'd already been pummeled by one of the refer-
ees, George Will, whose questioning revealed that the Marriott tale
was a hand-me-down figment from "Troopergate's" David Brock.
Newsweek had the same story, and Kurtz's article had raised all the
right ethical questions. By Sunday afternoon, *Dateline* and *Larry*

King Live had canceled Aldrich, and most of the follow-up focused on his shoddy sourcing and shady connections.

My War Room swan song was a success. Was it necessary? Hard to say. But a cardinal rule of the Clinton culture was, Never take political threats lightly.

On July 31, 1996, I feared it was a lesson learned too well. Over the previous year, the president had vetoed two Republican welfare reform bills that would have ended the federal government's guarantee of health and welfare benefits to poor children. Now, after restoring the entitlement to health care but not welfare, Congress was sending it back a third time. With the election only three months away and the final decision meeting only three hours away, Clinton faced a perilous choice.

"If he vetoes, he'll lose," Morris declared.

I was listening to Dick's desperate rant from the phone booth carved into the back corner of Panetta's office, where the morning staff meeting had just begun. Morris said his polls predicted that a veto of welfare reform would transform our projected fifteen-point November win into a three-point loss, and he begged me to switch sides and support the bill. Taking comfort from his anxiety, I refused. Dick had been bragging for days that Clinton was sure to sign the welfare bill, walking through the halls offering 10–1 odds against a veto to any of us willing to take his bet. The fact that he was this worried on the morning of the final decision gave me hope.

So did Hillary. In my last few phone calls with the first lady, I could tell she preferred a veto. Like her friend Marian Wright Edelman, president of the Children's Defense Fund, she feared the bill would effectively abolish the safety net and jeopardize millions of poor children. But she also kept referring to "the president's decision" — oddly formal, but somehow appropriate. After the failure of health care, and given the persistence of Whitewater, political prudence and the balance of power in their marriage weighed against a decisive Hillary intervention on welfare. She couldn't be positioned — publicly or privately — to take the fall if he vetoed the bill and the race went south. I had the sense that she was pointing out the flaws without being pushy. Maybe the lighter touch was working.

The atmosphere in the cabinet room that morning was self-consciously statesmanlike, as if we were gathered for a council of war. Which was appropriate. The decision to end a cornerstone of the New Deal was historic, and lives hung in the balance. "The objective reality is that people are going to get hurt," argued Housing and Urban Development Secretary Henry Cisneros, and Health and Human Services Secretary Donna Shalala cited a study that predicted up to eleven million families could suffer severe harm if Clinton signed the bill. Bob Reich, Bob Rubin, Laura Tyson, Harold Ickes, and Leon Panetta all seconded the veto recommendation. A smaller faction that included Rahm Emanuel and Mickey Kantor countered that killing the bill would cause more harm by perpetuating a failed system that trapped families in a cycle of dependency. As each cabinet member and staffer solemnly stated a position, the president took notes and played devil's advocate — challenging the bill's proponents on the cruelty of the cuts and its opponents on the irresponsibility of doing nothing. But he didn't tip his hand.

The strongest argument for signing came from domestic policy adviser Bruce Reed, a New Democrat of integrity and conviction who had developed Clinton's welfare policy since 1992. Calling it "a good welfare bill wrapped in a bad budget bill," he conceded that the deep cuts in food stamps and emergency benefits to legal immigrants were gratuitous and needed to be fixed. But he also insisted that the core welfare reform provisions — time limits and work requirements — were close to Clinton's original proposals; that changes in child care, child support enforcement, and the school lunch program made this a far better bill than the two Clinton had vetoed; and that we couldn't get a better deal if this one broke down. Finally, he said, a third veto would break faith with voters who took Clinton at his word when he promised in 1992 to "end welfare as we know it."

Bruce made a good case — and I said so when Clinton called on me. "It's a tough call," I began. Although I recommended a veto and said that I thought the benefit cuts to legal immigrants were unconscionable and un-American, any temptation I felt to mount a self-righteous soapbox was tempered by my complicity. In 1992, I had been eager to put millions of dollars of television advertising behind the phrase "end welfare as we know it," even though I knew full well that it sent a message far more powerful than, and somewhat contradictory to, the fine print of our proposal in *Putting People First*, which had promised more assistance to welfare recipients looking for work, not less. The policy arguments had all been made by the cabinet experts, so I used most of my time to answer the adviser not in the room. While conceding that a veto could cause "a quick five- or six-point drop," I argued that it would never cost us the race and that the president had always pulled through potentially unpopular decisions like Bosnia, the budget, and affirmative action by taking principled stands. The truth is, I wanted Clinton to be a hero — to take a political risk on behalf of people who had nowhere else to turn. Besides, I concluded, "signing the bill will cut the legs out from Democrats running against the extreme Gingrich Congress," and we needed them for a successful second term.

After more than two hours of discussion, Clinton retreated to the Oval with Panetta and Gore, the only other person in the room who hadn't said what he thought. I walked back to my office with Harold, and we waited for the decision together, still hoping. Neither of us knew what the president would do, or maybe that's just what we needed to believe. The uncertainty — the idea that Clinton was struggling toward a principled decision after reasoned deliberations — was somehow reassuring. To Clinton too. This was a decision he couldn't compartmentalize; before he could act, he had to convince himself he was doing the right thing for the right reasons. His heart urged a veto, while his head calculated the risk. They were reconciled by his will — a will to win that was barely distinguishable and basically inseparable from the conviction that what was best for the poor was for him to be president. *They* would have to trust his decision: Sign it now; fix it later.

Clinton's belief that the bill would end welfare as a political bogeyman and usher in an era of altruism struck me as a rationalization; his hope that a new Congress would restore the cuts seemed like wishful thinking. But a few weeks later at the Democratic convention, I faithfully repeated the talking points to help quell a rumored demonstration by liberal delegates over welfare reform. That was the trade-off. In return for a seat at that cabinet table, in return for the privilege of influencing issues you care about, in return for the rush of power and reflected glory, you defend the boss — fiercely, unapologetically, giving no ground. If you can't do it, you have to go.

But I don't want to resign. Not before we win again. It was a close call. Who am I to judge? And Clinton knows a lot more about welfare than you do, George. Besides, he already came through on the budget and affirmative action, and we can't risk losing the White House again. You can't expect 100 percent. Resigning with an election so close is just self-indulgent.

My own capacity for rationalization wasn't exactly underdeveloped, but most Democrats were making a similar calculation. The floor fight over welfare reform never caught fire. Democrats had to consider the alternative — a Republican president working with a Republican Congress — and they were too content to fight. With a resilient president riding to reelection on the back of a resurgent economy, this was a feel-good convention — a coronation. Nobody wanted to spoil the celebration.

Not even Morris could spoil the fun. The man who at our first dinner had said "I don't want any publicity. Being a man of mystery helps me work better" was holding a coming-out party in Chicago. He was on the cover of that week's *Time*, and he was granting a steady stream of interviews in which he described his brilliant engineering of Clinton's comeback. My natural jealousy was moderated a bit by my belief that he did deserve his share of credit for Clinton's recovery, and by the fact that he was making new internal enemies every day. It wasn't just the media tour; he was going through another manic phase. In his zeal for total control, he tried to replace both Hillary's and Gore's speeches with his own rapidly dictated drafts — speeches so over the top that Harry Thomason quipped, "Dick's gone bad. Someone's gonna have to put him down."

Little did he know that Morris was taking care of that himself. I got my first inkling that something was up late Monday afternoon, the first full day of the convention. The two of us were at the headquarters hotel, waiting for a speech prep with Hillary to begin. She never arrived, but while we were waiting, Dick confided to me that he might be the subject of a nasty personal story in the *Star* tabloid. "It didn't happen," he said, "but I think you should know that it's coming." I'd been around long enough to know that "It didn't happen" wasn't exactly a denial, but I didn't ask what the "it" was. I didn't want to know the details because I didn't want to be blamed if they leaked, and defending Dick against the tabloids wasn't part of my job description. If the story was published, he was on his own.

On Wednesday night at the convention center, Harold pulled me aside near the end of the night to say he'd heard a rumor that the next day's *New York Post* was going to run the *Star*'s story on Morris and a prostitute. But he wasn't sure, and I was too tired to wait up for it. The president's acceptance speech was the next night, and I wanted to be fresh for the prep. Thursday morning, I got up at 6:30 and called Dick for our daily conversation about the overnight polls.

"They're fine," he said. "But I'm resigning."

He didn't have to explain. The story must have appeared and been every bit as bad as he'd feared. "We started out as enemies," he said, "but now I really respect you."

"I'm sorry, Dick."

I didn't like Dick — hell, I hated him. I wanted him gone. But to face such a public disgrace on a day of such personal triumph seemed too cruel, too unusual, too Greek. No one should have to endure such a mythic turn of fate — even if it was his own fault. The feeling faded over the course of the day. As I learned the details of what he'd done — not just hiring the prostitute, but letting her listen in on his phone calls with the president — I became more angry at him for putting Clinton and our work at risk. But at Hillary's insistence, I tried not to show it. Fearing that Dick was troubled enough to commit suicide, she had issued strict instructions for all of us to avoid any public comment that might set him off.

When I arrived at Clinton's suite for the speech prep, he was already at the dining-room table, scribbling on the speech drafts spread before him. Concentrating on his speech, the president didn't mention Morris. Maybe it was my imagination, but he seemed relieved, almost lighthearted. On top again, he didn't need Dick now; the win would be his alone. We worked through the day as if Morris had never existed, and I had a hint of what I would feel in our first residence meeting after Dick's departure. It was all so simple. Panetta took Dick's chair and gave a perfunctory, thirty-second "Now that Dick is gone . . ." speech. That was that. I was there. Dick wasn't. I had won. But *Man*, I thought, *this is one cold-blooded business we're in.*

Two months later, two nights before Clinton's final presidential debate, a group of us were in the bar of the Albuquerque Holiday Inn reviewing the day's prep session over burgers and beer. Around midnight, an advance man found me to say the president was on the phone.

"You doin' anything?"

"No."

"Can you come up for a minute?"

The encounter I'd been dreading. That morning, *The New Yorker* had published David Remnick's profile of me, in which I openly discussed moving on before the start of the second term. I had been candid with Remnick, in part because I wanted to lock myself into leaving. But I thought I had been careful enough to avoid creating spin-off news stories. Apparently not. My plans were all over CNN and the AP wire, and I hadn't yet talked to the president. It had seemed presumptuous, and I was chicken. I wanted to put off this conversation as long as I could. Now Clinton was calling me on it.

When I entered the suite, he was sprawled on the bed in T-shirt and jeans, with the contents of his saddlebag briefcase — folders, briefing books, a couple of paperback mysteries, and a new hardcover by Gary Hart — spilled on the bedspread around him. I walked across the room to lean against the radiator on the far wall. CNN *Headline News* filled the awkward silence.

"So, how's this Remnick article?"

"It's not too bad," I replied. But searching for more comfortable ground, I quickly changed the subject. "The prep went well today," I said. "We're ahead of schedule. If you have a solid night Wednesday, the election is over." This was what I knew how to do with Clinton — relate through work, a candidate and his staff. The talk turned to his next cabinet. I advised him to pick at least one Republican, and we discussed his top three picks for secretary of state: George Mitchell, Madeline Albright, and the ever-elusive Colin Powell. But after a few minutes, Clinton stopped me.

"Now let's talk about you," he said. "Do you really want to leave? Nobody around here can do what you do."

I had steeled myself for just this moment. Clinton's personal magnetism had less power over me now. Watching it work on others still gave me a kind of clinical thrill, but I liked to think that I had become more a student of his seductive powers than their subject. He foiled that defense by tapping into my need to feel indispensable and saying exactly the right thing: *"Nobody around here can do what you do."* Then there was the fact that he was president. Early in our term, though I was still captured by Clinton's charisma, I hadn't had sufficient in-your-bones awe for the presidency itself — perhaps in part because we had beaten an incumbent. Over time, as I developed a more realistic view of Clinton the man, my respect for the office increased. My apprehension that night was that I wouldn't be able to say no to a president.

But I was also grateful to Clinton — for the chances he had given me and the things he had taught me, for his intelligence and fortitude, for his commitment to public service, for coming through on the biggest issues and becoming a better president every day. And I was grateful that night because he didn't pull rank. After I told him about being treated for burnout, he suggested that I take a six-month sabbatical and then come back to work. Thoughtful, but that wasn't how the White House worked. The conversation drifted. After ninety minutes, I reminded Clinton that he needed his sleep and prepared to leave — relieved. The president of the United States had told me he needed me, but he hadn't commanded my service. All I could have hoped for. On my way out, he asked me to reconsider his offer. "Of course," I said. But we both knew this was good-bye.

Election day 1996, I slept in. Around noon, I threw on some jeans and a baseball cap for an anonymous walk around Little Rock. I wanted lunch at Doe's, and to wander down Main Street to see the War Room. The space had been rented out for a corporate reception — re-created down to the headset from my phone and the little white sign Carville had hung on the wall: "Change vs. More of the Same . . ."

The late autumn haze carried me back to the day I first landed — to the mansion, their bedroom, that paint store where it all began. *Clinton's allergies will be acting up. Man, that seems like a long time ago. So much has happened. Ugly sometimes. Didn't get all we wanted. But the country's in good shape, and we did some good things.* . . . As I passed by the old train station, my reverie was interrupted by a shout: "Are you registered to vote in Little Rock?" A woman in a flowing white muumuu beneath a Medusa's tangle of dark hair rushed toward me with an offering. It was a business card with a caramel wrapped in gold foil stapled to the corner:

VOTE FOR CONNIE HAMZY

LITTLE ROCK CITY BOARD, POSITION 10 —

"TO REPRESENT THE CONCERNS OF THE WORKING POOR."

I looked down at the card, then back at her face. *Sweet, sweet Connie.* My first bimbo eruption. A candidate for city council. I was getting out; she was getting in.

Later that night, in the presidential suite of the Excelsior Hotel, I told Clinton about it. "Did she recognize you?" I shook my head. "Too bad, she might have flashed." Roaring, he repeated every detail from their moment in the North Little Rock Hilton. It was safe to laugh now.

Hillary was in the back bedroom, helping Chelsea get dressed. Just before I left for a victory lap with the network anchors, I knocked on her door. She peeked out, "Just a minute," then came into the hall. Only the two of us were there, separated by a wall from the suite where the returns were being announced and Clinton was holding court. This was our private good-bye. She gave me a hug, then held me at arm's length for an extra second, a hand on each of my shoulders, her eyes shining.

We smiled through the silence. Victory was vindication — even sweeter for her than for her husband. She had paid a higher price, taken harder hits, achieved fewer dreams. Now she'd have a second chance, and I wished her luck. She did the same for me. All the stresses and threats, all the suspicions and resentments, all the times the two of us had clashed because I blamed her for being too rigid and she blamed me for not being as "tough as Kennedy's men" — all that was behind us now. We had survived. We had won. All would be well.

"I love you, George Stephanopoulos."

"I love you too."

Staff no more, I walked out the door.

EPILOGUE   ON MY OWN

> It was the office, not the man. That was what the historians
> said, and for once the historians were right. Oh, what a place
> Washington was, when you were there on the inside. Right in
> tight, near the Oval Office, where it happened. He'd been there
> for eight years, an assistant, a President's man. Now he was on
> the outs. He hated being on the outs more than he hated any-
> thing. For a President's man habit died hard, and suddenly he
> was afraid.
>
> — Ward Just, "A Guide to the Architecture of Washington, D.C."

After four years, unlike Ward Just's character, I put myself on the
outs. Maybe that's why I wasn't afraid. Grateful for the privilege
of serving a president, relieved to be leaving in one piece, I left
feeling as lucky as I had the day it all began. I would miss being on
the inside, miss making decisions and trying to make a difference,
miss the events that made history and the intimate moments when
the White House felt like home. But I wouldn't miss carrying
everything inside, and I wouldn't miss being an assistant. For the
first time in my professional life, I wanted to be on my own.

I moved to New York for a new career as a writer, teacher, and
television commentator, and slowly adjusted to speaking publicly
without first calculating Clinton's position or how it would play.
Liberated from the crisis cycles of the White House, I learned how

to better balance my life; over time, I stopped taking antidepressant medication. But habit dies hard. After a presidential press conference, I'd leave a congratulatory message with Betty Currie, hoping Clinton would call. When I defended him publicly, Clinton would return the favor by tracking me down. That was enough — twenty minutes of that familiar, sleepy hoarseness talking about the issues streaming through his mind. For the length of a phone call, I could pretend to be a president's man.

Then, on a Sunday afternoon in September 1997, for the first time in months, I returned to the White House to visit Gene Sperling. We wandered around the empty West Wing and popped into my old office — Rahm's now — before stepping across the hall to the Roosevelt Room. Some visitors on a special tour peeked through the door at me with a look of recognition that said I belonged there, which only made me more aware that I didn't. Then Gene and I settled into a slouch perfected over hundreds of staff meetings: gazing at the ceiling with our necks nestled on the backs of our chairs and our knees crossed high against the edge of the wooden table. But our nostalgic talk was interrupted by an unmistakable series of high-pitched staccato beeps from the Secret Service station across the hall.

I bolted upright in my chair, ready to work, as a uniformed agent reached into the room to close the four-inch-thick door facing the Oval's formal entrance. The president was in. My heart beat more rapidly. My stomach floated with butterflies, the kind you get when you're walking down the street and spot a girl you lost but still love a couple of blocks ahead.

A year earlier, I would have walked into the Oval without thinking. During the year of my exile I never would have entered without asking. In each case, however, I would have known what was right at the time. My whole being was wrapped up in reading the rhythms of the White House and the moods of the man. I anticipated his needs and answered his questions before they were asked. I prided myself on being Clintonologist in chief. Need to know what's going on or advice on what to do? Come see me. That was the George that Gene knew best, so he couldn't understand why I was so flustered. To him, I was still Clinton's guy.

But as I stared at the door that had melded seamlessly into the wall, I knew that wasn't true anymore. I didn't know what to do. Walking in on the president during one of his rare moments alone seemed presumptuous. Walking by without saying hello seemed rude. I was suddenly shy, and slightly afraid. This was not my place anymore. Clinton was still president, but I could no longer maintain the illusion that he was somehow *my* president in some special way. Not knowing what to do at that moment was the surest sign that I didn't belong.

We went up to Sperling's office and talked for another hour. Clinton stayed at his desk and shuffled his papers the way he liked to do on Sunday afternoons. Then it was time to go. I had a plane to catch; Gene had work to do. I still hoped we would run into him; maybe I would poke my head into the Oval after all. But when we descended the single flight of stairs and peered around the corner, the door was open and the president was gone. So I returned my visitor's pass to the Northwest Gate and walked up Connecticut Avenue.

That was how my story was supposed to end. But on Wednesday, January 21, 1998, it seemed to start all over again.

Shortly before five A.M., I prepared to check out of the Tutwiler Hotel in Birmingham, Alabama. The night before I had given a talk at the University of Alabama that included my usual riff on the Clinton scandals. By the end of 1998, I confidently predicted, the president would win the Paula Jones case and Ken Starr would close shop without finding any wrongdoing by the Clintons on White-water, Travelgate, or Filegate. Now I was rushing home to teach my weekly class on the presidency at Columbia. But when I reached the front desk, the clerk handed me a phone. My new employers at ABC News were on the line. A big story was breaking with allega-tions about the president and a former White House intern named Monica Lewinsky. They'd had sex. Clinton might have told her to lie. There were tapes. Starr was investigating. Get to a studio im-mediately. I asked for a fax of the story and went upstairs to put on my suit.

That damn Newsweek *rumor was true.* The previous Saturday, while the president was being deposed in the Paula Jones case, my friends in the White House were worrying that the magazine was about to print something about Clinton and an intern. By the end of the day, *Newsweek* had told Rahm there was no story, and Rahm had told me that the president's deposition was a home run. Another false alarm. The next morning on *This Week*, when my colleague Bill Kristol aired the intern rumor, I jumped down his throat and accused him of bottom-feeding from Internet gossip columnist Matt Drudge, who had issued a late-night bulletin about *Newsweek's* internal deliberations. We quickly moved to other topics, and I hoped that the intern story would be another example of a storm cloud that evaporated under scrutiny. Later, on my way to Alabama, I called Betty Currie from a pay phone at the Atlanta airport with a message for Clinton: "Hang in there, and take Arafat to the Holocaust Museum," the other big story of the week.

By Wednesday morning, there was no other story. In the cab to ABC's Birmingham affiliate, I fixed on the *Post* headline — "Clinton Accused of Urging Aide to Lie" — then foraged through the story for exculpatory facts, logical leaps, and questionable assertions. But the telltale signs were all bad: Attorney General Reno had personally authorized Starr's request to investigate "allegations of suborning perjury, false statements, and obstruction of justice involving the president." *There must be some hard evidence.* Clinton's lawyer, Robert Bennett, denied "a relationship" between Lewinsky and Clinton but wouldn't comment on whether the two had talked about her testimony in the Jones case. *There must have been conversations between them.* Lewinsky's attorney, William Ginsburg, strangely refused to deny that his client had had a sexual relationship with Clinton. *Shit, they must have had sex. And there are tapes.* Hours of them, "according to sources," describing the affair in graphic detail, including some conversations in which Lewinsky recounted Clinton's and Vernon Jordan's "directing her to testify falsely in the Paula Jones case."

I borrowed the driver's cell phone to call the White House. But Rahm said he didn't know anything beyond what he'd read in the paper — and he sounded sick. His shaky voice brought me back to the worst moments of my old life. The afternoon in Little Rock when I heard Clinton on the Gennifer tapes. The night in New York when I learned about his draft notice. The morning in Washington when I read that Clinton had called his Arkansas troopers to keep them quiet. Blindsided again — and these were the most serious allegations yet. They were about the present, not the past. He was president; she was an intern. If Clinton had asked her to lie under oath, or lied under oath himself, he had broken the law.

A moment from a Sunday morning in late 1996 recurred to me. Monica had approached me as I walked from my apartment to the Starbucks next door. I hadn't seen her in nearly a year, but I vaguely remembered her as a pretty, busty, flirty intern I'd pass in the halls or see hanging out at Starbucks on weekends. A few times at work, she had tried to surprise me with a double-tall latte, but my assistant Laura Capps would stop her at the door. That morning, Monica had a question for me: "Does your president tell the truth?" I thought her phrasing was peculiar, but people stopped me on the street to say strange things all the time. After mumbling some answer like "He does his best," I bought my coffee and didn't think about it again.

Until now. When added to the leaks out of Starr's office, it seemed like more evidence against Clinton. Although I still found it almost impossible to imagine how a president of the United States could take such a risk, my gut told me the core of the story was true. As much as I wanted to believe Clinton, I didn't — and couldn't pretend that I did. As much as I owed him, I didn't believe that loyalty demanded lying, and I had a duty in my new life to give honest opinions. As much as I still liked the president and supported his work, I was livid. *How could he be so stupid? So reckless? So selfish?*

I reached the studio just as *Good Morning America* was going on the air. While the technicians fiddled with my microphone and earpiece, I reminded myself to stay balanced, to control both my anger at Clinton and my instinct to spin for him. *Don't accuse. Don't defend.*

Analyze. When anchor Lisa McRee questioned me, I said that I didn't know much about Monica or her relationship with Clinton, then added my assessment of the situation:

> These are probably the most serious allegations yet leveled against the president. If they're true, they're not only politically damaging, but it could lead to impeachment proceedings. But they're just questions right now, and that's why I think we do all have to take a deep breath before we go too far here.

I didn't think I had gone too far. Saying that proven charges of perjury, witness tampering, and obstruction of justice by the president of the United States *"could"* cause Congress to begin the impeachment process seemed to me like an understatement. But to the rest of the political world, it was a leading indicator. Hearing a former close adviser to the president use the "I word," however qualified, made them think, *"Even apologists like George think Clinton's lying this time."* The political newsletter *Hotline* made it the quote of the day. Worse, the *Wall Street Journal* editorial page cited me approvingly after years of snide attacks. Although my analysis was accurate, I hadn't realized when I said it that a single word would signal such a fundamental break with my past.

That first day felt like old times. Another Clinton crisis, another round of anxious calls. James joked about moving to Honduras. Rahm worried about his wife and new baby. Paul wondered most about what had really happened. All of us thought the situation was dire. None of us knew the whole truth. The only difference was that instead of being in the foxhole with my friends, I was calling from behind enemy lines — the headquarters of ABC News. They had a job to do, and so did I. On the phone, I was consoling them, but I was also reporting the story; they were venting their frustration but also spinning me. From the start, I cautioned Rahm not to tell me anything that he didn't want me to report, and our phone conversations had a new code: "Just friends" meant "off the record." We promised each other that we wouldn't let Clinton's craziness drive us apart but somehow knew that it would. While they were prep-

ping the president, I was analyzing his performance. While they dutifully went before the cameras to defend Clinton, I couldn't bring
myself to say I believed him.

I wondered what I would do if I were back inside. After five years
of getting burned in battles, after a year away from the fray, I didn't
believe that I could actually be drawn back into the psychology of
the barricade. But it wasn't hard to imagine the slide from skepticism to certainty, from conscientious objector to kamikaze warrior:
*I'd advise the president to come clean, and I'd resign if he didn't. . . .
Alone? Then you'd be the Brutus doing him in. You can't do that. . . .
Right, I'd stay for loyalty's sake, but I wouldn't speak out in his defense. . . . Impossible. You've been on the front lines for years; public silence
now would be condemnation. . . . OK, I'd defend Clinton but refuse to attack his accusers. . . . But they're lying about him. They set him up, and
Starr's out of control. This is war: If we don't destroy them, they'll destroy
us and everything we've worked to achieve. . . .* The truth is I couldn't
really know what I would do because I wasn't there — in the Oval,
inhaling that high-octane White House air, sitting in my usual
chair, resting my forearm on his broad oak desk as the president of
the United States looked me in the eye and put his hand on mine
and begged me to believe him just one more time.

Having that meeting with Clinton was the last thing I wanted,
but I tried to advise him from afar. On the second night of the
scandal, during a prime-time special on the "Crisis in the White
House," Peter Jennings gave me the chance.

Peter Jennings: "George, my assumption is that President Clinton has a lot better things to do at the moment than be watching
ABC television. But if he were watching you at the moment, what
would you tell him?"

George Stephanopoulos: "I would tell him, 'Mr. President, get
your story together, get it out as quickly as you can. You've been
through tough things before. You can weather this storm if you go
out and get your story together and answer all the questions to the
best of your ability.'"

I wanted to scream: *"Tell the truth. Take responsibility."* But "get
your story together" was as far as I could go without directly accusing Clinton of lying. Coming clean with the country wouldn't be

easy, but it was the right thing to do. The president was getting similar advice from my friends inside; from his friend and chief of staff, Erskine Bowles, from his former chief of staff Leon Panetta, from his former deputy chief of staff Harold Ickes. But at his moment of maximum peril, the president chose to follow the pattern of his past. He called Dick Morris. Dick took a poll. The poll said lie. It was out of Clinton's hands.

The next day, Clinton called in his cabinet and sent them out to defend him. *Why is he dragging the secretary of state into this?* That Sunday, I sat grimacing in the ABC control room as Paul Begala got pummeled by my fellow *This Week* panelists with questions he couldn't answer and presidential actions he couldn't explain. *How can Clinton do this to them?* By Monday, January 26, I watched the president wagging his finger in the Roosevelt Room ("I never had sexual relations with that woman . . .") with a kind of fascinated disgust. This was Clinton at his cold-blooded worst. Gone were the guilty tics of his past denials — the downcast eyes, the stutter, the dry throat and pale face that displayed a sense of shame and sorrow and vulnerability. Now, full of self-righteous fury, he was lying with true conviction. All that mattered was his survival. Everyone else had to fall in line: his staff, his cabinet, the country, even his wife.

I don't think Hillary knew about Monica until Clinton came home from the Jones deposition. That night, they canceled plans to have dinner with Erskine and Crandall Bowles, and Hillary later said, cryptically, that they had spent much of the weekend "cleaning out closets." But Clinton probably didn't come clean then either. I imagine he told Hillary that he slipped up but didn't stray — that he had befriended a troubled girlfriend of Betty Currie's, but it got a little out of hand because the girl was insecure, infatuated, and slightly crazy. She came on to him, began to imagine an affair. It got so bad she started to stalk him and repeated her fantasy to friends. Somehow the Jones lawyers heard about her. He stupidly tried to fix the situation himself: talked to her on the phone, met with her when she came to see Betty, asked Vernon to help her get a job and get her out of town. But he never had sex with her and never told her to lie.

How could Hillary buy that? How could she not? The alternative was too painful to admit — and not only because she cared about their political survival. Every marriage is a mystery, but it seemed to me that their bond had been strengthened by the intensity of their White House experience, that Hillary had fallen in love all over again with the boy from Arkansas who had become the president she dreamed he could be. By the time I left the White House, there was less whispering about screaming bouts on the second floor. Hillary hinted to *Time* that she and Bill had talked about adopting a second child, an unexpected revelation I would have dismissed if I hadn't also heard West Wing gossip about their trying to have a baby of their own. The last time I'd seen them together was in October 1997 at Hillary's fiftieth birthday party. The Ritz-Carlton ballroom was filled with their friends of a lifetime and Washington's power elite. Chelsea had flown home from her first term at Stanford to surprise her mom. As Hillary swirled around the dance floor in her husband's arms, surrounded by family and friends, she seemed as happy as I'd ever seen her.

Hillary had to believe him. It was harder this time, but she had to. She had to believe that as he'd grown in office he'd outgrown his past. She had to believe that he wouldn't risk their life's work for a fling with an intern only a few years older than their daughter. She had to believe that he loved her enough not to humiliate her. She had to do what she had always done before: swallow her doubts, stand by her man, and savage his enemies. On the *Today* show the morning of the State of the Union, Hillary sounded the trumpets for one more battle against the "right-wing conspiracy."

But I wasn't there to answer the call. I refused to vouch for Clinton's credibility, and I couldn't buy the party line that this was more about Clinton's accusers than his own actions — which meant I was the enemy now. That's the way it was with the Clintons: You were either for them or against them. I knew what being under siege was like, so I couldn't entirely blame them for feeling that way. But the first signs of my ostracism were disconcerting and painful. In early February, on the eve of a White House party to celebrate the fifth anniversary of Clinton's economic speech, I received a flurry of phone calls from Paul and Rahm to make sure I didn't accept the invitation mistakenly sent by the social office. They didn't want to risk a scene. I heard that as far as Clinton was concerned, I was now a nonperson — my name was not to be mentioned in his presence. As the White House settled into a strategy of stonewalling and denial, the rift widened. My commentary became more pointed, my tone more raw. The White House responded in kind, and my friendships became strained. A series of articles in which I was featured as a poster boy for betrayal appeared in several prominent publications.

Democrats called me an ingrate, arguing that I had a duty to swallow my doubts and defend the man who had "created" me. Journalists labeled me a hypocrite, arguing that I must have known about Clinton's affair with Monica, and that my past defenses of Clinton against similar charges made my present skepticism suspect. My former colleagues took a more subtle tack. Off the record, they suggested I was simply trying to please my new paymasters by being provocative; on the record, they explained away my dire predictions of where the scandal might lead as a symptom of my pessimistic and anxious "dark side."

There was just enough truth in each of the charges to get to me: I didn't think that Clinton had "created" me or that loyalty should require me to defend behavior I found abhorrent, but Clinton *had* given me the opportunity of a lifetime, and I *did* owe him some benefit of the doubt. I didn't think I was a hypocrite, because my defense of Clinton against past bimbo eruptions had been predicated on my belief that he wouldn't create new ones, but maybe I *was* complicit because when I worked for Clinton I had been willing to suspend my disbelief about some of his more suspect denials. Although I had never seen Clinton in a compromising position with Monica or any other woman, I may not have looked hard enough then because I didn't want to know the truth. I was sure the Monica story was true, and that Clinton was jeopardizing his presidency by covering it up, but what if I was wrong? What if I *was* just being "dark"? Maybe, just maybe, those floating trial balloons about Clinton's being guilty of nothing more than taking pity on a sweet-natured stalker were true.

Now I knew what it felt like to be on the other side of the White House spin machine. But my bouts of doubt were balanced by all the leaking details: Monica's thirty-seven White House visits, the late-night phone calls and gifts, the blue dress. So I steeled myself to the public criticism and became accustomed to reading hate mail from liberal Democrats instead of conservative Republicans. What bothered me far more was what I heard from my friends. Carville and I still talked several times a day, but after one *This Week* performance in which I looked and sounded more like a prosecutor than an analyst, he screamed at me: "Boy, you were tough this morning. It feels like you're pulling for the other side." Paul said I was acting like a father umpiring Little League who makes all the close calls against his own kid's team.

The truth hurts. There were times when I did start to pull for the other side. Although I wasn't proud of the feeling and tried to control it, I wanted to be right and wanted Clinton to pay a price. The longer he lied, the more it seemed as if he might get away with it, the more furious I became. I was angry at Clinton for selfishly risking his presidency on a foolish dalliance and arrogantly trying to fix it himself, for lying about it and sending others out to lie for him, for paralyzing his policy agenda and making his accusers look like prophets instead of fools. The "new covenant" heart of Clintonism now seemed hollow. Apparently the rule of personal responsibility applied to every American except the president himself.

My heart was getting hard, partly from self-righteousness, partly as a shield against sadness and shame. I realized that the intensity of my anger was both irrational and uncharitable, but I couldn't help it: I took Clinton's actions personally. For several years, I had served as his character witness. Now I felt like a dupe. I had done everything I could to make Bill Clinton president, and everything in my power to keep him there. Although I wasn't proud of all I'd done, I was proud of our accomplishments. But the scandal now cast a shadow over the whole endeavor, making it seem more like an experience to be explained than an adventure to be celebrated. Decisions I had defended in the past seemed more dishonorable now. The ultimate rationale for getting my hands dirty and doing what it took to win — from attacking Gennifer Flowers to working with Dick Morris to accepting welfare reform — was not just the thrill of the fight or my need to be on top, but also my belief that progressive ideals would be better protected as long as Clinton was president. If that was true, then Clinton didn't have a right to put his presidency at risk. He didn't have a right to betray those of us who had put our trust in him. He didn't have a right to compromise my compromises, to make me question whether helping him get elected was the best thing I ever did — or the worst.

All of these emotions boiled over on August 17, when Clinton addressed the nation after his grand jury appearance. For many who had chosen to believe him, this was the worst moment — now they had to start coping with feelings of anger, disillusionment, and betrayal. For Clinton, it was another missed opportunity. If he had acted against type; if he had apologized, acknowledged his wrongdoing, and accepted responsibility more forthrightly; if he had resisted the temptation to vent his rage against Starr in that forum on that night, the impeachment process would not have developed momentum. For me, it was a relief. Clinton's admission, however grudging and cramped, ended the futile debates about what he did and whether he deserved to be believed. It helped me put his failings back in perspective.

As angry as I was, I didn't believe that Clinton should be removed from office. In all of American history, through countless scandals petty and grand, only one president had resigned, only one president had been impeached. Despite being saturated with all the tawdry details, the country still wanted Clinton to stay. Resignation might have been an act of personal honor, I thought, but the obsessively abusive conduct of Clinton's prosecutors and their partisan accomplices was an argument for resistance. It shouldn't be easy to force a president from office. Starr's investigation demonstrated that Clinton lied under oath about his sexual relationship with Monica Lewinsky, but it did not prove that he obstructed justice. Although he humiliated himself, dishonored his presidency, and deserved to be punished, Clinton did not abuse presidential power in a way that justified impeachment. His crimes were more about the man than the office.

On September 21, my heart caught up with my head. The videotape of Clinton's grand jury testimony was about to be played to the whole country, and I was wired up in a small room at ABC, watching the monitor next to the television camera that would broadcast my commentary on Clinton's testimony.

The tape started to roll, and even before the questions began, it had the quality of an amateur porn flick: The fixed camera angle gave the room a generic look, the lighting was bright and unforgiving, the ambient noise and off-screen conversations made me feel as if I were eavesdropping on a private encounter caught by a hidden taping device. Most unnerving was the close-up of Clinton — the picture of a president of the United States alone and unprotected. No American flag, no presidential seal, no Oval Office desk. Just a man in a straight-backed chair, facing a grand jury of his peers and the prosecutors who had ruined his life. The picture screamed, *"No president is above the law."*

When the questions quickly turned to sex and Clinton began to read his public admission, I felt a tug inside. Maybe it came from seeing his reading glasses again — the old-fashioned half bifocals that we always encouraged Clinton to wear for photographs because they gave him a fatherly air. Now they just made him seem tired and old. Clinton's words were more annoying than moving. He was still trying to slide around the truth. But the whole scene was heartbreaking. For the first time in months, I began to sympathize with my former boss.

After reading his statement, Clinton removed his glasses and waited for the questions to resume. For a silent moment he was not on — not trying to charm, persuade, evade, or empathize, not relying on the ambivalent skills that had propelled him through a lifetime of political triumphs but also landed him in that room today. He was a man alone with his failings before the whole world, a man forced to confess sins that had devastated his family and undone the hopes of his life, a man ashamed. He sighed. His face fell, the last breath from an all-but-deflated balloon. Off camera, I quietly started to cry.

"Mister SPEAK-KERRR, the PRESIDENT of the UNITED STATES!"

Clinton followed the sergeant at arms into the House chamber shortly after nine P.M. on January 19, 1999, just as he always did — soaking up the applause, grabbing a few hands on each side of the aisle, impatiently eyeing the podium that held his State of the Union Address. The speech was sure to be a winner; it always was. But as he bounded toward the Speaker's chair and patted the air with his hands to quiet the crowd, Clinton seemed nervous to me — and who could blame him? A month earlier, in that same chamber, he had become the first elected president in American history to be impeached.

Acting with a recklessness that matched Clinton's, the Republican majority in the House had passed two impeachment articles on a near party-line vote, and they were paying a price. A year into the Monica scandal, their poll numbers were in the tank, while Clinton's were higher than ever. Two Republican Speakers had resigned; Clinton was still standing. He might never be able to erase the stain of impeachment, but neither would they. In Clinton's Senate trial earlier that day, White House counsel Charles Ruff had made a powerful opening argument for acquittal. Tonight, the president was mounting the podium in his own defense.

"My fellow Americans, I stand before you to report that the state of our union is strong." Never mentioning the issue that had consumed his presidency, but armed with an arsenal of popular proposals on everything from Social Security to health care to education to crime, Clinton made his own best case, doing what he did best. Halfway through, he even started toying with his Republican tormentors. When they clapped, he praised them for getting into the bipartisan spirit; when they sat on their hands through a surefire applause line, he shot them a competitor's glare — a look that said, *"You guys can pound me all you want. Tonight you're mine."* When he basked in the reflected heroism of Rosa Parks smiling from the balcony, he seemed like a man without a care in the world.

Sitting across town in what had become my usual chair at ABC, I had to laugh, delighting in the sheer political virtuosity of Clinton's performance — even the "I love you" he mouthed to Hillary as if the whole world wouldn't notice. "This is our moment," Clinton said as he drew to a close. And he was right. America was doing fine — better than fine, better than I ever could have imagined that morning six years ago, when I handed him his Inaugural Address minutes before he took the oath and promised the country to "force the spring." Now I watched from far away, enjoying the show but wondering too. Wondering what might have been — if only this good president had been a better man.

NOTE ON SOURCING

I did not keep a diary while I worked in the White House, but on about a dozen weekend afternoons at that time, I had a series of conversations with my friend Eric Alterman. Eric, who was working on his dissertation in American history at Stanford University, taped and stored these talks to create a historical record. After I left the White House he allowed me to use this material for my book. It could not have been written without his warm friendship, probing questions, rigorous criticism, and personal discretion.

I also tried to follow the advice given to me by William Safire. Early in my tenure, he encouraged me to jot down personal observations when I could and "throw the paper in a drawer." Several of these observations appear in this book.

The direct quotations in this book are real, not reconstructed. They come largely from my personal notes, Eric's tapes, and occasionally from secondary printed sources.

Other books written about Clinton and his presidency were invaluable as I prepared this account, most notably *On the Edge* and *Showdown*, by Elizabeth Drew; *The Agenda* and *The Choice*, by Bob Woodward; *First in His Class*, by David Maraniss; *Quest for the Presidency, 1992* and *Back From the Dead*, by *Newsweek*'s political team; *Behind the Oval Office*, by Dick Morris; *Blood Sport*, by James Stewart; *The System*, by Haynes Johnson and David Broder; and *Not All Black and White*, by Christopher Edley.

Finally, for each incident I chose to write about, I reviewed articles in the *Washington Post*, the *New York Times*, and other major periodicals. *The Public Papers of the Presidents* from 1993–1996 were also exceedingly helpful.

I used no classified material in preparing this book.

ACKNOWLEDGMENTS

I couldn't have written this book without the support, friendship, and advice of countless family and friends. To anyone I missed, I apologize in advance.

William Novak was the best writing coach a first-time author could ask for. From our first meeting through to the evening I read him the last line of my last draft, he was never more than a phone call away. He spent months in 1997 interviewing me for dozens of hours, transcribing the notes and helping me to organize my thoughts. When I actually began writing, I had the luxury of reading him my daily output over the phone and receiving his suggestions. Once the draft was completed, his edits helped clear away the clutter in my writing. Bill was also a good friend, reminding me that writer's block was not a permanent condition and welcoming me into his home. I'm also grateful to Linda and the rest of the Novak family for their hospitality, and a special thanks to Ben Novak for his fresh and careful read of an early draft.

If Bill Novak was my coach, my editor, Bill Phillips, acted like a good director. He pushed me to tell my story as I lived it, to feel the experience again, and to be honest with myself and my readers. There were times when I felt he understood the narrative even better than I did. Bill's vision and enthusiasm never failed to pump me up. I'm also grateful for the encouragement I received from Gladys Phillips, and the help of Nicole Hirsh. Little, Brown's publisher, Sarah Crichton, never failed to make me excited about the book, and I appreciate her patience and savvy.

Peter Osnos, publisher of *Public Affairs*, was a bluntly shrewd reader and wise counselor.

A number of close friends took the time to review, discuss, and improve my manuscript, including M. J. Rosenberg, Dan Porter-field, Karen Herrling, David Dreyer, Mark Steitz, Mark Halperin, Karen Avrich, Diana Silver, and Wendy Smith. Thanks also to Betsy Uhrig of Little, Brown for her meticulous copyediting. Barney Frank, Paul Begala, Gene Sperling, Mark Katz, and Michael Wald-man helped refresh my recollection about various episodes in the book. Whatever errors of judgment and fact remain are mine alone.

Columbia's Jenny Parker and Chris Glaros ran my life in a way that made it possible for me to write this book. In addition to orga-nizing my often chaotic schedule and managing my office, Jenny was a thoughtful reader and research assistant. Before heading west for Stanford Law School, Chris was both my teaching assistant at Columbia and research assistant on this book, reviewing thousands of pages of public records and making sure I got my facts straight. Both Jenny and Chris helped supervise interns Leora Hanser, Jacob Kupietzky, Nandini Ramnath, Margaret Connolly, Allison Mas-corro, James Frederick Carson, Jennifer Credidio, Georgia Aarons, John Ray Clemmons, Meena Untawale, Lauren Rosenberg, Stefan Davis, and Robert Mook. Thanks to all.

A special word also for Heather Beckel, Laura Capps, Emily Lentzner, Stacy Parker, and Marlene McDonald, who did such a good job as my assistants during the 1992 campaign and in the White House.

My agent and attorney, Bob Barnett of Williams and Connolly, is a good lawyer and good friend. Thanks also to Jackie Davies and Sylvia Faison.

And a final thank-you to Kirk O'Donnell and Ann Devroy. They taught me much about politics and life. I miss them both.

INDEX